STRIVE FOR A 5

Preparing for the AP® Biology Exam

to accompany

Principles of **Life**

SECOND EDITION

for the AP® course

Hillis • Sadava • Hill • Price

Franklin Bell • John Lepri

SINAUER ASSOCIATES

bfw high school
BEDFORD, FREEMAN, & WORTH

Franklin Bell, a Science Department faculty member at Mercersburg Academy, has taught AP® Biology since 1994. He leads AP® Biology teacher workshops and participates in the annual exam readings.

John Lepri, Professor of Biology at the University of North Carolina at Greensboro, researches and teaches physiology and has been involved with the AP® Biology program since 1991.

Strive for a 5: Preparing for the AP® Biology Exam to accompany
Principles of Life for the AP® course, **Second Edition**

Copyright © 2015 Sinauer Associates, Inc. All rights reserved.
This book may not be reproduced in whole or in part without permission of the publisher.

Address editorial correspondence to:
Sinauer Associates, Inc.
P.O. Box 407
Sunderland, MA 01375 U.S.A.
Internet: www.sinauer.com; publish@sinauer.com

Address orders to:
MPS / W.H. Freeman & Co. Order Department
16365 James Madison Highway, U.S. Route 15
Gordonsville, VA 22942 U.S.A. or call 1-888-330-8477

ISBN: 978-1-4641-8652-3

Printed in U.S.A.

4 3 2 1

This SFI label applies to the text paper.

AP® is a trademark registered and/or owned by the College Board, which was not involved in the production of, and does not endorse, this product.

Contents

Preface

Strive for a 5 is a study guide and test preparation workbook for use throughout your AP® Biology course. Following the *Principles of Life*, Second Edition for the AP® course chapter by chapter, it reinforces the textbook's key concepts and focuses on the AP® Biology curriculum's Big Ideas and Learning Objectives.

This *Strive for a 5* workbook includes four main sections:

An Overview of the Science Practices in AP® Biology

New for the second edition, this section provides an overview of the practices that are part of every question on the AP® exam. Scientists share seven fundamental methods when performing their work. These include modeling, applying mathematics, posing questions, designing experiments, analyzing data, using explanations and theories, and connecting related knowledge across many domains. These "Science Practices" are enforced throughout the AP® Biology curriculum and are emphasized at the end of each *Strive* chapter. This section of the *Strive for a 5* workbook explains the importance and application of every method.

Study Guide

The Study Guide section is presented in chapters that follow the *Principles of Life,* Second Edition textbook. Each opens with an overview of the corresponding textbook material. The AP® Biology curriculum's Big Ideas and Learning Objectives covered in the chapter are clearly stated. The guide presents key concepts from the textbook and follows them with a number of free-response exercises. Emphasis on describing, explaining, and analyzing helps students master every concept in preparation for the exam.

Preparing for the AP® Exam

This section provides a description of the AP® Biology exam and includes strategies to help students prepare for and take the test. There are study tips for students to apply during the months of preparation and strategies to use on test day. There's even a list of things to avoid while taking the test—things that can waste valuable time or lower a score.

Full-Length Practice Exams

New for the second edition, the workbook now concludes with two full-length practice exams (with answer keys), designed to look and feel just like the real exam. These were written by current AP® Biology teachers, many of whom are also readers for the AP® exam. All of the questions are aligned to the new standards and are keyed to specific Learning Objectives and Science Practices. Working through these exams under the appropriate time limits will give students valuable practice and can help them gain the confidence they need to walk into the exam room feeling fully prepared.

An Overview of the Science Practices in AP® Biology

All scientists share fundamental methods of doing their work. It is essential for you to understand and use these methods, or Science Practices, as they are described here and applied throughout this book.

Knowledge in the four Big Ideas of AP® Biology: evolution, energy transfer, communication, and complex systems, has been developed through the application of the Science Practices and continues to grow with continued use. In fact, the Science Practices take us beyond guesses and beliefs to a mindset where facts and theories serve as "the rules" guiding the expansion of all scientific knowledge. The AP® exam, itself, will frequently require you to demonstrate your ability to use these practices. To help you prepare, each chapter in *Strive for a 5* concludes with problems that apply one or more of the seven Science Practices.

The following is a condensed list of the Science Practices that you will use in your biology studies. A strong foundation in these will help you understand how science is conducted and will assist you in performing well on your biology exam.

Science Practice 1
Use representations and models to communicate about science and solve problems.

Science Practice 2
Use the appropriate mathematical operations to solve problems.

Science Practice 3
Ask the right scientific questions to guide your biology investigations.

Science Practice 4
Design effective experiments and collect meaningful data when solving problems.

Science Practice 5
Analyze data to evaluate whether or not the evidence suggests any new conclusions.

Science Practice 6
Work with scientific explanations and theories.

Science Practice 7
Connect and relate knowledge across many scales and domains.

Each of the Science Practices includes diverse methods and mechanisms that scientists use to do their work and to communicate their results. What follows is an explanation of each practice.

Science Practice 1 focuses on using models and other representations to present complex information in biology. The ability to create, interpret, and work with models greatly enhances the study of science and can be particularly useful in biology.

EXAMPLE: Models are of great importance for representing how evolution can alter phenotypes. A classic model to explore evolution shows light- and dark-colored moths sitting on light- and dark-colored trees. The moths' susceptibility to predation depends on their contrast against the light and dark backgrounds. A graph showing changes in light vs. dark moth survival as the background colors change would provide a clear model for discussing evolutionary mechanisms.

In some cases, you will be asked to construct a model. In others, you might be given instructions to interpret and describe the information provided by a model. You may even be given some components of a model and required to add others, as in the following diagram.

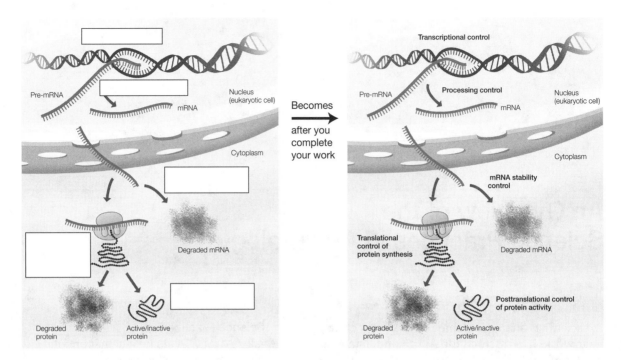

Models can be very helpful in the study of cells, which can be described as tiny membrane-covered bags filled with water, salts, and up to 75,000 different proteins. Because we are not able to produce a picture that includes 75,000 proteins, we use simplified drawings that emphasize the parts or proteins that are of interest for the phenomenon under consideration. A drawing like the one below shows a portion of a cell's membrane to communicate information clearly and focus viewers on the topic of interest. This is another application of Science Practice 1.

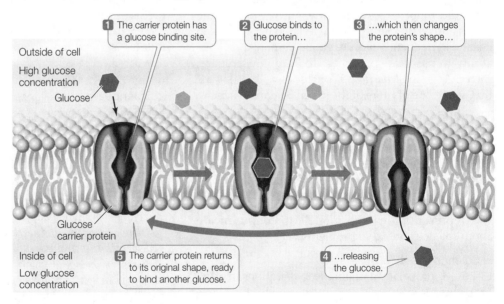

Models that represent interactions in biological systems typically emphasize numeric relationships between trophic levels. For example, drawings of tropic levels will show relatively few predators and many more plants than herbivores. You should be able to portray these differences and write a description that proves you understand the relationships. During your exam, show your understanding through drawings, and be sure to describe in words and sentences what your drawing or model represents. This can help you earn more credit.

TRY IT OUT: Models and representations can be powerful tools. You may recall in an earlier biology class being introduced to cellular reproduction, also known as mitosis. With a partner, examine the model below of a cell undergoing mitosis. What does it show well? What is not clearly shown? How could you refine this model to better illustrate important features or functions of mitosis?

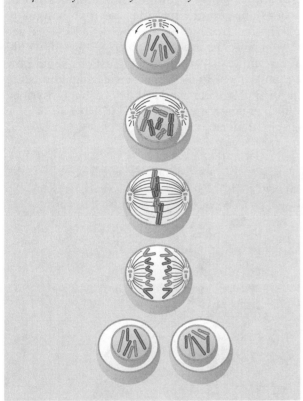

■ **Science Practice 2** is about using mathematical operations appropriately. Biology often requires the analysis of large numbers of events. Applying math, as with the Hardy–Weinberg equilibrium, offers the only approach for working with large amounts of data. Because biology is dependent on chemistry and physics, and chemistry and physics are dependent on math, you will be required to demonstrate your math skills on your exams. The best way to become proficient at using math in biology is to practice often.

EXAMPLE: Understanding water potential and using its related equation is important for studying the biology of cells and plants. A classroom experiment showing changes in the mass of potatoes soaked in fluids of differing osmolarity, for instance, requires you to calculate the amount of water gained or lost and make comparisons among osmolarities of the soaking solutions. Finding the rate of water movement across membranes requires calculating the slope of a line on a graph.

To help you apply Science Practice 2, the AP® Biology Equations and Formulas sheet appears inside the back cover of this guide and will also be included with the exam.

Some equations, such as the one for standard deviation, appear to be complex, but practice makes them easier to use. (The four-function calculator you are permitted to use on the AP exam is inadequate here, so you will not be asked to calculate this value.) $s = \sqrt{\dfrac{\sum (x_i - \bar{x})^2}{n-1}}$

Past exams have required the interpretation of data sets that include this information, so it is important that you understand what everything on the equation sheet represents and how each equation and formula is used to interpret data.

Monohybrid and dihybrid crosses will test your ability to understand the genes controlling given traits. Statistical testing, such as chi square testing, is essential for examining patterns of inheritance and for determining the frequency of an allele in a population. It is likely that you will be asked to calculate chi square on your final exam. $\chi^2 = \sum \dfrac{(o-e)^2}{e}$

TRY IT OUT: A male and a female rat were introduced to an island where no rats had previously lived. During the following year, the population grew to 800 individuals. This island has a carrying capacity of 2,000 and the rats have a maximum growth rate of 0.3. Locate the equation sheet inside the back cover of this book, and using the appropriate equation, calculate the growth rate for this population.

■ **Science Practice 3** is about asking appropriate questions when trying to understand biological phenomena. The best questions yield conclusive answers or lead to further investigations that will move you in the right direction, while vague questions often reveal confusion.

EXAMPLE: If you tried to design an experiment to answer the question, "How much energy is acquired from different fuel molecules?" you would have very little direction to help you focus your study. Instead, the more precise question, "Would a hungry animal get more energy from metabolizing fat or from metabolizing carbohydrates?" provides you with starting information to measure and analyze. This gets you much closer to drawing specific conclusions than would a question that is broad and vague.

Scientists who want to ask meaningful research questions first review the existing literature to learn what others have discovered. The results of this literature review guide the development of appropriate conditions and procedures for the design of new experiments. Experimental design, which always includes consideration of experimental controls, should specify an appropriate statistical analysis that will either support or contradict the hypothesis being addressed.

Examining evolutionary relationships among organisms can reveal patterns of evolutionary change that are modeled in phylogenetic trees and cladograms. It is important to ask appropriate questions about evolutionary relationships and be able to use phylogenetic trees in your answer.

Questions about genetic information require a high degree of specificity. You know from examining patterns of inheritance that even something as simple as dominant and recessive traits requires that you focus your questions. Think carefully about the data you need and the assumptions that must be met when considering questions concerning hereditary information.

Questions about biological systems, such as ecosystems, might include specific changes to particular trophic levels. Being able to trace movement of energy through an ecosystem would allow you to ask appropriate questions about how a change in one of the trophic levels might influence the overall structure and stability of that ecosystem. Which organisms are affected first? How are "ripple effects" understood?

TRY IT OUT: The food web below shows the complex relationships between the organisms of a grasslands community in Yellowstone National Park. One question you might ask to better understand these relationships is, "Which could survive without the others, producers or consumers?" What other questions could you ask about this community?

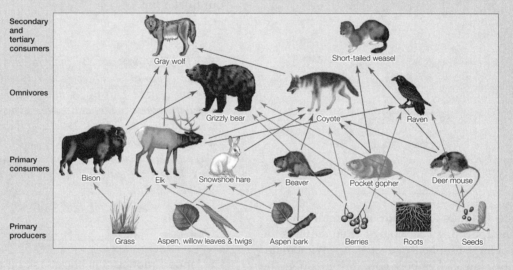

■ **Science Practice 4** directs your attention to data-collection strategies. How do you go about collecting and recording the information that will properly address the hypothesis you have carefully formulated?

EXAMPLE: Real life doesn't always allow us to impose stringent experimental treatments, making our powers of observation essential for learning about the world. For example, you may believe that an endangered population of birds depends on the availability of a certain type of cavity in an endangered species of tree. However, there might not be enough birds or trees left to do an actual

experiment, so you must make many observations from nature and try to develop facts needed to support or disprove your hypothesis.

To design your data-collection procedures for an experiment, you must first determine what you are going to manipulate and what you are going to measure. The condition that you manipulate, or change, is called the *independent variable* and is usually presented on the *x* axis. What you measure is called the *dependent variable*, because it is affected by, or *depends* on, the behavior of the independent variable. The dependent variable is typically shown on a graph's *y* axis. Experimental *controls* provide a fixed comparison to give your results validity. An experiment without a control is at risk of being dismissed due to the lack of a sound, real-world comparison. In class, you will likely be conducting experiments. When you do so, heed the rules about including control groups.

In an evolutionary inquiry, Science Practice 4 requires that you first examine an ecological setting or biological conditions that might affect reproduction and/or survival of a target species, and then determine which conditions most influence a particular phenotype. You need to ask the right question about the ecological setting (Science Practice 3). For example does a particular piece of body armor on some individuals better protect them from predation? Have you accounted for all of the selective pressures that could influence the evolution of that particular phenotype? Then you must collect data in such a way that your question will be answered; it is essential that you set up proper data-collection techniques.

The exam could require you to formulate specific questions about the pathway a key nutrient takes in a biological process, such as respiration for photosynthesis. Or you might be asked to design an experiment that tests the effects of temperature or pH on the activity of an enzyme in a pathway. You should be able to explain how you would use your results to answer your question. The ability to plan, carry out, and justify a selected data-collection strategy is the emphasis of Science Practice 4.

TRY IT OUT: Evidence suggests that high school students that start classes later in the day learn more and drive more safely than those who start the school day earlier. Determine the data you would need to gather to support this hypothesis. With a partner, discuss how you would collect and record your data.

■ **Science Practice 5** refers to the method by which you find meaning in the data you have collected. Graphing your data is often the first step in learning from your work. Remember which axis represents each condition, as noted above, and accurately label everything on your graph.

EXAMPLE: The activity of an enzyme catalyzing a reaction may increase as temperature begins to increase but then stops once a certain temperature has been exceeded. Though you may recognize this as the classic determination of optimal temperature for enzyme

activity, you should also provide a sentence or two that describes what is shown on the graph you have drawn. Assume that nothing is obvious; describe everything carefully, as points are earned in answers that more fully describe the findings, even if they seem obvious to you.

Once your graph is constructed, you need to extract meaning from it. You may be asked to judge the quality of a set of data, such as whether or not test tubes have been mislabeled or reagents have been accidentally omitted from the reaction mix. Other common examples to test your data analysis and presentation/interpretation skills are graphical representations of predator-prey relationships and competition between species for resources. Remember that you have to provide a thorough explanation for your answer.

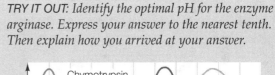

TRY IT OUT: Identify the optimal pH for the enzyme arginase. Express your answer to the nearest tenth. Then explain how you arrived at your answer.

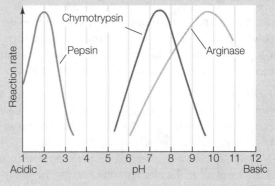

■ **Science Practice 6** is about the way we explain scientific observations, formulate solutions to science problems, and expand biological knowledge. In short, it addresses the fit between data and a scientific theory and the way new data allow a theory to be revised and refined for greater accuracy. Experiments must be very carefully designed, including adequate control groups. The data should fit into a clear conclusion that either supports or fails to support the hypothesis.

A theory is a set of principles and ideas about a scientific phenomenon. With Science Practice 6, science theories and knowledge become more accurate and useful as experiments progress.

EXAMPLE: The most important theory in biology, Charles Darwin's theory of natural selection, has an incredible range of supporting data. Its scope is broadening every day, as scientists continue to discover evidence of connections and changes that were unknown in Darwin's time.

An experiment requires that we first formulate a hypothesis about a scientific problem. This not only provides a reasonable and plausible explanation for a scientific observation, but the specific hypothesis poses detailed questions. It is important to understand that hypotheses are never proven; they are either supported or not supported. Be sure to identify a specific hypothesis when you formulate experiments, and be clear that your experiment will support, or fail to support, that hypothesis.

> *TRY IT OUT: In the previous problem, you were asked to identify the optimal pH for the enzyme arginase, which is 9.6. An important skill in science is the ability to provide a justification for your reasoning. In one or two sentences, further justify your reasoning, based on the diagram, for why 9.6 is an optimal pH for arginase.*

■ **Science Practice 7** requires that you demonstrate knowledge of the connections and relationships of biological phenomena across different scales and concepts and in diverse areas of scientific theory.

EXAMPLE: In a classic tale that demonstrates the importance of connecting data, a number of people standing in darkness put their hands on different parts of an elephant and describe to the others what they feel. No piece of data alone reveals what the animal is, but combining all of the observations enables the group to conclude that the animal being investigated is an elephant.

It can be challenging to comprehend the idea of scale. A very large elephant is made up of trillions of molecules produced by trillions of chemical reactions, some moving in one direction, some moving in the opposite direction. This requires you to shift your thoughts to a "population level." Similarly, piecing together evolutionary evidence requires you to consider hundreds of millions of years in which natural selection has operated, shaping the current observable phenotype.

A challenge in applying Science Practice 7 is working across different domains of scientific endeavor. For example, you may know that a certain plant or animal phenotype seems to have increased fitness. You may learn about the Mendelian pattern of genetic inheritance of the trait that increases fitness. You may find that the gene codes for a specific protein, and this protein can act as a switch for other genes to be expressed. In this example, you have spanned gene expression to evolutionary change.

> *TRY IT OUT: Evolution is a key idea of biology. Frequently, biology classes discuss evolution only from an organismal point of view, talking about how populations evolve. But change happens on other levels as well. With a partner, discuss where else we see evolution in biology. But remember, individuals themselves do not evolve.*

Finding an effective approach to developing valid answers to scientific questions is important in this course. You are always encouraged to ask questions, and your ability to state them in a scientifically appropriate framework will help you succeed in laboratory investigations and writing projects. Approach problem-solving with *cause-and-effect* thinking. Then choose your words carefully and express yourself clearly.

With the help of your textbook, this guide, and your classroom activities, you will obtain new skills for understanding how these Science Practices are utilized. You will then be able to use experiments to communicate scientific phenomena and solve scientific problems.

TRY IT OUT (answers)

Science Practice 1: The diagram could make better use of three dimensions. Shapes and colors could be more realistic. *(There are many possible answers to this question.)*

Science Practice 2: *144*

Science Practice 3: *(There are many possible answers to this question.)*

Science Practice 4: It would be useful to gather data—via research and/or surveys—on students in both early- and late-start schools. Sources would include test grades, rates of driving accidents and infractions, etc. Data could be presented in the form of graphs, and conclusions would be based on these graphs.

Science Practice 5: 9.6 or 9.7; The curve for arginase is highest at 9.6.

Science Practice 6: Because the curve for arginase peaks at a pH of 9.6, this is its optimal reaction rate.

Science Practice 7: Over evolutionary time, protein structures can be modified through mutations. Communities or organisms can change, and there are different successional patterns. *(There are many possible answers to this question.)*

Study Guide

to accompany

Principles of

SECOND EDITION

Hillis • Sadava • Hill • Price

1 Principles of Life

Chapter Outline

1.1 – Living Organisms Share Common Aspects of Structure, Function, and Energy Flow
1.2 – Life Depends on Organization and Energy
1.3 – Genetic Systems Control the Flow, Exchange, Storage, and Use of Information
1.4 – Evolution Explains the Diversity as Well as the Unity of Life
1.5 – Science Is Based on Quantitative Observations, Experiments, and Reasoning

Living organisms share many structures and functions as the result of having evolved from a common ancestor. This chapter provides you with collective ideas of how life, genetics, and evolution operate.

You will begin to see how scientists make observations and design experiments. This chapter will help you succeed with the activities and curiosity-driven efforts that make up the laboratory portion of your course. You will soon be thinking like a scientist and understanding better how science knowledge grows from experiments. At the end of this and every subsequent chapter review, **Science Practices & Inquiry** will support you in developing and refining your own testable predictions of natural phenomena and explaining the results of experiments.

Chapter 1 ties principally with the AP Biology Curriculum Framework's **Big Idea 1:** The process of evolution drives the diversity and unity of life.

The specific parts of the AP Biology curriculum that are covered in Chapter 1 include:

- **1.A.1:** Natural selection is a major mechanism of evolution.

- **1.B.1:** Organisms share many conserved core processes and features that evolved and are widely distributed among organisms today.

- **1.B.2:** Phylogenetic trees and cladograms are graphical representations (models) of evolutionary history that can be tested.

- **1.D.1:** There are several hypotheses about the natural origin of life on Earth, each with supporting scientific evidence.

- **1.D.2:** Scientific evidence from many different disciplines supports models of the origin of life.

Chapter Review

Concept 1.1 *is an overview of living organisms and how they are connected by their shared traits.*

1. Organisms share many conserved biological, chemical, and structural characteristics. Briefly outline the distinctive characteristics of life shared by all living organisms.

a. _____

b. _____

c. _____

d. _____

e. _____

f. _____

g. _____

h. _____

2. How do the shared characteristics on your list (in Question 1) provide evidence for evolution?

_____

_____

_____

_____

_____

_____

_____

_____

_____

3. There are several competing hypotheses about the evolution of early life on Earth, but as life evolved, all cells clearly had requirements for raw materials and energy transfers. Briefly explain how the earliest living cells obtained raw materials and accomplished energy transfers.

_____

_____

_____

_____

_____

_____

_____

_____

_____

_____

_____

4. Briefly describe and discuss how living organisms have altered the oxygen concentration in the atmosphere over the past three billion years.

_____

_____

_____

_____

_____

_____

_____

_____

_____

_____

5. Phylogenetic trees and cladograms are graphical representations (models) of evolutionary history that can be tested. In the figure below, the two vertical fill-in boxes represent endosymbiotic events; label one vertical box "mitochondria" and the other "chloroplasts." In each of the three horizontal boxes, write the name of the domain for that group of organisms.

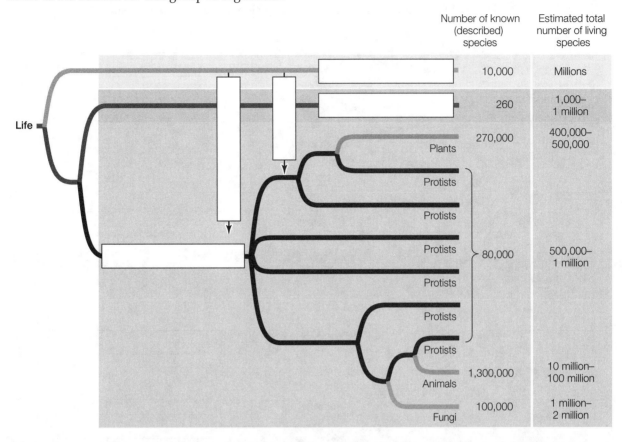

	Number of known (described) species	Estimated total number of living species
	10,000	Millions
	260	1,000–1 million
Plants	270,000	400,000–500,000
Protists		
Protists		
Protists	80,000	500,000–1 million
Protists		
Protists		
Protists		
Animals	1,300,000	10 million–100 million
Fungi	100,000	1 million–2 million

Concept 1.2 *shows how life depends on organization and energy.*

6. Consider these two organizational hierarchies:

atoms → organisms   populations → ecosystems

Describe one difference between the first hierarchy and the second. Then describe one similarity between the first hierarchy and the second.

_____

_____

_____

7. Dynamic regulation is required for maintaining homeostasis. Explain how a cellular mechanism that regulates the quantity of a biochemical product in a cell resembles the regulation of a heating and cooling system that keeps your room temperature comfortable.

_____

_____

_____

_____

_____

Concept 1.3 *helps you understand genetic information and its transmission from one generation to the next.*

8. In the fill-in boxes beside the figure below, label DNA, nucleotide, gene, and protein.

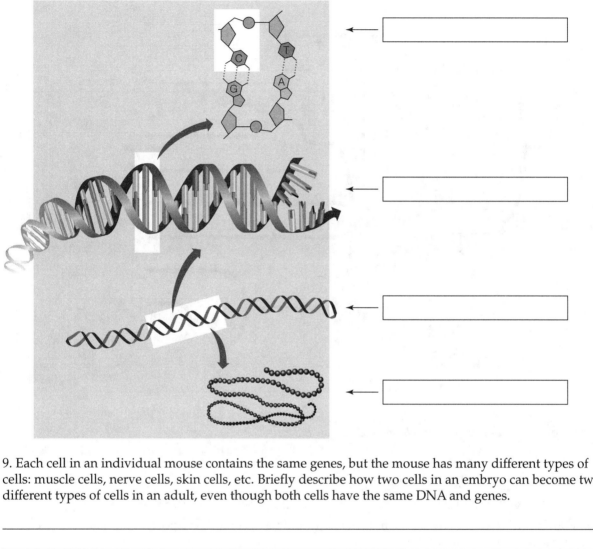

9. Each cell in an individual mouse contains the same genes, but the mouse has many different types of cells: muscle cells, nerve cells, skin cells, etc. Briefly describe how two cells in an embryo can become two different types of cells in an adult, even though both cells have the same DNA and genes.

_____
_____
_____
_____
_____
_____
_____
_____
_____
_____
_____
_____
_____
_____

Concept 1.4 *describes how evolution is the central unifying theme of biology and provides a framework for organizing how we think about living systems.*

10. "Theory" is an important term in science. How do scientists define a theory?

_____

_____

_____

11. Explain how evolution is both a fact and a theory.

_____

_____

_____

_____

_____

Concept 1.5 *focuses on how science is based on experiments, with observation, data collection, and analysis. Scientists are guided in their work by the principles of experimental design as they work to uncover the underlying characteristics of life.*

12. Biologist Tyrone Hayes and his co-workers investigated the effects of the herbicide atrazine on sexual development in frogs. In their experiments, they exposed each group of tadpoles to a specific amount of atrazine. To gain greater confidence in their results, they repeated each experiment multiple times for each treatment. Their observations suggest that frogs exposed to atrazine early in life developed multiple, mixed gonads or became demasculinized as a result.

Below is an excerpt describing the design of this experiment from the original paper, which can be found at www.pnas.org/content/99/8/5476.full.pdf+html.

> In Exp[eriment] 1, we exposed larvae to atrazine at nominal concentrations of 0.01, 0.1, 1.0, 10.0, and 25 parts per billion (ppb).... Concentrations were confirmed by two independent laboratories (PTRL West, Richmond, CA, and the Iowa Hygienic Laboratory, Univ. of Iowa, Iowa City, IO). All stock solutions were made in ethanol (10 ml), mixed in 15-gallon containers, and dispensed into treatment tanks. Controls were treated with ethanol such that all tanks contained 0.004% ethanol. Water was changed and treatments were renewed once every 72 h. Each treatment was replicated 3 times with 30 animals per replicate (total of 90 animals per treatment) in both experiments. All treatments were systematically rotated around the shelf every 3 days to ensure that no one treatment or no one tank experienced position effects. Experiments were carried out at 22°C with animals under a 12-h–12-h light-dark cycle (lights on at 6 a.m.).

Identify the following elements in the atrazine experiment.

a. Independent variable: _____

b. Range of the independent variable: _____

c. Dependent variable: _____

d. Control: _____

e. Constant conditions: _____

f. Repeated trials: _____

Science Practices & Inquiry

In the AP Biology Curriculum Framework, there are seven **Science Practices**. In this chapter, we focus on **Science Practice 4:** The student can plan and implement data collection strategies to answer a particular scientific question. More specifically, we look at **Science Practices 4.1** and **4.2:** The student can justify the selection of the kind of data needed and design a plan for collecting data to answer a particular scientific question.

Question 13 asks you to design a controlled experiment using goldfish as a model organism. One of the most important activities for scientists is to be able to design and conduct controlled experiments. A key component of any biology class is the laboratory experience; students must be able to design and plan experiments using inquiry.

13. After looking at many types of fish food available at a local store, a friend asks you which would make his goldfish grow faster, flake fish food or shrimp pellets. Design a controlled experiment to test this question.

(Hint: You are not simply writing the procedures in an experiment. In paragraph form, discuss all of the elements, a. through f., in Question 12. Begin by identifying your independent and dependent variables and writing a hypothesis. Your experimental design should include many goldfish in separate containers.)

2 The Chemistry and Energy of Life

Chapter Outline

2.1 – Atomic Structure Is the Basis for Life's Chemistry
2.2 – Atoms Interact and Form Molecules
2.3 – Carbohydrates Consist of Sugar Molecules
2.4 – Lipids Are Hydrophobic Molecules
2.5 – Biochemical Changes Involve Energy

Living organisms, such as birds and fish, are made up of cells—collections of molecules that work together. Interacting atoms make up the molecules, and it is necessary for you to understand a few details about atoms and molecules if you are going to be able to understand life. All life exists at the expense of its surrounding environment and is dependent on biochemical transformations of matter. These transformations occur within the laws of thermodynamics, specifying that energy is neither created nor destroyed and that disorder (entropy) increases during transformations.

Chapter 2 continues the consideration of **Big Idea 1**. Specific parts of the AP Biology curriculum that are covered in Chapter 2 include:

- **1.D.2:** Scientific evidence from many different disciplines supports models of the origin of life.

This chapter also begins your exploration of **Big Idea 2**, wherein you examine energy use by cells as you begin to catalogue the molecular building blocks of life processes. Included are:

- **2.A.1:** All living systems require constant input of free energy.

- **2.A.3:** Organisms must exchange matter with the environment to grow, reproduce, and maintain organization.

The chapter introduces **Big Idea 4**: Biological systems interact, and these systems and their interactions possess complex properties. Specifically, it addresses:

- **4.A.1:** The subcomponents of biological molecules and their sequence determine the properties of that molecule.

- **4.B.1:** Interactions between molecules affect their structure and function.

- **4.C.1:** Variation in molecular units provides cells with a wider range of functions.

Chapter Review

Concept 2.1 *reviews some details about atomic structure in order to understand how molecules function in living organisms.*

1. For each of the following, provide the number of electrons, protons, and neutrons, and the atomic number in its elemental form. Look for the information in your textbook or on a periodic table of the elements.

	electrons	protons	neutrons	atomic number
a. hydrogen	_____	_____	_____	_____
b. carbon	_____	_____	_____	_____
c. oxygen	_____	_____	_____	_____
d. phosphorus	_____	_____	_____	_____

Concept 2.2 *explains how molecules result from interactions between atoms.*

2. Arrange the following atomic interactions from strongest to weakest: van der Waals forces, covalent bonds, hydrogen bonds, ionic bonds.

_____ > _____ > _____ > _____

3. Define *cation*.

_____

_____

4. Define *anion*.

_____

_____

5. Using sodium chloride as an example, explain how electron imbalances cause atoms to interact with one another.

_____

_____

_____

_____

6. Name the molecule shown by the two models at the right.

_____

Explain how the electrons of these atoms are affected by their atomic interaction, and describe what this does to the distribution of charge around the molecule.

_____

_____

_____

_____

_____

7. Drawings (A) and (B) are shown at different magnifications. They represent three molecules, two of which are interacting with each other and a third that is interacting with itself. Explain the interactions in each. Then explain why you think (A) and (B) have either the same number of atoms or a different number of atoms.

   a. Interactions in (A) _____

_____

_____

_____

b. Interactions in (B) _____

_____

_____

c. (A) and (B) have (the same/a different) number of atoms because _____

_____

_____

_____

d. More atoms are represented in drawing _____ because _____

_____

_____

_____

8. The two chemicals at the right are found in the body and differ in their solubility in water. One is quite soluble, and the other is much less soluble. Explain this by completing the sentences below.

(A)

(B)

a. Choice _____ is more water-soluble because _____

_____

_____

_____

b. Choice _____ is less water-soluble because _____

_____

_____

_____

Concept 2.3 *explains how carbohydrates, or sugar molecules, yield chemical energy when catabolized (taken apart). Many organisms, including plants, catabolize glucose and other sugars to liberate energy for their own use. Plants also synthesize sugars by using solar energy and environmental sources of carbon dioxide and water.*

9. Solar energy drives _photosyn thesis_ in green plants, resulting in the synthesis of _glucose_____, a monosaccharide. Sucrose is a disaccharide resulting from the formation of a _glycosidic_____ linkage between two monosaccharides. The starch molecule, also known as _polysaccharide_is an even larger polymer of the products of these synthetic processes, and the most abundant member of this group on Earth is _cellulose_____.

10. Number the carbons in the figure at the right.
    What are the names of these two monosaccharides?

    <u>Ribose</u>
    <u>   Deoxyribose</u>

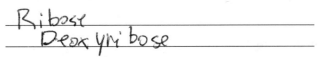
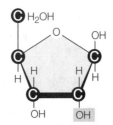
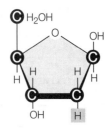

Concept 2.4 *explains that lipids (fats) are large storage molecules that do not dissolve readily in water.*

11. Refer to the models below.

    a. Provide labels for the four different areas of the molecule, indicated by the four shaded blocks on
       each representation. (Two models are shown.)

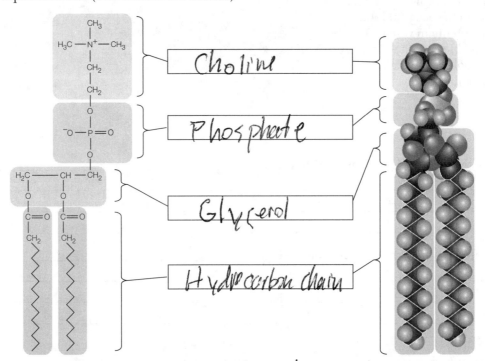

Choline

Phosphate

Glycerol

Hydrocarbon chain

    b. The hydrophobic tail includes <u>hydrocarbon chains</u>

    c. The hydrophilic head includes <u>choline and phosphate</u>

12. Steroids and other fatty substances pass readily through most cellular membranes because
    <u>They are ~~hydrophilic~~ hydrophobic</u>

Concept 2.5 *explains how energy for life comes from biochemical changes in molecules.*

13. Anabolic steroids are drugs that are sometimes misused by people who want to increase their athletic prowess. Describe what is meant by *anabolic* in this term.

A complex molecule formed by linking simple molecules.

Science Practices & Inquiry

There are seven **Science Practices** in the AP Biology Curriculum Framework. In this chapter, we focus on **Science Practice 6:** The student can work with scientific explanations and theories. More specifically, we look at **Science Practice 6.2:** The student can construct explanations of phenomena based on evidence produced through scientific practices.

Questions 14–17 ask you to construct explanations based on evidence of how variations in molecular units provide cells with a wider range of functions (**Learning Objective 4.22**).

In 1953, Stanley Miller and Harold Urey set up an apparatus, depicted at the right, to simulate Earth's early atmosphere. The gases they added in their original setup were methane (CH_4), ammonia (NH_3), hydrogen (H_2), water (H_2O), carbon dioxide (CO_2), and nitrogen gas (N_2). Energy was added by passing a spark across two electrodes and by boiling the reactants. After one week of continuous sparking and boiling of this "primordial soup," several amino acids—including aspartic acid, glycine, and alanine—were found in the condensed fluid from the apparatus.

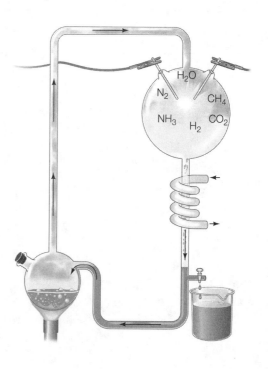

The final lines from the original paper state:

> In this apparatus an attempt was made to duplicate a primitive atmosphere of the earth, and not to obtain the optimum conditions for the formation of amino acids. Although in this case the total yield was small for the energy expended, it is possible that, with more efficient apparatus … this type of process would be a way of commercially producing amino acids. A more complete analysis of the amino acids and other products of the discharge is now being performed and will be reported in detail shortly.

14. Define *abiogenesis*.

The theory that life can arise spontaneously from nonliving molecules, under certain conditions.

15. Define *biogenesis*.

The theory that life or living organisms can only be created from other living organisms and not from nonliving molecule or matter

16. Explain whether or not abiogenesis and biogenesis were demonstrated in the Miller–Urey experiment.

_____

_____

_____

17. Discuss this claim: "The Miller–Urey apparatus proves that life originated in a primordial sea."

_____

_____

_____

_____

_____

_____

_____

_____

_____

_____

_____

3 Nucleic Acids, Proteins, and Enzymes

Chapter Outline

3.1 – Nucleic Acids Are Informational Macromolecules
3.2 – Proteins Are Polymers with Important Structural and Metabolic Roles
3.3 – Some Proteins Act as Enzymes to Speed Up Biochemical Reactions
3.4 – Regulation of Metabolism Occurs by Regulation of Enzymes

As you saw in Chapter 2, smaller molecules (monomers) can bond together to form larger molecules (macromolecules). Chapter 3 focuses on the relationships between two related groups of monomers: the nucleic acids and the proteins. In later chapters, you will see that proteins form the structural components of many cells and serve as the enzymes that speed up many metabolic processes in the cells.

Chapter 3 continues the consideration of **Big Idea 1** and investigates **Big Idea 3** and **Big Idea 4**. You study the structure of RNA and DNA and examine proteins and enzymes. Specific parts of the AP Biology curriculum covering **Big Idea 1:** The process of evolution drives the diversity and unity of life, include:

- **1.D.2:** Scientific evidence from many different disciplines supports models of the origin of life.

Specific parts of the AP Biology curriculum that address **Big Idea 3:** Living systems store, retrieve, transmit and respond to information essential to life processes, include:

- **3.A.1:** DNA, and in some cases RNA, is the primary source of heritable information.

Specific parts of the curriculum covering **Big Idea 4:** Biological systems interact, and these systems and their interactions possess complex properties, include:

- **4.A.1:** The subcomponents of biological molecules and their sequence determine the properties of that molecule.

- **4.B.1:** Interactions between molecules affect their structure and function.

Chapter Review

Concept 3.1 *explains how the nucleic acids DNA and RNA are polymers of nucleotides connected each to the next by a bond called a phosphodiester linkage. These macromolecules are used by cells to code genetic information because the sequence of nucleotides determines the sequence of amino acids in proteins. The structures of proteins, in turn, determine their structural, enzymatic, and other functions.*

1. Identify the three major differences between RNA and DNA.

   a. _Sugar Group (DNA is deoxyribose, RNA ribose)_
   b. _____
   c. _____

2. Explain the difference between a polynucleotide and an oligonucleotide. Give an example of each.

   _____
   _____
   _____
   _____

3. In the diagram at the right, identify and label *all* of the following:

     two 3′ ends
     two 5′ ends
     four purine bases
     four pyrimidine bases
     ten hydrogen bonds
     six phosphodiester bonds

This drawing is an example of (circle one):

     (DNA)   RNA

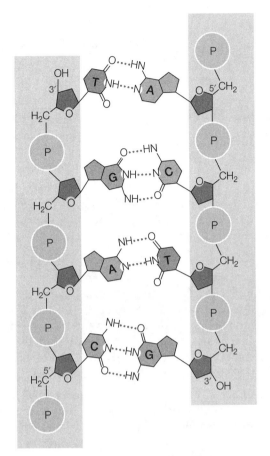

4. DNA sequences are frequently compared between two groups of organisms to determine how closely they are related in terms of their evolutionary past. For example, the Asian and African elephants were believed to be the only two living species of elephants. However, recent DNA testing showed enough DNA differences between Africa's forest and savanna elephants to identify them as two separate species. Explain why DNA sequences, but not carbohydrates or lipids, are used for this type of taxonomic analysis.

Since the DNA strands are complementary, its preferred.

Concept 3.2 *explains how proteins are macromolecules comprised of amino acids linked together by peptide linkages. Proteins serve many diverse roles, including structural, metabolic, enzymatic, and regulatory. There are at least four levels of protein structure.*

5. There are 20 different amino acids in humans. You do not need to memorize all 20, but you should know the structure of a generalized amino acid. At the right, draw a generic amino acid, using the letter "R" to designate a generic side chain, and be sure to include and label the carboxyl group and the amino group.

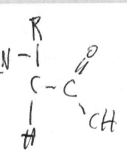

6. Explain how 20 different amino acids permit 75,000 different proteins to be found in humans.

All humans have unique protein.

7. Most proteins have at least four levels of physical structure. Briefly describe each level below, and identify where it is found in a protein molecule.

a. Primary: _____
_____

b. Secondary: _____
_____

c. Tertiary: _____
_____

d. Quaternary: _____
_____

8. Draw structural representations of glutamic acid and lysine.

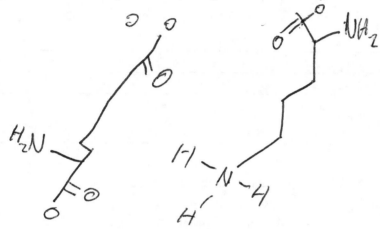

a. Which has two carboxyl groups? _____ Circle and label all carboxyl groups.

b. Which has two amino groups? _____ Circle and label all amino groups.

c. In the space below, draw a dipeptide composed of lysine and glutamic acid bound together by a peptide bond. Identify the peptide bond with an arrow.

9. Different sequences of amino acids in proteins are the cause of different structures and functions of various proteins. A mutational change in the genetic code for a protein can change the sequence of amino acids that are peptide-bonded together during protein synthesis. Using the amino acids shown, explain what might happen to the structure of a protein for each of the substitutions described below.

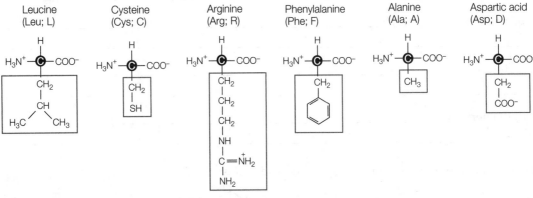

a. Leucine substituted for cysteine:

_____

_____

_____

b. Arginine substituted for phenylalanine:

_____

_____

_____

c. Alanine substituted for aspartic acid:

_____

_____

_____

10. Identify which one of the two proteins shown at the right includes quaternary structure, and explain your choice.

_____

_____

_____

_____

_____

(A)   (B)

11. A solution was made of water, salts, and enzymes (functional proteins). After adding a strong acid, the enzymes no longer functioned as reaction catalysts. Explain how adding the strong acid altered the proteins' structures and functions. Be sure to include the following terms in your answer: protons, three dimensional structure, carboxyl groups, polarity, tertiary structure, and denaturation.

_____

_____

_____

_____

Concept 3.3 *focuses on one of the major roles of proteins, that of enzymes or biological catalysts. Enzymes speed up some of the biochemical reactions of life by lowering the activation rate of such reactions.*

12. Explain how an enzyme can speed up a chemical reaction between two substrate molecules.

_____

_____

_____

_____

_____

13. On the graph below, label the following: the energy state of the products, the energy state of the reactants, the amount of energy of activation for the catalyzed reaction, and the amount of energy of activation for the uncatalyzed reaction.

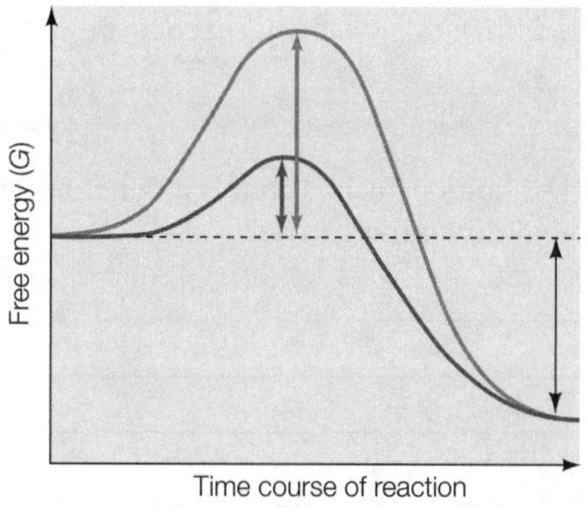

Time course of reaction

14. The diagram below represents the enzyme sucrase. The specificity of most enzymes is such that each only "recognizes" very particular substrates. Using your knowledge of protein structure, explain how sucrase binds to the disaccharide sucrose but does not bind to most other disaccharides.

_____

_____

_____

_____

_____

_____

_____

_____

15. An "induced fit" occurs when enzymes change their shape as a result of binding to a substrate. Explain how binding to a substrate can cause an enzyme to change its shape.

_____

_____

_____

_____

16. Which of these three molecules—DNA, RNA, and protein—most likely operated prior to the appearance of the other two molecules? Explain how your choice of the earliest "proto-life" chemical can serve more than one function.

_____

_____

_____

17. Explain the difference between cofactors and coenzymes in relation to the different functions of different proteins.

_____

_____

_____

Concept 3.4 _notes that regulation of enzymes allows organisms to more precisely maintain a constant internal state, a process called homeostasis. In addition to regulation, enzymes are affected by many environmental factors, including pH and temperature._

18. Regulation is an important part of homeostasis. What is a benefit of an organism being able to regulate an enzyme's activity, such as the breakdown of glucose?

_____

_____

_____

19. Which picture in the diagram below is an example of allosteric regulation? Explain.

(A) Competitive inhibition

(B) Noncompetitive inhibition

Science Practices & Inquiry

Chapter 3 addresses **Science Practice 4:** The student can plan and implement data collection strategies appropriate to a particular scientific question. This exercise is based more specifically on **Science Practice 4.1:** The student can justify the selection of the kind of data needed to answer a particular scientific question, and **Science Practice 4.2:** The student can design a plan for collecting data to answer a particular scientific question.

20. Edward Stone's letter to the Royal Society, dated 1763, detailed his ideas on aspirin as a painkiller. Stone tested 50 people to formulate his ideas. Design a sample that a scientist like Edward Stone could use for modern-day research in the drug industry. You may wish to research double-blind studies and include this in your design.

_____
_____
_____
_____
_____
_____
_____
_____
_____
_____
_____
_____
_____
_____
_____
_____
_____
_____
_____
_____
_____
_____
_____
_____
_____
_____

4 Cells: The Working Units of Life

Chapter Outline

You already know that living organisms are made up of cells. Think of cells as small, water-filled balloons holding the mixture of proteins, ions, and other molecules that is necessary for life. In this chapter you learn about intracellular organelles that compartmentalize biochemical activities necessary for cellular life. Not all cells have these organelles. In fact, the most numerous cells on the planet, those of the *Archaea* and *Bacteria*, lack organelles, and this absence of organelles is a defining characteristic of simple, ancient cells called prokaryotic cells. Eukaryotic cells, such as those in our bodies, are larger in size and have numerous membranous internal structures. These are the organelles. By relegating certain types of processes to certain types of organelles, eukaryotic cells are extremely efficient.

Chapter 4 spans all four of the **Big Ideas** in the AP Biology Curriculum Framework. Try to develop your understanding across these ideas.

Big Idea 1 recognizes that evolution ties together all parts of biology. In Chapter 4 we look at a theory for the development of cell complexity with:

• **1.D.2:** Scientific evidence from many different disciplines supports models of the origin of life.

Big Idea 2 recognizes that the utilization of free energy and use of molecular building blocks are characteristic fundamentals of life processes. Specifically, Chapter 4 includes:

• **2.A.3:** Organisms must exchange matter with the environment to grow, reproduce, and maintain organization.

• **2.B.3:** Eukaryotic cells maintain internal membranes that partition the cell into specialized regions, including the rough endoplasmic reticulum, mitochondria, chloroplasts, Golgi apparatus, nucleus, and smooth endoplasmic reticulum.

Big Idea 3 recognizes that living systems store, retrieve, and transmit information essential to life processes. Specifically, Chapter 4 lays this groundwork by including:

• **3.D.2:** Cells communicate with each other through direct contact with other cells or from a distance via chemical signaling. Examples include immune cells and plasmodesmata between plant cells.

Big Idea 4 recognizes that biological systems interact in complex ways. Chapter 4 includes:

• **4.A.2:** The structure and function of subcellular components, and their interactions, provide essential cellular processes.

Chapter Review

Concept 4.1 *introduces the idea that multicellular life forms contain billions of cells. These cells come from pre-existing cells, and they are the basic units of most life forms. The principles that apply to single cells apply to whole organisms. Just like whole organisms, cells can stay alive and persist only when nutrients are available and waste materials do not reach dangerous or toxic levels. The size of cells is limited by how quickly materials can cross the membranes on the surface.*

1. Most cells are quite small. Limits on cell size are related to limits on the rate of movement of "good stuff in" and "bad stuff out" across cell membranes. Movement rates are greatly influenced by the surface area-to-volume ratio of the cells.

Imagine three cube-shaped cells. Given the dimensions shown for each cube-shaped cell here, calculate that cell's surface area, its volume, and its surface area-to-volume ratio.

	10 µm	20 µm	100 µm
Surface area (SA)			
Volume (V)			
SA:V ratio			

2. As the amount of a membrane-crossing toxin increases around the outside of the three cube-shaped cells in the above diagram, which cell would be the first to have an enriched concentration of the toxin in its center (core) region? Explain your answer using the surface area-to-volume ratio.

_____

_____

_____

_____

_____

3. Use this logarithmic scale to determine how many 100 µm cells you would have to stack on top of each other to make the stack as tall as an athlete of 2 m height. (*Hint*: 2 m = _____ µm)

| 0.1 nm | 1 nm | 10 nm | 100 nm | 1 µm | 10 µm | 100 µm | 1 mm | 1 cm | 0.1 m | 1 m | 10 m | 100 m | 1 km |

_____

_____

_____

_____

_____

How many 10 µm prokaryotic cells would be needed to reach the same height? _____

Concept 4.2 *shows how the nucleoid region in prokaryotic cells serves the same hereditary functions served by the membrane-bound nucleus in eukaryotic cells.*

4. Explain how prokaryotes, despite lacking cellular organelles, are able to carry out many of the same enzymatically catalyzed biochemical conversions that eukaryotes carry out.

_____

_____

_____

_____

_____

_____

5. Describe, in general terms, the structural components of ribosomes, including a brief explanation of their function. Explain whether ribosomes are present only in eukaryotes, only in prokaryotes, or in both eukaryotes and prokaryotes. A drawing might be helpful, but make sure you explain the drawing.

_____

_____

_____

_____

_____

_____

6. Humans, perhaps unjustly, claim credit for inventing the wheel. Discuss the argument that prokaryotes using their flagella long preceded the human "invention" of the wheel.

_____

_____

_____

_____

_____

_____

7. Some models wrongly portray the prokaryotic cell as a plastic bag of alphabet soup with a golf ball included to represent the nucleus. Discuss how this model is not a good representation of a prokaryotic cell, and be sure to discuss the cytoskeleton in your answer.

_____

_____

_____

_____

_____

_____

_____

Concept 4.3 *explains that the nucleus in a eukaryotic cell serves the same hereditary functions served by the nucleoid region in a prokaryotic cell. Eukaryotic cells also have many other cellular organelles.*

8. Many hormones, such as insulin, are proteins secreted by cells. Describe the structure and function of four cellular organelles needed for the synthesis and secretion of protein signals.

_____

_____

_____

_____

_____

_____

9. Identify the two primary groups of molecules that interact to become ribosomes, and include a description of where ribosomes are synthesized in eukaryotic cells.

_____

_____

_____

_____

10. One of your fellow classmates tells you, "The mitochondrion is the site where ingested glucose molecules are made into ATP molecules." Kindly point out the error of your classmate's statement by offering a statement that is more correct. (*Hint:* Is glucose biochemically converted to ATP?)

_____

_____

_____

_____

Concept 4.4 *explains how the cytoskeleton of eukaryotic cells provides strength and coordinates movement.*

11. Describe how the cilia-based movement of a paramecium is similar to, yet different from, movement by an amoeba.

_____

_____

_____

_____

12. Compare eukaryotic flagella and cilia in terms of structural size and in number present, using *Euglena* with flagella *versus* ciliated *Paramecium* as examples.

_____

_____

_____

_____

13. The longest cells of eukaryotes, as you might guess, are found as neurons in giraffes. Such cells can be two or more meters in length. The length of such cells includes an impressive mechanism for moving proteins from one end of the cell to the other. Describe the intracellular transport system, including vesicles, microtubules, and motor-proteins, for such long and thin cells.

_____

_____

_____

_____

_____

_____

Concept 4.5 *discusses how cells can interact with other cells and send and receive chemical signals at specialized regions on the surface of the cell.*

14. Correct and expand on this statement: "Adjacent plant cells are joined together by walls made up of only phospholipid molecules and proteins."

_____

_____

_____

_____

15. Correct and expand on this statement: "Sugar molecules hold adjacent animal cells together."

_____

_____

_____

16. Specialized connections between adjacent cells in your heart hold them together closely so that blood does not leak out between the cells as the heart dynamically pumps your blood. The pressure of pumping would blow apart adjacent cells, were they not held tightly together by a second specialized connection. Furthermore, coordinated pumping activity of these cells relies on a third specialization between them. Describe how these three types of intercellular connections (shown at the right) work together in the functioning heart.

_____

_____

_____

_____

_____

_____

17. What do the characteristics of prokaryotic cells tell us about how the first eukaryotic cells originated? Using your knowledge of cellular organelles, create a model (flow chart) showing the steps involved in the evolution of eukaryotic cells from a chemical-rich environment.

Science Practices & Inquiry

In the AP Biology Curriculum Framework, there are seven **Science Practices**. In this chapter, we focus on **Science Practice 2**: The student can use mathematics appropriately. More specifically, we will use **Science Practice 2.2**: The student can apply mathematical routines to quantities that describe natural phenomena.

Question 18 addresses **Science Practice 2** by using your knowledge of math to enhance your understanding of biology. The ability to relate math to biology is important. You will calculate a surface area-to-volume ratio, then use this information to explain how cells of different sizes might eliminate wastes or procure nutrients faster by diffusion (**Learning Objective 2.6**). Why are cells the size they are?

18. Calculate the ratio (SA : V) of surface area (SA) to volume (V) for a cube with dimensions typical of eukaryotic cells (i.e., cells that are 0.1 mm in length on each side). Explain why bacteria need to divide well before they grow to the size of eukaryotic cells.

_____
_____
_____
_____
_____
_____
_____
_____

5 Cell Membranes and Signaling

Chapter Outline

5.1 – Biological Membranes Have a Common Structure and Are Fluid
5.2 – Passive Transport across Membranes Requires No Input of Energy
5.3 – Active Transport Moves Solutes against Their Concentration Gradients
5.4 – Large Molecules Cross Membranes via Vesicles
5.5 – The Membrane Plays a Key Role in a Cell's Response to Environmental Signals
5.6 – Signal Transduction Allows the Cell to Respond to Its Environment

Living organisms, such as birds and fish, are made up of cells. These cells are collections of molecules that work together. Surrounding each cell is a plasma membrane that serves as a boundary between the cell and the environment. The cell membrane is much more than a just a boundary, because it includes proteins that regulate what goes into or out of the cell.

Intercellular communication is essential for multicellular forms of life. It provides precision in homeostasis, serves as the site of self-recognition and cell defense (immune system), and responds to changes in the environment. Proteins in membranes serve as receptors for many communication messages from other cells.

Chapter 5 emphasizes **Big Idea 3** but also includes some of **Big Idea 2** and **Big Idea 4**.

Big Idea 2 states that the utilization of free energy and the use of molecular building blocks are characteristic of all life. Specific parts of the AP Biology curriculum that are covered in Chapter 5 include:

• **2.B.1:** Cell membranes are selectively permeable due to their structure.

• **2.B.2:** Growth and dynamic homeostasis are maintained by the constant movement of molecules across membranes.

Big Idea 3 states that living systems store, retrieve, transmit, and respond to information essential to life processes. Chapter 5 explains cell communication, addressing:

• **3.B.2:** A variety of intercellular and intracellular signal transmissions mediate gene expression.

• **3.D.1:** Cell communication processes share common features that reflect a shared evolutionary history.

• **3.D.3:** Signal transduction pathways link signal reception with cellular response.

• **3.D.4:** Changes in signal transduction pathways can alter cellular response.

Big Idea 4 states that biological systems interact in complex ways. Specifically Chapter 5 includes:

• **4.C.1:** Variation in molecular units provides cells with a wider range of functions.

Chapter Review

Concept 5.1 *explains that membranes surrounding cells have a common structure through all forms of life: a phospholipid bilayer that is embedded with proteins, and carbohydrates that serve several functions. Additional characteristics of membranes include a thick, hydrophobic middle layer as well as inner and outer layers. The inner and outer layers are thin and have hydrophilic properties.*

1. On the diagram below, label the following: phospholipid, cholesterol, cytoskeleton, cell interior (cytoplasm), integral protein, peripheral protein, and carbohydrate. In the space below the figure, explain what information you would use to determine which side of the membrane faces the inside of the cell and which side faces the extracellular environment.

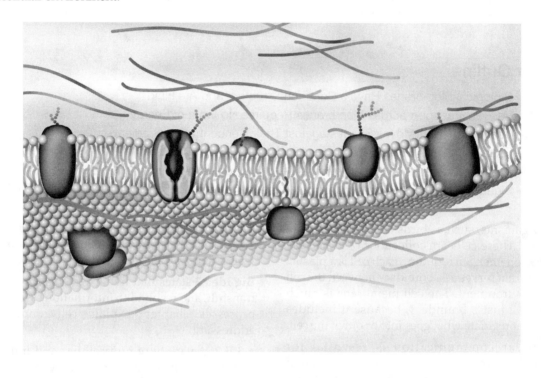

_____

_____

_____

_____

2. Descriptions of the plasma membrane often refer to a "fluid mosaic" model. Provide evidence that the membrane is "fluid," and describe the "mosaic" of this model.

_____

_____

_____

_____

3. Explain how the structure of an individual phospholipid molecule allows these molecules to form a membrane with a nonpolar/hydrophobic middle layer and polar/hydrophilic inner and outer layers.

_____

_____

_____

_____

4. Describe one physical factor and one chemical factor that influence membrane fluidity.

_____

_____

5. In addition to phospholipids, many other molecules have both polar and nonpolar regions. For a large protein that spans the phospholipid membrane, describe how this characteristic facilitates its correct placement in membranes. Add an amphipathic protein embedded in the membrane to the diagram at the right . Label the polar and nonpolar regions of both the membrane and the large protein.

_____

_____

_____

_____

6. Explain how some organisms cope with the temperature extremes of hot summers and cold winters by altering the biochemical composition of membranes.

_____

_____

_____

_____

7. Describe the two major structural components and one function of glycoproteins.

_____

_____

_____

_____

Concept 5.2 *explains that kinetic energy drives the movement of substances from an area of high concentration to an area of low concentration. Diffusion is the term that describes such movement across cell membranes. Not all molecules readily diffuse across membranes, because the molecular size and polarity of a molecule determine whether or not it can enter the phospholipid bilayer. Osmosis is the diffusion of water across membranes.*

8. In the example at the right, a drop of ink was placed into a bowl of gelatin. Explain how the ink diffused throughout the gel even though there were no currents to help move it around.

_____

_____

_____

_____

_____

9. Describe two differences between passive transport and active transport.

_____

_____

_____

_____

10. Briefly explain how each of the following factors can alter the diffusion rates of solutes across membranes.

 a. Size of the diffusing solute: _____

 _____

 _____

 _____

 b. Temperature: _____

 _____

 _____

 _____

 c. Concentration gradient: _____

 _____

 _____

 _____

11. Some topical anesthetics dissolve into the membranes of sensory neurons to reduce their activity. Describe two structural properties of an anesthesia-inducing molecule that would make it a likely candidate for this route of anesthetic effect.

 _____

 _____

 _____

12. Even though water can readily move across many natural membranes, explain why it might be expected to move slowly or not at all through artificial membranes constructed without proteins.

 _____

 _____

 _____

13. The three terms below are used when comparing solute concentration on either side of a cell membrane. Define each term and describe how that condition might affect a cell's shape.

 a. Isotonic: _____

 _____

 _____

 _____

 b. Hypotonic: _____

 _____

 _____

 _____

 c. Hypertonic: _____

 _____

 _____

 _____

14. Facilitated diffusion refers to a special type of transport. For example, the entry of glucose into the muscles in your body is considered facilitated diffusion. Is this type of transmembrane movement an example of active transport or passive transport? Explain why.

_____

_____

_____

_____

15. After several days without watering, plants tend to wilt. When a wilted plant is watered, it will often return to its normal shape. Explain how cells and water movements are involved in the transition from wilted to not wilted.

_____

_____

_____

_____

16. Explain how the carrier protein in the diagram below is facilitating the diffusion of a molecule. Include an explanation for why the protein is needed.

_____

_____

_____

_____

Concept 5.3 *considers active transport and describes the movement of substances against their chemical concentration gradient, which requires energy.*

17. Describe the primary chemical process that occurs inside the cell to drive active transport.

_____

_____

_____

_____

_____

18. Complete the table below:

	Simple diffusion	Facilitated diffusion (channel or carrier protein)	Active transport
Cellular energy required?			
Driving force			
Membrane protein required?			
Specificity			

19. The Na^+–K^+-ATPase is the most active and widespread active-transport system in the human body. Add labels and processes on the diagram below to describe how this pump functions.

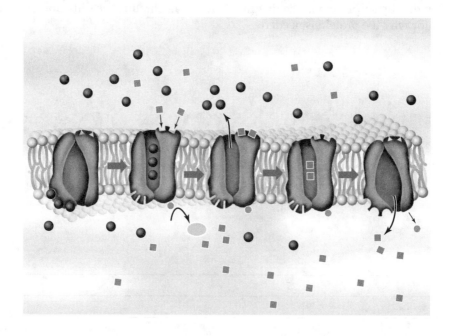

Concept 5.4 *examines how many large molecules cannot cross membranes via transporters embedded in membranes; rather, such compounds enter or leave cells via vesicles, in a process called endocytosis or exocytosis, respectively.*

20. Explain the similarities and differences between phagocytosis and pinocytosis.

_____

_____

_____

_____

_____

21. Describe receptor-mediated endocytosis, using details that explain whether this process meets the criteria for active transport or passive transport.

_____

_____

_____

_____

_____

_____

Concept 5.5 *explains how some hormones (e.g., insulin and many other signals from outside the cell) are received and alter the cell's activity. This process is called a signal transduction. In order to respond, the cell must have a specific receptor that is modified by the stimulus. Once a receptor in the membrane is activated by the signal, it sets off a series of biochemical changes within the cell. These pathways are sequences of events and chemical reactions that lead to a cell's response to a signal. This ability to respond to the environment is critical to the organism's or cell's ability to maintain precision in its homeostatic mechanisms.*

22. Describe the three major steps in cell signaling.

_____

_____

_____

23. Different receptor proteins for different signals are found either on the membrane of the cell or in the cytoplasm of the cell, implying that the signal must enter the cell. Give an example of each receptor type below, and discuss the properties of the ligand (signal molecule) that activates this receptor.

    a. Intracellular receptor protein: _____

_____

_____

_____

_____

    b. Membrane-bound receptor protein: _____

_____

_____

_____

_____

24. If a cell has no proteins in its membrane, will it be able to respond to any environmental stimuli? Explain your answer.

_____

_____

_____

_____

_____

Concept 5.6 *shows how physical or chemical signals initiate responses from cells that have a signal transduction pathway for that signal. For example, signals that modify receptor proteins in membranes rapidly initiate a series of biochemical changes within the cell. The pathways affected by these biochemical changes are typically components in a signaling cascade that amplifies and distributes responses by effector proteins in the cell.*

25. Complete the diagram below showing an example of a signal cascade.

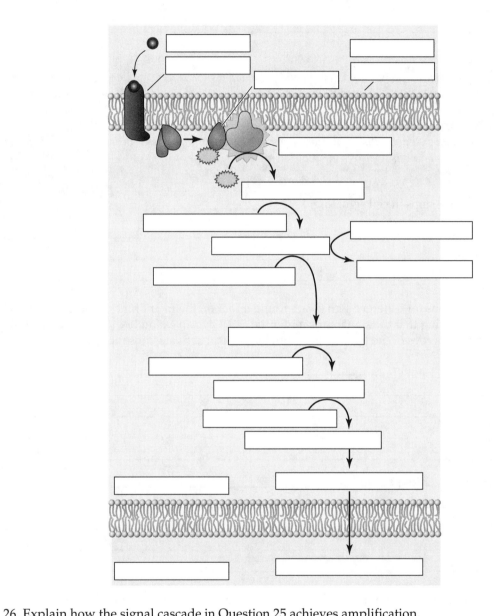

26. Explain how the signal cascade in Question 25 achieves amplification.

_____

_____

_____

_____

_____

_____

27. Describe how the signal cascade in Question 25 is terminated after the necessary response has been obtained.

_____

_____

_____

_____

_____

Science Practices & Inquiry

In the AP Biology Curriculum Framework, there are seven **Science Practices**. In this chapter, we focus on **Science Practice 1:** The student can use representations and models to communicate scientific phenomena and solve scientific problems; **Science Practice 3:** The student can engage in scientific questioning to extend thinking or to guide investigations within the context of the AP course; and **Science Practice 7:** The student is able to connect and relate knowledge across various scales, concepts, and representations in and across domains.

Question 28 ties **Science Practices 1, 3, and 7** together by asking you to use representations and models to pose scientific questions about the properties of cell membranes and selective permeability based on molecular structure. You need to construct models that connect the movement of molecules across membranes with membrane structure and function (**Learning Objectives 2.10 and 2.11**).

Question 29 focuses on **Science Practices 3 and 7**. This question asks you to generate scientific questions involving cell communication as it relates to the process of evolution and to describe how organisms exchange information in response to internal changes or environmental cues (**Learning Objectives 3.32 and 3.42**).

28. Below is a diagram of the caffeine molecule.

   a. Label the parts of the molecule that make it difficult for caffeine to enter the cell.

   b. Caffeine acts by binding to a receptor on the cell surface. Explain why it does not enter the cell.

_____

_____

_____

_____

_____

29. The drug ouabain inhibits the activity of the Na^+–K^+ pump. A nerve cell is incubated in ouabain. Create a table in which you predict what would happen to the concentrations of Na^+ and K^+ inside the cell, as a result of the action of ouabain. Explain.

_____

_____

_____

_____

_____

_____

_____

_____

_____

_____

_____

_____

_____

_____

6 Pathways that Harvest and Store Chemical Energy

Chapter Outline

Plants use sunlight-driven photosynthesis to synthesize carbohydrates. The energy released from taking apart (catabolizing) these carbohydrates is a primary source of chemical energy for both plants and animals. A sequence of controlled enzyme-catalyzed pathways allows these catabolic chemical reactions to operate without causing excessive damage.

Some of the energy made available from the catabolism of carbohydrates and other fuel molecules drives the synthesis of adenosine triphosphate (ATP). Inside the cells, ATP molecules function as a form of energy currency; the hydrolysis of ATP, an exergonic reaction that yields adenosine diphosphate (ADP) and a phosphate ion, liberates a small amount of chemical energy, some of which activates the biochemical reactions needed in cells. This small energy transfer "nudges" biochemical reactions that support life.

The two primary means of maintaining ATP supplies are substrate-level phosphorylation and oxidative phosphorylation. In substrate phosphorylation, a phosphate group on an organic molecule is transferred to ADP, restoring it to ATP. This pathway makes ATP quickly, but phosphorylated organic molecules are present in only limited quantity in cells, so it is only a short-term solution to increased ATP demand. Oxidative phosphorylation, which bonds ADP to free phosphate ions in a process linked to the activity of the respiratory chain in mitochondria, makes a lot of ATP, but it requires continual access to oxygen and reduced coenzymes. The reduced coenzymes are NADH and $FADH_2$. The reduced coenzymes are continuously supplied by the ongoing catabolism of glucose and its metabolites via glycolysis and the citric-acid cycle, while oxygen molecules come from the environment.

Big Idea 1 recognizes that evolution ties together all parts of biology. Chapter 6 reviews energy transfers that are conserved across all categories of animals and plants. It also briefly considers the ways that agriculture and fermented beverages developed among early humans. The specific parts of the AP Biology curriculum that are covered in Chapter 6 include:

- **1.D.1:** There are several hypotheses about the natural origin of life on Earth, each with supporting scientific evidence.

Big Idea 2 focuses on free energy and the use of molecular building blocks that are fundamental to life processes. Specific parts of the AP Biology curriculum that are covered in Chapter 6 include:

- **2.A.1:** All living systems require constant input of free energy (e.g., the Calvin cycle, glycolysis, the Krebs cycle, and fermentation).

- **2.A.2:** Organisms capture and store free energy for use in biological processes (e.g., NADP in the reactions of photosynthesis and the importance of oxygen in cellular respiration).

Big Idea 4 states that biological systems interact in complex ways. Specific parts of the AP Biology curriculum that are covered in Chapter 6 include:

- **4.A.2:** The structure and function of subcellular components, and their interactions, provide essential cellular processes.

- **4.C.1:** Variation in molecular units provides cells with a wider range of functions (e.g.,the role of chlorophyll in photosynthesis).

Chapter Review

Concept 6.1 *introduces how ATP, reduced coenzymes, and chemiosmosis play important roles in biological energy metabolism. The energy needed for many biochemical reactions in cells is provided by the hydrolysis of ATP, yielding ADP and either phosphorylated proteins or inorganic phosphate (hydrogen phospahate; commonly abbreviated as P_i). As ATP is "used" in this way, it is also being continuously produced by two processes, substrate phosphorylation and oxidative phosphorylation.*

In substrate phosphorylation, phosphate groups on proteins and other molecules are transferred to ADP to quickly restore ATP supplies. Although substrate phosphorylation rapidly delivers ATP, the supply of phosphorylated substrates that can "give up" phosphate groups in this manner is limited.

In contrast, ATP production resulting from oxidative phosphorylation yields much more ATP, although oxidative phosphorylation requires more ingredients: oxygen, reduced coenzymes (NADH and $FADH_2$), and, of course, ADP and P_i. The mitochondrion is the intracellular organelle where most of the components of oxidative phosphorylation are found.

The catabolism of fuel molecules, such as glucose, supports both pathways of ATP production, yielding energy transfers that result in substrate phosphorylation and that produce the reduced coenzymes needed for oxidative phosphorylation. As NADH and $FADH_2$ are oxidized, this energy transfer develops a gradient of hydrogen ions (H^+) inside the mitochondrion. The gradient provides energy transfer to an enzyme, ATP synthase, accelerating its rate of binding ADP and P_i, thereby making ATP.

1. Discuss this statement: The hydrolysis of ATP to support an anabolic process includes both endergonic and exergonic reactions, depending on which perspective one takes: the hydrolysis of ATP or the formation of anabolic products.

_____

_____

_____

_____

2. The diagram at the right shows the conversion of compound AH to compound A and the conversion of compound B to compound BH, with interconversions of NAD+ and NADH. To each of the four boxes, add either "oxidation" or "reduction." Explain your label choices.

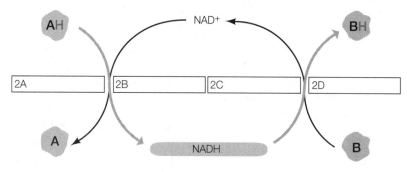

    a. Box 2A: _____

_____

    b. Box 2B: _____

_____

    c. Box 2C: _____

_____

    d. Box 2D: _____

_____

3. Use the figure to the right as a guide to answering the following questions regarding these molecules:

propanoic acid	propanol	propane
C_2H_5COOH	C_3H_7OH	C_3H_8

| Methane (CH_4) | Methanol (CH_3OH) | Formaldehyde (CH_2O) | Formic acid ($HCOOH$) | Carbon dioxide (CO_2) |

Most reduced state
Highest free energy

Most oxidized state
Lowest free energy

    a. Which compound is in the most reduced state? _____

    b. Which compound has the lowest free energy? _____

    c. Which compound is in the most oxidized state? _____

    d. Which compound has the highest free energy? _____

Concept 6.2 *describes how carbohydrate catabolism in the presence of oxygen releases a large amount of energy. In cellular respiration, the fuel molecule under consideration is usually glucose, a monosaccharide carbohydrate. The catabolic pathways are well studied:*

$$Glycolysis \rightarrow Pyruvate\ oxidation \rightarrow Citric\ acid\ (Krebs)\ cycle$$

Along the catabolic pathways, ATP is made directly by substrate phosphorylation. Reduced coenzymes are also produced, thus supporting oxidative phosphorylation, a process that generates considerably more ATP synthesis than does substrate phosphorylation.

4. Explain how the following two membrane-embedded proteins in mitochondria simultaneously influence the gradient of hydrogen ions and ATP synthesis.

    a. Proton pump _____

    _____

    _____

    _____

    b. ATP synthase _____

    _____

    _____

    _____

5. The complete catabolism of glucose can yield an energy transfer up to 686 kcal/mol. Indicate whether each of the following statements is true or false, then explain your answer.

    a. All 686 kcal/mol is directly transferred to ATP synthesis.
       TRUE FALSE [*choose one, then explain*]

    _____

    _____

    _____

b. Less than half of the 686 kcal/mol is directly transferred to ATP synthesis.
    TRUE   FALSE   [*choose one, then explain*]

_____

_____

_____

c. Only 10% of the 686 kcal/mol is directly transferred to ATP synthesis, in accordance
    with the principles of thermodynamics.
    TRUE   FALSE   [*choose one, then explain*]

_____

_____

_____

6. Assume that the diagram at the right refers to the
catabolism of one glucose molecule.

Draw arrows to show where NADH and FADH$_2$ are
generated. Include the number of each produced.
Then, add arrows to show where the reduced
coenzymes participate in energy-transfer reactions.

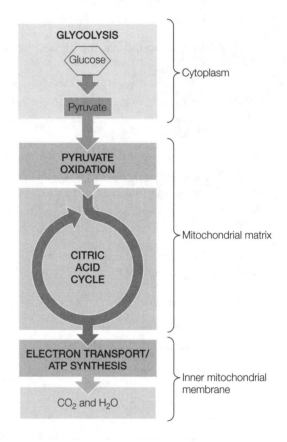

7. Starting with *three* molecules of glucose, insert the appropriate numbers in the blanks below, assuming
complete catabolism with oxygen available.

a. _____   molecules of ATP must be hydrolyzed to start the process.

b. _____   molecules of NADH are produced.

c. _____   molecules of FADH$_2$ are produced.

d. _____   molecules of ATP are produced via substrate phosphorylation.

e. _____   molecules of water are produced in the electron transport chain.

f. _____   molecules of carbon dioxide are released from the process.

Concept 6.3 *examines how carbohydrate catabolism in the absence of oxygen releases a small amount of energy. Organisms that live in conditions in which molecular oxygen is periodically unavailable or is never available use the process called fermentation to reoxidize NADH to NAD⁺. Without NAD⁺, glycolysis and all subsequent steps of catabolism come to a halt, and ATP production stops. Complex organisms like ourselves, as well as some microbes, produce lactic acid or lactate as a byproduct of fermentation, whereas yeasts and some plants produce an alcohol known as ethanol as a byproduct of fermentation.*

8. Lactic acid fermentation and alcoholic fermentation both result in alterations to three-carbon pyruvate molecules. Which of these two fermentation pathways converts pyruvate to the smaller catabolites? Provide specific details.

_____

_____

_____

_____

_____

Concept 6.4 *explains how catabolic and anabolic pathways are integrated. Changes in cellular activity and in the availability of fuel molecules occur frequently in nature. During lean times or under high metabolic activity, energy transfers occur by breaking down a variety of fuel molecules, allowing for the catabolism of proteins, fats, and carbohydrates. By contrast, in times of plenty, cellular reserves are restored through anabolism. For example, many types of smaller molecules can be converted to lipids. In addition, the storage-polymer of glucose, called glycogen, is synthesized in muscle and liver.*

9. Carbohydrates are not the only source of fuel molecules. Identify two additional pools of fuel molecules whose catabolism can yield energy transfers that result in ATP synthesis. For each of the two categories of fuel molecules you've identified, briefly describe how the molecules are utilized, and comment on any similarities to glucose catabolism.

    a. Fuel-molecule pool 1: _____

_____

_____

_____

    b. Fuel-molecule pool 2: _____

_____

_____

_____

10. Catabolism and anabolism are intrinsically linked together in your body. Describe what happens to quantities of each of the molecules below during times with plenty of access to food *and* during times with limited access to food.

    a. Glucose _____

_____

_____

_____

b. Lipids _____

_____

_____

_____

c. Proteins _____

_____

_____

_____

11. Cells of the brain and the heart are highly specialized to carry out specific functions in the body, and their metabolic needs must be met, or death will soon follow. Part of this specialization includes reliance on glucose as a key fuel molecule. Explain how glucose is made available to the brain and heart during times when carbohydrates are not readily available.

_____

_____

_____

_____

_____

_____

Concept 6.5 *studies photosynthesis, and shows how light energy is converted to chemical energy. Most plants do not appear to eat, yet they grow. Until it became clear to scientists that plants take up carbon dioxide from the environment and use solar energy to fuel sugar synthesis, it was thought that most of their growth was fueled by things they take from the soil. During "light reactions" of photosynthesis, sunlight's energy activates chlorophyll molecules to capture light energy in the synthesis of ATP and NADPH. As these compounds accumulate, water molecules are catabolized, liberating hydrogen ions sufficient to build a chemiosmotic gradient similar to that in mitochondria. Molecular oxygen is a byproduct of photosynthesis. Energy released during ATP hydrolysis and the oxidation of NADPH drive the "Calvin cycle," in which carbohydrates such as glucose are made (see Concept 6.6).*

12. Photosystem I and photosystem II are directly activated by different wavelengths of photon energy. Describe each and discuss their interdependence.

a. Photosystem I: _____

_____

_____

_____

_____

_____

b. Photosystem II: _____

_____

_____

_____

_____

Concept 6.6 *examines how photosynthetic organisms use chemical energy to convert* CO_2 *to carbohydrates. Carbon dioxide, ATP, and NADPH are the key requirements for the synthesis of sugars by plants. The light reactions of photosynthesis generate ATP and NADPH (Concept 6.5), and* CO_2 *is taken up from the environment, especially from the atmosphere, via the leaves of plants.*

13. Briefly describe each of the three major segments of the Calvin cycle, noting the key components needed in each segment.

_____

_____

_____

_____

_____

_____

_____

_____

_____

14. Explain the claim that Rubisco (RuBP) is the most abundant protein on the planet, by describing its role in the Calvin cycle.

_____

_____

_____

_____

_____

_____

_____

_____

15. A student says that because plants can carry out photosynthesis, they do not need cellular respiration. His lab partner argues that photosynthesis without respiration is a wasted effort. Who is correct? Explain your answer.

_____

_____

_____

_____

_____

_____

_____

_____

Science Practices & Inquiry

In the AP Biology Curriculum Framework, there are seven **Science Practices**. In this chapter, we focus on **Science Practice 6:** The student can work with scientific explanations and theories. More specifically, we focus on **Practice 6.2:** The student can construct explanations of phenomena based on evidence produced through scientific practices.

Question 16 asks you to construct explanations of the mechanisms and structural features of cells that allow organisms to capture, store, or use free energy (**Learning Objective 2.5**) and to construct explanations based on scientific evidence as to how interactions of subcellular structures provide essential functions (**Learning Objective 4.5**).

16. In the absence of electron transport, an artificial H^+ gradient is sufficient for ATP synthesis in cellular organelles. In an experiment, chloroplasts were isolated from plant cells and incubated at pH 7. The chloroplasts were then subjected to six different conditions. They were incubated with ADP, phosphate (P_i), and magnesium ions (Mg^{2+}) at pH 7 and at pH 3.8. The chloroplasts were then incubated at pH 3.8 with one of the four components (ADP, P_i, Mg^{2+}, chloroplasts) missing.

ATP formation was measured using luciferase, which catalyzes the formation of a luminescent (light-emitting) molecule if ATP is present. Here are the data from the original paper:

a. Circle the control reaction in the table.

b. Use the control data to correct the raw data for the experimental reaction mixtures and complete the table.

Reaction #	Mixture Description	Luciferase activity (light emission)	
		Raw data	Corrected data
1	Complete, pH 3.8	141	
2	Complete, pH 7.0	12	
3	Complete, pH 3.8 – P_i	12	
4	Complete, pH 3.8 – ADP	4	
5	Complete, pH 3.8 – Mg^{2+}	60	
6	Complete, pH 3.8 – chloroplasts	7	

c. Summarize the results of the experiment. _____
_____
_____

d. Explain why ATP production dropped in the absence of P_i. _____
_____
_____

e. Explain why ATP production could be negative in this experiment. _____
_____
_____

f. Discuss where the free energy comes from to drive the production of ATP. _____
_____
_____

7 The Cell Cycle and Cell Division

Chapter Outline

A cell, like any other living thing, does not live forever. The continuity of life in a single-celled organism requires that it produce copies. Multicellular organisms start life as a single "parent" cell and then produce many, many "offspring" cells during growth and development.

To understand cell replication, you must learn how DNA is duplicated in a parent cell and then evenly shared between two offspring cells. After the duplication and segregation of DNA are complete, the parent cell physically splits into two offspring cells, each enclosed by its own membrane via a process called *cytokinesis*.

Binary fission and mitosis are the two primary mechanisms by which cells produce copies of themselves. Prokaryotes are unicellular organisms that typically contain only one chromosome, and they achieve cell duplication via binary fission. The DNA in the chromosome is copied end-to-end, with one copy ending up on one side of the cell and the other copy on the other. As this separation occurs, the cell membranes grow toward the middle of the parent cell to effectively pinch it in half, with each half receiving one complete copy of the chromosome. In contrast, eukaryotic cells undergo mitosis. Because they have multiple chromosomes, the copying of these individual molecules of DNA must be synchronized and coordinated. After copying is complete, the two full sets of chromosomes must be moved to opposite ends of the parent cell before it separates into two offspring cells.

The phases of the cycle of eukaryotic cell duplication make up the cell cycle. The cell (e.g., a liver cell involved in metabolism) grows and carries out its normal function during the G1 phase of the cell cycle. At some point, a growth regulator protein called cyclin activates the cellular machinery that replicates DNA. This is known as the S phase of the cycle, as in DNA synthesis. The next phase of the cycle, during which the components needed for mitosis are made, is called the G2 phase. At the end of the G2 phase, the stage is set for mitosis. Mitosis proceeds, and the cell cycle moves from interphase to prophase, during which distinct duplicated chromosomes are microscopically visible. Next, the duplicated chromosomes line up across the middle of the cell during metaphase, and they are pulled to opposite poles during anaphase. Finally, during telophase, each set of chromosomes becomes surrounded by nuclear membranes, and during cytokinesis, the membranes enclose each new cell.

Eukaryotes that reproduce sexually gain the evolutionary benefits of mixing together the genes of two different parents, resulting in offspring that are not identical to either parent. In this scenario, the parents' reproductive systems have cells that undergo two nuclear divisions, producing haploid cells called gametes via the process of meiosis. Gametes are cells with only one copy of the otherwise paired chromosomes that are typical of diploid cells. The gametes become fused into a single diploid cell, called a zygote, as a result of mating. As in previous chapters, you have seen many new terms. Two of these—*haploid* and *diploid*—are very important to understanding the nature of life cycles of living organisms.

You should now realize that cell reproduction is highly regulated; otherwise, living organisms would use up all of their resources and perish. When regulation breaks down, uncontrolled growth and cancer can result.

Chapter 7 concludes with a description of cell death, which takes place either by extensive damage to the cell, killing it outright, or by the initiation of genetic programming that results in hydrolytic destruction. This "genetically regulated cell death" is called apoptosis. It can protect an individual from a spreading infection and facilitate the recycling of cellular materials.

In the AP Biology Curriculum Framework, Chapter 7 develops **Big Idea 2**, invoking regulatory mechanisms of living organisms, but it is more directed at understanding **Big Idea 3**, information transfer.

Big Idea 2 states that utilization of free energy and use of molecular building blocks are characteristic of life processes. Chapter 7 discusses the signals that initiate cell duplication and cell death. Specific parts of the AP Biology curriculum that are covered in Chapter 7 include:

• **2.C.1:** Organisms use feedback mechanisms to maintain their internal environments and respond to external environmental changes.

Big Idea 3 states that living systems store, retrieve, transmit, and respond to information essential to life processes. Chapter 7 lays the groundwork for examining cellular reproduction. Specifically, Chapter 7 includes:

• **3.A.2:** In eukaryotes, heritable information is passed to the next generation via processes that include the cell cycle and mitosis or meiosis plus fertilization.

• **3.C.1:** Changes in genotype can result in changes in phenotype.

• **3.C.2:** Biological systems have multiple processes that increase genetic variation.

Chapter Review

Concept 7.1 *examines how different life cycles use various modes of cell reproduction. The reproduction of cells is the basis for the continuity of life. Cells reproduce through both sexual and asexual means. Diploid cells carry two sets of homologous chromosomes, one from each parent. Mitosis replicates all of these chromosomes identically to create a new cell via asexual reproduction. In sexual reproduction, meiosis halves the diploid number of chromosomes, creating haploid gametes. When two gametes unite to create a new generation, a single-celled diploid zygote results and proceeds to mitosis.*

1. Identify the three major reasons for the reproduction of cells.

   a. _____

   b. _____

   c. _____

2. The clonal production of identical cells is called _____

3. Discuss the possible consequences of the inexact duplication of DNA.

   _____

   _____

   _____

4. Describe the differences between haploid and diploid cells, and identify the processes by which these two types of cells are produced.

   _____

   _____

   _____

   _____

   _____

   _____

   _____

   _____

5. Discuss the formation of the diploid cell known as the zygote.

_____

_____

_____

_____

6. Briefly describe what happens to a zygote after it is formed, assuming success in its first week.

_____

_____

_____

_____

7. Complete the life-cycle diagrams shown by writing meiosis, fertilization, zygote, spore, gamete, mature organism, haploid, alternation of generations, and diploid in the correct boxes. Write mold, plant, or animal on the line below the appropriate diagram.

8. Describe the relative advantage of asexual reproduction over sexual reproduction during prolonged periods of favorable environmental conditions and abundant resources.

_____

_____

_____

_____

9. Discuss the relative advantage of sexual reproduction over asexual reproduction during prolonged periods of varying environmental conditions with fluctuations in resource availability.

_____

_____

_____

_____

Concept 7.2 *explores how both binary fission and mitosis produce genetically identical cells. Asexual reproduction by either method produces such cells. In single-celled organisms, such as the amoeba, this is how new amoeba arise. For multicellular organisms, such as birds and insects, mitosis is the mechanism of growth and development or repair and replacement of dead, dying, or worn-out tissues.*

10. Briefly describe each of the four key events that are common to both binary fission and mitosis.

    a. _____
    _____

    b. _____
    _____

    c. _____
    _____

    d. _____
    _____

11. Describe two ways that binary fission differs from mitosis.

_____
_____
_____
_____
_____
_____
_____

12. Compare cytokinesis in plant and animal cells.

_____
_____
_____
_____
_____
_____
_____

13. The diploid ($2n = 6$) cell shown below is in interphase, prior to DNA replication. In the circles below, draw the five steps of mitosis that this cell would undergo during replication.

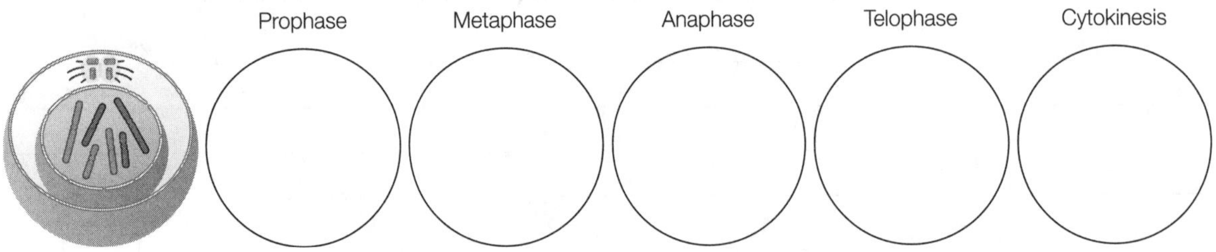

Prophase   Metaphase   Anaphase   Telophase   Cytokinesis

14. The interphase of the cell cycle is divided into three distinct phases: G1, S, and G2. Briefly describe what happens during each part of interphase.

a. G1: _____

_____

b. S: _____

_____

c. G2: _____

_____

15. Draw a chromosome that has two chromatids, and label the centromere and sister chromatids.

16. In the circles at the right, draw the nuclear contents of a cell with $2n = 8$ at the beginning and end of the S phase of interphase.

Beginning of S phase   End of S phase

17. Assume that a mutation in a cell results in nonfunctional proteins needed for the kinetochore to function properly. Describe what would happen to that cell during attempted duplication.

_____

_____

_____

_____

_____

Concept 7.3 *explains how cell reproduction is under precise control. Cell reproduction requires access to nutrients and space and is closely regulated by signaling mechanisms. A single-celled species with unregulated reproduction would likely soon exceed the carrying capacity of its environment and would starve to death. In a multicellular organism, cell reproduction is closely regulated to maintain the forms and functions of different parts of the body. Cancer is largely a disease of deregulated mitosis, and rapidly growing tumors deprive other body parts access to nutrients and waste removal.*

18. Identify and describe the key restriction point of the cell cycle. Identify the phase where this regulation takes place.

_____

_____

_____

_____

_____

_____

_____

19. Explain the biochemical actions of protein kinases in controlling the cell cycle.

_____

_____

_____

_____

_____

_____

_____

_____

_____

20. The cyclin-CDK complexes regulate the cell cycle by many of the mechanisms described in previous chapters. Briefly explain how each mechanism below plays a role in the regulation of the G1 (restriction point) checkpoint of interphase.

a. Allosteric regulation: _____

_____

b. Gene expression: _____

_____

c. Protein synthesis: _____

_____

d. Signal transduction: _____

_____

e. Cell division: _____

_____

Concept 7.4 *describes how meiosis halves the nuclear chromosome content and generates diversity among offspring. Meiosis forms haploid gametes that unite to initiate the next generation. Meiosis also results in offspring that are inexact copies of any one parent, providing fodder for natural selection as the environment or ecosystem changes. Without meiosis, each new generation would be a clone of the previous generation and would be at a disadvantage to react to changes in the environment. Crossing over and independent assortment rearrange existing genetic variation between gametes, while other meiotic errors can create new variation, often leading to cancer and other diseases.*

21. Meiosis serves several important purposes for sexual reproduction. Describe what would happen if each of the following did *not* occur prior to sexual reproduction.

a. Chromosome number reduced: _____

_____

_____

b. A complete set of chromosomes made: _____

_____

_____

c. Genetic diversity generated: _____

_____

_____

22. Complete the chart below, comparing mitosis and meiosis.

	Mitosis	Meiosis
Number of daughter cells		
Chromosome number of parent cell	____n	____n
Chromosome number of daughter cell	____n	____n
Number of nuclear divisions		
Pairing of homologous chromosomes? (Yes/No)		
Daughter nuclei are genetically identical? (Yes/No)		

23. Identify and describe two processes that cause daughter nuclei formed during meiosis to be genetically different.

_____

_____

_____

_____

_____

_____

24. Calculate the quantity of each of the following for an organism with a diploid number of $2n = 12$.

a. Chromatids at prophase of mitosis: _____

b. Chromosomes at metaphase of mitosis: _____

c. Centromeres at prophase of meiosis I: _____

d. Chromosomes in a gamete: _____

e. Chromosomes in a skin cell: _____

f. Daughter nuclei after mitosis: _____

g. Chromosomes after meiosis I: _____

Concept 7.5 *explains why programmed cell death is a necessary process in living organisms. Cells die in two primary ways. Necrosis occurs when cells die of starvation, are cut open (wounded), or are poisoned. This frequently causes inflammation, which is the redness and swelling we associate with an injury. More often, cell death is due to apoptosis, a genetically programmed series of events.*

25. Explain the difference between apoptosis and necrosis. Give an example of each.

_____
_____
_____
_____
_____
_____
_____

26. Why is apoptosis important to the normal, healthy development of an organism? Give an example of when and where it occurs in humans.

_____
_____
_____
_____
_____
_____
_____

27. Explain how a caterpillar forms a cocoon and then develops into a moth, as shown in the figure at the right.

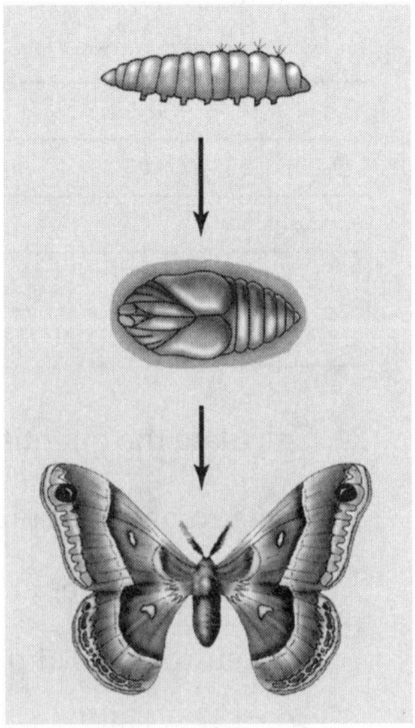

_____
_____
_____
_____
_____
_____
_____
_____
_____
_____
_____
_____

28. Two types of proteins implicated in the regulation of the cell cycle are oncogene proteins and tumor suppressors. Briefly describe the role that each plays in cancer.

a. Oncogene proteins: _____

_____

b. Tumor suppressors: _____

_____

Science Practices & Inquiry

In the AP Biology Curriculum Framework, there are seven **Science Practices**. In this chapter, we focus on **Science Practice 6:** The student can work with scientific explanations and theories; and **Science Practice 7:** The student is able to connect and relate knowledge across various scales, concepts, and representations in and across domains.

Question 29 focuses on **Science Practice 6,** asking you to construct an explanation, using visual representations or narrative, as to how DNA in chromosomes is transmitted to the next generation via mitosis or meiosis followed by fertilization.

29. In an elegant set of experiments, Rao and Johnson (published in *Nature*, 1970) determined some of the important elements of cell cycle regulation. Rao and Johnson fused together mammalian cells at different times of the cell cycle (G1, S, and G2). After fusion, the nuclei were monitored and the time required for mitosis to occur was measured. Below are three of their experiments with the results. For each, write a two- or three-sentence conclusion about what the experiment shows.

a. Fusion of S-phase cells with G2-phase cells

Result: Chromosome replication continued in the S nucleus, while the G2 nucleus was unable to synthesize DNA.

Conclusion: _____

_____

_____

b. Fusion of S-phase cells with G1-phase cells

Result: The G1 nuclei rapidly moved into S phase.

Conclusion: _____

_____

_____

c. Fusion of G1-phase cells with G2-phase cells

Result: The entry of the G2 nucleus into mitosis was delayed.

Conclusion: _____

_____

_____

Question 30 looks at **Science Practice 7**, asking you to represent the connection between meiosis and increased genetic diversity necessary for evolution (**Learning Objective 3.10**).

30. An organism has a diploid number of $2n = 6$. Draw diagrams of chromosomes in the nuclei of this organism as it produces gametes through meiosis. Explain how these gametes are genetically unique.

_____

_____

_____

_____

_____

_____

_____

_____

8

Inheritance, Genes, and Chromosomes

Chapter Outline

Genetic inheritance is explainable and predictable. Once you are familiar with the field's specialized vocabulary you will be able to accurately describe how the inherited characteristics of organisms (e.g., round versus wrinkled garden peas studied by Gregor Mendel in the 19th century) are based on what the parent generation provided to their offspring.

In the simple case of seed appearance in peas, there are two alleles, or alternate forms of the gene. One of the seed-appearance alleles codes for a protein that results in a round and smooth appearance on the surface of the seed. Another codes for a protein that results in a wrinkled and irregular appearance. By interbreeding "true-breeding" round-seed–producing plants with "true-breeding" wrinkled-seed–producing plants to produce F_1 offspring, Mendel found that *all* of the seeds in the F_1 offspring were round and smooth. "True-breeding" means that, after many generations, the offspring of members of the strain always have the same appearance as the parent and are assumed to be genetically identical. (Mendel did not know about DNA and proteins.)

An important detail from Mendel's studies is that the appearance (phenotype) of the pea seeds in his crosses was either round or wrinkled, not something in between. This shows that even if an individual pea plant inherited the allele for wrinkled seeds from one parent, receiving an allele for round and smooth seeds from the other parent results in all of the offspring's seeds being round and smooth. Thus, we say that the allele for round seed appearance is dominant over the recessive allele for wrinkled seed appearance. Such knowledge gives us predictability for what seeds will look like in offspring, provided we know about their parents and the inheritance patterns of the genes they have.

Geneticists utilize several systems for symbols of genes; we will utilize a simple system by describing the alleles for seed appearance in peas in the following

way. The uppercase "S" represents the dominant allele for round and the lowercase "s" represents the recessive allele for wrinkled. By custom, most alleles are abbreviated by the first letter(s) of the dominant allele. Here, "S" indicates "smooth."

The greatest breakthrough Mendel made was not in the demonstration of simple dominant and recessive traits of garden pea phenotypes. Rather, it was what happened when he bred together the round F_1 offspring. These F_1 seeds and the plants that grew from them must have received one allele for round and one allele for wrinkled. Today we know that this is true because when producing gametes (pollen and ova in plants), only one of the two alleles for a gene will be present in any given gamete. Thus, there will be some pollen with a round allele for the gene for coat appearance and other pollen with the wrinkled allele, with the same either/or situation being true for the ova. When breeding the F_1 plants together to make the F_2 generation, Mendel kept track of how many smooth seeds were produced among the F_2 plants and noted that 75 percent of the F_2 plants were smooth and round while the other 25 percent were wrinkled. Mendel examined tens of thousands of peas to reach his results.

The possible genotypes for seed appearance in the F_2 offspring described above is limited to this set: SS, Ss, sS, and ss. Recall that each parent contributes one of the alleles in its offspring. Any F_2 plant with a single "S" will produce round seeds, the dominant trait, and we see that there are three such combinations: SS, Ss, and sS. By the same rule, there is only one combination of alleles, ss, that will result in wrinkled seeds. Therefore, there are three times as many round seeds (75 percent) as there are wrinkled seeds (25 percent) in the F_2 generation.

In addition to explaining straightforward genetics, there are some tricks of nature presented in this chapter. For example, mitochondria and chloroplasts are organelles that almost exclusively come from the maternal parent because the gametes of females, the ova, are much larger cells than sperm. The larger cells are the ones that provide mitochondria and chloroplasts, as pollen and spermatozoa are generally too small to carry any cargo other than the primary genetic information. Since mitochondria and chloroplasts have some genes (and therefore, DNA) of their own, the "mother" is typically the sole source of mitochondria and chloroplast genes.

Chapter 8 covers aspects of **Big Idea 3 and Big Idea 4**. **Big Idea 3,** stating that living systems store, retrieve, transmit, and respond to information essential to life processes, is the dominant theme of the chapter. Specific parts of the AP Biology curriculum that are covered in Chapter 8 include:

- **3.A.3:** The chromosomal basis of inheritance provides an understanding of the pattern of passage (transmission) of genes from parent to offspring.
- **3.A.4:** The inheritance pattern of many traits cannot be explained by simple Mendelian genetics.
- **3.C.2:** Biological systems have multiple processes that increase genetic variation.
- **3.C.3:** Viral replication results in genetic variation, and viral infection can introduce genetic variation into the hosts.

Big Idea 4 states that biological systems interact in complex ways. Specifically, this chapter includes:

- **4.C.2:** Environmental factors influence the expression of the genotype in an organism.

Chapter Review

Concept 8.1 *describes how genes are particulate and are inherited according to Mendel's laws. Key vocabulary terms in genetics that you need to be familiar with include: character, trait, parental generation (P), first filial generation (F_1), second filial generation (F_2), test cross, monohybrid cross, dominant, recessive, allele, homozygous, heterozygous, dihybrid cross, phenotype, genotype, law of segregation, Punnett square, law of independent assortment, and pedigree analysis.*

1. What can be deduced from the observation that all offspring have the phenotype of only one of the parents when two true-breeding animals with different traits are bred?

_____

_____

_____

_____

2. Predict and explain the expected result on the F_1 from breeding one type of wheat that is homozygous for the dominant allele of a particular trait with another strain that is homozygous for the recessive allele of that trait.

_____

_____

_____

_____

3. Explain the importance of Mendel's observations of the F_2 generation after he completed his careful observations of the F_1 generation.

_____

_____

_____

_____

Concept 8.2 *explains how alleles and genes interact to produce phenotypes. Over the long term, it is clear that there have been many changes in the appearance of plants and animals. For example, the phenotype of today's human beings is likely quite different than the human phenotype of 200,000 years ago. We don't need to wait for 10,000 generations of breeding, however, before we see changes in phenotypes. A single gene with two or more alleles can result in two or more phenotypes. An allele present in 99 percent or more of the phenotypes seen in nature is labeled as the "wild" type allele of the gene, with alternate, uncommon alleles labeled as "mutants." In addition, the phenotype might be under the control of several genes that act in different patterns of expression when present in different combinations of alleles.*

Match one of the following terms to each of the examples in Questions 4 through 7. Then explain how that demonstrates that phenotypic effect.

epistasis   dominance   codominance   incomplete dominance

4. True-breeding round peas bred with true-breeding wrinkled peas produced offspring that were all round.

Matching term: _____ Explanation: _____
_____
_____
_____
_____

5. True-breeding white-flowered snapdragons bred with true-breeding red-flowered snapdragons produced offspring that were all pink-flowered.

Matching term: _____ Explanation: _____
_____
_____
_____
_____

6. A man with blood type A and a woman with blood type B produce a daughter of blood type O.

Matching term: _____ Explanation: _____
_____
_____
_____
_____

7. A male Labrador retriever with a black coat and a female Labrador retriever with a chocolate coat produce a puppy that has a yellow coat.

Matching term: _____ Explanation: _____
_____
_____
_____
_____

Concept 8.3 *examines how genes are carried on chromosomes. The seven phenotypic traits selected by Mendel for detailed study are examples of the simple dominant/recessive pattern of trait characterization. His idea that there are two "determinants" of each trait mesh well with later observations that chromosomes exist as pairs in cells (except in sperm and ova). Thus it was recognized, and later demonstrated, that one determinant can be on one chromosome, while the other member of the chromosome pair might have the same or another determinant.*

We now know that DNA, the genetic code, is arranged in the form of the chromosomes that are found in the nucleus of eukaryotic cells. The "law of independent assortment" most directly applies to genes that reside on different chromosomes, as genes that are on different chromosomes are inherited independently of one another.

Not all genes are on different chromosomes, of course, and in general, two different genes that are located on the same chromosome are more likely to be inherited together than are two different genes that are located on different chromosomes. Thus, genes on the same (autosomal) chromosome are said to be "linked" in their pattern of inheritance. Linkage by virtue of sharing space on the same chromosome does not forever bind two genes to be inherited together. In the production of gametes, it is possible for genes to undergo recombination when exchanged between homologous chromosomes, in a process called "crossing over." Crossing over does not occur with sex chromosomes.

For the special case of genes located on the X and Y (sex) chromosomes, it is impossible for exchange between X and Y chromosomes. Among flies and humans, each male offspring (XY sex chromosomes) will have a Y chromosome identical to its paternal parent's Y chromosome. Each male offspring must also receive an X chromosome from its maternal parent. Although the Y chromosome has only a very limited number of genes, which are related to the differentiation of the testes, the X chromosome contains many, many more genes, and therefore the maternal parent determines more of the male offspring's traits than does the paternal parent, especially if the allele is recessive. Note that a male with a mutation or rare allele on the X chromosome can indeed pass along that mutation or rare allele, but only to his female offspring.

8. Plant scientists studying inheritance in sweet peas developed two true-breeding strains of peas, one with purple flowers and the other with red flowers. When these two strains were crossed, all of the F_1 were purple. Another trait of interest was pollen grain appearance. For this, two true-breeding strains were produced, one strain yielding long (tube-like) pollen grains and the other, round pollen grains. When these two strains were crossed, all of the offspring had long pollen grains.

Predict the flower color and pollen shape of 1,000 members of the F_1 generation for a mating between true-breeding purple-flowered, long-grained pollen peas and true-breeding red-flowered, round-grained pollen peas.

_____

_____

_____

_____

_____

Now predict the flower color and pollen shape of 1,000 members of the F_2 generation, resulting from corssing F_1 plants above, and assuming Mendel's law of independent assortment applies to the flower and pollen traits.

_____

_____

_____

_____

_____

Predict the flower color and pollen shape of 1,000 members of the F_2 generation if Mendel's law of independent assortment did *not* apply to the flower and pollen traits. This is considered to be the alternate hypothesis to the previous prediction.

_____

_____

_____

_____

9. Steroid hormones (gonadal androgens), such as testosterone, lead to differentiation of the male reproductive system. However, if the receptors for the hormones are non-functional due to a mutation in the gene for the androgen-receptor protein, a condition called "complete androgen insensitivity" is likely to develop and result in a female-like external phenotype. Note that all affected individuals have a Y chromosome that is typically normal. The syndrome is not seen in genetic (XX) females, however. Speculate on the chromosomal location of the mutation that causes this developmental abnormality, and explain your answer fully.

_____

_____

_____

_____

10. Thomas Hunt Morgan reported on many different genetic crosses he made with fruit flies, including several scenarios of eye color inheritance. Red eye color is dominant (R) over white eye color (r). Show all possible genotypes, including sex, that can be formed by the cross of a white-eyed female (X^rX^r) with a red-eyed male (X^RY), and give an explanation for the eye color in each of the offspring.

_____

_____

_____

_____

11. The karyotype figure at the right shows the chromosomes of a person with Down syndrome, a trisomy in which there are more than the usual number of chromosome copies.

Circle the trisomy in the karyotype, and describe the errant inheritance process that resulted in its presence. (*Hint*: Consider whether the trisomy more likely results from an error in mitosis or an error in meisosis.)

Courtesy: National Human Genome Research Institute

_____

_____

_____

_____

_____

_____

Concept 8.4 *examines how prokaryotes can exchange genetic material. Most prokaryotes reproduce asexually by cloning (binary fission) and have only a single chromosome that is located in the cytosol of their cells. Evolution of prokaryotes is strongly driven by mutational changes in DNA, but there exist a limited number of ways that gene exchange between individuals can occur, even without sex. Bacteria can form a connection between two organisms, called a sex pilus. After DNA is moved through pili or conjugation tubes, segments of the DNA can be interchanged between the two genomes, via bacterial conjugation and genetic recombination. In a second variation of gene exchange, plasmid DNA of bacteria, a small circle of DNA independent of the larger segment of DNA in the chromosome, can move between bacteria and result in DNA transfer between individuals.*

12. A patient was admitted to a hospital infected with a "new" pathogenic strain of *E. coli* that shows resistance to antibacterial soap. Discuss how the new *E. coli* likely acquired the resistance trait.

_____

_____

_____

_____

_____

_____

13. During the next week, identify every product you use that is sold as "antibacterial." Do you think it is wise to make so many of these products widely available? Explain.

_____

_____

_____

_____

_____

_____

Science Practices & Inquiry

In the AP Biology Curriculum Framework, there are seven **Science Practices**. In this chapter, we focus on **Science Practice 1:** The student can use representations and models to communicate scientific phenomena and solve scientific problems; **Science Practice 2:** The student can use mathematics appropriately; **Science Practice 3:** The student can engage in scientific questioning to extend thinking or to guide investigations within the context of the AP course; **Science Practice 6:** The student can work with scientific explanations and theories; and **Science Practice 7:** The student is able to connect and relate knowledge across various scales, concepts, and representations in and across domains.

Questions 14 and 15 ask you to analyze the empirical outcomes from genetic crosses in order to extract knowledge about the pattern of inheritance of genes. Question 16 provides data you will use to estimate the proximity of two genes.

In a completely hypothetical case, assume that "yogurt flies" were recently discovered in the International Space Station, and that these flies complete their life cycle in only 90 hours, making them ideal for genetic experiments. The astronauts observe variations in fly phenotypes. With lots of time on their hands, the astronauts decide to run some genetic crosses to see if inheritance patterns in space match those back on Earth.

14. First, they cross a true-breeding female with a purple abdomen to a true-breeding male with a pink abdomen. Here are the results of that cross:

	Females	Males
Purple abdomen	787	774
Pink abdomen	0	0

Being careful scientists, they arrange another cross, a true-breeding female with a pink abdomen to a true-breeding male with a purple abdomen. Here are the results of that cross:

	Females	Males
Purple abdomen	646	702
Pink abdomen	0	0

Discuss the inheritance pattern shown.

_____

_____

_____

_____

_____

_____

_____

15. The scientists test another trait by crossing strains. First, they cross a true-breeding female with four antennae to a true-breeding male with two antennae. Here are the results of that cross:

	Females	Males
Four antennae	827	904
Two antennae	0	0

Seeking balance, they do the reciprocal cross: mating a true-breeding female with two antennae to a true-breeding male with four antennae. Here are the results of that cross:

	Females	Males
Four antennae	757	0
Two antennae	0	690

Discuss this second example of an inheritance pattern and compare it with the results on abdomen color.

_____

_____

_____

_____

_____

16. A fruit scientist conducted genetic experiments to breed a pomegranate that is juicier and that stays fresh longer on the grocery shelf. She isolated two genes, *F* and *J*. She developed and then crossed these two lines of pomegranate shrubs: *FfJj* × *ffjj*.

Predict what the cross would yield in percentages of offspring type if the genes are not linked (i.e., they are subject to Mendel's law of independent assortment). Write your percentages in the table.

%	offspring of the *FJ* type
%	offspring of the *Fj* type
%	offspring of the *fJ* type
%	offspring of the *fj* type

a. Explain why you chose these percentages.

_____

_____

_____

_____

The actual results of her cross were:

518 offspring of the *FJ* type (38%)

175 offspring of the *Fj* type (13%)

168 offspring of the *fJ* type (13%)

491 offspring of the *fj* type (36%)

1,352 total offspring

b. Discuss what these data suggest about the linkage and the distance between genes *F* and *J*.

_____

_____

_____

_____

_____

_____

9 DNA and Its Role in Heredity

Chapter Outline

9.1 – DNA Structure Reflects Its Role as the Genetic Material
9.2 – DNA Replicates Semiconservatively
9.3 – Mutations Are Heritable Changes in DNA

In this chapter we examine the structure and function of another macromolecule, DNA. DNA is a nucleic acid that is responsible for transmitting heredity from one generation to another. It occurs as a double-stranded helix, typically packaged in the form of a chromosome. DNA replication occurs in a semiconservative fashion, meaning that each of the two "new" DNA copies have one strand of the original DNA and one strand that is newly synthesized. Although the vast majority of DNA copying is exact and precise, changes in DNA, *mutations*, frequently occur. Some mutations are small and inconsequential, while others change the organism and can result in the complete rearrangement of a chromosome.

As you read this chapter, pay particular attention to the experimental evidence presented. This evidence reveals how we know what we know about DNA. Many of the DNA research experiments were "wet lab" procedures, like those of Rosalind Franklin, Maurice Wilkins, Hershey and Chase, and Meselson and Stahl. Some scientists, including Watson and Crick, did little to no experimentation but rather built models based on the work of numerous experiments by others. Both experimentation and modeling are important scientific practices.

Chapter 9 emphasizes **Big Idea 3**, but it also considers the idea of emergent properties in **Big Idea 4**.

Big Idea 3 states that living systems store, retrieve, transmit, and respond to information essential to life processes. Chapter 9 lays the groundwork for heredity with its discussion of the structure and function of DNA. Specific parts of the AP Biology curriculum that are covered in Chapter 9 include:

- **3.A.1:** DNA, and in some cases RNA, is the primary source of heritable information.

- **3.A.4:** The inheritance pattern of many traits cannot be explained by simple Mendelian genetics.

- **3.C.1:** Changes in genotype can result in changes in phenotype.

- **3.C.2:** Biological systems have multiple processes that increase genetic variation.

- **3.C.3:** Viral replication results in genetic variation, and viral infection can introduce genetic variation into the hosts.

- **3.D.1:** Cell communication processes share common features that reflect a shared evolutionary history.

Big Idea 4 states that biological systems interact in complex ways. Specifically, Chapter 9 includes:

- **4.A.1:** The subcomponents of biological molecules and their sequence determine the properties of that molecule.

Chapter Review

Concept 9.1 *explains how DNA structure reflects its role as the genetic material. DNA is found in chromosomes as a double-stranded helix. It is a nucleic acid, containing the nucleotides adenine (A) paired with thymine (T), and cytosine (C) paired with guanine (G). The two strands of DNA are antiparallel, meaning that the code of each strand is "read" in the direction opposite that of the other strand. The complementary pairing arrangement (A with T; C with G) stabilizes the double helix.*

1. Describe the major contributions to the discovery of the specific structure of DNA by the following scientists:

   a. Hershey and Chase: _____

   _____

   _____

   _____

   b. Erwin Chargaff: _____

   _____

   _____

   _____

   c. Rosalind Franklin: _____

   _____

   _____

   _____

   d. Watson and Crick: _____

   _____

   _____

   _____

2. Define bacterial transformation, and discuss how studies of this phenomenon influenced DNA research.

   _____

   _____

   _____

   _____

   _____

3. In living organisms, the amount of adenine is equal to the amount of thymine, and the amount of cytosine is equal to that of guanine. A researcher measured the amount of adenine in a cell and found it to be 15 percent of the DNA. Calculate the amounts of the other nucleotides, and report the percent of each.

4. Explain why the molecular ratio of A+T to C+G is always the same within a single species, yet differs across species.

   _____

   _____

   _____

   _____

   _____

5. Explain how the double helical structure of DNA allows for each of the following:

a. Storage of genetic information: _____
_____
_____

b. Precise replication during the cell division cycle: _____
_____
_____

c. Susceptibility to mutations: _____
_____
_____

d. Expression of the coded information as phenotypes: _____
_____
_____

Concept 9.2 *explains that DNA replicates semiconservatively. The two antiparallel strands of DNA are held together by weak hydrogen bonds. During DNA replication, these bonds are pulled apart as DNA polymerase assembles complementary base pairs to form a new double strand of DNA.*

6. The diagram below shows a strand of DNA being replicated. Label the following: a phosphate, sugar, nitrogenous base, DNA polymerase, growing strand, and template strand. For each strand, label the 5′ and 3′ ends.

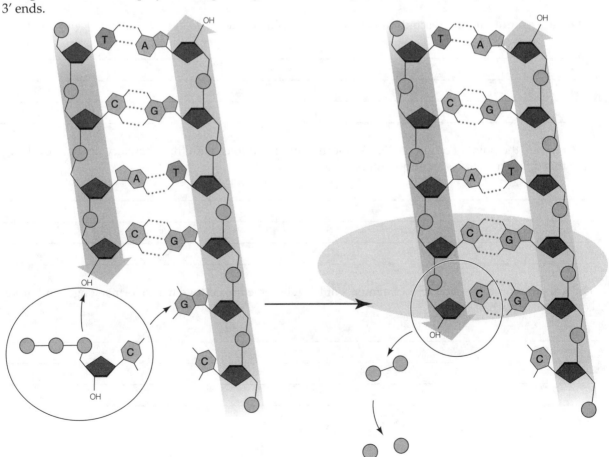

7. In the diagram for Question 6, the strand on the left shows the impending addition of a cytosine with three phosphates attached. Two of the phosphates will ultimately become detached. What result is achieved by the departure of the two phosphate groups?

_____

_____

_____

_____

8. Briefly describe the function of each of these enzymes in DNA replication.

    a. Primase: _____

_____

_____

_____

    b. DNA polymerase: _____

_____

_____

_____

    c. Ligase: _____

_____

_____

_____

9. Discuss continuous and discontinuous replication, using the terms *leading strand* and *lagging strand*.

_____

_____

_____

_____

10. Compare the point of origin of DNA replication in prokaryotes with that of eukaryotes, and explain how this difference serves an important function.

_____

_____

_____

_____

11. Explain how adjacent Okazaki fragments of DNA become linked together to form a longer and more continuous stretch of DNA.

_____

_____

_____

_____

12. Describe how the telomeres, the ends of chromosomes, are shortened each time a chromosome replicates.

_____

_____

_____

_____

_____

_____

13. Explain how telomeres help prevent the loss of genetic material during replication.

_____

_____

_____

_____

_____

14. Define the function of telomerase, and describe what types of cells are particularly dependent on its continual function.

_____

_____

_____

_____

_____

_____

15. Describe the mechanism by which PCR proceeds, and discuss one example of PCR's use.

_____

_____

_____

_____

_____

16. Imagine that you need to amplify (copy) a single gene from a eukaryotic organism with eight chromosomes. Describe the materials you will need, and state the function of each.

_____

_____

_____

_____

_____

17. The diagram below shows two strands of DNA ready for replication.

  a. Draw in the DNA on the continuous side being formed by DNA polymerase.

  b. Draw in two Okazaki fragments on the discontinuous side, one that is formed and a second that is still being formed by DNA polymerase. Label the spot to be filled in by ligase.

Concept 9.3 *describes how mutations are heritable changes in DNA. Mutations can occur by the substitution of single nucleotides or by rearrangement of large segments of chromosomes.*

18. Discuss whether adult-onset skin cancer in a tanning-bed fanatic is caused by a somatic mutation or by germline mutation.

_____

_____

_____

_____

_____

19. Explain the difference between silent mutations and loss-of-function mutations. Which type is more common?

_____

_____

_____

_____

_____

20. Describe and discuss the differences between point mutations and chromosomal mutations.

_____

_____

_____

_____

_____

21. Identify five different mutagens that are in your everyday environment, and indicate how you might avoid each.

a. _____

b. _____

c. _____

d. _____

e. _____

22. Describe the type of mutations that provide the raw material for natural selection. Explain your answer.

_____

_____

_____

_____

23. Discuss how PCR was used to examine the DNA of Neanderthal people.

_____

_____

_____

_____

_____

_____

_____

24. If you search the Internet for images of Neanderthals, you will find many older images that depict them as dumb, ape-like, inferior human beings. This more recent drawing depicts Neanderthals as more like modern humans. Explain why this newer image is likely to be more accurate.

_____

_____

_____

_____

_____

_____

_____

_____

_____

_____

Science Practices & Inquiry

In the AP Biology Curriculum Framework, there are seven **Science Practices**. In this chapter, we focus on **Science Practice 2:** The student can use mathematics appropriately, and **Science Practice 6:** The student can work with scientific explanations and theories. This exercise is based more specifically on **Science Practice 2.2:** The student can apply mathematical routines to quantities that describe natural phenomena; and **Science Practice 6.4:** The student can make claims and predictions about natural phenomena based on scientific theories and models.

Question 25 asks you to use a mutation rate to perform a calculation and then generate a scientific explanation on this topic using your knowledge of genetics. Scientists frequently draw on their knowledge to explain phenomena in our world. In this case, you are asked to explain a mutation rate, based on your knowledge of the human genome (**Learning Objective 3.6**).

25. In the April 30, 2010, issue of *Science*, J. C. Roach, *et al.*, reported that the mutation rate for humans is approximately 1.1×10^{-8} mutations per base pair in the haploid genome. Humans have a diploid genome of 6×10^9 base pairs.

   a. Calculate the number of mutations in each new child. Show your work.

   b. Explain why the majority of these spontaneous mutations have no effect on most children.

   _____

   _____

   _____

   _____

   _____

   _____

   _____

10 From DNA to Protein: Gene Expression

Chapter Outline

In Chapter 10, we make the transition from stored information, which is generally in the form of DNA, to the retrieval of that information, usually by the synthesis of "effector" proteins (polypeptides) that change what is happening in and around the cells of living organisms. The overall sequence is:

$$DNA \xrightarrow{\text{transcription}} RNA \xrightarrow{\text{splicing}} mRNA \xrightarrow{\text{translation}} Polypeptide$$

Once the transcription of the DNA code to the RNA code is complete, RNA modification occurs, and the exon sequences of RNA get spliced back together, producing messenger RNA (mRNA). The mRNA departs from the nucleus and moves to the ribosomes, where it guides protein synthesis. Proteins, or polypeptides, are often modified within cells to become specific effector proteins. These modifications occur after translation has been completed.

Regulating which DNA sequences (i.e., genes) are transcribed to make RNA sequences is most directly controlled in the cells by signals called *transcription factors*. Each of us, male or female, has enough genetic information to make most of the male and female parts of the reproductive system. So why do most individuals have only male *or* female organs? We make only the reproductive parts we need because the expression of genetic information is closely regulated by our sex-specific transcription factors. In the case of reproductive development, hormones and other signals ensure that the correct genes are expressed.

Chapter 10 expands on your understanding of **Big Idea 3**, concerning the nature of information transfer in living organisms. Specifically, Chapter 10 includes:

- **3.A.1:** DNA, and in some cases RNA, is the primary source of heritable information.

Chapter Review

Concept 10.1 *describes how genes code for proteins. Enzymes were an obvious and measurable category of proteins for early researchers, whose observations led to the hypothesis that genetically determined diseases are often based on mutations in the genes that code for enzymes. Subsequent work led to the one gene–one protein hypothesis. Today we understand this better as the one gene–one polypeptide relationship, because many functional proteins (e.g., insulin) are fragments of much larger polypeptides (e.g., preproinsulin).*

1. On the diagram below, label DNA, pre-mRNA, tRNA, ribosome, translation, polypeptide, and transcription.

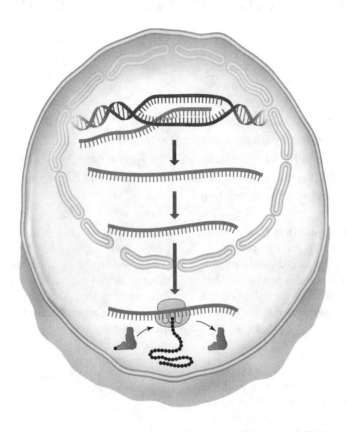

2. Describe the structure and function of mRNA, rRNA, microRNA, and tRNA.

_____

_____

_____

_____

_____

_____

_____

3. A dog was taken to a veterinary clinic because she had become increasingly lethargic. A blood test determined that the dog had very low levels of the steroid hormones produced by the adrenal glands, especially cortisol. The veterinarian's diagnosis was "a mutation in the cortisol gene." Explain why this characterization is inaccurate, given that steroid hormones are lipids. Speculate on a way that a genetic mutation could result in low levels of steroid hormones.

_____

_____

_____

_____

_____

_____

4. Describe the genetic condition of a person who has sickle-cell disease. Provide specific details about which gene is mutated, and include information about the polypeptide that has been altered by the mutation. Compare the effects of being heterozygous versus homozygous for the mutation.

_____
_____
_____
_____
_____
_____
_____

Concept 10.2 *explains how gene expression begins with the transcription of DNA to make RNA. Transcription of DNA begins with the association of the enzyme RNA polymerase with the DNA template. The necessary "ingredients" for transcription include free nucleoside triphosphates (ATP, GTP, CTP, and UTP) that are incorporated into the RNA strand being built by RNA polymerase moving along the DNA sequence. Transcription follows this sequence: initiation → elongation → termination. As transcription proceeds, each base in the DNA template strand pairs with its complementary nucleoside phosphate, which is then incorporated into the RNA. Here is a short example of that complementarity:*

3'-T-C-A-A-G-T-5' in DNA results in 5'-A-G-U-U-C-A-3' in RNA

The start of transcription along a strand of DNA is determined by the presence of a promoter sequence in the DNA, and RNA polymerase binds here. The next part of the sequence specifies the "start" codon UGA in the RNA. Elongation of RNA proceeds until a "stop" codon (UAA or UAG) is specified. While still in the nucleus, pre-mRNA receives a GTP-cap on its 5' end, and a poly-A tail on its 3' end; these modifications enhance RNA stability and later facilitate mRNA exiting from the nucleus and binding to ribosomes to start protein synthesis.

5. Mutations can have many different effects on the outcome of a gene's expression.

    a. Describe two possible impacts on a gene's expression resulting from a mutation in the promoter region of that gene.

_____
_____
_____
_____

    b. Describe two possible impacts on a gene's expression resulting from a mutation in the stop codon of that gene.

_____
_____
_____
_____

6. Describe what happens to "intron" and "exon" sequences as pre-mRNA is processed.

_____
_____
_____
_____

7. Describe the functions of the GTP cap and the poly-A tail on mRNA.

____

____

____

____

Concept 10.3 *describes how the genetic code of RNA is translated, driving the specific sequence of amino acids that are incorporated into newly synthesized proteins. The ribosomes "translate" the mRNA code by using it to determine which amino acid gets placed at which position in newly synthesized proteins. More specifically, the mRNA code consists of sequences of triplets of ribonucleotides (three bases in length) called codons. Each mRNA codon determines which amino acid will be added onto the linear sequence of the amino-acid chain that is the backbone of the growing polypeptide.*

8. Use the table below to characterize the peptide product by translating the mRNA fragment shown below the table.

First letter	Second letter: U	Second letter: C	Second letter: A	Second letter: G	Third letter
U	UUU UUC Phenyl-alanine UUA UUG Leucine	UCU UCC UCA UCG Serine	UAU UAC Tyrosine UAA Stop codon UAG Stop codon	UGU UGC Cysteine UGA Stop codon UGG Tryptophan	U C A G
C	CUU CUC CUA CUG Leucine	CCU CCC CCA CCG Proline	CAU CAC Histidine CAA CAG Glutamine	CGU CGC CGA CGG Arginine	U C A G
A	AUU AUC AUA Isoleucine AUG Methionine; start codon	ACU ACC ACA ACG Threonine	AAU AAC Asparagine AAA AAG Lysine	AGU AGC Serine AGA AGG Arginine	U C A G
G	GUU GUC GUA GUG Valine	GCU GCC GCA GCG Alanine	GAU GAC Aspartic acid GAA GAG Glutamic acid	GGU GGC GGA GGG Glycine	U C A G

5′ AUG UUU CAG CGA GGA UGA 3′

____

9. Describe how the result would change if the above sequence were altered so that the sixth base from the 5′ end was switched to G.

____

____

____

____

____

10. Describe how the result would change if the above sequence were altered so that 19th base from the 5' end was switched to A.

_____
_____
_____

11. Even though the amino acid serine is specified by UCU, UCC, UCA, UCG, AGU, and AGC, is it said that the genetic code is not ambiguous. Explain.

_____
_____
_____

12. Explain the comment "the genetic code is nearly universal" in terms of evolutionary ancestry.

_____
_____
_____

13. Explain how the human gene for insulin can be inserted into an *E. coli* bacterium to produce human insulin for medicinal purposes.

_____
_____
_____

14. What distinguishes the impacts of silent mutations from those of nonsense mutations?

_____
_____
_____
_____

Concept 10.4 *describes that the translation of the genetic code occurs when transfer RNA (tRNA) molecules deliver amino acids to ribosomes. Amino acids are carried on specialized RNA carriers known as tRNA. Each tRNA molecule includes a triplet sequence of RNA that is complementary to, and will bind with, a particular codon of mRNA, triggering the delivery of the tRNA's amino-acid cargo to the growing polypeptide. After that delivery is complete, the remnants of the tRNA leave the ribosome, and the mRNA code is then moved along to the next codon, which specifies the next tRNA to bind and leave its amino acid for the growing polypeptide.*

15. Explain the relationship between codons and anticodons, and describe where they interact.

_____
_____
_____
_____
_____
_____

16. Describe how more than one ribosome can be active in the process of translating a piece of mRNA.

_____

_____

_____

_____

_____

_____

17. For the ribosome shown at the right, state the anticodon sequence for the next tRNA to bind (at the bottom of the figure), then use the table in Question 8 to determine which amino acid will be incorporated into the peptide next.

_____

_____

_____

_____

18. Compare the actions of RNA polymerase and ribosomes.

_____

_____

_____

_____

_____

_____

_____

_____

_____

_____

Concept 10.5 _describes how proteins are modified after translation. When the mRNA has been translated up to a "stop" codon (UAA, UAG, or UGA), the polypeptide is released from the ribosome and either used as is or modified by other parts of the cell. Three major categories of posttranslational modification can take place. First, proteolytic enzymes could cut a long polypeptide into smaller proteins. Second, carbohydrates might be added onto the polypeptide, especially in proteins that play a role in cellular identity. Third, phosphorylation could covalently modify the protein, thus altering its shape and function._

19. Secreted proteins, including insulin and other hormones, typically interact with at least two membrane-bound organelles prior to their secretion from the source cell. Describe the activities of these two organelles in terms of preparing the polypeptide for secretion out of the source cell.

_____

_____

20. Describe the possible roles of RNA processing and posttranslational modification in explaining the observation that human insulin, with only 51 amino acids, is in fact a product of the INS gene, which has nearly 40,000 base pairs.

_____

_____

_____

21. On the diagram below, label RER, phospholipid bilayer, mRNA, polypeptide, and ribosome.

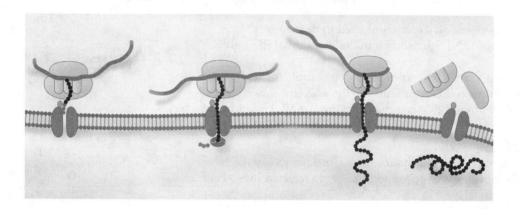

Science Practices & Inquiry

In the AP Biology Curriculum Framework, there are seven **Science Practices**. In this chapter, we focus on **Science Practice 1:** The student can use representations and models to communicate scientific phenomena and solve scientific problems. More specifically, we focus on **Practice 1.2:** The student can describe representations and models of natural or man-made phenomena and systems in the domain. We also cover **Science Practice 6:** The student can work with scientific explanations and theories. More specifically, we focus on **Practice 6.4:** The student can make claims and predictions about natural phenomena based on scientific theories and models.

Question 22 asks you to describe representations and models illustrating how genetic information is translated into polypeptides (**Learning Objective 3.4**), while question 23 asks you to predict how a change in a specific DNA or RNA sequence can result in changes in gene expression (**Learning Objective 3.6**).

22. Researchers have determined that a short-chain polypeptide signal (nuclear localization signal, or NLS) comprised of eight amino acids must be part of the central sequence of a protein if it is to enter the nucleus. When the NLS-protein complex docks with a pore in the nuclear membrane, the signal causes the pore to open. The sequence for this NLS peptide is: -Pro-Pro-Lys-Lys-Lys-Arg-Lys-Val-.

a. Explain why methionine could not be part of NLS.

_____

_____

b. Write out one mRNA strand that could produce this sequence.

_____

_____

c. Write out the DNA sequence that this mRNA sequence comes from.

_____

_____

d. Is this the only possible DNA sequence that could code for this NLS? Explain your answer.

_____

_____

_____

_____

23. The results of an experiment used to determine the function of the NLS are shown in the diagram at the right.

In scenario Y, an NLS-protein–red-dye complex that was injected into a cell is later found in the nucleus. In scenario Z, the protein–red-dye complex, lacking the NLS peptide, is injected into the cell, and it is later found only in the cytoplasm.

For each of the three scenarios below, predict where the NLS-protein complex will be found after being injected into a cell, and explain why.

a. A cytosolic protein, normally found only in the cytoplasm, is bound to an NLS.

_____

_____

_____

_____

_____

b. A nuclear protein is attached to a mutated form of an NLS that is missing its final valine.

_____

_____

_____

_____

_____

c. A nuclear protein is attached to an NLS that was produced from the DNA sequence TAC-GGG-GGT-TTT-TTC-TTC-GCT-TAC-CAC-stop.

_____

_____

_____

_____

_____

11 Regulation of Gene Expression

Chapter Outline

11.1 – Many Prokaryotic Genes Are Regulated in Operons
11.2 – Eukaryotic Genes Are Regulated by Transcription Factors
11.3 – Gene Expression Can Be Regulated via Epigenetic Changes to Chromatin
11.4 – Eukaryotic Gene Expression Can Be Regulated after Transcription

The DNA code is the transcription template for making RNA, which is then processed to make mRNA. The mRNA code is translated at the ribosomes to guide the synthesis of a polypeptide or a protein. Most of the cells of an organism carry the full set of that organism's DNA code.

The expression of different genes is what leads to the specialization of the thousands of kinds of cells in the human body (e.g., liver cells, skin cells, bone cells). In addition to encoding cell types, DNA encodes the messages necessary to repair cells, maintain homeostasis, regulate cell death, and address a host of other activities. Inducible genes, operons, transcription factors, posttranscriptional factors, and the cell's environment all work together in a dynamic fashion to maintain homeostasis and maximize the cell's functions.

Chapter 11's coverage of the AP Biology Curriculum Framework encompasses three of the **Big Ideas**.

Big Idea 2 states that the utilization of free energy and the use of molecular building blocks are characteristic of processes fundamental to life. Chapter 11 looks at regulation of DNA and gene expression. Specifically, Chapter 11 addresses:

• **2.C.1:** Organisms use negative feedback mechanisms to maintain their internal environments and respond to external environmental changes.

Big Idea 3 states that living systems store, retrieve, transmit and respond to information essential to life processes. Chapter 11 continues discussing DNA and includes the regulation of DNA. Chapter 11 includes:

• **3.B.1:** Gene regulation results in differential gene expression, leading to cell specialization.

Big Idea 4 states that biological systems interact in complex ways. Continuing with the theme of regulation, Chapter 11 considers the effects of the environment as well. Specifically, Chapter 11 addresses:

• **4.C.2:** Environmental factors influence the expression of the genotype in an organism.

Chapter Review

Concept 11.1 *examines how gene regulation can involve positive and/or negative regulation. The general label "transcription factor" is given to a regulatory protein that binds to DNA and activates or prevents transcription. Operons serve in transcriptional regulation for prokaryotes. They allow prokaryotes to conserve energy and resources by expressing genes only when their protein products are needed. Viruses, particularly bacteriophages, provide a convenient model to study transcription regulation. Viruses infect bacteria and turn them into virus factories by shutting down bacterial gene transcription and rapidly stimulating genome replication.*

1. It has long been suspected that alcoholism in some families includes a genetic influence. Briefly describe the recent discovery of the genetic underpinnings of alcoholism in studies of lab rats.

_____

_____

_____

_____

_____

2. In the diagram below, label and identify the five potential points (shown as arrows) for the regulation of gene expression.

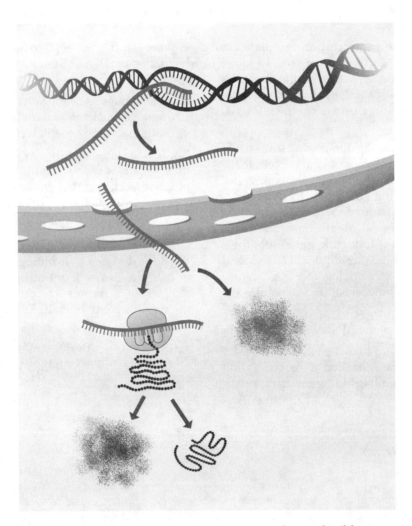

3. Explain the primary difference between a constitutive gene and an inducible gene, and provide an example of each.

_____

_____

_____

_____

_____

4. Describe the three primary parts of the *lac* operon.

a. _____

_____

b. _____

_____

c. _____

_____

5. Explain why the *trp* operon is described as a repressible operon, and discuss how this regulatory function is important to a bacterial cell.

_____

_____

_____

_____

6. Describe two features of bacteria that make them especially useful for studying the mechanisms of gene regulation.

_____

_____

_____

_____

7. Explain why viruses are not considered cellular organisms.

_____

_____

_____

_____

8. Explain how the four types of viruses are distinguished by differences in their genetic material.

_____

_____

_____

_____

_____

9. Describe the lytic and lysogenic phases of viral reproduction.

_____

_____

_____

_____

_____

10. Genetic mutations are useful in analyzing the control of gene expression. In the *lac* operon of *E. coli*, gene *i* codes for the repressor protein, P_{lac} is the promoter, *o* is the operator, and *z* is the first structural gene; (+) means wild type/normal; (−) means mutant/nonfunctional. Using the diagram below for reference, fill in the table by writing "YES" or "NO" to describe the presence of transcription in different genetic and environmental conditions.

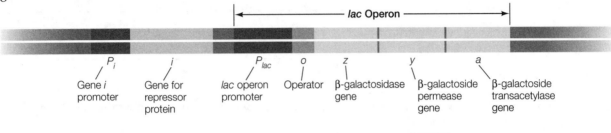

	Operator	
P_i	i	P_{lac}	o	z	y	a
Gene *i* promoter	Gene for repressor protein	*lac* operon promoter	Operator	β-galactosidase gene	β-galactoside permease gene	β-galactoside transacetylase gene

	z Transcription level	
Genotype	**Lactose present**	**Lactose absent**
$i^- P_{lac}^+ o^+ z^+$		
$i^+ P_{lac}^+ o^+ z^-$		
$i^+ P_{lac}^- o^+ z^+$		
$i^+ P_{lac}^+ o^- z^+$		

Concept 11.2 *explains how eukaryotic gene regulation can be even more complex than operon control of prokaryotic gene regulation. While operons are sometimes found in eukaryotes, genes are regulated at several other points as they are transcribed to RNA.*

11. Explain why transcription factors are found more commonly in eukaryotes than in prokaryotes.

_____

_____

_____

_____

_____

_____

_____

12. Describe all the necessary components that must be present before RNA polymerase II can transcribe a segment of eukaryotic DNA.

_____

_____

_____

_____

_____

_____

_____

13. In the diagram below, label the following: DNA, TATA box, transcription initiation site, promoter, transcription factors, and RNA polymerase II.

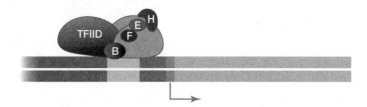

14. Describe the chemical matching between a transcription factor and the specific DNA sequence to which it binds.

_____

_____

_____

_____

15. Discuss the concept of "induced fit" as it applies to a transcription factor binding to DNA.

_____

_____

_____

_____

_____

_____

16. Discuss the importance of precision in the coordination of gene expression.

_____

_____

_____

_____

_____

_____

17. Explain how HIV uses RNA as its genetic material but still uses DNA for insertion as a provirus.

_____

_____

_____

_____

_____

_____

_____

_____

Concept 11.3 *explains how epigenetics and the environment also regulate genes. These influences can be passed down through multiple generations.*

18. Describe two ways that epigenetic changes to DNA can alter gene expression, and describe how these changes can be inherited despite the lack of changes in the parent's DNA sequence.

a. _____

_____

_____

_____

_____

_____

b. _____

_____

_____

_____

_____

_____

_____

19. Early in life, identical twins behave very similarly and are often difficult to tell apart. As they age, subtle differences appear, and as they reach middle age, the differences become more distinct. Explain how this can occur at a molecular level with reference to their shared DNA.

_____

_____

_____

_____

_____

_____

_____

_____

_____

_____

_____

_____

_____

Concept 11.4 *examines regulation of gene expression in the steps that follow transcription, including alternative RNA splicing and the control of mRNA translation. Farther along the sequence, the longevity of a protein product in the cell is also regulated by proteasomes, which degrade proteins when they are no longer useful to a cell.*

20. In *Drosophila*, sex is determined by a gene that has four exons, which we will designate 1, 2, 3, and 4. In the female embryo, splicing generates two active forms of the protein, one containing information from exons 1 and 2 and one containing information from exons 1, 2, and 4. In the male embryo, the protein contains information from all four exons (1, 2, 3, and 4), but the protein is inactive. Draw a diagram that represents this process, using the one below as a model.

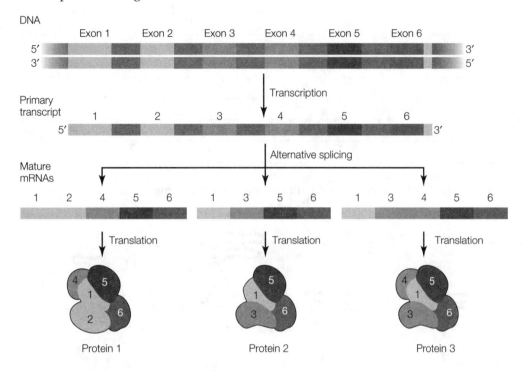

21. Explain how it is that humans have only about 24,000 genes but at least 85,000 different mRNA sequences.

_____

_____

_____

_____

_____

_____

_____

_____

_____

_____

22. In the figure below, label targeted protein, ubiquitin, and proteasome.

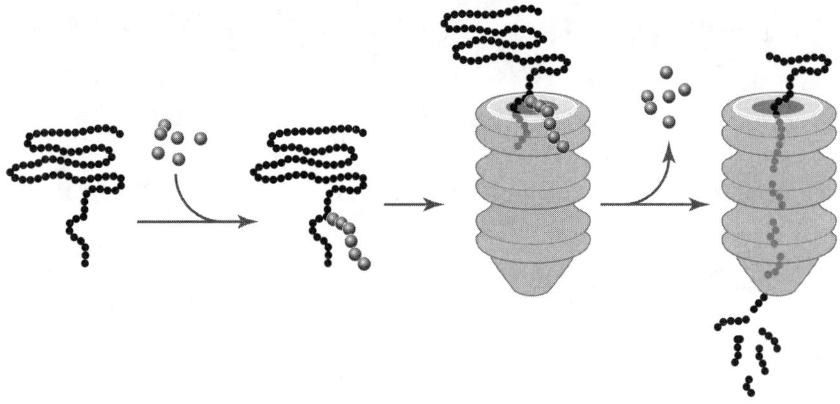

23. Explain the role of ubiquitin as shown in the figure for Question 22.

_____

_____

_____

_____

_____

_____

_____

24. Explain how microRNA (miRNA) can act in gene silencing.

_____

_____

_____

_____

_____

_____

_____

25. Complete the table below for the different types of gene regulation.

	Location in cell	Molecule(s) acted on	Example
Operons			
Transcription factors			
Translational			
Epigenetics			
Chromatin remodeling			
miRNA			
Alternative splicing			

Science Practices & Inquiry

In the AP Biology Curriculum Framework, there are seven **Science Practices**. In this chapter, we focus on **Science Practice 7:** The student is able to connect and relate knowledge across various scales, concepts, and representations in and across domains. More specifically, we focus on **Science Practice 7.1:** The student can connect phenomena and models across spatial and temporal scales.

Question 26 asks you to describe the connection between the regulation of gene expression and observed differences between individuals in a population (**Learning Objective 3.19**).

26. In a breeding experiment, fruit flies showed unusual growths on their eyes. This trait lasted for eleven to thirteen generations before breeding resulted in normal fruit flies.

   a. Could this change have occurred due to a mutation or change in the DNA sequence? Why or why not?

   _____

   _____

   _____

   _____

   _____

   _____

   _____

   b. Explain how this change could continue for generations and then disappear.

   _____

   _____

   _____

   _____

   _____

   _____

   _____

12 Genomes

Chapter Outline

Chapter 12 draws attention to the genome. An organism's genome is the complete DNA sequence that constitutes its full set of genes plus the rest of its DNA. Mistakes in the copying of DNA (*mutations*) provide evolutionary possibilities in the face of environmental uncertainty. Natural selection's effects are especially apparent at the level of the phenotype, but as phenotypic variation is largely based on variation in the genome, genomic studies provide detailed evolutionary insight into life's variations. Genomic analysis allows detailed studies of gene/protein structure/function, which demonstrate key evidence for the presence of evolutionary connections among all living organisms.

Genomes have been characterized for many viruses, prokaryotes, and eukaryotes. Prokaryotic cells are produced via binary fission, and each resulting cell typically has the full set of genes as well as other DNA. Cell replication, called *mitosis* in eukaryotes, includes copying all of an organism's DNA so that each eukaryotic cell has the full genome. Viruses have the capacity to take advantage of, and even insert DNA into, the genomes of both prokaryotes and eukaryotes. Genomic analysis provides detailed examples of viral enhancement of host genomes.

Chapter 12 includes material characterized in **Big Idea 3**. The heritable information in cells that effects change is their genes (i.e., their DNA or genome). The genome typically includes much more information than a single cell might use, but different information (different genes) in the genome can be activated in response to different signals found in the environment. These responses usually promote homeostasis in the organism. Specific parts of the AP Biology curriculum that are covered in Chapter 12 include:

- **3.A.1:** DNA, and in some cases RNA, is the primary source of heritable information.

- **3.A.3:** The chromosomal basis of inheritance provides an understanding of the pattern of passage (transmission) of genes from parent to offspring.

- **3.C.3:** Viral replication results in genetic variation, and viral infection can introduce genetic variation into the hosts.

Chapter Review

Concept 12.1 *discusses the methods for sequencing genomes and analyzing gene products. The "instructions for life" are found in every cell that has the full complement of DNA. Sequencing the genome started as an expensive and laborious process, but it has been greatly accelerated by automated techniques. Even so, DNA is typically an incredibly long molecule; the single DNA molecule that comprises human chromosome one has 246,000,000 base pairs.*

Genomic studies provide insight into protein structure and function, as proteins are among the direct products of gene expression. More than one protein can be the product of a gene being expressed; one large protein from a single gene can be cut up into several smaller proteins, each of which might serve a different role in the cell. For the approximately 24,000 genes in the human genome, there are about 75,000 proteins known. Because many proteins serve as enzymes in the synthesis of lipids and other biomolecules, the analysis of the full set of active biomolecules has its own label: metabolomics.

(continued)

Genomic analysis spans many areas of interest, including evolutionary biology, molecular details of genetic function in health and disease, RNA functions, open reading frames, intron analysis, protein synthesis, and chromosome stability. Comparing DNA sequences provides insight into the molecular basis of evolutionary changes that cause related organisms to separate from their common ancestor. Recall that certain parts of the DNA sequence code specifically for the start and stop of transcription, and you will appreciate how far genomic analysis has advanced in a short amount of time.

1. On the diagram below, label terminator of transcription, promoter of transcription, centromere, telomere, RNA polymerase, and mRNA. Then add a labeled bracket for the open reading frame.

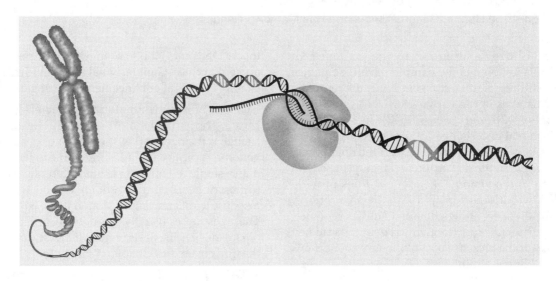

2. On the diagram below, label mRNA, phenotype, genome, metabolome, proteome, and genes.

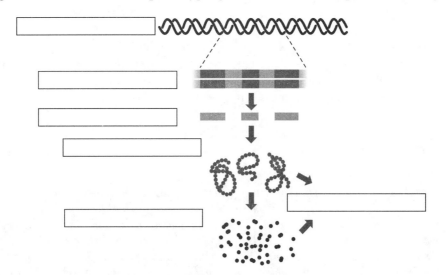

Concept 12.2 notes that prokaryotic genomes are relatively small, compact, and diverse. Organisms are broadly described as either eukaryotes or prokaryotes, with the latter including bacteria and all of the other microbes that lack membrane-bound organelles. Genomic packaging in the prokaryotes is typically minimal and compact, taking place on a single chromosome. In fact, the first genome to be fully sequenced was that of a prokaryote. The first synthetic genome/organism assembled by biologists was also prokaryotic in most of its characteristics.

(continued)
Very few prokaryotic genes have introns, suggesting efficiency in gene expression by these haploid organisms. Genomic analysis of different prokaryotes has revealed the evolutionary expansion of key functions, such as molecular uptake of nutrients from the environment and the metabolism of fuel molecules. It is also apparent that some sets of base sequences move around in the DNA and can be loaded onto plasmids, greatly enhancing biotechnology-based efforts to understand life.

3. Imagine that you are studying two strains of related bacteria: one is non-pathogenic but has antibiotic resistance, and the other is pathogenic but lacks antibiotic resistance. Speculate on the possible consequences of contamination in these two strains if you were to rely only on antibiotic soaps to "sterilize" your hands and equipment while going back and forth between the bacterial strains.

_____

_____

_____

_____

_____

_____

4. *Escherichia coli* has 4,288 protein-coding genes, 243 energy-metabolism genes, and 427 genes with products that take up molecules from the environment, whereas *Mycoplasma genitalium* has only 482, 31, and 34 genes in those categories, respectively. Discuss the differences between these two prokaryotes from a genomic viewpoint.

_____

_____

_____

_____

_____

_____

Concept 12.3 *reviews the large and complex genomes of eukaryotes. The packaging of the eukaryotic genome is necessarily complex, due to its large size and greater number of genes compared to prokaryotes. Eukaryotic DNA is packaged in structures clearly recognized as chromosomes. Many parts of eukaryotic DNA are not transcribed and/or translated and thus serve purposes other than coding for proteins (e.g., telomeres and spacers). Eukaryotes are diploid, with two copies of each gene present in each cell (except for the haploid gametes, sperm, and egg). Among animals, developmental genes are broadly shared, reflecting a conserved evolutionary history in the genes controlling development.*

5. Construct an argument to explain why the claim that DNA codes for proteins is too limited to provide a good description of "life's instruction book."

_____

_____

_____

_____

_____

6. Complete the table below by filling in the appropriate genomic characteristics of prokaryotes and eukaryotes.

	Prokaryotes	Eukaryotes
Complexity		
DNA location		
Chromosomes		
RNA splicing		
Size (number of base pairs)		
Number of gene copies		
Proportion of DNA that is translated		
Number of genes		

7. Discuss the claim that viruses directly increase genomic variation in prokaryotes and eukaryotes. Include a discussion of transposons in your answer.

_____

_____

_____

_____

_____

_____

8. In analyzing the genomes of diverse eukaryotes, scientists have found many stretches of gene duplication. Assume that an original DNA sequence is associated with an essential protein, and that the duplicate sequence is no longer identical to the original sequence. Discuss gene duplication as an evolutionary opportunity for changing the phenotype.

_____

_____

_____

_____

_____

_____

_____

Concept 12.4 *describes the many applications of human-genome study. Human DNA includes some six billion base pairs, packaged in 23 pairs of chromosomes. Genomic diversity is small; humans are much more alike than they are different, with 97 percent of DNA sequences being identical from one person to the next.*

9. A newspaper story reported that the genomes of persons with African–American ancestry have fewer genetic components for resistance to malarial infection, compared to the genomes of persons with African-only ancestry. Describe methodology that could have been used to generate these results.

_____

_____

_____

_____

_____

_____

_____

10. Following up on the finding described in Question 9, discuss the idea that African–Americans have faced different selective pressures than those faced by Africans.

_____

_____

_____

_____

_____

_____

_____

_____

11. If you knew the heights of 100 people whose individual genomes had been fully sequenced, how could you use the sequencing information to determine how height is passed on from one individual to another?

_____

_____

_____

_____

_____

12. Consider the population of people described in Question 11. Describe challenges you might have in drawing satisfactory conclusions about differences in their intelligence.

_____

_____

_____

_____

_____

_____

Science Practices & Inquiry

In the AP Biology Curriculum Framework, there are seven **Science Practices**. In this chapter, we focus on **Science Practice 6:** The student can work with scientific explanations and theories. More specifically, we focus on **Science Practice 6.4:** The student can make claims and predictions about natural phenomena based on scientific theories and models.

Question 13 provides you with enough information to justify the claim that humans can manipulate heritable information by identifying at least two commonly used technologies (**Learning Objective 3.5**).

13. Discuss two technologies that researchers can use to manipulate heritable information. Identify each technology, explain how it is used, and then give an example of its use.

_____

_____

_____

_____

_____

_____

_____

_____

_____

_____

_____

_____

_____

_____

_____

_____

_____

_____

_____

13 Biotechnology

Chapter Outline

13.1 – Recombinant DNA Can Be Made in the Laboratory
13.2 – DNA Can Genetically Transform Cells and Organisms
13.3 – Genes Come from Various Sources and Can Be Manipulated
13.4 – Biotechnology Has Wide Applications

In this chapter we examine how humans genetically modify organisms. From domesticating dogs and cats to selecting crops that produce the best yields, we have been manipulating genomes for thousands of years. More recently, we have learned how to insert the DNA of one organism into another organism, creating recombinant DNA.

Restriction enzymes, ligase, and gel electrophoresis are all associated with recombinant DNA, using techniques that you may have practiced in your laboratories. Inserting recombinant DNA into living organisms results in *transformed* or *transgenic* organisms. The majority of soy products in modern agriculture are derived from transgenic soybean plants that have genes to protect them from herbicides. These genetically modified organisms (GMOs) have attracted concern about unintended effects, generating close scrutiny and experimentation.

Biotechnology also allows the manipulation of an organism's own genes to address questions in biology. Which genes are turned on and off in any

given cell? How can we block the expression of a gene, such as the uncontrolled growth of cancer cells? Projects within the scope of biotechnology range from replacing organs and controlling cancer to producing high-yield crops and breeding organisms to clean up toxins in the environment.

Within the AP Biology Curriculum Framework, Chapter 13 focuses primarily on **Big Idea 3**. Though this chapter features only one of the **Big Ideas**, it is important that you make connections across the others. For instance, consider how the expression of DNA is regulated and how humans control this expression.

Big Idea 3 states that living systems store, retrieve, transmit, and respond to information essential to life processes. Chapter 13 discusses biotechnology and how we can manipulate genomes. Specific parts of the AP Biology curriculum that are covered in Chapter 13 include:

- **3.A.1:** DNA, and in some cases RNA, is the primary source of heritable information.

Chapter Review

Concept **13.1** *examines how restriction enzymes isolated from bacteria are used to cut DNA fragments, producing fragments with "sticky ends" that can be joined to other DNA segments. These fragments can be separated by size using gel electrophoresis. After cutting open a plasmid with restriction enzymes, a DNA fragment can be sealed into place by using the ligase enzyme.*

1. Explain why the process of brewing beer is an example of biotechnology.

_____

_____

_____

_____

_____

2. Restriction enzymes are sometimes called "the immune system of bacteria." Explain how restriction enzymes can protect bacteria from viruses.

_____
_____
_____
_____
_____
_____

3. How does a bacterium protect its own DNA from being cleaved by restriction enzymes?

_____
_____
_____
_____
_____

4. Explain how sticky ends are used to join DNA from two different organisms.

_____
_____
_____
_____
_____

5. Describe the type of atomic interaction between sticky ends that holds together two recently joined fragments of DNA.

_____
_____
_____
_____
_____

6. Compare the rearrangement of DNA during meiosis to the production of recombinant DNA.

_____
_____
_____
_____
_____

7. Plasmids are small, circular pieces of DNA. A particular plasmid (pUC 19) is cut with the *Ava*II restriction endonuclease (enzyme). The pUC 19 plasmid has 26,867 base pairs (bp). The *Ava*II cuts the plasmid at two locations: 1837 bp and 2059 bp.

   a. The circle at the right represents the DNA sequence of a pUC 19 plasmid. Draw a map of this plasmid, showing the location of the cuts described above. Then calculate the size of each fragment.

   b. In one of the lanes on the gel diagram at the right, sketch the results you would expect to see if the fragments from above were run using gel electrophoresis. Label the positive end and the negative end.

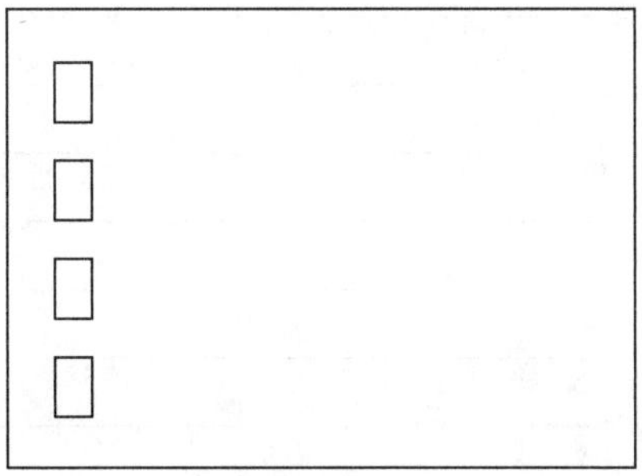

8. Single-stranded DNA of 12 kilobase (KB), or 12,000 bp, is cut by restriction enzymes A and B, as shown.

Condition	Sizes of Fragments (KB)
Enzyme A	2, 10
Enzyme B	2, 10
Enzymes A + B	2, 8

   a. In three of the lanes on the gel diagram at the right, show the expected results of the three cuts representing gel electrophoresis used for DNA separation. Be sure to label each lane.

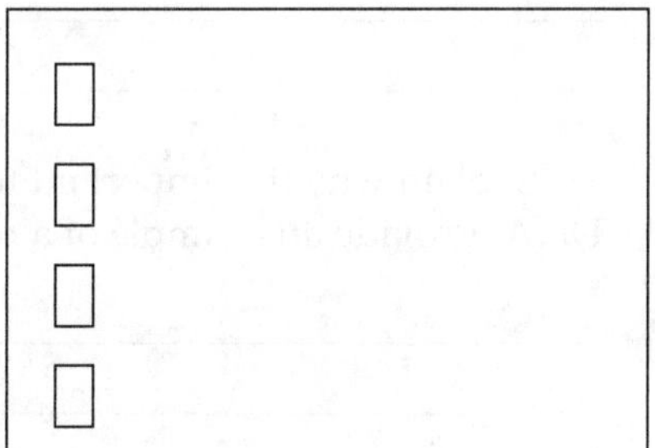

   b. Draw a linear map of this DNA and indicate where each enzyme cuts the DNA.

Concept 13.2 *explains how recombinant DNA is inserted into an organism so that the organism will express the recombinant gene. There are many techniques for doing this, including the use of plasmids as vectors and the transformation of bacteria. Resistance to antibiotic genes and green fluorescent genes are often used as markers to screen for organisms that have been transformed in this manner.*

9. Describe the advantage of using yeast instead of bacteria as a model organism for the introduction of recombinant DNA.

10. Explain the benefits of using a viral vector in the place of a plasmid vector.

11. Explain why it is important to use recombinant "reporter genes" to identify host cells with recombinant DNA. Provide an example of a reporter gene used in this way.

12. Outline the steps that a researcher would follow to insert a foreign piece of DNA into a plasmid.

_____

_____

_____

_____

_____

_____

_____

_____

_____

13. A researcher has a small gene that she wants to insert into *E. coli* for expression. This gene has been cut on both ends with the *Eco*RI restriction enzyme. The researcher obtained a plasmid vector that includes the following functional genes:

- β-galactosidase gene (*lacZ*) that codes for an enzyme that can convert the colorless substrate X-gal into a bright blue product
- a gene for resistance to the antibiotic ampicillin (*amp*)

The *Eco*RI restriction enzyme site on the *lacZ* gene was cut to insert the small gene of interest. The researcher grew *E. coli* bacteria with the following treatments:

- no plasmid added
- plasmid alone
- recombinant plasmid (gene added inside the *lacZ* gene site)

a. Draw the uncut and the recombinant plasmids below, showing the differences.

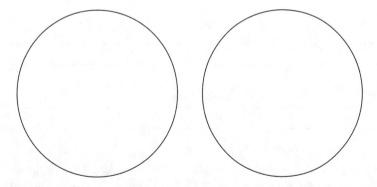

b. Complete the table below by describing the results the researcher would expect to see after growing the *E. coli* bacteria on media containing X-gal and the antibiotic ampicillin.

Treatment	Selection by ampicillin (colonies present or absent)	Color of colonies if present (blue or white)
Grown with no plasmid		
Transformed with plasmid		
Transformed with recombinant plasmid		

Concept 13.3 *reviews some of the molecular methods for manipulating gene expression, including the selection or creation of DNA for amplification, the detection of expressed genes, and the artificial regulation of gene expression.*

14. Use the figure at the right to explain how knockout genes are produced. Label five parts of the figure (a, b, c, d, and e) as you refer to them in your discussion.

_____

_____

_____

_____

_____

_____

_____

_____

_____

_____

_____

_____

_____

15. How does antisense RNA regulate the expression of DNA?

_____

_____

_____

_____

_____

_____

Concept 13.4 *surveys some applications of biotechnology. Examples include the production of human insulin and human growth hormone by bacteria, the improvement of agricultural crops, and bioremediation techniques to clean up environmental disasters.*

16. Give three reasons why biotechnology provides an advantage over more traditional plant-breeding techniques.

_____

_____

_____

_____

_____

17. Many people oppose inserting genes from one organism into another to produce genetically modified organisms (GMOs). Describe three scientific concerns about GMOs.

_____

_____

_____

_____

_____

_____

_____

_____

_____

_____

_____

Science Practices & Inquiry

In the AP Biology Curriculum Framework, there are seven **Science Practices**. This chapter addresses **Science Practice 6:** The student can work with scientific explanations and theories. More specifically, we focus on **Practice 6.4:** The student can make claims and predictions about natural phenomena based on scientific theories and models.

Question 18 asks you to recall how proteins are assembled by a cell, including how their shapes are formed during production. It may be helpful to review chaperonins before answering *Part a*, reminding yourself of the close relationship of structure and function. *Part b* requires you to apply your knowledge of biotechnology techniques. There are many tools you could use to answer this question; it is important to explain what property of the molecule is being tested or analyzed by the technique (**Learning Objectives 3.5 and 3.6**).

18. Organic chemists frequently substitute one functional group for another on a large molecule to make minor changes to the molecule. Cocaine, for example, has four functional groups that can be substituted for or deleted to make different pharmaceutical drugs of various potencies.

   a. Explain why changing one amino acid to alter a protein's function is not as easy as changing a functional group on a large molecule.

_____

_____

_____

_____

_____

_____

_____

_____

_____

b. Identify two biotechnology techniques that could be used to determine whether or not an experimentally induced change in a single amino acid of a protein change was successful.

_____

_____

_____

_____

_____

_____

_____

_____

14   Genes, Development, and Evolution

Chapter Outline

14.1 – Development Involves Distinct but Overlapping Processes

14.2 – Changes in Gene Expression Underlie Cell Fate Determination and Differentiation

14.3 – Spatial Differences in Gene Expression Lead to Morphogenesis

14.4 – Changes in Gene Expression Pathways Underlie the Evolution of Development

14.5 – Developmental Genes Contribute to Species Evolution but Also Pose Constraints

Most organisms start life as a single cell. The interplay between the genes and the materials inside and around the cells sets in motion a precisely regulated pattern of development from which a mature organism takes shape. The material found inside the cell depends on the location and time of that cell's appearance in the developing organism. In this way, spatial and temporal differences in gene regulation result in spatial and temporal patterns of organ and limb development. As a result of these patterns, everything develops at the right time and in the right place. Spatial and temporal differences in development influence, and are influenced by, the evolution of species differences.

Developmental biology is strong support for **Big Idea 2**, which notes that biological systems utilize free energy and molecular building blocks to grow, to reproduce, and to maintain dynamic homeostasis. Specific parts of the AP Biology curriculum that are covered in Chapter 14 include:

- **2.E.1:** Timing and coordination of specific events are necessary for the normal development of an organism, and these events are regulated by a variety of mechanisms.

Understanding the networks and cascades of signaling that direct developmental biology strongly supports **Big Idea 3**, which is based on information flow in living systems. Chapter 14 also addresses:

- **3.B.2:** A variety of intercellular and intracellular signal transmissions mediate gene expression.

- **3.D.2:** Cells communicate with each other through direct contact with other cells or from a distance via chemical signaling.

Finally, **Big Idea 4**, biological systems interact with complexity, is a fundamental underpinning in developmental biology. Specifically, Chapter 14 includes:

- **4.A.3:** Interactions between external stimuli and regulated gene expression result in specialization of cells, tissues, and organs.

Chapter Review

Concept 14.1 *describes how development involves distinct but overlapping processes. The zygote is the single cell formed by the union of the gametes in sexually reproducing species, and mitosis is the process that gives rise to more cells. Determination of any individual cell's "fate" happens early in its development, and groups of cells can differentiate to become specific structures with specific functions. Morphogenesis proceeds, resulting in the formation of body parts and organs. Growth typically occurs over a much longer part of the organism's lifespan. Cells that are labeled "totipotent" can differentiate to become any part of an organism, whereas cells that are "multipotent" have a more limited array of developmental possibilities.*

1. The schematic drawing at the right shows possible surgical manipulations to non-human embryos. In scenario A, which provides background, the oval-shaped embryo at the top normally gives rise to the embryo form below it. Briefly explain what is shown in scenarios B and C, and compare the impact of these two scenarios on our knowledge of fate determination. The shading of the embryos and embryo parts is an important clue.

Early embryo Donor   Older embryo Donor

Transplant   Transplant

Host   Host

Normal fate

(A)   (B)   (C)

_____

_____

_____

_____

_____

_____

_____

2. Discuss two reasons why model organisms, such as fruit flies and *Brassica* plants, have proven so useful in research studies conducted by developmental biologists.

_____

_____

_____

_____

_____

3. The team that cloned Dolly the sheep used a nucleus from a mammary epithelium (ME) cell. They also tried cloning by transplanting nuclei from fetal fibroblasts (FB) and embryos (EC), with these results:

Stage	Number of attempts that progressed to each stage		
	ME	FB	EC
Egg fusions	277	172	385
Embryos transferred to recipients	29	34	72
Pregnancies	1	4	14
Live lambs	1	2	4

a. Calculate the percentage survival of eggs from fusion to birth, and comment on the efficiency of cloning.

_____

_____

_____

b. Compare the efficiencies of cloning using different nuclear donors. What can you conclude about the ability of nuclei at different stages to be totipotent?

_____

_____

_____

_____

_____

4. The French flag model of early development holds that chemical gradients of morphogens across developing tissues influence regional gene expression, leading to specific patterns in the emerging organism. A morphogen called *Sonic hedgehog* plays an important role in the formation of the vertebrate nervous system. Briefly describe how the French flag model, shown at the right, might be used to generate testable ideas in developmental studies of nerves in vertebrate embryos.

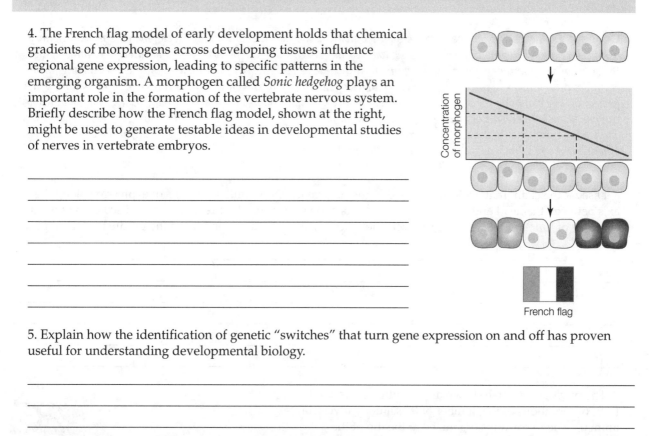

French flag

_____

_____

_____

_____

_____

_____

_____

5. Explain how the identification of genetic "switches" that turn gene expression on and off has proven useful for understanding developmental biology.

_____

_____

_____

6. Discuss the observation that Hox genes are present in all animals and have a positional expression pattern during development, which guides cell fates.

_____

_____

_____

_____

7. A fruit fly with the *Antennapedia* mutation grows a leg where an antenna should be. Explain this homeotic mutation in general terms. Include changes in the expression patterns of Hox and related genes.

_____

_____

_____

_____

_____

Concept 14.4 *explains that gene-expression pathways underlie the evolution of development. The evolutionary perspective on developmental biology has advanced largely through the observations that diverse organisms use the same or very similar regulatory mechanisms during development. Much of the diversity we see among forms of different organisms is the result of small changes in the timing or the place of the expression of regulatory gene networks. For example, the observation that chimpanzees and humans are so closely related in genotype but not in phenotype is the result of many similarities and differences in species-specific patterns of gene expression. An additional example is that a longer interval for the expression of a particular gene can result in the elongation or other changes in a limb, as in the long neck of the giraffe.*

8. Discuss the claim that evolution-related regulatory genes show similar patterns of expression along the axis between the head and the abdomen in insects and vertebrates. Be sure to include a discussion of what category of function (e.g., signals, transcription factors, or filaments) is present in the products of these genes.

_____

_____

_____

_____

_____

9. The phylogenetic tree shown at the right was derived from observations of the number of legs among invertebrate animals. The five groups organized at the top of the drawing have six legs each, and the four groups below them have eight or more legs. Explain the genetic implications of the small circle drawn on the tree at the key branch point for the evolution of changes in the number or location of legs.

_____

_____

_____

_____

_____

_____

_____

_____

10. In many animals, eye formation during development is under the control of a genetic switch and a transcription factor. Here are partial DNA sequences for the control gene from two organisms:

Mouse *Pax6* gene: 5′-GTA TCC AAC GGT TGT GTG AGT AAA ATT-3′
Fruit fly *eyeless* gene: 5′-GTA TCA AAT GGA TGT GTG AGC AAA ATT-3′

a. Calculate the percentage of identity (identical bases) between the two DNA sequences.

_____
_____
_____

b. Use the genetic code to determine the amino acid sequences encoded by the two regions, and calculate the percentage of similarity between the two proteins.

_____
_____
_____

c. The fruit fly and mouse had a common ancestor about 500 million years ago. Comment on your answers to *Part a* and *Part b*, above, in terms of the evolution of developmental pathways.

_____
_____
_____
_____
_____

Concept 14.5 *explains how developmental genes contribute to species evolution but also pose constraints. The "genetic toolkit" describes the limited set of developmentally important genes on which natural selection has acted to generate variability in form and function. Examination of the genetic toolkit supports the conclusion that evolution acts on genes that are already present, rather than inventing new ones.*

11. Historically, it was thought that any two species with large differences in form and function must have huge differences in the genes that regulate their development patterns. Discuss whether this hypothesis has been widely supported or weakened by the data collected during more recent studies of developmental gene expression.

_____
_____
_____
_____

12. Stickleback fish that live in the ocean develop a pelvic spine that makes it difficult for predators to swallow them. A key gene is required for development of this spine. Suppose that two freshwater populations of sticklebacks from different regions never develop the pelvic armor. Present two hypotheses, one to help determine whether the loss of the armor is due to identical genetic changes in the gene or to different changes in the gene. For the latter, comment on the concept of parallel phenotypic evolution.

_____
_____
_____
_____

Science Practices & Inquiry

In the AP Biology Curriculum Framework, there are seven **Science Practices**. In this chapter, we focus on: **Science Practice 1:** The student can use representations and models to communicate scientific phenomena and solve scientific problems, and **Science Practice 6:** The student can work with scientific explanations and theories. Specifically, the student uses evidence to justify a claim that a variety of phenotypic responses to a single environmental factor can result in different genotypes within the population (**Learning Objective 4.25**). We also address **Science Practice 7:** The student is able to connect and relate knowledge across various scales, concepts, and representations in and across domains.

13. The drawing below shows wings of pterosaurs, birds, and mammals. Draw circles around these subsets of skeletal entities in the drawing: humerus, radius and ulna, metacarpals, and phalanges. Then connect your circles with lines to show the homologous parts.

Discuss how these similarities demonstrate that the wing was not a completely novel "invention" of nature each time it developed.

15 Processes of Evolution

Chapter Outline

Evolution explains the interrelatedness of all of the different species of microbes, plants, and animals. Some commonalities of life include the genetic code, the similarity of developmental genes, and similar biochemical processes (glycolysis) across the phyla. In this chapter, we examine the history of thought on life's mechanisms of change, derived from the analytical observations and ideas of Charles Darwin.

Evolution's factual basis is that organisms have always changed and are still changing today. Evidence of evolutionary change comes from analysis of fossils, biochemistry, homologous structures, and biogeography, and the direct observation of change. Today, as we observe active evolution in the development of antibiotic-resistant bacteria and pesticide-resistant insects, we ask, "How have these changes occurred over long periods of time?" This is the theoretical side of evolutionary study. It is important to remember that a theory is not just a random thought or idea. Rather, a theory is a well-developed idea, repeatedly tested with experiments, and it provides a cohesive framework for analysis.

The basis of evolutionary theory, which explains how populations change over time, was first proposed by Darwin and Alfred Russell Wallace. The success of their ideas hinged on the idea of natural selection. Darwin observed that there is variation among the members of any species and that not all members of each species survive to reproduce. Only those members of a species that are well adapted thrive enough to reproduce and to pass their genes on to the next generation. Thus, some variants of form are passed from generation to generation, resulting in evolution, a change over time.

A primary source of new variation in a population is mutation of DNA, resulting in offspring that have a DNA sequence that is different from that of their parent or parents. In addition, genetic variation results from meiosis, nonrandom mating, gene flow, and genetic drift. These changes can be estimated by counting the frequencies of traits and genes in a population. The Hardy–Weinberg theorem is more about non-evolution than evolution, as it states that in order for a population to "not evolve" over time, five conditions must exist: no mutations, no gene flow, no environmental impact on survival, random mating, and a very large (infinite) population size. The Hardy–Weinberg conditions are not obtained in nature, except in contrived settings set up by humans, so evolution proceeds.

Changes in the phenotype of a population over time can follow distinct patterns, including stabilizing, directional, or disruptive selection. These changes are assessed by observations of phenotypes or observable behaviors. The changes underlying these phenotype changes can be seen in the genes of organisms or genomes. Sequencing DNA or proteins and then looking at mutation rates is used to research the evolution of genomes. These techniques have provided many new insights into evolutionary theory and the interrelationships of different organisms, including the splitting of prokaryotes into two groups and the creation of a new level of classification called the *domain*.

The emphasis in Chapter 15 is primarily on **Big Idea 1**, but some of **Big Idea 4** is addressed, as well.

The specific parts of the AP Biology curriculum covering **Big Idea 1:** The process of evolution drives the diversity and unity of life, recognizes that evolution ties together all parts of biology, include:

- **1.A.1:** Natural selection is a major mechanism of evolution.

- **1.A.2:** Natural selection acts on phenotypic variations in populations.
- **1.A.3:** Evolutionary change is also driven by random processes.
- **1.A.4:** Biological evolution is supported by scientific evidence from many disciplines, including mathematics.

- **1.C.3:** Populations of organisms continue to evolve.

Specifically, the curriculum addressing **Big Idea 4:** Biological systems interact, and these systems and their interactions possess complex properties, includes:

- **4.C.3:** The level of variation in a population affects population dynamics.

Chapter Review

Concept 15.1 *introduces evolutionary theory and the ideas of Darwin, Wallace, and others.*

1. Explain in evolutionary terms why a different flu vaccine is developed each year.

_____

_____

_____

_____

2. Explain the meaning of *theory* in the context of atomic theory and evolutionary theory.

_____

_____

_____

_____

3. Charles Darwin noted that the species of South America's temperate regions were more similar to the species of South America's tropical regions than they were to the species of Europe's temperate regions. Explain how this observation guided his evolutionary thinking.

_____

_____

_____

_____

_____

_____

4. In addition to observing biological specimens, Darwin also read a book about geology by Charles Lyell. Discuss how Lyell's concepts of geological time and space influenced Darwin's biological considerations of life on Earth.

_____

_____

_____

_____

_____

5. Describe two ways that the discovery of genes and chromosomes affected evolutionary theory.

_____

_____

_____

_____

_____

_____

Concept 15.2 *examines the primary mechanisms of evolution, including mutation, gene flow, genetic drift, and nonrandom mating.*

6. Explain the phrase "individuals do not evolve, populations do."

_____

_____

_____

_____

_____

7. Describe the origin of new genetic variation in the genetic code.

_____

_____

_____

_____

8. It has been observed that 10 percent of the Japanese population has blood type AB. Discuss this observation using the terms *allele, gene frequency,* and *gene pool.*

_____

_____

_____

_____

_____

_____

_____

_____

9. Describe one difference and one similarity between artificial selection and natural selection, and explain how each influenced Darwin's writings on evolution.

_____

_____

_____

_____

_____

10. Darwin made the two key observations presented below. Explain how each supports his concept of natural selection.

a. Populations have a large amount of variation within them. _____

_____

_____

_____

_____

b. Most individuals that are born do not survive to reproduce. _____

_____

_____

_____

_____

11. In northern Canada, there are two large herds of caribou that seldom encounter each other. Speculate on the amount of gene flow between these populations.

_____

_____

_____

_____

_____

_____

12. Explain how the bottleneck principle relates to conservation problems for endangered species.

_____

_____

_____

_____

_____

13. While observing wild birds, a fellow student asks, "Why are male cardinals such a brilliant red? Doesn't that make them more visible to predators?" Use your knowledge of sexual selection to answer how the predation risk of high visibility might be offset.

_____

_____

_____

_____

_____

Concept 15.3 *describes how we can measure evolutionary change with the Hardy–Weinberg equilibrium principle.*

14. Identify the five principles of the Hardy–Weinberg theorem that must be true for a population to be in genetic equilibrium.

a. _____

_____

b. _____

_____

c. _____

_____

d. _____

_____

e. _____

_____

15. Assume that a local population of birds experiences immigration of additional birds of the same species from another country each winter, and that there is a limited amount of breeding during those winters. For each of the five principles of the Hardy–Weinberg theorem, explain why it would be impossible for the local population *not* to evolve.

a. _____

_____

b. _____

_____

c. _____

_____

d. _____

_____

e. _____

_____

16. Discuss the challenge to evolutionary theory based on the fact that many populations of organisms appear to be stable and unchanging from year to year and many of their genotypes are not significantly changing from Hardy–Weinberg expectations.

_____

_____

_____

_____

_____

Concept 15.4 *considers the interaction of genes with each other and with the environment to create shifts in the phenotoypes of a population based on selection.*

17. A biologist finds a population of small arthropods on a Pacific island with white sand beaches between black lava flows. Most of the arthropods are either dark gray or very light gray, but less than 10 percent of the population is an intermediate gray color. Identify this pattern of selection, and discuss how it might operate in this manner.

_____

_____

_____

_____

18. In lizards, it has been shown that there is an optimum size egg for survival: eggs that are too big or too small are not adaptive. Identify this pattern of selection and discuss this example.

_____

_____

_____

_____

Concept 15.5 *describes specific processes that operate at the level of genes and genomes. One of the most important examples in this section is called the* heterozygote advantage.

19. Discuss the claim that a heterozygote advantage promotes genetic diversity within a population.

_____

_____

_____

_____

_____

20. Explain whether or not a neutral mutation affects the phenotype of an individual.

_____

_____

_____

_____

21. Much of the DNA in eukaryotes is noncoding, in that proteins are not produced using it as a template. For many years, the noncoding DNA was called "junk" DNA, but recent work shows that it has several important functions. Identify two possible functions of noncoding DNA.

_____

_____

_____

_____

Concept 15.6 *discusses how new genes with novel functions can form in a population.*

22. Sexual reproduction generates diverse combinations of genes within a population. However, not all species reproduce sexually, revealing some of the drawbacks of sexual reproduction. Discuss three of these drawbacks.

_____

_____

_____

_____

_____

_____

23. Two "endosymbiotic" organelles in eukaryotes appear to have resulted from lateral gene transfer from prokaryotes. What new benefits did these organelles confer on the recipients?

_____

_____

_____

24. Give an example of gene duplication in an organism, and discuss how the duplication appears to be the basis for evolutionary change.

_____

_____

_____

_____

_____

Concept 15.7 *examines how knowledge of evolutionary theory is used to combat disease, benefit agriculture, and study protein function.*

25. Explain the evolutionary thinking behind the advice to farmers to use different herbicides in consecutive years.

_____

_____

_____

26. Discuss how genomic databases allow for better detection and treatment of diseases.

_____

_____

_____

_____

Science Practices & Inquiry

In the AP Biology Curriculum Framework, there are seven **Science Practices**. In this chapter, we focus on **Science Practice 2:** The student can use mathematics appropriately. More specifically, we focus on **Science Practice 2.2:** The student can apply mathematical routines to quantities that describe natural phenomena.

Question 27 asks you to apply mathematical methods to data and predict what will happen to the human population in the future (**Learning Objective 1.3**). Most of the Science Practice questions up to this point have been free-response questions. The redesigned AP Biology exam has a multiple-choice portion and a set of grid-in items that require you to apply mathematics to biological concepts. An equation sheet, similar to the one inside the back cover of this workbook, will give you the commonly used equations, such as the Hardy–Weinberg principle that is used in the question below.

27. Cystic fibrosis is an autosomal recessive genetic disorder. This disease occurs in 0.4 out of 1,000 children born in the United Kingdom. Calculate the percent of carriers in the UK, and record your answer in the grid provided. Express your answer to the hundreth of a percent.

16 Reconstructing and Using Phylogenies

Chapter Outline

It is challenging to tell the full story of the amazing diversity of life; many attributes of living organisms are so different that the task seems hopelessly complex. Complications include an incredibly long passage of time, far removed from our daily experience of seconds, minutes, and hours, and we have only an incomplete record of all changes. Nonetheless, there are many, many similarities between organisms, both living and dead, and these provide clues used by biologists to follow the many branches in the vast tree of life.

Much as a family tree traces a family's generations over time, phylogenetic trees trace evolutionary history. A family tree includes the names of family members, whereas a phylogenetic tree is built with the units of taxonomic categories, such as orders and species. Phylogenetic trees reveal evolutionary history, and they permit us to make predictions about

what might be possible as life responds to the never-ending changes in environmental and other selection pressures.

The specific parts of the AP Biology curriculum in Chapter 16 addressing **Big Idea 1**: The process of evolution drives the diversity and unity of life, include:

- **1.A.4**: Biological evolution is supported by scientific evidence from many disciplines, including mathematics.

- **1.B.1**: Organisms share many conserved core processes and features that evolved and are widely distributed among organisms today.

- **1.B.2**: Phylogenetic trees and cladograms are graphical representations (models) of evolutionary history that can be tested.

Chapter Review

Concept 16.1 *examines how all of life is connected through its evolutionary history. Try to imagine the long personal history that led you to what you're doing right now. If you were to create your family tree, the logic and simplicity of your family pedigree would become clear. The same approach works with the history of relationships that preceded today's diverse plants and animals.*

Evidence of species interconnectedness is particularly compelling when it comes to examining genomes, which are a kind of "molecular registry" of evolution. Relationships within a particular level of taxonomic organization are depicted using simple phylogenetic trees. Typically, these "trees" are presented sideways, with most branching on the right side of the tree, and time (usually in unspecified and varying intervals) along the horizontal axis. The branch-points in phylogenetic trees indicate occasions where one group developed a substantial difference from its ancestral group, justifying its placement away from a straight linear sequence of genetic inheritance.

1. Refer to the phylogenetic tree at the right.

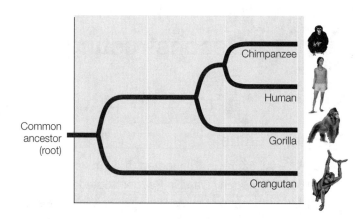

a. What clades are indicated in the tree? _____

_____

_____

b. Choose the taxonomic branching that occurred most recently, and justify your selection.

_____

_____

_____

c. Discuss the reasons why one of the organisms depicted would be interested in its evolutionary relationships to the other three organisms.

_____

_____

_____

2. Homologous structures are of great use in determining evolutionary relationships. Explain the homology that is present in each pair of items below.

a. The spinal cord of a shark and that of a chimpanzee: _____

_____

_____

_____

b. The wing of a bird and that of a bat: _____

_____

_____

_____

c. A vision-related gene in fruit flies that is identical to that in mice: _____

_____

_____

_____

Concept 16.2 *examines how phylogeny can be reconstructed by examining the traits of organisms. The physical and other traits of organisms help us organize groups to reveal evolutionary relationships. Such analyses are built on two assumptions: 1) There hasn't been any convergent evolution (i.e., a "new" trait arose only once in the set of organisms selected for analysis), and 2) Traits of interest were not lost over the evolutionary interval under consideration.*

Information that is used to construct phylogenetic trees and cladograms includes morphology (physical features of traits, such as flowers), patterns seen during development (such as Hox genes in vertebrate and invertebrate development), behaviors (such as similar mating calls in varied frog populations), and molecular sequences in genes of interest, especially mitochondrial and chloroplast genes.

3. Use data from the table below to label the small dots in the phylogenetic tree with the appropriate derived traits.

EIGHT VERTEBRATES AND THE PRESENCE OR ABSENCE OF SOME SHARED DERIVED TRAITS								
	Derived trait							
Taxon	Jaws	Lungs	Claws or nails	Gizzard	Feathers	Fur	Mammary glands	Keratinous scales
Lamprey (outgroup)	−	−	−	−	−	−	−	−
Perch	+	−	−	−	−	−	−	−
Salamander	+	+	−	−	−	−	−	−
Lizard	+	+	+	−	−	−	−	+
Crocodile	+	+	+	+	−	−	−	+
Pigeon	+	+	+	+	+	−	−	+
Mouse	+	+	+	−	−	+	+	−
Chimpanzee	+	+	+	−	−	+	+	−

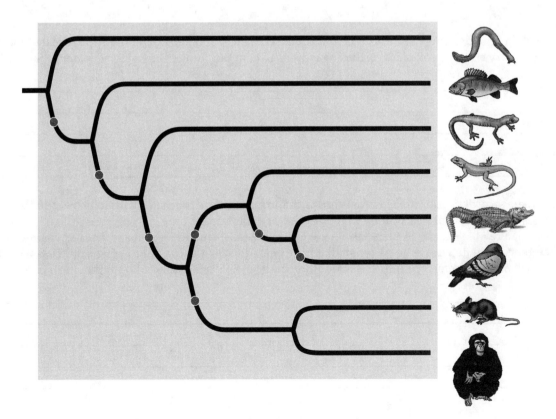

4. *Parsimony* refers to the way a particular analysis, among many analyses, generates the simplest possible solution to a problem. Describe what parsimony means in the context of Question 3.

_____

_____

_____

5. Though their body shapes are similar, snakes and worms have substantially different evolutionary histories. Discuss how this convergence might have occurred, and suggest additional data that could be sought in determining the differences in their evolutionary lineages.

_____

_____

_____

6. Explain why phylogenetic trees based on gene sequences are more accurate in showing evolutionary relationships than phylogenetic trees based on morphology.

_____

_____

_____

Concept 16.3 *explores how phylogeny makes biology both comparative and predictive. Phylogenetic analysis of organisms that appear to be similar has often shown that they arrived at such similarity via convergent evolution, rather than simply being closely related to one another.*

Knowing phylogenetic pathways helps us see the broad scope of evolutionary change, but it also reveals some of its limitations. Such knowledge is used in choosing genes from wild plants to engineer into domestic plants and in analyzing patterns of pathogen diversification. Therefore, phylogeny is of considerable value in solving the problems faced by our species.

7. Explain how protein analyses can help meet the challenge of determining the approximate time that an evolutionary change took place, including a discussion of the "molecular clock of protein changes."

_____

_____

_____

_____

8. Female swordtail fish (*Xiphophorus*) show a mating preference for males with long swordtails, suggesting that sexual selection for longer tails over evolutionary time has occurred. Even though the males of a related species of platyfish do not have long tails, females of that species demonstrate a preference to mate with male platyfish that have been fitted with artificial long tails. Discuss what the females' mating preference suggests about the phylogenetic background of both groups of fish.

_____

_____

_____

_____

9. Discuss how studies of the "molecular clock of DNA changes" allowed an estimate of the specific year of origin for the human immunodeficiency virus.

_____

_____

_____

_____

Concept 16.4 *explains how phylogeny has become the basis of biological classification. Making sense of the immense biological diversity requires us to examine the relationships of all organisms. Phylogenetic analysis is really evolutionary history, and with it, we know more about the possible directions that evolution may take in the future, with or without our help. The development of taxonomic rules will result in the most parsimonious and accurate description of evolutionary consequences: speciation.*

10. Describe the Linnaean binomial nomenclature of your own species.

_____

_____

_____

_____

_____

11. Place the taxonomic terms *order, genus, family, species, class, phylum, kingdom* in correct sequence, from most inclusive to most specific.

_____

_____

_____

12. Explain why it is essential that each group of organisms included in genetic databases has an accurate and specific taxonomic identity.

_____

_____

_____

_____

_____

_____

13. An article in a recent newspaper placed humans in the genus *sapiens*. Explain why this is inaccurate and why *sapiens* cannot be used by itself.

_____

_____

_____

_____

_____

Science Practices & Inquiry

In the AP Biology Curriculum Framework, there are seven **Science Practices**. In this chapter, we focus on **Science Practice 5:** The student can use mathematics appropriately. More specifically, we focus on **Science Practice 5.3:** The student can evaluate the evidence provided by data sets in relation to a particular scientific question.

Question 14 provides an opportunity to evaluate evidence and find patterns and relationships. We examine characteristics of animals that spend most of their time in water, and we attempt to determine their evolutionary relationships (**Learning Objective 1.9**).

14. Sharing aquatic habitats suggests a shared evolutionary heritage, but there are many other things to consider. Here we will survey traits of four animals with aquatic lifestyles: sponges, fish, newts, and whales. Sponges do not have circulatory systems, fish have two-chambered hearts, aquatic newts have three-chambered hearts, and whales have four-chambered hearts. Sponges, fish, and newts are poikilothermic (cold-blooded), whereas whales are homeothermic (warm-blooded). Sponges reproduce both asexually and sexually; when reproducing sexually, sponges shed gametes externally. The fish and newt shed their gametes externally; internal fertilization, internal development (gestation, or pregnancy), and nursing of offspring are reproductive characteristics of whales. Sponges do not have true tissues, while fish, newts, and whales do.

   a. Create a table to describe these animals and their characteristics.

   b. Draw a phylogenetic tree using this information.

   c. Indicate on your cladogram where each of the characteristics arose. Then provide an evolutionary justfication for where you placed the characteristics.

   _____

   _____

   _____

   _____

17 Speciation

Chapter Outline

Chapter 17 uses biological concepts to explore the meaning of the term "species." We define a species as a group of organisms that are potentially or actually interbreeding and can produce fertile offspring. This concept does have limitations and is not particularly useful for examining fossils or bacteria and asexual organisms, so other definitions of species are used in those situations. Species typically change very slowly over time as they respond to changes in their environment. Thus, the formation of a new species typically requires some form of an isolating event that prevents the flow of genes from one group to another. When this happens, a new species can result.

Isolating events can be as simple as a population migrating to the other side of a mountain range or a tectonic plate forming a barrier between two groups of a species. This is called allopatric speciation, and it results from a physical separation of the groups that cuts off genetic exchange between the groups. This is the most common mode of speciation in animals. Sympatric speciation appears to be less common, but it occurs when a new species arises without physical separation between the groups that diverge to form distinct species. Sympatric speciation has occurred frequently in plants.

After a barrier to gene flow is established, differences in gene frequencies and types of mutations can build up in the separated populations. On a molecular level, genetic incompatibility can create two groups that cannot produce offspring with each other, even if they were to try to mate. Recall that a zygote is the first new cell of a sexually produced organism. Prezygotic and postzygotic isolating mechanisms serve to further reinforce the genetic isolation between species. Prezygotic isolating mechanisms prevent the union of sperm and egg to form a zygote. On those few occasions when a viable zygote has formed between two different species, postzygotic isolating mechanisms occur when the resulting hybrid is weak, malformed, or sterile.

Specific parts of the AP Biology curriculum in Chapter 17 covering **Big Idea 1**: The process of evolution drives the diversity and unity of life, include:

- **1.C.1:** Speciation and extinction have occurred throughout the Earth's history.

- **1.C.2:** Speciation may occur when two populations become reproductively isolated from each other.

- **1.C.3:** Populations of organisms continue to evolve.

Chapter Review

Concept 17.1 *discusses the definition of species. There are many definitions, all of which attempt to describe biological diversity and to define this most descriptive level of classification.*

1. Below are pictures of four small fishes found in the eastern United States.

For each of the species concepts below, describe the evidence that would be used to determine whether these fishes are separate species.

a. Morphological species concept: _____

_____

_____

_____

b. Biological species concept: _____

_____

_____

_____

c. Lineage species concept: _____

_____

_____

_____

2. Which of the three species concepts in Question 1 is most useful for describing asexually reproducing organisms? Explain.

_____

_____

_____

3. Captive tigers and lions can be mated under certain conditions but will produce sterile offspring. Why are these two organisms considered to be different species?

_____

_____

_____

Concept 17.2 *examines the idea that the accumulation of several mutations in the genetic composition of a population can result in reproductive incompatibility with similar populations; the end products of genes must be able to work together. If multiple gene changes create reproductive incompatibility, then reduced fitness or even lethal changes may result.*

4. After two groups of a species become isolated, mutations can quickly accumulate in each of the separated groups. Discuss how the resulting combinations of genes, such as that shown for two genes in the diagram, may have deleterious effects on a zygote formed by mixing gametes of the separate groups together.

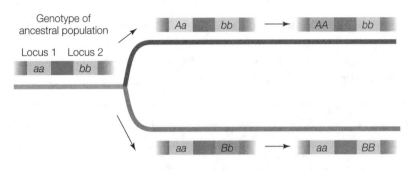

_____

_____

_____

_____

_____

_____

_____

5. The diagram at the right shows modifications of the chromosomes of an original species (A) after two subgroups (B and C) became distinct from Species A.

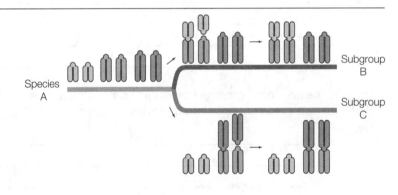

Assume that all three of the groups shown are sexually reproducing species that form gametes via meiosis. Sketch what would happen when the gametes of subgroup B are united with those of subgroup C, then discuss whether or not speciation is possible among these three groups.

_____

_____

_____

_____

_____

Concept 17.3 *examines how groups of a population can split and become divided over time with geographic isolation (allopatric speciation) or without (sympatric speciation).*

6. Read the opening passage of Chapter 17 (page 343 in your textbook) to learn about the cichlid fishes of Lake Malawi.

    a. Some cichlids populate the sandy areas of the lake, and some populate the rocky areas. Does this represent allopatric or sympatric speciation? Explain. _____

_____

_____

_____

    b. In the rocky area, some of the cichlids evolved into plankton eaters, while others became algae eaters. Does this suggest allopatric or sympatric speciation? Explain. _____

_____

_____

_____

7. Distinguish autopolyploidy and allopolyploidy, and explain how sympatric speciation can result from each condition.

_____

_____

_____

_____

8. Describe how road construction could lead to allopatric speciation. Would a new road be expected to have the same effect for all animal species in a given area?

_____

_____

_____

_____

_____

_____

_____

Concept 17.4 *explains that prezygotic and postzygotic processes reinforce the isolation of separate species.*

9. Define "zygote," and briefly discuss the origination of gametes and how they then form a zygote.

_____

_____

_____

_____

_____

10. Your textbook gives several examples of prezygotic and postzygotic isolating mechanisms (shown in parentheses below). For each of the mechanisms given, provide another example, not found in Chapter 17, and explain how the isolating mechanism keeps the two species from hybridizing.

    a. Mechanical isolation (orchids and wasps): _____

_____

_____

_____

    b. Temporal isolation (leopard frogs): _____

_____

_____

_____

    c. Behavioral isolation (frog calls, coloration of cichlids in Lake Malawi, columbine flowers and pollinators, *Phlox*): _____

_____

_____

_____

    d. Habitat isolation (cichlids of Lake Malawi, *Rhagoletis* flies): _____

_____

_____

_____

    e. Gametic isolation (sea urchins): _____

_____

_____

_____

    f. Low viability of hybrid adults (*Bombina* toads): _____

_____

_____

_____

    g. Hybrid infertility (mule and horse): _____

_____

_____

_____

11. For many years, two populations of orioles in the United States were considered to be separate species. Now, most bird books list them as one species. What evidence would researchers need to have collected to make this change in classification?

_____

_____

_____

_____

_____

Science Practices & Inquiry

In the AP Biology Curriculum Framework, there are seven **Science Practices**. In this chapter, we focus on **Science Practice 4**: The student can plan and implement data collection strategies appropriate to a particular scientific question. More specifically, we focus on **Science Practice 4.1**: The student can justify the selection of the kind of data needed to answer a particular scientific question, and **Science Practice 4.2**: The student can design a plan for collecting data to answer a particular scientific question. We also address **Science Practice 6**: The student can work with scientific explanations and theories. We focus on **Science Practice 6.4**: The student can make claims and predictions about natural phenomena based on scientific theories and models.

In *Parts a* and *b* of question 12, you will use data from two real populations and explain why they represent separate species (**Learning Objective 1.22**). *Part c* asks you to design a plan for collecting data to investigate the scientific claim that speciation and extinction have occurred throughout Earth's history (**Learning Objective 1.21**) and to justify the selection of data that address questions related to reproductive isolation and speciation (**Learning Objective 1.23**).

12. When interbred, domestic horses (*Equus caballus*; $2n = 64$) and donkeys (*Equus asinus*; $2n = 62$) produce either a mule or a hinny, both of which are infertile hybrids ($2n = 63$).

Two groups of horses were found to have different numbers of chromosomes. Przewalski's horse (*Equus ferus przewalskii*, $2n = 66$) is an ancient horse formerly found only in Mongolia. This horse is now thought to be extinct in the wild, but it survives in many zoos. Crosses between the domestic horse (*E. caballus*, $2n = 64$) and Przewalski's horse produce fertile offspring that appear normal in phenotype.

   a. Explain why the offspring of horses and donkeys are infertile. Be sure to include a discussion of meiosis and gametes. _____

   _____

   _____

   _____

   b. Though domestic horses and Przewalski's horses create fertile offspring, they are considered different species. Explain this. _____

   _____

   _____

   _____

   c. Imagine that Przewalski's horses have been reintroduced to Mongolia and are thriving in large numbers. Populations of domestic horses live in areas bordering the Przewalski horse range. Design an experiment to determine whether these two groups of horses are different species. Describe the type of data you would need to collect to make this determination. _____

   _____

   _____

   _____

   _____

   _____

   _____

   _____

   _____

18 The History of Life on Earth

Chapter Outline

18.1 – Events in Earth's History Can Be Dated
18.2 – Changes in Earth's Physical Environment Have Affected the Evolution of Life
18.3 – Major Events in the Evolution of Life Can Be Read in the Fossil Record

It's time to think about time. Understanding the impressive evolutionary changes of plants and animals requires you to think far beyond the lifespan of a human being, as life on Earth started long ago, was punctuated by five major extinctions, and will continue on for a very long time to come.

To organize our thinking about evolutionary time, Earth's geological history has been mapped out into four major intervals, called *eras*, starting 4,500,000,000 years ago (4.5 bya). Each era is subdivided into periods. While it is true that intense cataclysms (e.g., volcanoes, meteors, continental crashes, etc.) shaped life on Earth, it is also true that life shaped Earth—especially Earth's atmosphere—yielding

more evolutionary opportunities. Puzzling through the evidence, the fossils, the geological changes, and the calculations allows us to see some of life's experimentation, including the dead ends and, perhaps, some of our planet's future opportunities.

In Chapter 18, specific parts of the AP Biology curriculum covering **Big Idea 1:** The process of evolution drives the diversity and unity of life, include:

- **1.A.4:** Biological evolution is supported by scientific evidence from many disciplines, including mathematics.

- **1.C.1:** Speciation and extinction have occurred throughout Earth's history.

Chapter Review

Concept 18.1 *explains how events in Earth's history can be dated. Imagine having an immense trash can into which you place all of your disposable items throughout your lifetime. Someone could sort through the layers, or strata, in the trash, and find out what you did last week, two years ago, and when you were five years old. In doing so, they could put together a picture of how you and your world have changed over the years. It is the same with fossils in ocean sediments: the oldest forms of life are in the bottom layer, and the newer forms are closer to the top. Analyzing the layers that have accumulated over the years tells us much about the history of life on Earth.*

The cooling rate of a recently deceased individual has been thoroughly studied in forensic science, so the temperature of a corpse is an important clue to an investigator at a murder scene. Just as heat energy dissipates when it is no longer being produced, elemental isotopes decay in a measureable way over time, albeit over a much longer period, and provide important clues that "date" rocks and other materials of interest to those focused on analyzing Earth's past.

1. Radioisotopic elements in igneous rock decay at predictable rates, as shown in the table below.

Radioisotope	Decay product	Half-life (years)	Useful dating range (years)
Carbon-14 (^{14}C)	Nitrogen-14 (^{14}N)	5,700	100 – 60,000
Uranium-234 (^{234}U)	Thorium-230 (^{230}Th)	80,000	10,000 – 500,000
Uranium-235 (^{235}U)	Lead-207 (^{207}Pb)	704 million	200,000 – 4.5 billion
Potassium-40 (^{40}K)	Argon-40 (^{40}Ar)	1.3 billion	10 million – 4.5 billion

For the samples listed in *Parts a* and *b*, use the table below to select the radioisotope that should be measured to best estimate the age of the samples. Explain your answers.

a. Alleged Permian sample: _____

_____

_____

_____

_____

_____

_____

_____

_____

b. Alleged Quaternary sample: _____

_____

_____

_____

_____

_____

_____

_____

TABLE 18.1	Earth's Geological History		
Eon	Era	Period	Onset
Phanerozoic (~0.5 billion years long)	Cenozoic	Quaternary (Q)	2.6 mya
		Tertiary (T)	65.5 mya
	Mesozoic	Cretaceous (K)	145.5 mya
		Jurassic (J)	201.6 mya
		Triassic (Tr)	251.0 mya
	Paleozoic	Permian (P)	299 mya
		Carboniferous (C)	359 mya
		Devonian (D)	416 mya
		Silurian (S)	444 mya
		Ordovician (O)	488 mya
		Cambrian (C)	542 mya
Proterozoic	Collectively called the Precambrian (~4 billion years long)		2.5 bya
Archean			3.8 bya
Hadean			4.5–4.6 bya

Note: mya, million years ago; bya, billion years ago.

2. Suppose that the sample you dated in Question 1a was found in igneous rock two meters above a dinosaur fossil. Explain how this information would affect your assessment of the geological age of the alleged Permian sample.

_____

_____

_____

_____

3. Suppose that the sample you dated in Question 1b was found in rock two meters above a dinosaur fossil. Explain how this information would affect your assessment of the geological age of the alleged Quaternary sample.

_____

_____

_____

_____

Concept 18.2 *examines how changes in Earth's physical environment have affected the evolution of life. The movement of the continental land masses has been an important influence on the distribution of plants and animals. Just as sheets of ice can move on water, plates of Earth's surface, or crust, move around on a bed of very hot molten rock. You probably know that these continental drifts can cause earthquakes. They are also instrumental in determining where volcanoes occur and in what direction ocean currents flow, thus influencing temperatures across the Earth. In addition to its own restlessness, Earth has been struck by extraterrestrial objects of varying sizes, possibly including an immense meteorite that caused mass extinctions. Furthermore, the organisms on the planet, especially the plants, have had a major effect on the amount of oxygen in the atmosphere.*

4. Discuss how climate changes can be associated with large reductions in sea level that coincide with mass extinctions of marine life.

_____

_____

_____

5. Describe the hypothesis of current global climate change, and discuss how having an unusually cold winter fails to refute the hypothesis.

_____

_____

_____

_____

6. Iridium is fairly uncommon in the clay soils on Earth's surface. It is more abundant, however, in a thin layer of the Cretaceous–Tertiary boundary sample created 65 million years ago, when a mass extinction took place. Discuss this finding.

_____

_____

_____

_____

7. Describe how life on Earth has impacted the concentration of oxygen in the atmosphere at each of the following times:

    a. 2 billion years ago: _____

_____

_____

    b. 1 billion years ago: _____

_____

_____

    c. 500 million years ago: _____

_____

_____

    d. 250 million years ago: _____

_____

_____

Concept 18.3 *describes how major events in the evolution of life can be read in the fossil record. Fascination with dinosaurs is widespread, likely because the artistic models of these animals, based on fossil evidence, reveals animals that are so large and so strange that it is difficult to imagine them inhabiting our Earth. But fossils are evidence for many other kinds of plants and animals that can factor into solving the puzzles of evolutionary history. Unfortunately, the fossil record is only a tiny representation of the planet's past flora and fauna, since very few dying organisms end up in conditions appropriate for fossilization processes to occur.*

8. Around 500 million years ago, the Cambrian explosion in the number of plants and animals on Earth was in bloom. At the end of the Devonian period 150 million years later, a massive extinction occurred. This was followed by the "invasion of the land," as vertebrates began to move onto land and into drier habitats. Discuss the changes that produced the opportunity for a land invasion by animals.

_____
_____
_____
_____
_____

9. Consider the hypothesis that the invasion of the land occurred at the end of the Devonian period. Describe the types of fossil evidence of animal morphology that would support this hypothesis.

_____
_____
_____
_____
_____

10. Describe the primary geologic factors at work for each of these milestones of evolution:

a. 250 million years ago: _____
_____
_____
_____

b. 225 million years ago: _____
_____
_____
_____

c. 175 million years ago: _____
_____
_____
_____

d. 100 million years ago: _____
_____
_____
_____

Science Practices & Inquiry

In the AP Biology Curriculum Framework, there are seven **Science Practices**. In this chapter, we focus on **Science Practice 5**: The student can perform data analysis and evaluation of evidence. More specifically, we focus on **Science Practice 5.1:** The student can analyze data to identify patterns or relationships.

Question 11 asks you to analyze data related to questions of speciation and extinction throughout Earth's history (**Learning Objective 1.20**).

11. The graph below shows the number of families of organisms over time.

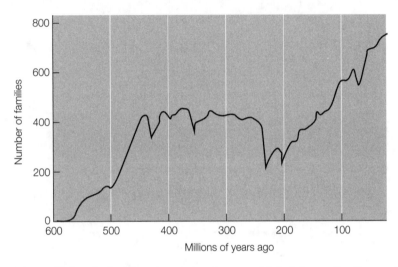

a. Select four intervals that include major extinctions, and label the extinctions with arrows.

b. Explain how a major extinction can impact the surviving species, that is, the survivors that do not go extinct.

_____

_____

_____

_____

_____

_____

_____

_____

_____

_____

_____

_____

_____

19 Bacteria, Archaea, and Viruses

Chapter Outline

19.1 – Life Consists of Three Domains That Share a Common Ancestor
19.2 – Prokaryote Diversity Reflects the Ancient Origins of Life
19.3 – Ecological Communities Depend on Prokaryotes
19.4 – Viruses Have Evolved Many Times

In this chapter we begin our study of the diversity of life. The chapter opens with an introduction to the three domains of life. There are obvious distinctions between eukaryotes and prokaryotes. Though you cannot see Bacteria and Archaea individuals without a microscope, the differences between the Bacteria and the Archaea are equally dramatic. The major distinctions are biochemical in nature, with some variation in the size and structure of ribosomes and the structure of their membrane lipids.

As the AP Biology course content does not include many details of taxonomy and classification, the important lessons of this chapter include the evolutionary lineages of organisms from a prokaryotic predecessor and the idea that phylogenetic trees show evolutionary history. Whether or not a particular bacterium stains Gram-positive or Gram-negative is less important than understanding that major biochemical processes, such as glycolysis, are conserved through the phyla. Prokaryotes utilize diverse metabolic processes, including chemoheterotrophy and photoheterotrophy. Focus on how different organisms produce ATP and obtain carbon atoms for anabolic reactions.

Additionally, the prokaryotes play many vital roles in ecosystems. Early prokaryotes liberated enough molecular oxygen gas into the atmosphere to allow the evolution of aerobic respiration. Without nitrogen-fixing bacteria, there would be insufficient quantities of nitrates available for plants to thrive. The cycling of nutrients by bacteria acting as decomposers is critical to many ecosystems. As symbionts and pathogens, bacteria are also important to larger organisms: they help cattle digest grasses and produce vitamins B_{12} and K in the intestine.

Chapter 19 concludes with viruses, which some biologists classify as non-living and others as acellular. Viruses, which replicate very efficiently and mutate frequently, make up an important group of pathogenic organisms. A virus is classified by type of genetic material and whether it is single- or double-stranded. Retroviruses regenerate themselves by reverse transcription, producing complementary DNA from the viral RNA genome and replicating it. Given its impact on human populations, HIV is one retrovirus that is important for us to understand.

Chapter 19 spans **Big Idea 1** and **Big Idea 2**. Here, we see an introduction to classification and the evolutionary relationships of bacteria to eukaryotes. Specific parts of the AP Biology curriculum covering **Big Idea 1**: The process of evolution drives the diversity and unity of life, include:

- **1.B.1:** Organisms share many conserved core processes and features that evolved and are widely distributed among organisms today.

- **1.B.2:** Phylogenetic trees and cladograms are graphical representations (models) of evolutionary history that can be tested.

Parts of the curriculum addressing **Big Idea 2**: Biological systems utilize free energy and molecular building blocks to grow, to reproduce, and to maintain dynamic homeostasis, include:

- **2.E.3:** Timing and coordination of behavior are regulated by various mechanisms and are important in natural selection.

Chapter Review

Concept 19.1 *examines the commonalities and differences across the three domains of life. Evolutionarily, the last common ancestor of all three domains probably lived on Earth approximately 3 billion years ago. Over the past 3 billion years, organisms have evolved a diversity of metabolic pathways and differentiated into three major groups.*

1. Describe and discuss four attributes shared by all living organisms.

_____

_____

_____

_____

_____

_____

_____

_____

_____

_____

_____

2. Discuss why all living things share the features you identified in Question 1.

_____

_____

_____

_____

3. Explain how binary fission in prokaryotes is both similar to and different from mitosis in eukaryotes.

_____

_____

_____

_____

_____

_____

4. Eukaryotes have membrane-bound organelles where specific biochemical reactions take place. How do prokaryotes accomplish these tasks without using highly specialized organelles, specifically lysosomes, mitochondria, and endoplasmic reticula?

_____

_____

_____

_____

_____

5. Describe and discuss two types of evidence supporting the idea that all three domains of life have a common ancestor.

_____

_____

_____

_____

_____

_____

6. The diagram below shows the phylogenetic relationships among various bacteria. Discuss the similarity of genes found in the Archaea and the Bacteria to those of eukaryotes, citing evidence presented in the diagram to justify your logic.

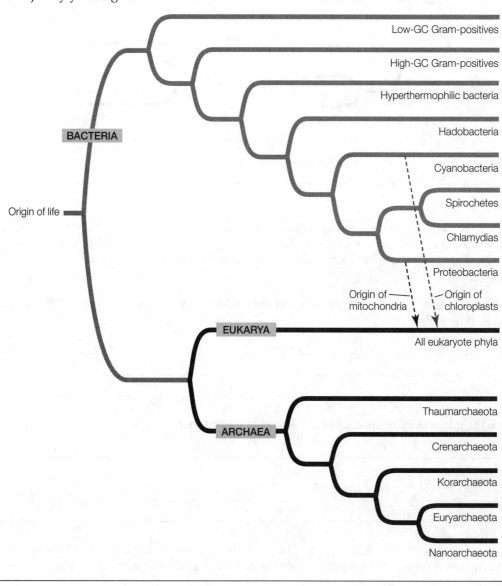

_____

_____

_____

_____

7. Consider the statement: "Bacteria are primitive life forms that are more than 3 billion years old." Do you agree or disagree? Explain your answer, keeping in mind the diversity of today's prokaryotes.

_____

_____

_____

_____

_____

_____

8. Below are two possible cladograms showing the relationships of four species. What would be needed to determine the relationship between B, C, and D?

_____

_____

_____

Concept 19.2 *reviews the taxonomy and classification of prokaryotes, issues beyond the scope of the AP Biology curriculum. However, understanding the extreme habitats in which different bacteria flourish can give us insights into shared biochemical pathways and teach us about useful biotechnology tools.*

9. The keyboard you are typing on or the pen you are holding may or may not have any Archaea and/or Bacteria on it. Why is this?

_____

_____

_____

10. Describe the importance of spores to the bacteria that form them.

_____

_____

_____

_____

11. Most animal classification involves physical features or behavioral characteristics. Describe the key feature that was used originally to separate Archaea and Bacteria into separate domains.

_____

_____

_____

_____

12. One frequently encounters unfamiliar words in science textbooks. For instance, a sentence in *Principles of Life* states: "These ether linkages are a synapomorphy of archaea."

a. Define *synapomorphy* as used in an evolutionary context.

_____

_____

_____

_____

_____

b. Synapomorphy occurs when a trait is shared by two or more ancestors and their common ancestor but not by the ancestor of the common ancestor. Complete the phylogenetic tree below, showing how it might look with two species that have a common trait. Use shaded circles to show a shared trait and unshaded circles to show the lack of this trait.

13. Describe how the membranes of archaea are unique among prokaryotes.

_____

_____

_____

_____

_____

_____

_____

Concept 19.3 *notes that prokaryotes flourish everywhere and are important members of ecosystems.*

14. Discuss and compare the metabolism of obligate and facultative anaerobes, then classify humans using this terminology.

_____

_____

_____

_____

_____

_____

_____

15. Complete the table below:

Category	Energy source	Carbon source	Example
Photoautotrophs			
Photoheterotrophs			
Chemolithotrophs			
Chemoheterotrophs			

16. Use the categories in the table above to classify the following:

_____ Humans

_____ A fungus decomposing a rotting tree

_____ A plant absorbing CO_2 and producing sugars

_____ An organism that lives in complete darkness and cannot utilize CO_2 but is able to produce its own sugars

17. Compare the reactions of nitrogen-fixing bacteria with those of nitrifying bacteria.

_____

_____

_____

_____

18. In an aquarium, fish excrete ammonia as a waste product. Describe the types of bacteria that convert the ammonia to nitrates.

_____

_____

_____

_____

19. A fellow student complains that there are too many bacteria in the world and all surfaces in the classroom should be treated with antibiotic spray.

a. How would you explain to the student why very few of the bacteria are able to hurt him?

_____

_____

_____

_____

b. If all surfaces in the room were sprayed with the same antibiotic spray every day, what effect would this have on the bacteria populations?

_____

_____

_____

Concept 19.4 *focuses on viruses and their importance to other organisms. Evolutionarily, viruses probably evolved multiple times as either escaped genetic elements or highly reduced parasites.*

20. Viruses are generally classified into four large groups: those with DNA, those with RNA, and those with single- stranded or double-stranded genetic material. Explain why most biologists believe that these groups are *not* monophyletic.

_____

_____

_____

_____

_____

_____

_____

21. Explain why some biologists view viruses as parasitic organisms.

_____

_____

_____

_____

_____

_____

22. Explain quorum sensing and why it is important to bacteria from the perspective of natural selection. (*Hint*: You may want to reread the opening page of the chapter.)

_____

_____

_____

_____

_____

_____

_____

_____

_____

Science Practices & Inquiry

In the AP Biology Curriculum Framework, there are seven **Science Practices**. In this chapter, we focus on **Science Practice 6:** The student can use representations and models to communicate scientific phenomena and solve scientific problems. More specifically, we focus on **Science Practice 6.1**: The student can justify claims with evidence.

Questions 23 and 24 ask you to justify the scientific claim that organisms share many conserved core processes and features that evolved and are widely distributed among organisms today (**Learning Objective 1.16**).

23. Draw a diagram showing how a retrovirus infects a host cell and completes its life cycle. Label all the different forms of genetic material that are utilized.

24. Describe and discuss evidence that viruses evolved recently from other living organisms, rather than being an ancient form of life.

_____

_____

_____

_____

_____

_____

_____

_____

_____

_____

_____

_____

_____

_____

_____

_____

_____

20 The Origin and Diversification of Eukaryotes

Chapter Outline

20.1 – Eukaryotes Acquired Features from Both Archaea and Bacteria

20.2 – Major Lineages of Eukaryotes Diversified in the Precambrian

20.3 – Protists Reproduce Sexually and Asexually

20.4 – Protists Are Critical Components of Many Ecosystems

Chapter 20 explores an early question challenging evolutionary biologists: How did living organisms gain such complexity? When you encounter an unfamiliar organism, here are some questions to think about: What does it look like? How does its metabolism work? What is its mode of reproduction? These broad functional questions will help you identify the biological characteristics of most use.

In Chapter 20, the specific parts of the AP Biology curriculum covering **Big Idea 1:** The process of evolution drives the diversity and unity of life, include:

• **1.B.2:** Phylogenetic trees and cladograms are graphical representations (models) of evolutionary history that can be tested.

Chapter Review

Concept 20.1 *shows how eukaryotes "acquired" features from both Archaea and Bacteria. Having explored the single-celled Archaea and Bacteria in Chapter 19, this section reviews the cellular transitions hypothesized to have led from simple cells of Archaea and Bacteria to the more complex cells of the Eukarya. First, it appears that size limits on diffusion and metabolism were barriers to single cells with smooth surfaces, and the infolding of the cell's surface resulted in an increased surface area for exchange between the cell and its environment. Second, the DNA of prokaryotes, bound to a small piece of membrane, became encircled by that membrane, leading to the eukaryotic nucleus. Third, larger cells engulfed other smaller cells, and their life cycles became united as they prospered together—the endosymbiotic theory that explains eukaryotic complexity.*

1. Describe the hypothesized non-endosymbiotic relationship between the diffusion requirements of cells and the development of Golgi apparatus, the smooth endoplasmic reticulum, and the rough endoplasmic reticulum.

_____

_____

_____

_____

2. Describe the hypothesized endosymbiotic relationship between a bacterium and the eukaryotic mitochondrion. Include in your discussion the role of the bacteria in detoxification metabolism.

_____

_____

_____

_____

3. Describe the hypothesized endosymbiotic relationship between the metabolism of a cyanobacterium and the first photosynthetic eukaryotes.

_____

_____

_____

_____

4. Describe the structural characteristics suggesting a formerly independent lifestyle for the following organelles:

  a. Mitochondria: _____

  _____

  _____

  _____

  b. Chloroplasts: _____

  _____

  _____

  _____

5. Compare and discuss the DNA of Bacteria and Archaea with the DNA of eukaryotes.

_____

_____

_____

_____

_____

6. Compare and discuss primary and secondary endosymbiosis.

_____

_____

_____

_____

_____

7. Discuss your agreement or disagreement with the statement: "The evolutionary development of photosynthetic eukaryotes was likely preceded by the development of mitochondria." Explain your reasoning.

_____

_____

_____

_____

_____

Concept 20.2 *explains how major lineages of eukaryotes diversified in the Precambrian. Protists are the eukaryotes of interest in this chapter. "Protista" is not a formal taxon, but the term is used to suggest that these organisms are not the traditional plants, animals, and mushrooms we see in everyday life. Even though memorizing taxonomy is not required in the AP Biology curriculum, this chapter includes some phylogenetic trees that you should be able to read and understand without memorizing.*

8. Freshwater *Paramecium* would explode if you deactivated a specific organelle. Name the structure, and describe how it works.

_____
_____
_____
_____
_____
_____
_____
_____

9. In spite of their amazingly diverse forms, diatoms follow one of two simple body plans. Describe both plans and discuss whether humans follow either of them.

_____
_____
_____
_____
_____
_____
_____
_____
_____

10. A fellow student, using a high-powered microscope, discovers a unicellular organism in a water sample taken from the creek behind your school. Suggest some visual landmarks she should look for to determine whether or not this unicellular organism is a eukaryote.

_____
_____
_____
_____
_____
_____
_____
_____

11. Explain how this phylogenetic tree shows that "protists" does not refer to a formal taxonomic group.

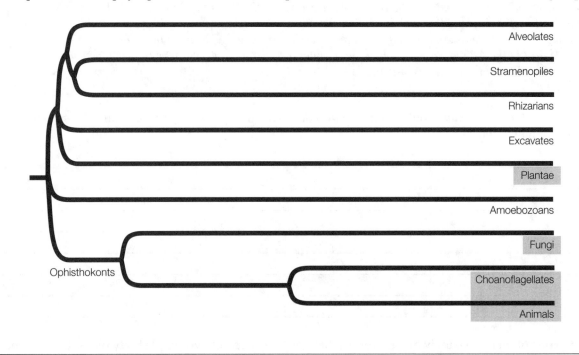

_____
_____
_____
_____
_____

Concept 20.3 *explores variations among protists: some reproduce sexually and others, asexually. Recall that asexual reproduction is similar to a clone factory, wherein progeny are nearly fully identical to the parent. Some protists exchange DNA without producing offspring. Others engage in sexual reproduction, and these can include prominent diploid and haploid stages of development, yielding insight into "the alternation of generations" characteristic of these and many other forms of more complex eukaryotes.*

12. Explain how some protists "have sex" without undergoing reproduction.

_____
_____
_____
_____
_____

13. Explain how some protists undergo reproduction without "having sex."

_____
_____
_____
_____
_____

14. Explain alternation of generations. Is this part of your own life pattern?

_____
_____
_____
_____
_____
_____
_____
_____
_____

Concept 20.4 *explains how protists are critical components of many ecosystems and are incredibly bountiful. Despite their small size, their byproducts are abundantly obvious, whether at the beach or deep in a petroleum well.*

15. "Tidal blooms" occur in the ocean when certain plankton species become especially abundant. Explain how toxins produced under "bloom" conditions can make it into the human food chain, even though we don't intentionally eat protists.

_____
_____
_____
_____
_____
_____
_____
_____
_____
_____

16. Describe the relationship between protists and petroleum.

_____
_____
_____
_____
_____
_____
_____
_____
_____
_____
_____

Science Practices & Inquiry

In the AP Biology Curriculum Framework, there are seven **Science Practices**. In this chapter, we focus on **Science Practice 3**: The student can engage in scientific questioning to extend thinking or to guide investigations within the context of the AP course. More specifically, we focus on **Science Practice 3.1:** The student can pose scientific questions.

Question 17 asks you to pose scientific questions about a group of organisms whose relatedness is described by a phylogenetic tree or cladogram in order to 1) identify shared characteristics, 2) make inferences about the evolutionary history of the group, and 3) identify character data that could extend or improve the phylogenetic tree (**Learning Objective 1.17**).

17. The phylogenetic tree (gene tree) at the right shows the evolutionary relationships of rRNA gene sequences isolated from the nuclear genomes of humans, yeast, and corn; an archaeon (*Halobacterium*), a proteobacterium (*E. coli*), and a cyanobacterium (*Chlorobium*); and from the mitochondrial and chloroplast genomes of corn. Use the gene tree to answer the questions that follow.

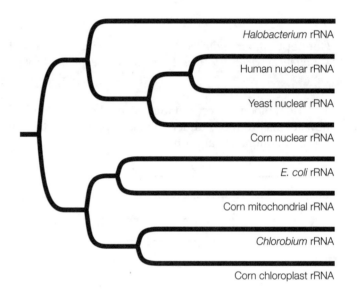

Halobacterium rRNA

Human nuclear rRNA

Yeast nuclear rRNA

Corn nuclear rRNA

E. coli rRNA

Corn mitochondrial rRNA

Chlorobium rRNA

Corn chloroplast rRNA

a. Why aren't the three rRNA genes of corn one another's closest relatives? _____

_____

_____

_____

b. Where on the tree would rRNA genes from human and yeast mitochondrial genomes be placed?

_____

_____

c. What other characteristics might you analyze in order to improve the gene tree? _____

_____

_____

_____

21 The Evolution of Plants

Chapter Outline

21.1 – Primary Endosymbiosis Produced the First Photosynthetic Eukaryotes
21.2 – Key Adaptations Permitted Plants to Colonize Land
21.3 – Vascular Tissues Led to Rapid Diversification of Land Plants
21.4 – Seeds Protect Plant Embryos
21.5 – Flowers and Fruits Increase the Reproductive Success of Angiosperms

In this chapter we examine the evolution of land plants. The opening page of the chapter provides historical intrigue to the relationships among the different groups of plants, especially the insights of Darwin regarding the adaptations of orchids. Though plant taxonomy and reproduction are not specified in the AP Biology Curriculum Framework, the evolutionary relationships among plants and the survival of plants on land are important biological concepts.

Invasion of land by plants features the evolution of several adaptations, including the cuticle, stomata, gametangia, a protected embryo, protective pigments, and thick spore walls. Later adaptations

of vascular plants include xylem, phloem, tracheids, and the evolution of the seed, which brought the gymnosperms and related plants to dominance. With the evolution of flowers and fruits, the angiosperms gained a major advantage in reproduction over other plants.

In Chapter 21, specific parts of the AP Biology curriculum covering **Big Idea 1:** The process of evolution drives the diversity and unity of life, include:

• **1.B.2:** Phylogenetic trees and cladograms are graphical representations (models) of evolutionary history that can be tested.

Chapter Review

Concept 21.1 *describes the evolution of land plants, beginning with early green algae.*

1. After observing an orchid with a foot-long (30 cm) nectar tube in the flower, Charles Darwin predicted the discovery of a moth with a very long proboscis. Several years later, a sphinx moth that pollinates this flower was discovered. Explain the logic that Darwin used to make his prediction.

_____

_____

_____

_____

_____

_____

_____

_____

_____

_____

2. Examine the diagram below. The dots represent new evolutionary features that gave the plants a reproductive advantage. Label each dot with its feature.

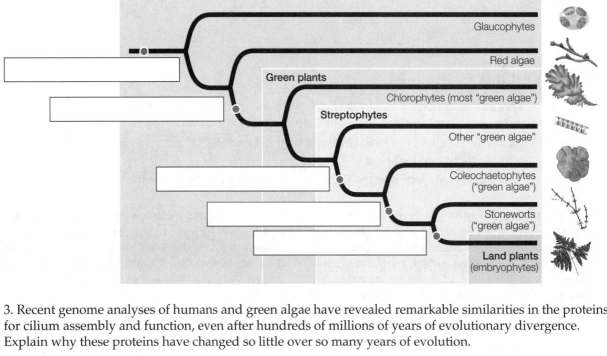

3. Recent genome analyses of humans and green algae have revealed remarkable similarities in the proteins for cilium assembly and function, even after hundreds of millions of years of evolutionary divergence. Explain why these proteins have changed so little over so many years of evolution.

_____

_____

_____

_____

_____

_____

_____

_____

Concept 21.2 _examines the evolution of land plants from algae living in marginal habitats along shorelines._

4. A plant's life on land is much more unpredictable than plant life in a body of water. Describe four aspects of life on land that make terrestrial environments difficult places for plants to grow.

_____

_____

_____

_____

_____

_____

_____

_____

5. Describe the two key processes needed for reproduction by the alternation of generations.

_____

_____

_____

_____

_____

_____

_____

6. For plants whose gametes are produced by mitosis rather than meiosis, explain the role of meiosis in the alternation of generations.

_____

_____

_____

_____

_____

_____

_____

7. A fellow student tells you that he has discovered a new species of moss that grows over six feet tall. Explain why this organism is probably classified in a group of plants other than mosses.

_____

_____

_____

_____

_____

_____

Concept 21.3 *describes how the evolution of vascular tissue in land plants led to diversified plant forms.*

8. Identify the two major types of vascular tissues in plants and describe the function of each.

_____

_____

_____

_____

_____

_____

_____

9. The evolution of a cellulose-digesting enzyme in fungi likely occurred after the evolution of land plants, and the metabolic activity of the fungi caused the formation of fossil fuels. Explain how coal and oil form and why they are considered nonrenewable resources.

_____

_____

_____

_____

_____

_____

Concept 21.4 *studies the evolution of the seed and its importance to the gymnosperms and angiosperms.*

10. Describe the sporophyte and the gametophyte in a reproducing angiosperm, and discuss the function of each.

_____

_____

_____

_____

_____

_____

11. Describe pollen grains and discuss their function in angiosperm reproduction. Explain how pollen can survive for many years.

_____

_____

_____

_____

_____

_____

Concept 21.5 *examines the reproductive advantages of the fruit and the flower among the angiosperms.*

12. Is pollen unique to angiosperms or gymnosperms? Provide details in your answer.

_____

_____

_____

_____

_____

_____

13. Draw a cladogram (phylogenetic tree) showing the evolution of pollen grains in angiosperms and gymnosperms, as well as their ancestors. Clearly identify the point at which pollen grains evolved.

14. Draw a cell ($2n = 6$), and then add drawings of three subsequent mitosis cycles, each abnormal due to the lack of cytokinesis. (You do not need to draw each phase of mitosis.) Show the total $2n$ number and the number of nuclei present in the final cell.

15. Explain the difference between pollination and fertilization in plants. Draw a cross section of a flower, and show where each process occurs.

Science Practices & Inquiry

In the AP Biology Curriculum Framework, there are seven **Science Practices**. In this chapter, we focus on **Science Practice 1**: The student can use representations and models to communicate scientific phenomena and solve scientific problems. More specifically, we focus on **Science Practice 1.1:** The student can create representations and models of natural or man-made phenomena and systems in the domain.

Question 16 asks you to create a phylogenetic tree or simple cladogram that correctly represents evolutionary history and speciation from a provided data set (**Learning Objective 1.19**).

16. Below are some characteristics found among four groups of plants.

	Movement to land	Presence of chlorophyll *a*	Vascular system	Inversion in chloroplast DNA	Seeds	Flowers
A	+	+	+	+	+	+
B	+	+	+	+	+	−
C	+	+	+	+	−	−
D	+	+	−	−	−	−

   a. Using the data, draw a phylogenetic tree for these organisms.

   b. Indicate on your cladogam the most likely place that each characteristic in the table evolved.

22 The Evolution and Diversity of Fungi

Chapter Outline

22.1 – Fungi Live by Absorptive Heterotrophy
22.2 – Fungi Can Be Saprobic, Parasitic, Predatory, or Mutualistic
22.3 – Major Groups of Fungi Differ in Their Life Cycles
22.4 – Fungi Can Be Sensitive Indicators of Environmental Change

The opening of this chapter demonstrates the relevance of understanding natural selection. When Alexander Fleming discovered that mold contaminating his bacterial growth plates inhibited the growth of the bacteria, he launched the discovery of the first antibiotic drug, penicillin. It took almost twenty years for chemists to isolate the new antibiotic and create a stable version that could be used in modern medicine. Once they did, penicillin ushered in a new age of modern medicine, greatly reducing the number of complications and deaths from infections. Subsequently, blindly killing as many bacteria as possible led us to our current state of antibiotic overuse. As a result, new forms of antibiotic-resistant bacteria have become abundant through natural selection.

The evolutionary relationships among different organisms and fungi are important biological concepts, even though the taxonomy and the diverse reproductive patterns of fungi included in Chapter 22 are not in the AP Biology Curriculum Framework. However, the evolution of fungi as absorptive heterotrophs, and the symbiotic relationships of many fungi with other organisms, are worthy of your attention. The vocabulary used to describe fungi might be new to you, but you should be able to apply what you've already learned about other living organisms: form arises during development and serves to meet the metabolic and reproductive functions of the organism.

The scope of Chapter 22 includes **Big Idea 1** and **Big Idea 2** in the AP Biology Curriculum Framework.

The specific parts of the AP Biology curriculum covering **Big Idea 1:** The process of evolution drives the diversity and unity of life, include:

- **1.A.2:** Natural selection acts on phenotypic variations in populations.

- **1.B.2:** Phylogenetic trees and cladograms are graphical representations (models) of evolutionary history that can be tested.

The specific parts addressing **Big Idea 2:** Biological systems utilize free energy and molecular building blocks to grow, to reproduce, and to maintain dynamic homeostasis, include:

- **2.E.2:** Timing and coordination of physiological events are regulated by multiple mechanisms.

Chapter Review

Concept 22.1 *introduces the fungal lifestyle. Most fungi are absorptive heterotrophs, meaning they secrete digestive enzymes onto their intended food, releasing nutrients that can be absorbed for use. The primary "body" of a fungus is called the mycelium that is made up of individual filaments called hyphae.*

1. Explain the following terms of fungal structure:

a. hyphae _____

b. mycelium _____

c. septa _____

2. Explain how heterotrophy by humans is similar to that by fungi.

_____

_____

_____

_____

_____

3. Explain how heterotrophy by humans is different from that by fungi.

_____

_____

_____

_____

_____

4. Compare septate and coenocytic hyphae (shown) to multicellular plants and animals in the way they solve the problem of being multinucleate.

_____

_____

_____

_____

_____

_____

_____

_____

_____

_____

Concept 22.2 *compares feeding patterns among different fungi. Many fungi (saprobes) feed on organic material in dead animals and plants, releasing carbon into the carbon cycle. Other fungi are parasitic. Several fungi have mutualistic relationships with other organisms, such as lichens and mycorrhizae. Lichens are a symbiotic relationship between algae and fungi, and mychorrhizae are an association between fungi and vascular plants.*

5. Lichens are mutualistic relationships between fungi and algae. Describe the contributions of each partner in this relationship and how this arrangement allows lichens to colonize and thrive on bare rock.

_____

_____

_____

_____

_____

6. Not all fungi are as pleasant or benign as lichens or mycorrhizae. The fungus shown at the right (*Arthrobotrys dactyloides*) is a predator that traps small nematodes in soil. Explain how this fungus is still an absorptive heterotroph.

_____

_____

_____

_____

_____

_____

_____

7. Many plants and fungi are associated in mycorrhizae. A gardener starts some seeds in a pot with sterile soil that has all the nutrients needed to grow plants, but finds that the plants are small compared with those grown in a nearby garden. Explain the effects of the two types of soil as they relate to the gardener.

_____

_____

_____

_____

_____

_____

_____

_____

_____

_____

Concept 22.3 *compares the many and varied life cycles of different fungi. While it is not important to memorize the life cycles of the various groups, you should be aware that fungi, and many other organisms, can regulate physiological processes in response to external signals.*

8. Explain where a mycologist should look for the dikaryotic mycelium of a club fungus if the fungus is dependent on environmental moisture for its reproduction and growth.

_____

_____

_____

_____

_____

9. Using the diagram below, describe the life cycle of a fungus in terms of how much time it is in haploid or diploid form.

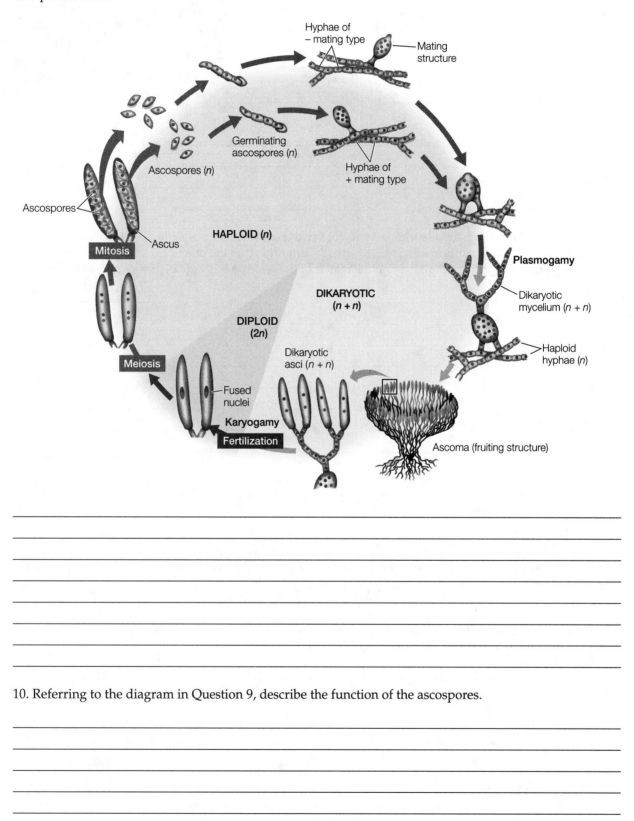

_____

_____

_____

_____

_____

_____

_____

_____

_____

10. Referring to the diagram in Question 9, describe the function of the ascospores.

_____

_____

_____

_____

_____

Concept 22.4 *describes how fungi can be used to study and solve environmental problems.*

11. Propose a method for an environmental scientist to monitor air quality using lichens. Explain your logic.

_____

_____

_____

_____

_____

_____

_____

_____

_____

_____

_____

_____

_____

_____

_____

12. A forester proposed that the difficulty and expense of a reforestation project after a tree harvest may be reduced by retaining viable communities of mycorrhizal fungi. Explain how this could be done.

_____

_____

_____

_____

_____

_____

_____

_____

_____

_____

_____

_____

_____

_____

_____

Science Practices & Inquiry

In the AP Biology Curriculum Framework, there are seven **Science Practices**. In this chapter, we focus on **Science Practice 1:** The student can use representations and models to communicate scientific phenomena and solve scientific problems. More specifically, we focus on **Science Practice 1.1:** The student can create representations and models of natural or man-made phenomena and systems in the domain.

Question 13 asks you to create a phylogenetic tree or simple cladogram that correctly represents evolutionary history and speciation from a provided data set (**Learning Objective 1.19**).

13. Below is a phylogenetic tree showing the relationships between choanoflagellates (protists), animals, and fungi. Draw a new phylogenetic tree showing the relationships between plants, humans, bacteria, and fungi. Label the shared derived characteristics for each group.

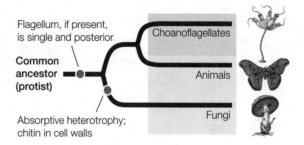

23 Animal Origins and Diversity

Chapter Outline

Chapter 23 reviews evolutionary relationships among the animal groups. Beginning with the sponges, the chapter reviews each of the major phyla, their characteristics, and their evolutionary adaptations, including developmental patterns and body plan developments.

Most of the information in this chapter is outside of the scope of the AP Biology Curriculum Framework, so memorizing the many phyla and characteristics is not necessary. However, information related from this and other chapters might be provided in exam questions as background information in order to assess your understanding of concepts and science practices. Familiarize yourself with terms and ideas so you will recognize them in the context of a paragraph or diagram in an exam question.

The most important material in Chapter 23 relates to **Big Idea 1,** which recognizes that evolution ties all parts of biology together. This chapter summarizes the major branches of the evolutionary history of animals. The specific parts of the AP Biology curriculum covering **Big Idea 1:** The process of evolution drives the diversity and unity of life, include:

• **1.B.2:** Phylogenetic trees and cladograms are graphical representations (models) of evolutionary history that can be tested.

Chapter Review

Concept 23.1 *begins with an overview of the animal phyla and their characteristics.*

1. Discuss the difficulties that scientists face when trying to classify the numerous taxa of insects.

_____

_____

_____

_____

2. Tree canopies in tropical forests are rich in unclassified species of insects. Explain why there is a high diversity of insects in the tropics, basing your logic on natural selection as the mechanism for evolutionary diversification.

_____

_____

_____

_____

3. Describe and discuss two reasons that the animal phyla are considered to be monophyletic.

_____

_____

_____

_____

_____

_____

_____

4. Based on the phylogenetic tree below, identify three characteristics common to both echinoderms and ctenophores.

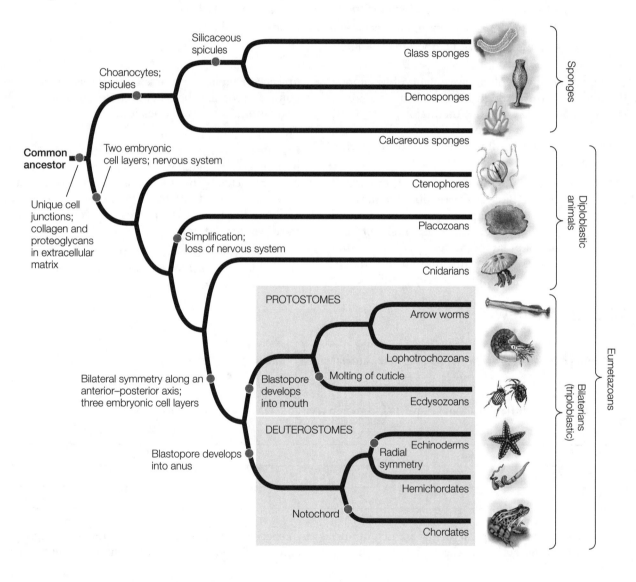

_____

_____

_____

_____

5. Referring to the phylogenetic tree in Question 4, identify four characteristics common to both chordates and arrow worms.

_____

_____

_____

_____

_____

6. Discuss the differences and similarities among the characteristics you identified in Questions 4 and 5.

_____

_____

_____

_____

7. Describe the primary difference between radial and bilateral symmetry.

_____

_____

_____

_____

_____

8. Describe the primary difference between protostomes and deuterostomes, and explain which group includes humans.

_____

_____

_____

_____

_____

9. Describe the primary difference between pseudocoelomates and acoelomates.

_____

_____

_____

_____

_____

10. Discuss the principle evolutionary advantage provided by the development of segmentation in the body plans of animals.

_____

_____

_____

_____

Concept 23.2 *reviews the major animal groups outside of the Bilateria.*

11. Bilateria comprises a very large group of animals but does not include sponges. Discuss the characteristics of the bilataria and explain why sponges are not included in this group.

_____

_____

_____

_____

_____

12. Many sponges reproduce both sexually and asexually. Describe how a sponge reproduces asexually.

_____

_____

_____

_____

_____

Concept 23.3 *examines the highly diverse protostomes. Though their body plans are extremely varied, they are all bilaterally symmetrical animals with two major derived traits: an anterior brain that surrounds the entrance to the digestive tract, and a ventral nervous system consisting of paired or fused longitudinal nerve cords. Other aspects of protostome body organization differ widely from group to group. Though the common ancestor of the protostomes likely had a coelom, subsequent modifications of the coelom distinguish many protostome lineages. In at least one protostome lineage (the flatworms), the coelom has been lost (that is, the flatworms reverted to an acoelomate state). Some lineages are characterized by a pseudocoel.*

13. The onychophorans are often considered to be a transitional animal group, leading to the evolution of the arthropods. Describe two evolutionary adaptations that would make the organism at the right a true arthropod.

_____

_____

_____

_____

_____

14. Rotifers evolved anatomical features to enhance food gathering and digestion. Identify one new feature and discuss how it increased digestive capacity. Explain how this is related to reproductive success.

_____

_____

_____

_____

15. In a handful of rich soil, you could find hundreds or even thousands of nematodes. Identify and briefly describe three benefits of nematodes to humans and/or the environment.

_____

_____

_____

_____

_____

_____

Concept 23.4 *discusses the arthropods, a group that might include a billion billion (10^{18}) living individuals on the planet at this moment. There are nearly two million species of insects, showing that their consequences of evolutionary changes among arthropods are extraordinary.*

16. Describe how the jointed appendages of arthropods have contributed to their evolutionary success in colonizing terrestrial habitats.

_____

_____

_____

_____

_____

_____

17. Distinguish between complete and incomplete metamorphosis. From an evolutionary perspective, explain which one likely evolved first.

_____

_____

_____

_____

_____

_____

Concept 23.5 *considers the diversity among the three major clades of deuterostomes.*

18. Describe the main characteristic that differentiates protostomes from deuterostomes.

_____

_____

_____

_____

_____

19. Chordates have three derived features that are apparent at some point during development, though some marine chordates, the sea squirts and the lancelets, do not all show these features during all stages of life. Describe the features and their appearances in the sea squirts and lancelets.

_____

_____

_____

_____

_____

_____

_____

_____

_____

_____

20. Echinoderms have two unique structural features, an internal skeleton and a water vascular system. Describe each and comment on its contribution to the success of these organisms.

_____

_____

_____

_____

_____

_____

21. The hagfish and lampreys were lumped together as "jawless fishes" in early classification efforts. Refer to the diagram below to explain why they are no longer classified together.

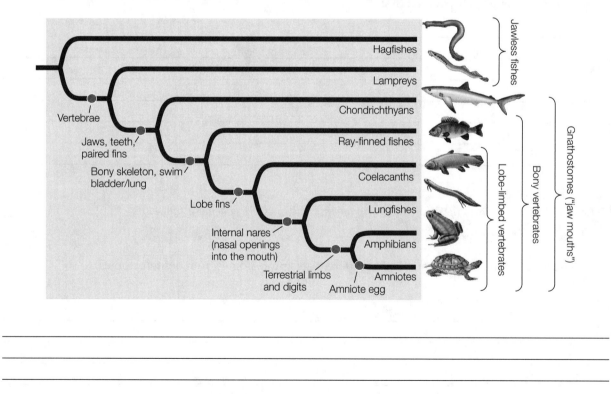

_____

_____

_____

22. Describe three features of substantial evolutionary benefit that set the ray-finned fishes apart from the chondrichthyans (cartilaginous fishes).

_____

_____

_____

_____

_____

_____

_____

_____

Concept 23.6 *describes the evolutionary adaptations of vertebrates that allowed them to colonize land.*

23. Discuss two of the reproductive adaptations that allowed animals to successfully move out of water and onto land.

_____

_____

_____

_____

_____

_____

24. Discuss the two key features that distinguish mammals from other vertebrate phyla.

_____

_____

_____

_____

_____

_____

25. Describe the three patterns of reproduction in the three classes of mammals.

_____

_____

_____

_____

_____

_____

_____

_____

_____

26. Birds were recently reclassified as a taxonomic group more closely related to reptiles and dinosaurs than to mammals. The classification of turtles is still fairly uncertain. Explain why some classifications are tentative and subject to change.

_____

_____

_____

_____

_____

_____

_____

Concept 23.7 *provides an overview of primate evolution.*

27. Explain the adaptive importance of each of the following hominid characteristics:

a. Brain size _____

_____

_____

b. Bipedal motion _____

_____

_____

c. Grasping fingers _____

_____

_____

28. It is often mistakenly claimed that humans evolved from modern-day apes. Describe three similarities shared by humans and chimpanzees, and provide a more accurate statement about their evolution.

_____

_____

_____

_____

_____

_____

_____

_____

_____

_____

_____

_____

_____

_____

29. Complete the chart below. Your teacher may ask you to expand this chart to include other phyla or features such as body cavities, protostomes or deuterostomes, symmetry, sensory organs, skeletal or support systems, or movement.

Phylum	Example	Symmetry	Digestion	Excretion	Respiration	Reproduction	Nervous system			
Porifera										
Platyhelminthe										
Nematoda										
Mollusca										
Annelida										
Arthropoda										
Echinodermata										

30. Using the chart in Question 29, discuss the evolution of the nervous system from the sponges to the primates.

_____

_____

_____

_____

_____

_____

_____

_____

_____

_____

_____

_____

_____

_____

_____

_____

_____

_____

_____

_____

_____

_____

_____

_____

_____

_____

_____

_____

_____

_____

_____

Science Practices & Inquiry

In the AP Biology Curriculum Framework, there are seven **Science Practices**. In this chapter, we focus on **Science Practice 1**: The student can use representations and models to communicate scientific phenomena and solve scientific problems. More specifically, we focus on **Practice 1.1**: The student can create representations and models of natural or man-made phenomena and systems in the domain.

Question 31 asks you to create a phylogenetic tree or simple cladogram that correctly represents evolutionary history and speciation from a provided data set (**Learning Objective 1.19**).

31. The characteristics in the table below are found among four groups of animals.

	Spiral Cleavage	Chitonous Outer Skin	Specialized Segments	Bilateral Symmetry
Mollusks	+	–	–	+
Annelids	+	–	–	+
Onychophorans	–	+	–	+
Arthropods	–	+	+	+

Using the data, draw a cladogram for these organisms. Indicate clearly where each characteristic most likely evolved.

24 The Plant Body

Chapter Outline

24.1 – The Plant Body Is Organized and Constructed in a Distinctive Way
24.2 – Apical Meristems Build the Primary Plant Body
24.3 – Many Eudicot Stems and Roots Undergo Secondary Growth
24.4 – Domestication Has Altered Plant Form

Chapter 24 describes the development and the anatomy of plants. Apply what you have already learned about other living organisms: form arises during development and serves to meet the metabolic (vegetative) and reproductive functions of the organism. Unlike animals, many plants have root and apical meristems that remain embryonic and can grow throughout life. Information about plants is abundant in the AP Biology Curriculum Framework.

People have studied plants extensively over the millennia. Empirical data from experiments on plants are plentiful, and plant experiments offer many opportunities to test your knowledge of **Science Practices**, including the graphing and analysis of different treatments on plant physiology.

Chapter 24 includes content about ways humans have artificially selected plants over time to increase agricultural yield and improve food quality. The specific parts of the AP Biology curriculum covering **Big Idea 1:** The process of evolution drives the diversity and unity of life, include:

• **1.A.2**: Natural selection acts on phenotypic variations in populations.

Parts of the curriculum addressing **Big Idea 4:** Biological systems interact, and these systems and their interactions possess complex properties, include:

• **4.A.4**: Organisms exhibit complex properties due to interactions between their constituent parts.

Chapter Review

Concept 24.1 *reviews the parts of plants, with a focus on the development and anatomy of flowering plants. Plant cells are surrounded by cell walls, and the cells are usually totipotent in terms of development potential. The root system, which develops from the root apical meristem, is largely underground. It supplies the plant with water and soil-borne nutrients needed for growth and maintenance. The shoot system develops into the stems, leaves, and flowers.*
Plants have three tissues systems: The dermal system is the outer covering of the plant. The ground tissue system is where photosynthesis takes place and where the plant's supporting mechanism is found. The vascular system includes the xylem network, which distributes minerals and water from the roots; and the phloem network, which distributes carbohydrates, the products of photosynthesis, throughout the plant for use as fuel molecules or for storage in starch.

1. The following list includes some of the anatomical parts that a water molecule might pass through during its movement from the soil to a location where it becomes involved in the reactions of photosynthesis. Fill in the boxes by showing the following parts: *leaf vascular tissue, root dermal tissue, leaf ground tissue,* and *root ground tissue,* in the correct root-to-shoot sequence.

| soil → | | → | | → | | → | | → | photosynthesis |

2. Briefly explain, in general terms, how the protein components in root cells differ from the protein components in leaf cells.

_____

_____

_____

_____

3. Discuss how cells taken from the growing root tip on a carrot plant can be cultured with growth factors and nutrients in a supportive medium to make a full carrot plant, including roots, stems, leaves, and flowers.

_____

_____

_____

_____

4. Discuss the mechanism by which the leaves of an individual species of plant can take very different shapes when grown in different environmental conditions.

_____

_____

_____

_____

_____

_____

5. The roots, stems, and leaves of a plant are considered to be organs. Using a specific example, explain how their coordinated interactions provide essential biological activities.

_____

_____

_____

_____

_____

_____

Concept 24.2 *describes the mechanisms of development and differentiation in plants. Plants and animals differ in how they develop and function. While animals use their mobility to forage for food, plants stay in place and grow toward resources, both above and below the ground. Plant shoots grow toward sunlight, and roots grow toward water and minerals in the soil. In most animals, growth is determinate: it ceases when the adult state is reached. Some plant organs, including most leaves and flowers, show this characteristic. By contrast, the growth of roots and shoots is indeterminate, an open-ended process that can be lifelong.*

Apical meristems produce primary growth, giving rise to the primary plant body. All seed plants have a primary plant body. Primary growth results in the formation and lengthening of shoots and roots. Lateral meristems produce secondary growth, resulting in the secondary plant body. Secondary growth increases plant thickness and occurs in woody eudicots, such as trees and shrubs. Monocots typically do not undergo secondary growth.

6. Compare the long-term growth potential of cells in the apical meristem with that of cells in a newly emerged leaf.

_____

_____

_____

_____

7. Discuss the observation that desert plants in arid conditions produce a thicker extracellular matrix (cuticle) than do non-desert plants growing in a very moist environment.

_____

_____

_____

_____

8. Describe two of the selective advantages of indeterminate growth, both above and below the ground, for a plant such as the poison ivy vine.

_____

_____

_____

_____

_____

_____

9. For all multicellular organisms, coordination between systems is essential. Explain how the vascular tissue of a plant and the mesodermal tissue of a leaf are similar to the respiratory and circulatory systems of an animal.

_____

_____

_____

_____

_____

_____

_____

Concept 24.3 _explains how the roots and stems of some eudicots develop a secondary plant body, the tissues of which we commonly refer to as wood and bark. These tissues are derived by secondary growth from the two lateral meristems. The first, the vascular cambium, produces cells that make up secondary xylem (wood) and secondary phloem (inner bark). The second, the cork cambium, produces mainly waxy-walled protective cells, some of which become the outer bark._

10. Deciduous trees drop their leaves in the fall and grow new leaves in spring. Discuss what this implies for the location of apical meristem in such species.

_____

_____

_____

_____

_____

_____

_____

11. Describe the relationship between the annual rings in a tree trunk and the age of the tree, and explain how the annual rings are used to approximate past climatic patterns.

_____

_____

_____

_____

_____

_____

_____

_____

_____

Concept 24.4 _begins to describe the many ways that humans have selectively altered plants by artificial selection. The predecessor of modern corn plants is pictured as a relatively simple grass, one that makes a considerably smaller energetic investment in seed production, compared to a modern-day ear of corn._

12. The yield of corn from domesticated corn plants has increased tremendously over the past 100 years. Unfortunately, this has come with increased disease susceptibility in these plants. Discuss this "cost" of artificial selection.

_____

_____

_____

_____

_____

_____

_____

Science Practices & Inquiry

In the AP Biology Curriculum Framework, there are seven **Science Practices**. In this chapter, we focus on **Science Practice 3**: The student can engage in scientific questioning to extend thinking or to guide investigations within the context of the AP course. More specifically, we focus on **Science Practice 3.3**: The student can evaluate scientific questions.

Question 13 asks you to evaluate scientific questions concerning organisms that exhibit complex properties due to the interaction of their constituent parts (**Learning Objective 4.8**).

13. In an experiment that lasted 60 days, seeds were sprouted and grown in wet or arid conditions. Above-ground (shoots) and below-ground (roots) mass was measured every 10 days, producing the data shown in Table 1.

	Mean shoot and root mass (grams) of sprouts over 60 days					
	10 days	20 days	30 days	40 days	50 days	60 days
WET						
shoots	3.2	3.3	3.8	4.4	6.2	8.1
roots	2.4	2.5	2.9	3.3	4.5	6.0
ARID						
shoots	3.0	3.3	3.5	3.8	4.1	4.4
roots	2.4	3.0	4.2	6.1	6.6	7.5

a. Graph the data, using four curves. Be sure to label the axes and show the units of measurement.

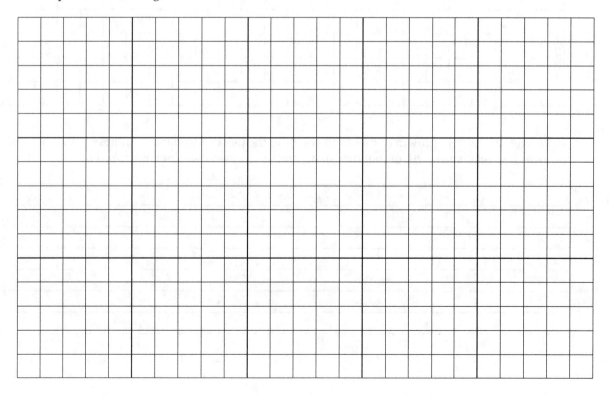

b. For each condition, and at each point in time, calculate the ratio of root growth to shoot growth (i.e., root mass divided by shoot mass), and fill in the table below.

	Calculated root-to-shoot ratio					
	10 days	**20 days**	**30 days**	**40 days**	**50 days**	**60 days**
WET						
ARID						

c. Graph the root-to-shoot ratios.

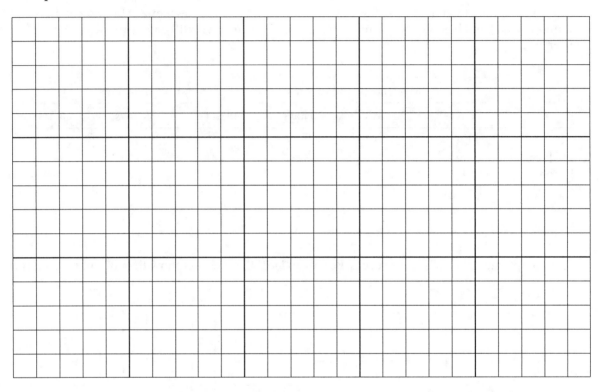

d. Discuss the relative growth of roots and shoots in the two experimental conditions used here, including relative growth of root meristems and apical meristems in your answer.

_____

_____

_____

_____

_____

_____

_____

_____

_____

_____

e. Speculate, without mentioning specific chemicals, what caused the plant to grow in the different patterns you observed in your graphs.

_____

_____

_____

_____

_____

_____

_____

_____

f. Discuss one evolutionary advantage of plants growing in different patterns, based on what you observed in your graphs.

_____

_____

_____

_____

_____

_____

_____

_____

g. Describe which part of the plant would have the highest concentration of sugars when subjected to a chemical assay to measure carbohydrates.

_____

_____

_____

_____

_____

_____

_____

25 Plant Nutrition and Transport

Chapter Outline

25.1 – Plants Acquire Mineral Nutrients from the Soil
25.2 – Soil Organisms Contribute to Plant Nutrition
25.3 – Water and Solutes Are Transported in the Xylem by Transpiration–Cohesion–Tension
25.4 – Solutes Are Transported in the Phloem by Pressure Flow

Plants are autotrophic organisms that acquire carbon from atmospheric carbon dioxide, using energy from the sun. Oxygen is released by plants as a byproduct of photosynthesis, but oxygen is also absorbed from the atmosphere by plants and used in respiration, especially during the evening hours and other periods of darkness. Plants also acquire nutrients from soil and ground water through their roots. Though mineral cycles are not part of the AP Biology Curriculum Framework, it is important to understand that human manipulation and disruption of mineral cycles, via agricultural fertilizers, can lead to undesirable environmental changes.

Most terrestrial plants interact with fungi in structures called mycorrhizae, which promote the absorption of nutrients and water by the plants' roots. Some plants also sustain relationships with nitrogen-fixing bacteria that convert atmospheric nitrogen (N_2) to a usable form of nitrogen (NO_3^-) that plants can absorb. These relationships between plants and organisms are coordinated by the signaling compatibilities between the plants and these other organisms.

Xylem and phloem are tissues that transport substances throughout the plant. Water is transported in xylem from the roots up through the leaves. The movement of water is governed by the evaporation of water from leaves, thus providing a pull (transpiration—cohesion—tension) to move water up from the roots; water molecules form hydrogen bonds that make them "stick" together, much like a long line of cars in a train. Phloem is the tissue that moves the sugars produced by photosynthesis to their destinations throughout the plant from an area of high pressure (source) to one of low pressure (sink).

In Chapter 25, the specific parts of the AP Biology curriculum covering **Big Idea 2:** Biological systems utilize free energy and molecular building blocks to grow, to reproduce, and to maintain dynamic homeostasis, include:

- **2.A.3**: Organisms must exchange matter with the environment to grow, reproduce, and maintain organization.

Chapter Review

Concept 25.1 *describes how plants acquire mineral nutrients from the soil. Some of the minerals move into the roots as a result of ion exchange, an ATP-dependent process that "pumps" hydrogen ions (H^+) out of the root, where the hydrogen ion "trades places" with cations that are then taken up by the roots.*

1. Identify three ways that the growth of plants benefits humans.

_____

_____

_____

_____

2. Identify three ways that the growth of plants benefits other organisms.

_____

_____

_____

_____

3. Explain how plants use each of the following materials.

  a. Carbon dioxide (CO_2): _____

_____

_____

  b. Oxygen gas (O_2): _____

_____

_____

  c. Water (H_2O): _____

_____

_____

  d. Nickel (Ni): _____

_____

_____

  e. Nitrogen gas (N_2): _____

_____

_____

  f. Nitrogen-oxygen ions (NO_3^-, NO_2^-): _____

_____

_____

4. Design and describe an experiment to show the effect of carbon dioxide (CO_2) uptake on plant growth. Be sure to include a hypothesis, a control, and at least two constants in your design.

_____

_____

_____

_____

_____

_____

_____

_____

_____

_____

_____

_____

5. Through ion exchange, epidermal root cells dislodge cations bound to clay particles by pumping protons out of the cell. Does this represent active or passive transport? Explain.

_____

_____

_____

_____

Concept 25.2 *discusses how fungi aid the uptake of water and nutrients in plants, and explains the importance of nitrogen-fixing bacteria in nitrogen capture.*

6. Researchers grew lemon seedlings in soils that contained 0 g, 12 g, or 24 g of phosphate fertilizer. In each of the three fertilizer conditions they grew the seedlings with and without fungi that associate in the mycorrhizae. The table below shows the mean dry weight of the seedlings after six months.

Phosphate fertilizer (g)	Mycorrhizal addition	Mean dry weight of seedlings (g)
0	No	1
0	Yes	10
12	No	28
12	Yes	166
24	No	20
24	Yes	210

a. Summarize the results of this experiment.

_____

_____

_____

_____

b. Identify the independent and dependent variables in this experiment.

_____

_____

_____

_____

c. Identify three other features that the experimenters would have held constant in this experiment.

_____

_____

_____

_____

7. Explain how a plant's mycorrhizae expand the surface area that is available for water absorption from the soil.

_____

_____

_____

8. Our atmosphere is almost 80 percent N_2 gas. Explain why N_2 cannot be used directly by plants.

_____

_____

_____

9. Describe how plants use the nitrates they absorb through their roots.

_____

_____

_____

_____

Concept 25.3 *explains how plants absorb water from the environment and how xylem transports water throughout the plant.*

10. Draw two water molecules next to each other, showing regions of polarity and hydrogen bonding.

11. Two of the primary variables that affect water potential (ψ) are shown by the formula $\psi = \psi_p + \psi_s$. Explain what ψ_p and ψ_s represent in this equation.

_____

_____

_____

_____

12. Water potential is described in terms of the concentration of water molecules in a compartment. Describe how adding salt to water reduces that solution's concentration of water molecules.

_____

_____

_____

_____

_____

13. Describe the barrier that impedes the diffusion of most ions across a plant cell's membrane.

_____

_____

_____

_____

_____

14. Explain what is wrong with the following statement: Water in the root flows faster through the apoplastic pathway (via cell walls) than through the symplast pathway (via cytoplasm and plasmodesmata); thus, the majority of the water entering the xylem flows only through the apoplastic pathway.

_____

_____

_____

_____

_____

15. The transpiration–cohesion–tension mechanism explains how water streams up a tall tree to its leaves, where much of it is then lost to the atmosphere. Explain how each component in this mechanism functions.

   a. Transpiration: _____

_____

_____

_____

   b. Cohesion: _____

_____

_____

_____

   c. Tension: _____

_____

_____

_____

16. Discuss how the structure of a guard cell allows it to open and close a stoma.

_____

_____

_____

_____

17. Most water potential values are negative. Describe a way to generate a positive water potential value.

_____

_____

_____

_____

18. Compare the water potential of the atmosphere (–55.0 MPa) with that of soil water (–0.3 MPa). Explain why these values are negative.

_____

_____

_____

_____

_____

_____

_____

Concept 25.4 *explains how phloem transports sugars throughout the plant.*

19. Define each term below in the context of the movement of sugars through a plant. Give an example of each.

a. Source: _____

_____

_____

b. Sink: _____

_____

_____

20. While trimming grass with a weed whacker, a person accidently cut a groove in the bark around the base of a tree. The tree survived for a few months but died the following spring. Explain why the tree eventually died.

_____

_____

_____

_____

_____

_____

_____

21. Explain how the movement of phloem sap from one part of a plant to another is considered to be an example of both active and passive transport.

_____

_____

_____

_____

_____

_____

_____

22. Explain how plant growth depends on other organisms.

_____

_____

_____

_____

_____

_____

_____

_____

23. Describe crop rotation and explain how this practice helps farmers produce food in a more sustainable manner.

_____

_____

_____

_____

_____

_____

_____

_____

Science Practices & Inquiry

In the AP Biology Curriculum Framework, there are seven **Science Practices**. In this chapter, we focus on **Science Practice 2:** The student can use mathematics appropriately. More specifically, we focus on **Science Practice 2.2:** The student can apply mathematical routines to quantities that describe natural phenomena.

Question 24 asks you to model the exchange of molecules between an organism and its environment and the subsequent use of these molecules to build new molecules (**Learning Objective 2.19**). An equation sheet, provided inside the back cover of this book and with the exam, includes the commonly used equations and conversions you will need to solve problems like this one.

(*Hint*: When you are writing an answer to a free-response question with multiple parts, write each part separately and clearly label all parts.)

24. While shopping at a food store, you pick up two tomatoes: one is marked *organic* and is priced at $2.37 per pound. The other is marked *conventional* and is priced at $1.75 per pound.

   a. Explain any differences in the actual make-up of the two tomatoes.

_____

_____

_____

_____

_____

_____

b. Calculate the cost for two kilograms of each tomato type. (One pound = 0.45 kilograms)

c. Approximately 13 gallons of water are needed to produce each tomato. If there are 4.3 tomatoes per pound, calculate how much water is used to produce two kilograms of tomatoes.

d. Explain any differences in the impact on the environment caused by the growth of these two tomatoes.

_____

_____

_____

_____

_____

_____

_____

e. Which tomato would you buy? Why?

_____

_____

_____

_____

_____

26 Plant Growth and Development

Chapter Outline

26.1 – Plants Develop in Response to the Environment
26.2 – Gibberellins and Auxin Have Diverse Effects but a Similar Mechanism of Action
26.3 – Other Plant Hormones Have Diverse Effects on Plant Development
26.4 – Photoreceptors Initiate Developmental Responses to Light

The germination of a dormant seed and its growth into a leafy green plant with flowers is a magnificent drama. In this area of biology, cause-and-effect thinking and careful experimentation have contributed greatly to our understanding of how the expression of the information coded in the plant genome is precisely orchestrated by environmental and hormonal signals.

The AP Biology Curriculum Framework does not include the names and mechanisms of the many plant hormones that have been identified, but some basic ideas about signaling are reinforced in this chapter. For example, hormones are chemical signals that are released by cells and then received by receptor proteins on other cells, also known as target cells. As a result of the hormone binding to the receptor protein, the biochemical reactions in the target cell are altered, typically in a way that is of benefit to the organism. Furthermore, the activation of light-sensitive chemicals in plants influences their hormonal and genetic responses, coordinating metabolism, growth, and reproduction.

Chapter 26 includes topics in **Big Idea 2** and **Big Idea 3**. The specific parts of the AP Biology curriculum covering **Big Idea 2**: Biological systems utilize free energy and molecular building blocks to grow, to reproduce and to maintain dynamic homeostasis, include:

• **2.E.1**: Timing and coordination of specific events are necessary for the normal development of an organism, and these events are regulated by a variety of mechanisms.

The specific parts addressing **Big Idea 3**: Living systems store, retrieve, transmit, and respond to information essential to life processes, include:

• **3.B.2**: A variety of intercellular and intracellular signal transmissions mediate gene expression.

Chapter Review

Concept 26.1 *describes some of the factors that control seed dormancy. Dormancy typically involves a tough seed coat, but chemical inhibitors can also establish dormancy. Upon the appropriate environmental stimulation or disruption of the seed coat, the seed germinates to form a sprout, which sends a growing root tip toward the soil and a growing plant stem toward the open air and sunlight. Various environmental and chemical factors determine the differentiation and development of the plant from the sprout.*

1. Discuss why the surface of some garden seeds needs to be physically scratched (scarified) before most of the seeds will sprout.

_____

_____

_____

_____

_____

2. Explain how too much scratching of the seed can greatly impair its ability to sprout. Include discussion of the seed coat and the embryo in your answer.

_____

_____

_____

_____

_____

3. Discuss why scarified seeds need to be placed in a moist environment before sprouting will take place.

_____

_____

_____

_____

4. Despite making adequate scratches on seeds from his dogwood tree, followed by proper soaking, William finds that his dogwood seeds will not sprout. To slow bacterial growth on the wet seeds, he puts them in his refrigerator for safekeeping. Alas, he forgets about them until three months later. He takes the seeds out and keeps them wet for another week, and this time all of the seeds germinate. Discuss three physical factors that might be responsible for the sprouting of these dogwood seeds.

_____

_____

_____

_____

_____

_____

_____

Concept 26.2 *describes six kinds of growth hormones in plants. You should focus on the overall messages about signaling, rather than trying to remember all of the details presented in this section. First, chemical signals come from a source that synthesizes them in response to an environmental cue. The signals that are released by the source cells travel to target cells, where target is defined by the presence of the appropriate receptor protein needed to receive the signal. The binding of the signal and the receptor activates a response in the target cell, yielding a biochemical change, such as enzyme activation or altered gene expression, in the cells.*

5. Charles Darwin and his son Francis grew grass seedlings where the light source was kept on only one side of the sprout. The sprouts grew toward the light in a response called *phototropism*. Today we know that higher levels of the plant hormone auxin cause elongation of growing plant cells, compared to such cells exposed to lesser concentrations of auxin. Speculate in detail about whether auxin was produced symmetrically *or* asymmetrically in Darwin's phototropism by grass seedlings. Include receptor proteins, and consider auxin's effects on cell elongation in your answer.

_____

_____

_____

_____

6. The downward growth of root tips of the sprouted grass described above, called *gravitropism*, is also mediated by auxin. Speculate in detail about whether auxin is produced symmetrically *or* asymmetrically in the root tips of grass seedlings. Include receptor proteins, and consider auxin's effects on cell elongation in your answer.

_____

_____

_____

_____

_____

_____

7. Gibberellins stimulate starch hydrolysis in plants. Describe the general function of starch in plants. Then predict the expected level of gibberellin activity in a germinated seed, compared with that of a plant that is undergoing a high rate of photosynthesis. Explain your predictions.

_____

_____

_____

_____

_____

_____

8. In an experiment conducted 20 years ago, researchers reported that auxin treatment of plant cells led to increased levels of mRNA. Discuss the meaning of this observation in terms of signal transduction and the mechanism of action for auxin's effects on its target cells.

_____

_____

_____

_____

_____

_____

9. Suppose that both dwarf and excessively tall plants were found to have mutations in a gene active in the auxin signaling. However, the mRNA sequences of the two mutated genes and their protein products were found to differ. Given that a protein can have more than one functional domain, propose an explanation for how two different mutations of the same gene can have such different effects.

_____

_____

_____

_____

_____

_____

Concept 26.3 *expands on the survey of chemical signals used by plants in growth, metabolism, and reproduction. For example, ethylene is a gas that promotes fruit ripening and senescence in plants. It is possibly the most widely used plant hormone, in the practical and applied sense. Cytokinins (inhibit elongation) and brassinosteroids (enhance growth) are also reviewed here, along with abscisic acid (inhibits growth).*

10. Discuss the science behind the saying, "one rotten apple spoils the whole barrel."

_____

_____

_____

_____

_____

11. Radishes and other root crops produce an abundance of cytokinins, the signals that inhibit the elongation of the roots. Auxins are signals that are active in the elongation of roots and stems. Discuss whether or not it is likely that both types of signal would be active in the same plant.

_____

_____

_____

_____

_____

_____

12. Steroid hormone responses in animals are the classic example of signals that alter gene expression; steroid hormones bind to receptor proteins in the nucleus of the target cells, and the hormone-receptor complex acts as a transcription factor. In some plants, the brassinosteroids are signals whose receptors are found only on cell membranes. Discuss whether or not the brassinosteroids are likely to have the same mechanism of action as the steroid hormones of animals.

_____

_____

_____

_____

_____

13. Abscisic acid is often regarded to have the opposite action of the gibberellins. Given that gibberellins stimulate starch hydrolysis in plants, predict the activity level of abscisic acid during seed germination. Explain your prediction.

_____

_____

_____

_____

Concept **26.4** *directs our discussion to the non-photosynthetic effects of light on plants. For example, light exposure of particular wavelengths can activate or inhibit seed germination. Furthermore, flowering responses of many plants are dependent on changes in the light/dark cycle to which they are exposed. In both cases, light-sensitive chemicals in the plants are altered upon exposure to the appropriate light, thus signaling the cells to alter their patterns of growth and activity. Many of these responses are categorized as photomorphogenesis, a term suggesting that light exposure changes the shape of the plant.*

14. Suppose that three possible pigments (compounds F, G, and H) have been identified in the grass seedlings discussed in Question 5, and Darwin's ancestors want to get to the bottom of the phototropism reaction. Compound F is activated by green light (500 nm), Compound G is activated by yellow light (540 nm), and Compound H is activated by red light (650 nm).

Given the results shown in the graph, where the slender stems shown (B) represent phototropism or non-phototropism, predict which pigment (F, G, or H) is most justified for further study as "the phototropism pigment." Explain your answer based on the results shown in the figure.

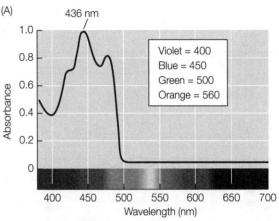

The absorbance curve shows how a mixture of the three pigments absorbs light across the spectrum of visible light.

_____

_____

_____

_____

_____

_____

_____

_____

_____

_____

_____

_____

_____

_____

_____

15. Phytochrome (P) is a blue pigment that exists in one of two alternating forms. When exposed to broad-spectrum light, it is converted to P_{fr}. At night, or when exposed to far-red light, it is converted to P_r, which is considered to be the default, inactive state of the pigment. By contrast, P_{fr} is the signal that triggers numerous light-dependent responses (e.g., seed germination, flowering, and shoot development). At sunset, most of the phytochrome is in the P_{fr} form, but as the night progresses, it is slowly converted, in a time-dependent manner, to the P_r form. The P_{fr} form is an activator of transcription factors and is a transcription factor in its own capacity as well. Discuss the theory that the ratio $P_{fr} : P_r$ is an important signal in plants that flower/fruit seasonally, and explain how this could work.

16. Cockleburs are called "short-day flowering plants" because their flowering stage begins when day length shortens to less than 13 hours, such as in the latter half of the summer. In an experiment, cockleburs were grown under a light cycle with 16 hours of light alternating with 8 hours of dark (16L : 8D) to the developmental stage, where flowering was possible but not yet underway. These plants were then separated into three rooms (P, Q, and R). Room P had its light cycle set to 16L : 8D, and its plants did not flower. Room Q had its light cycle set to 12L : 12D, and its plants flowered. Room R had its light cycle set to 11L : 6D : 1L : 6D (think of the lights in room R being turned on for one hour in the middle of the "night"). The plants in room R did not flower, even though there were 12 hours of darkness in every 24-hour cycle. Discuss these results, and explain why they occurred.

Science Practices & Inquiry

In the AP Biology Curriculum Framework, there are seven **Science Practices**. In this chapter, we focus on **Science Practice 1:** The student can use representations and models to communicate scientific phenomena and solve scientific problems. More specifically, we focus on **Science Practice 1.4:** The student can use representations and models to analyze situations or solve problems qualitatively and quantitatively.

Question 17 asks you to use a graph or a diagram to analyze situations or solve problems (quantitatively or qualitatively) that involve timing and coordination of events necessary for normal development in an organism (**Learning Objective 2.32**).

17. Refer to the figure below.

INVESTIGATION

CONCLUSION

Red light and far-red light reverse each other's effects.

ANALYZE THE DATA

Seven groups of 200 lettuce seeds each were incubated in water for 16 hours in the dark. One group was then exposed to white light for 1 minute. A second group (controls) remained in the dark. Five other groups were exposed to red (R) light for one minute and/or far-red (FR) light for four minutes. All the seeds were then returned to darkness for 2 more days. The table shows the number of seeds that germinated in each group.

Condition	Seeds germinated
1. White light	199
2. Dark	17
3. R	196
4. R then FR	108
5. R then FR then R	200
6. R then FR then R then FR	86
7. R then FR then R then FR then R	198

a. Calculate the percentage of seeds that germinated in each case.

b. What can you conclude about the photoreceptors involved? _____

18. The data in Question 17 demonstrate that some of the old-fashioned or heirloom varieties of certain lettuce plants germinate only when exposed to light of a certain wavelength. Put this observation in the context of evolutionary adaptation to explain why a seed's exposure to light is needed for germination to proceed. (*Hint*: Think about light competition from taller plants.)

27 Reproduction of Flowering Plants

Chapter Outline

27.1 – Most Angiosperms Reproduce Sexually

27.2 – Hormones and Signaling Determine the Transition from the Vegetative to the Reproductive State

27.3 – Angiosperms Can Reproduce Asexually

In Chapter 27, the term *alternation of generations* is used to describe the primary reproductive pattern in angiosperm plants. "Alternation" refers to a plant's progression from diploid to haploid forms as offspring are generated. To imagine this happening in humans, sperm and/or egg cells would have to grow by mitosis into multicellular forms. This does not happen with humans or most other animals, but it does happen in all plants. The multicellular haploid form in angiosperms is typically small, consisting of only a few cells within the flower of the sporophyte, as the multicellular diploid phase is known. Pollen is the male gametophyte and the embryo sac is the female gametophyte.

Plant flowering and reproduction are coordinated by plant hormones (chemical signals), but you do not need to memorize the names or specific roles of these hormones. Photoperiodism, however, is an important concept, as it determines the timing of seasonal flowering for many plants.

Chapter 27 notes that some plants can reproduce asexually. Asexual reproduction is efficient, especially for an organism in a predictable environment. There are three known means of asexual reproduction: Apomixis is the asexual production of seeds, vegetative propagation generates clones of the parent, and agricultural grafting physically connects different plants together.

Chapter 27 focuses on **Big Idea 2**. The specific parts of the AP Biology curriculum covering **Big Idea 2**: Biological systems utilize free energy and molecular building blocks to grow, to reproduce, and to maintain dynamic homeostasis, include:

- **2.A.1**: All living systems require constant input of free energy.

- **2.C.1**: Organisms use feedback mechanisms to maintain their internal environments and respond to external environmental changes.

- **2.E.2**: Timing and coordination of physiological events are regulated by multiple mechanisms.

Chapter Review

Concept 27.1 *discusses sexual reproduction and describes the alternation of generations. At the time of zygote formation (sperm and egg joining), double fertilization of nearby cells produces the nutritive endosperm that will be included in the seed.*

1. Distinguish between the two terms in each pair below.

   a. Perfect flower and imperfect flower: _____

   _____

   _____

   b. Complete flower and incomplete flower: _____

   _____

   _____

    c. Carpel and stamen: _____

_____

_____

    d. Gametophyte and sporophyte: _____

_____

_____

    e. Seed and fruit: _____

_____

_____

2. Explain why a pollen grain is considered to be an immature gametophyte.

_____

_____

_____

_____

3. Katie came across a pine tree that had large pine cones only in the upper half of the tree. She concluded that these were female cones that formed in the top of the tree to protect themselves against fertilization from the pollen of the smaller male cones in the bottom half of the tree. Design an experiment to determine whether or not Katie is correct.

_____

_____

_____

_____

_____

_____

_____

_____

_____

_____

_____

_____

_____

_____

4. Discuss the adaptive value of producing sweet fruits.

_____

_____

_____

_____

_____

_____

5. Coevolution explains that some species evolve defenses, whereas others evolve mechanisms to overcome defenses. The avocado fruit is buttery and sweet, yet the single seed inside is large and hard to crack open. Avocado seeds present a possible evolutionary anachronism, having evolved their size and hardness well before humans started eating them. In fact, no living animals are known to eat them. Propose an explanation as to why this seed evolved its large size and became so difficult to crack.

_____

_____

_____

_____

_____

_____

_____

_____

_____

_____

_____

_____

_____

6. Most plants do not self-pollinate, in spite of how easy this might be. Explain.

_____

_____

_____

_____

7. Complete the table below.

	Humans	Lily, a perfect angiosperm flower
Site of production of male gametes		
Site of production of female gametes		
Process that produces the haploid form		
Process that produces the diploid organism		
Location of fertilization		
Number of fertilizations		

8. Label each term below on the diagram at the right. Then briefly explain its function.

a. Antipodal cells: _____

_____

_____

b. Polar nuclei: _____

_____

_____

c. Egg cell: _____

_____

_____

d. Synergids: _____

_____

_____

e. Ovary: _____

_____

_____

f. Ovule: _____

_____

_____

Concept 27.2 *describes some of the events that signal a plant to transition from vegetative growth to the formation of flowers. The change from producing leaves and stems with indeterminate growth to a floral meristem is the result of a cascade of gene expression, triggered by changes in the light-dark cycle, especially in plants adapted to seasonal climates.*

9. "Short-day" and "long-night" might seem to be equivalent descriptors of plants that flower in autumn. Identify the more accurate of these, and explain why you chose it.

_____

_____

_____

_____

_____

10. A friend whose house is close to a busy, well-lit street planted several short-day chrysanthemums outside her front door, but they did not bloom, even as day length shortened. Suggest an explanation for this.

_____

_____

_____

_____

11. Briefly discuss why flowering is preceded by a "cascade" of gene expression.

_____

_____

_____

_____

_____

_____

_____

12. Not all plants utilize day or night length as a flowering cue. Identify and briefly discuss two other triggers for flowering.

_____

_____

_____

_____

_____

_____

13. Flowering in some varieties of the plant *Arabidopsis* is triggered by the light cycle experienced by the leaves rather than that experienced by the apical meristem. It appears that the protein called florigen, made in the leaves, mediates the flowering response. Discuss what components would be needed for such a communication system to function in this manner.

_____

_____

_____

_____

_____

_____

_____

_____

Concept 27.3 *explains how plants can reproduce asexually, essentially yielding cloned copies of the parental stock.*

14. Explain the term totipotency and its relevance to asexual reproduction.

_____

_____

_____

_____

_____

15. Design an experiment to show that dandelions do not cross-pollinate with other dandelions but still produce many seeds.

_____

_____

_____

_____

_____

_____

_____

16. Complete the table below for flowering plants.

	Asexual reproduction	**Sexual reproduction**
Advantages		
Disadvantages		
Example		

17. Citrus farmers produce seedless oranges by grafting trees and by apomixis.

   a. Explain why a farmer's intervention is needed for the plants to reproduce.

_____

_____

_____

_____

_____

_____

   b. Discuss how you could improve on the qualities of the seedless orange. (_Hint_: Recall what the source of new variation is.)

_____

_____

_____

_____

_____

_____

_____

Science Practices & Inquiry

In the AP Biology Curriculum Framework, there are seven **Science Practices**. In this chapter, we focus on **Science Practice 6**: The student can work with scientific explanations and theories. More specifically, we focus on **Practice 6.1:** The student can justify claims with evidence.

Questions 18 asks you to discuss how free energy is required for living systems to maintain organization, to grow, or to reproduce; to note that multiple strategies exist in different living systems; and to relate ideas from Chapters 6 and 27 as you consider the energy needs of plants (**Learning Objective 2.2**). You may wish to review the concept of free energy before answering the question.

18. As plants grow, they require an input of free energy.

   a. Describe the source of the free energy for plant growth, and explain how that energy is transferred by the plant's activities.

   _____

   _____

   _____

   _____

   _____

   _____

   _____

   _____

   b. Explain how energy transfers are necessary for growth.

   _____

   _____

   _____

   _____

   _____

   _____

   _____

   _____

   _____

   c. Strawberries can reproduce asexually by runners throughout the summer, but as fall approaches, they begin to form flowers. Explain the benefits of asexual and sexual reproduction from an energetic standpoint.

   _____

   _____

   _____

   _____

   _____

   _____

   _____

28 Plants in the Environment

Chapter Outline

28.1 – Plants Have Constitutive and Induced Responses to Pathogens
28.2 – Plants Have Mechanical and Chemical Defenses against Herbivores
28.3 – Plants Adapt to Environmental Stresses

Plants would seem to lead an idealized and peaceful existence, transpiring water and minerals as needed, exchanging gases with the atmosphere, and generally just soaking up the sunshine to enable photosynthesis. But pathogens, predators, and environmental stress are never far away. Plants are not defenseless in the face of such attacks; they often manage to maintain growth, metabolism, and reproduction, even while under attack, as described in Chapter 28.

The names and mechanisms of the many plant defenses listed in this chapter are outside of the AP Biology Curriculum Framework. Even so, you can reinforce your understanding of the **Big Ideas** as you read the chapter, particularly **Big Idea 2, Big Idea 3,** and **Big Idea 4.**

The specific parts of the AP Biology curriculum covering **Big Idea 2:** Biological systems utilize free energy and molecular building blocks to grow, to reproduce, and to maintain dynamic homeostasis, include:

- **2.C.1**: Organisms use feedback mechanisms to maintain their internal environments and respond to external environmental changes.

- **2.D.3**: Biological systems are affected by disruptions to their dynamic homeostasis.

- **2.D.4**: Plants and animals have a variety of chemical defenses against infections that affect dynamic homeostasis.

The parts of this chapter that are focused on **Big Idea 3:** Living systems store, retrieve, transmit, and respond to information essential to life processes, include:

- **3.D.2**: Cells communicate with each other through direct contact with other cells or from a distance via chemical signaling.

- **3.E.1**: Individuals can act on information and communicate it to others.

The specific parts supporting **Big Idea 4:** Biological systems interact, and these systems and their interactions possess complex properties, include:

- **4.C.3**: The level of variation in a population affects population dynamics.

Chapter Review

Concept 28.1 *describes some of the protective features on the surface of plants, including thick and waxy materials that can protect against pathogens and aid in water conservation. These features are called constitutive protection, and they are always present in the plant. Figure 28.1 in the textbook directs your attention to the pathogens at the molecular and cellular levels and shows that pathogen detection can lead to changes in gene expression, including genes that aid the plant's defenses. This second category of protection is called induced protection, as the arrival of the pathogen caused the changes.*

1. Many pepper plants infected by bacteria express resistance genes; some bacteria, in turn, express genes that defeat this resistance. Discuss the possible "evolutionary arms race" between peppers and their bacterial pathogens, including the ability of peppers to detect bacterial pathogens and the ability of the bacteria to remain undetected.

_____

_____

_____

_____

_____

_____

2. Physical isolation at an infection site refers to plants evoking signals to kill the plant cells surrounding an area of infection. Explain how this might help the plant survive the pathogen attack.

_____

_____

_____

_____

_____

_____

3. Some plant defenses depend on the development of systemic acquired resistance, which is initiated by salicylic acid. Assuming that changes in gene expression are needed for systemic acquired resistance, and that salicylic acid is produced locally, describe the possible chain of events leading to changes in gene expression throughout the plant.

_____

_____

_____

_____

_____

_____

4. Examination of the leaf at the right reveals dark spots where a fungal infection has killed the tissue. These spots are completely surrounded by boundaries of dead tissues, called necrotic lesions. The necrotic lesions are due to the expression of plant genes for programmed cell death, also known as apoptosis. Explain why it is adaptive for the plant to create the boundaries around the edges of the infected sites.

Necrotic lesion

_____

_____

_____

_____

_____

Concept 28.2 *describes mechanical and physical defenses found among plants. Many examples take the form of "chemical warfare" directed against herbivorous insects. The chemicals are often called secondary metabolites, and many of these, such as nicotine, are of considerable interest to humans.*

5. Some plants synthesize secondary metabolites that are very similar to amino acids but have one or more critical changes in chemical composition. Explain how these amino acid–like compounds function in defense against herbivores by affecting protein structure in the herbivore that consumes them.

_____

_____

_____

_____

_____

_____

_____

_____

_____

6. Find a plant that you believe has constitutive anatomical features that reduce herbivore impact. Describe the structure of the feature, and speculate on its evolutionary origin—that is, was it formerly a stem, a leaf, or something else?

_____

_____

_____

_____

_____

_____

_____

_____

Concept 28.3 *describes the adaptations that plants use for coping with environmental stress. The discussion includes constitutive adaptations of plants, as well as stress-induced changes that aid survival. Phytoremediation, the ability of plant roots to extract contaminants from soils, is being used as a tool for cleaning up the environment.*

7. In arid environments, some plants persist poorly when they reach their adult form. Explain the reproductive pattern and life history of such plants, considering that even arid environments have rainy seasons.

_____

_____

_____

_____

_____

_____

8. Plants with adaptations for long-term continuous survival of the adult form in a desert or other arid condition are often called xerophytes. For each of the following, describe one structural adaptation, and discuss how this adaptation aids the survival of the xerophyte.

a. Leaf size: _____

_____

_____

_____

b. Leaf cuticle: _____

_____

_____

_____

c. Water-storage systems: _____

_____

_____

_____

d. Roots: _____

_____

_____

_____

9. Abscisic acid is formed in the roots of drought-stressed plants. Explain how this compound affects the leaves of the plant and how this response aids in water conservation.

_____

_____

_____

_____

_____

_____

_____

_____

_____

_____

_____

_____

_____

_____

_____

_____

_____

_____

Science Practices & Inquiry

In the AP Biology Curriculum Framework, there are seven **Science Practices**. In this chapter, we focus on **Science Practice 5:** The student can perform data analysis and evaluation of evidence. More specifically, we focus on **Science Practice 5.3:** The student can evaluate the evidence provided by data sets in relation to a particular scientific question.

Question 10 asks you to evaluate data that show the effect(s) of changes in concentrations of key molecules on negative feedback mechanisms (**Learning Objective 2.17**).

10. The *Arabidopsis* gene *cor15a* is thought to be under the control of a promoter that responds to environmental conditions. The *cor15a* protein is an enzyme that appears to reduce membrane damage at cold temperatures. The levels of the enzyme that this gene is coded for were measured after plants were grown at room temperature and then transferred to one of three conditions of varying environmental temperature (2°C, 19°C, and 75°C). The data are shown below.

Hours after transfer	ENZYME ACTIVITY Units/g of protein		
	2°C	**19°C**	**75°C**
0	0.21	0.55	0.22
12	3.21	0.35	0.14
24	5.66	0.51	0.03
36	9.65	0.45	0.06
48	10.10	0.60	0.01
72	11.44	0.49	0.00

a. Plot the data with hours after transfer on the *x* axis and enzyme activity on the *y* axis. Be sure to label the axes. Provide three labeled curves, one for each temperature.

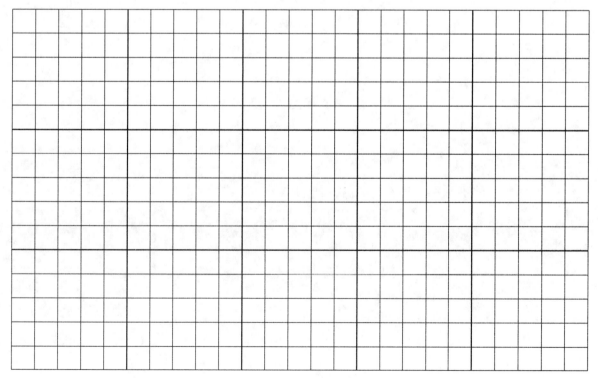

b. Write a description of what the data show regarding the expression of the *cor15a* gene.

_____

_____

_____

_____

_____

_____

_____

_____

_____

_____

c. Evaluate the meaning of the data collected from plants moved to 75°C.

_____

_____

_____

_____

_____

_____

_____

_____

_____

_____

29 Fundamentals of Animal Function

Chapter Outline

Chapter 29 provides an overview of metabolism and homeostasis, discussing how and why animals regulate their internal environments. Long-term changes in metabolic phenotype allow animals to respond successfully to changes in nutritional and environmental conditions.

Metabolism refers to the sum of all biochemical reactions in a living organism. Because they lack photosynthetic abilities, animals must gain the energy needed to sustain life by eating other organisms. The chemical breakdown (*catabolism*) of foods is the source of energy transfers that accomplish synthesis (*anabolism*), temperature regulation, and movement. Metabolism can be viewed within a single cell, as nearly all cells synthesize ATP, or in total, from the organismal perspective. Single-celled organisms and small flat or thin organisms rely on diffusion and transport of materials across cell membranes to get nutrients in and wastes out. However, diffusion is slow over distances larger than a cell, so multicellular and complex animals rely on more elaborate systems to balance their inputs and outputs.

Homeostasis is the dynamic maintenance of optimal conditions in the internal environment. Organisms have a "set point" for physiological variables, such as body temperature, and the concentration of H^+ (pH), buffers, ions, gases (O_2 and CO_2), and glucose in body fluids. Maintaining these physiological variables as close as possible to the optimal set point requires coordination of different body systems, a communication function carried out by nerves and hormones. "Sensors" in the body constantly monitor physiological variables, and when the variables stray from the optimal value, "effectors" work to correct the course. The activity of effectors is controlled—accelerated or slowed—by signals from the nervous and endocrine systems. Feedback from the sensors guides the effectors. As the sensors monitor information, negative or positive feedback regulation is activated. Negative feedback is the most common stabilizing force, and in this context, negative is not a bad thing. Rather, negative feedback assures that the effectors do not overshoot the set point, much like a thermostat in a house turns off the heat after detecting that enough heat has been delivered. Positive feedback, on the other hand, amplifies a response, and is less common. Childbirth and emptying body cavities (such as urination) are two activities where positive feedback is needed.

Chapter 29 includes discussion about the regulation of body temperature. Animals produce heat as a byproduct of metabolism and can gain or lose heat by radiation, convection, conduction, and evaporation. *Ectothermy*, taking on the temperature of the environment, and *endothermy*, maintaining a set body temperature, use different mechanisms to deal with heat gain and loss.

As you study the information in this chapter, focus on the "regulation viewpoint." How does the organism sense the departure from the set point (i.e., what is the physical stimulus)? What is the cause-and-effect response to the stimulus? What effectors bring the organism back toward the set point? Using this viewpoint as a lens, you can study the regulation of most systems in biology.

Chapter 29 emphasizes **Big Idea 2**, but **Big Idea 4** is considered as well. The specific parts of the AP Biology curriculum covering **Big Idea 2**: Biological systems utilize free energy and molecular building blocks to grow, to reproduce, and to maintain dynamic homeostasis, include:

• **2.A.1**: All living systems require constant input of free energy.

- **2.A.3**: Organisms must exchange matter with the environment to grow, reproduce, and maintain organization.
- **2.B.2**: Growth and dynamic homeostasis are maintained by the constant movement of molecules across membranes.
- **2.C.1**: Organisms use feedback mechanisms to maintain their internal environments and respond to external environmental changes.
- **2.C.2**: Organisms respond to changes in their external environments.

- **2.D.1**: All biological systems from cells and organisms to populations, communities, and ecosystems are affected by complex biotic and abiotic interactions involving exchange of matter and free energy.
- **2.D.2**: Homeostatic mechanisms reflect both common ancestry and divergence due to adaptation in different environments.

The specific parts covering **Big Idea 4**: Biological systems interact, and these systems and their interactions possess complex properties, include:

- **4.B.2**: Cooperative interactions within organisms promote efficiency in the use of energy and matter.

Chapter Review

Concept 29.1 *addresses how animals eat to obtain energy and chemical building blocks. In most ecosystems, sunlight is the primary energy input. Plants and algae use some of the light energy in sunlight to carry out photosynthesis and build organic compounds from simple precursors. However, animals are heterotrophs—organisms that require preformed organic molecules as food. They eat organic matter, such as starch or fat, that other organisms have synthesized. These animals get their energy by breaking the chemical bonds of these organic compounds, and they build their tissues from the same compounds.*

1. Describe the energetic difference between heterotrophs and autotrophs.

_____

_____

_____

_____

2. Define energy in a biological context.

_____

_____

_____

_____

_____

3. Draw a flow chart that shows how energy is absorbed, used, and converted between its different forms as it moves from the sun to heat energy emitted by a cow eating grass.

Concept 29.2 *examines how an animal's energy needs depend on physical activity and body size. How much energy does an animal need? This is a complicated question, because animals use energy for many different purposes. Every cell and tissue in an animal's body uses chemical energy every day to maintain its own internal organized state. Cells and tissues also use energy to do additional types of physiological work. When animals run, for example, their skeletal muscles use energy to generate mechanical forces for locomotion. An animal's heart muscle uses energy to pump blood. After a meal, the digestive tract uses energy to synthesize digestive enzymes and propel the ingested food through the gut. Applying this concept, we look at how total energy use is measured.*

4. Skates and sharks belong to the same group of animals, the cartilaginous fish. Which is likely to require more food over a given time period: a group of 60 skates, each of 1 kg body mass; or a pair of sharks, each of 30 kg body mass?

_____

_____

_____

_____

5. The graph at the right shows the metabolic rate for a bird as it flies at different speeds.

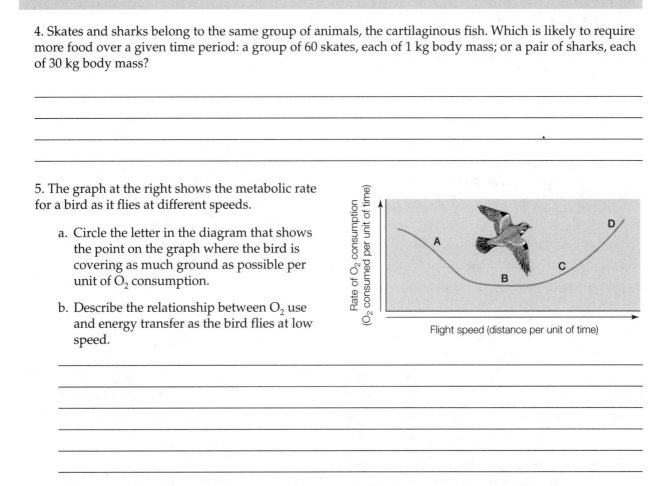

a. Circle the letter in the diagram that shows the point on the graph where the bird is covering as much ground as possible per unit of O_2 consumption.

b. Describe the relationship between O_2 use and energy transfer as the bird flies at low speed.

_____

_____

_____

_____

_____

_____

_____

Concept 29.3 *addresses how animals regulate their bodies in response to temperature changes. This section also includes a discussion of Q_{10}, which is a measure of the temperature sensitivity of a reaction. As a concept, Q_{10} is not in the AP Biology Curriculum Framework, but it is a quick way to compare different organisms' sensitivity to temperature changes, and it is an effective example of Science Practices.*

6. Define homeostasis, and explain why maintaining homeostasis is important.

_____

_____

_____

_____

_____

7. Propose an explanation for why most physiological reactions proceed more slowly when the temperature decreases.

_____

_____

_____

_____

8. Describe how biochemical reactions speed up as temperature increases but then cease to operate at high temperatures. Use and explain the term "denature" in your answer.

_____

_____

_____

_____

9. The graph at the right shows how body temperature changes in an endotherm (mouse) and an ectotherm (lizard) when environmental temperature changes. Summarize the information portrayed in the graph.

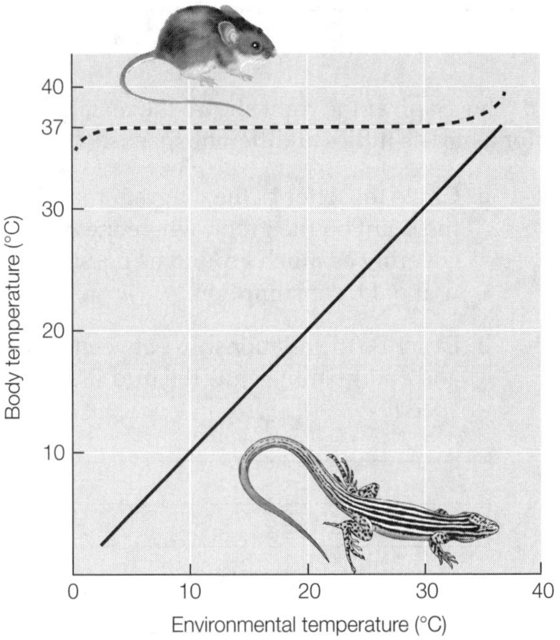

_____

_____

_____

_____

_____

_____

_____

_____

_____

10. The graph at the right shows how the metabolic rates of an endotherm (mouse) and an ectotherm (lizard) react to changes in environmental temperature. Compare the metabolic rates of the mouse and the lizard and discuss the differences between them.

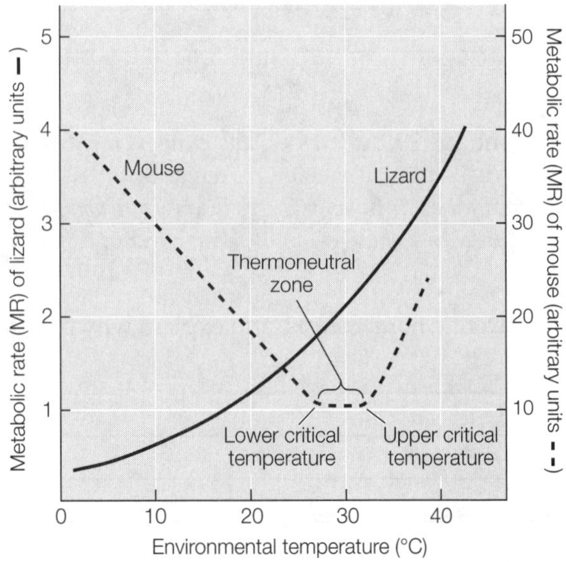

_____

_____

_____

_____

_____

_____

_____

11. Give three examples of ectotherms that use behavioral changes to help regulate body temperature. Describe each behavior and discuss how it affects body temperature.

_____

_____

_____

_____

_____

_____

_____

_____

12. Give two examples of endotherms that use behavioral changes to help regulate body temperature. Describe each behavior and discuss how it affects body temperature.

_____

_____

_____

_____

_____

13. Give two examples of endotherms that use physiological (non-behavioral) changes to help regulate body temperature. Describe each behavior and discuss how it affects body temperature.

_____

_____

_____

_____

_____

14. Both ectotherms and endotherms can regulate heat loss and gain with behavioral adaptations, while endotherms can also utilize metabolic mechanisms to regulate heat loss and gain. Discuss how humans regulate body temperature, discussing one physiological mechanism and one behavioral mechanism.

_____

_____

_____

_____

_____

_____

_____

15. Draw two flow charts showing the mechanisms of heat exchange in humans, one during exposure to a cold environment and one during exposure to a hot environment. Include in each diagram one behavioral response, two physiological responses, and the negative feedback systems at work, including sensors and effectors.

Concept 29.4 *explains how multicellular organisms utilize a division of labor through systems of organs to maintain homeostasis. Life requires the transfer of matter and energy, and this exchange is optimized through evolution, which provides organisms with the greatest likelihood of successful reproduction. For a multicellular animal, such as a human, the transfers of matter typically involve solutes moving as follows:*

Environment ⟷ Organism ⟷ Blood ⟷ Interstitial fluid ⟷ Active cells

16. Describe some of the benefits of multicellular organisms having specialized tissues.

_____

_____

_____

_____

_____

_____

_____

_____

17. Describe the interactions of the four separate tissue types in the stomach.

_____

_____

_____

_____

_____

_____

_____

_____

18. Jellyfish do not have internal systems of organs. Compare how humans and jellyfish solve the problem of getting nutrients to, and waste products away from, their internal cells.

_____

_____

_____

_____

_____

_____

_____

_____

_____

_____

Concept 29.5 *explains how the phenotypes of individual animals can change during their lifetimes. Though the genotype of an individual animal is constant for the animal's entire life, changes in phenotype, or observable characteristics, occur. This is called phenotypic plasticity. When an individual's phenotype changes as a result of long-term exposure to a particular environment, the individual is said to acclimate or acclimatize to that environment.*

19. Phenotypic plasticity occurs at many different levels as organisms acclimate to their surroundings. For each example below, write *yes* or *no* to tell whether the change is an example of phenotypic plasticity.

_____ The size of an ant depends on its role in the colony (soldier or non-soldier).

_____ A poikilotherm increases its metabolic rate as the environmental temperature increases.

_____ Small mammals living in colder climates for longer than a week increase the amount of brown adipose tissue in their bodies.

_____ Plants increase the amount of salicylate and other anti-herbivore toxins when caterpillars start feeding on them.

_____ The map butterfly produces an orange form in the spring and a drab gray form in the fall.

_____ Dandelions (common lawn weeds) vary the size of their roots depending on the nutrients available in the soil.

_____ A mutation forms a new protein that is better able to carry hemoglobin in an organism.

Concept 29.6 *explains the control mechanisms needed for coordination of physiology. The nervous and endocrine systems are the principal systems that control or regulate the ways tissues and organs interact throughout an animal's body. In addition, there are systems in individual cells that control cellular processes, such as biochemical reactions and cell division. The importance of these mechanisms is emphasized dramatically when controls fail. Cancer reflects a failure of cell division control.*

20. For each situation described below, identify the feedback as either negative or positive, and explain your choice.

a. As you eat, your stomach secretes an inactive enzyme precursor called *pepsinogen*. As pepsinogen is converted to the active enzyme pepsin, it triggers the activation of other pepsinogen molecules. Through this cascade effect, your food-filled stomach creates enough active pepsin molecules to digest the proteins you have ingested.

_____
_____
_____
_____

b. Cells along blood vessels have sensory neurons that measure the stretch caused by blood flow against the vessel walls, thus being part of a blood-pressure monitoring system. When blood pressure decreases during dehydration, thirst is stimulated.

_____
_____
_____
_____

c. Upon injury to a blood vessel, the platelets change shape and clump together, releasing compounds that cause more platelets to accumulate.

_____

_____

_____

_____

21. Certain sensory cells are neurons that increase their activity when stretched. Describe a situation in which information from stretch-sensitive neurons is used as negative feedback and a second situation in which it is used as positive feedback.

_____

_____

_____

_____

_____

_____

_____

_____

_____

_____

_____

_____

_____

_____

_____

_____

_____

_____

_____

_____

_____

_____

_____

_____

_____

_____

_____

_____

Science Practices & Inquiry

In the AP Biology Curriculum Framework, there are seven **Science Practices**. In this chapter, we focus on **Science Practice 5:** The student can perform data analysis and evaluation of evidence, **Science Practice 6:** The student can work with scientific explanations and theories, and **Science Practice 7:** The student is able to connect and relate knowledge across various scales, concepts, and representations in and across domains. More specifically, we focus on **Science Practice 5.1:** The student can analyze data to identify patterns or relationships, **Science Practice 6.1:** The student can justify claims with evidence, **Science Practice 6.4:** The student can make claims and predictions about natural phenomena based on scientific theories and models, and **Science Practice 7.2:** The student can connect concepts in and across domain(s) to generalize or extrapolate in and/or across **Enduring Understandings** and/or **Big Ideas**.

Question 22 considers organismal reactions in a scenario where the temperature is changed. It also addresses the ways organisms use negative feedback for homeostasis of body temperature (**Learning Objectives 2.15 and 2.16**). You will have to make predictions about how organisms use negative feedback mechanisms to maintain their internal environment (**Learning Objective 2.18**). You will need to analyze data to detect patterns and relationships between an abiotic factor and an organism (**Learning Objective 2.24**).

22. The data below were recorded during an experiment in which the temperature of the hypothalamus (T_H) of a ground squirrel was cooled while the animal's metabolic rate (MR) was measured. T_H is given in °C, and MR is given in calories per gram of body mass per minute.

Temperature of hypothalamus (T_H, °C)	Metabolic rate (MR, calories/g body mass/minute)
39.5	0.040
39.0	0.041
38.5	0.040
38.0	0.038
36.5	0.038
36.0	0.040
35.5	0.060
35.0	0.080
37.5	0.041
37.0	0.039
34.5	0.110
34.0	0.140

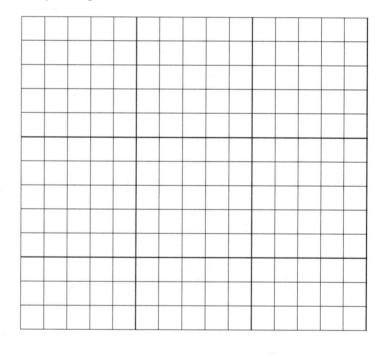

a. Plot the data on the grid.

b. Summarize the trends shown in your graph.

_____

_____

_____

_____

_____

c. Determine the threshold temperature for the metabolic-heat-production response from your graph, and describe what happens at this temperature.

_____

_____

d. Describe what these experimental results suggest about the function of the hypothalamus.

_____

_____

_____

_____

_____

e. Predict how the outcome of this experiment would differ if the tested animal were an ectothermic organism, such as a turtle.

_____

_____

_____

_____

_____

_____

_____

_____

_____

_____

_____

_____

_____

_____

_____

30 Nutrition, Feeding, and Digestion

Chapter Outline

Animals are heterotrophs, meaning they acquire their nutrition from eating other organisms. The catabolism of many of the ingested and absorbed molecules transfers energy used for metabolic needs, whereas other absorbed molecules are used as specific (anabolic) nutrients as cells synthesize proteins, membranes, and other materials. The reactions that hydrolyze and break apart food molecules for energy transfer are catabolic reactions. Anabolic reactions, in contrast, are those that use nutrients to form the proteins, lipids, and structural carbohydrates that the animal uses to build its body.

Memorizing the many micronutrients and macronutrients is not part of the AP Biology Curriculum Framework. Rather, develop your general understanding of how nutrients are utilized in organisms. Vitamins are coenzymes or parts of coenzymes important in our diet. Minerals may be required in large quantities (e.g., calcium needed for bone health and for muscle and neural functioning). Other minerals, like molybdenum, are found in only a few enzymes.

Digestive systems break apart large molecules (macromolecules) so that smaller products can be absorbed into the organism. Complex eukaryotic digestive systems with two openings evolved from ancestors with a simple digestive system with only one opening. The simplest systems are called gastrovascular cavities and are found in organisms like jellyfish and flatworms. A major evolutionary advancement was the development of the one-way digestive system. Simple organisms with a one-way system are the annelids or segmented worms. As you examine the digestive system, be sure to pay careful attention to how the structure of an organ complements its function. An example is that the folded lining of the stomach and three distinct overlapping muscle layers are specialized for squeezing and mixing the stomach, and they maximize the surface area for absorption.

The pancreas is a major exocrine gland, with its many digestive enzymes secreted into the intestine. It is also an important endocrine gland, secreting hormones, including insulin and glucagon, that regulate glucose concentration in the blood. The secretion of these hormones is a classic example of negative feedback, with high levels of glucose initiating the release of insulin, thereby increasing the rate of glucose absorption into many cells. If glucose levels in the blood are low, the heart and the brain are at risk of damage, so the pancreatic hormone glucagon is released. Glucagon stimulates liver cells to break down glycogen and release glucose.

The three physiological systems included in the AP Biology Curriculum Framework are the nervous, immune, and endocrine systems. Though it is not one of these, the digestive system is frequently used to illustrate how systems obtain nutrients and eliminate waste, exhibit cooperative behavior, and perform enzyme action, regulation, structure and function. It also offers a good example of the specialization of organs and the evolution of structures.

Chapter 30 has concepts that span **Big Idea 2** and **Big Idea 4**. The specific parts of the AP Biology curriculum covering **Big Idea 2**: Biological systems utilize free energy and molecular building blocks to grow, to reproduce, and to maintain dynamic homeostasis, include:

- **2.A.1**: All living systems require constant input of free energy.

- **2.A.2**: Organisms capture and store free energy for use in biological processes.

- **2.A.3**: Organisms must exchange matter with the environment to grow, reproduce, and maintain organization.

- **2.C.1**: Organisms use feedback mechanisms to maintain their internal environments and respond to external environmental changes.

- **2.D.2**: Homeostatic mechanisms reflect both common ancestry and divergence due to adaptation in different environments.

- **2.D.3**: Biological systems are affected by disruptions to their dynamic homeostasis.

The specific parts covering **Big Idea 4:** Biological systems interact, and these systems and their interactions possess complex properties, include:

- **4.A.4**: Organisms exhibit complex properties due to interactions between their constituent parts.

- **4.B.2**: Cooperative interactions within organisms promote efficiency in the use of energy and matter.

- **4.C.2**: Environmental factors influence the expression of the genotype in an organism.

Chapter Review

Concept 30.1 *introduces the requirement of heterotrophs to obtain external nutrition. Food provides them with both nutrition and essential minerals and vitamins.*

1. Identify each process below as either anabolic (A) or catabolic (C).

_____ Enzymatic digestion of a protein into amino acids

_____ Producing starch from glucose

_____ Conversion of hydrogen peroxide into water and oxygen gas

_____ Hydrolysis of a carbohydrate

_____ Building muscle tissue

2. Humans' average basal metabolic rate is 1,600 kcal/day. Walking burns five times as many calories as resting, and jogging burns eight times as many calories as resting. Calculate the time required to burn off the calories ingested from each of the following:

	Calories	Resting	Walking	Jogging
Starbucks Peppermint Mocha Frappuccino with whole milk and whipped cream, venti	540			
Chipotle Barbacoa Burrito with rice, beans, cheese, sour cream, and guacamole	1,180			
Dominos Brooklyn Deluxe pizza, 1 slice	335			

3. Describe why a 100 percent fat-free diet is virtually impossible to attain and is also an unhealthy choice.

_____

_____

_____

_____

Concepts 30.2 and 30.3 *examine the digestive systems of different animals, beginning with the gastrovascular cavity of jellyfish. One-way, or tubular, guts have an opening at each end, improving efficiency and allowing for specialization of various organs. The digestive system also plays a key role in determining the nutritional value of foods.*

4. Describe two evolutionary advantages of a one-way (complete) digestive system over a gastrovascular cavity.

_____

_____

_____

_____

_____

_____

5. Most organisms with gastrovascular cavities lack a circulatory system. Explain why they do not need one.

_____

_____

_____

_____

_____

_____

_____

6. Very few birds are herbivores, though some birds eat only seeds that are high in oils. Explain why a diet of oily seeds could be the most effective diet for an avian herbivore.

_____

_____

_____

_____

7. Briefly compare the digestive tracts of carnivores with those of herbivores.

_____

_____

_____

_____

_____

_____

_____

Concept 30.4 *discusses how food is digested in the vertebrate gut. Motility of the gut and secretion/activity of digestive enzymes and fluids are introduced.*

8. Explain how a person standing on his or her head is able to drink a glass of water.

_____

_____

_____

_____

9. Explain the function of bacteria living in a termite's gut.

_____

_____

_____

10. If the lining of a human's small intestine were laid out flat, it would likely cover the area of a tennis court. Explain the reason for the organ to be so large, and describe how such a large organ can be squeezed into your abdomen.

_____

_____

_____

_____

11. Complete the table below by describing what happens to each major nutrient in the parts of the digestive system given.

	Carbohydrates	Proteins	Lipids
Mouth			
Stomach			
Small intestine			
Large intestine			

12. Explain the role of each of the following in the digestion process.

a. Bile: _____

_____

_____

_____

_____

b. Saliva: _____

_____

_____

_____

_____

c. Teeth: _____

_____

_____

_____

_____

d. Water: _____

_____

_____

_____

_____

_____

13. Discuss how a person should modify his or her diet after gallbladder removal, and include a rationale for each modification in your answer.

_____

_____

_____

_____

_____

_____

_____

_____

_____

_____

_____

_____

Concept 30.5 *reviews the regulation of the distribution and use of nutrients in the body. Hormones and neurons are important signaling components in the coordination of gut activities.*

14. Complete the diagram at the right by placing the letter of each of the following in the correct blank.

    A. Breakdown of glycogen in liver

    B. Metabolic energy production, glycogen synthesis

    C. Increase in circulating insulin

    D. Increase in circulating glucagon

    E. Release of glucose to blood

    F. Stimulation of pancreas to secrete glucagon

    G. Stimulation of pancreas to secrete insulin

    H. Uptake of glucose by cells

    I. Rise in blood glucose level

    J. Drop in blood glucose concentration

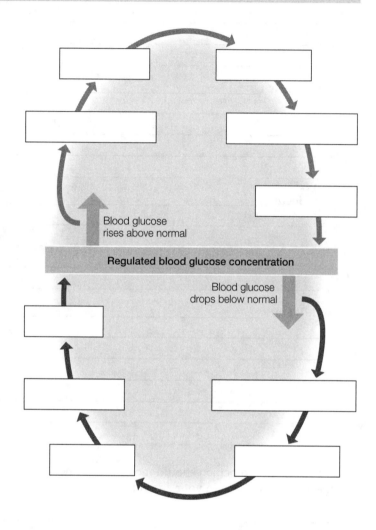

15. Describe the effects of insulin signaling that characterize insulin as an anabolic hormone.

_____

_____

_____

_____

_____

_____

_____

_____

_____

_____

_____

16. Predict which of these conditions would allow you to measure glucagon at its peak concentration in the blood: during rest, after a high carbohydrate meal, after an overnight fast, or during times of stress. Explain your choice.

_____

_____

_____

_____

_____

17. For each situation below, identify whether it demonstrates positive or negative feedback, and explain your answer.

a. Pancreatic enzymes are produced and secreted as inactive forms called zymogens. The zymogen trypsinogen is converted to its active form, trypsin, by enterokinase. Trypsin then activates other trypsinogen molecules.

_____

_____

_____

_____

_____

_____

_____

_____

b. Acidic chyme stimulates cells in the duodenum to release secretin, which slows the release of chyme from the stomach.

_____

_____

_____

_____

_____

_____

c. Ingested proteins in the stomach cause the release of acid and pepsinogen. The biochemical effects of these compounds lead to the release of even more acid and pepsinogen.

_____

_____

_____

_____

_____

_____

Science Practices & Inquiry

In the AP Biology Curriculum Framework, there are seven **Science Practices**. In this chapter, we focus on **Science Practice 5**: The student can perform data analysis and evaluation of evidence. More specifically, we focus on **Science Practice 5.3**: The student can evaluate the evidence provided by data sets in relation to a particular scientific question. We also consider **Science Practice 6**: The student can work with scientific explanations and theories. More specifically, we focus on **Science Practice 6.4**: The student can make claims and predictions about natural phenomena based on scientific theories and models.

Parts a and b of Question 18 ask you to evaluate data that show the effect(s) of changes in concentrations of key molecules on negative feedback mechanisms (**Learning Objective 2.17**). *Parts c and d* ask you to predict the effects of a change in an environmental factor on the genotypic expression of the phenotype (**Learning Objective 4.24**).

18. In house mice, the *Ob* gene codes for the protein leptin, a satiety factor secreted by fats cells. Leptin appears to signal the brain to stop eating when enough food has been consumed to assure adequate adipose tissue. The recessive *ob* allele is a mutant allele, resulting in the absence of leptin. Mice that are *ob/ob* do not experience satiety. They eat incessantly and become obese.

In an experiment, leptin was purified and injected into *ob/ob* and *Ob/Ob* (wild-type) mice daily. The data in the table were collected before the injections began (baseline) and 10 days later.

	Baseline		Day 10	
Characteristic measured	*ob/ob*	*Ob/Ob*	*ob/ob*	*Ob/Ob*
Food intake (g/day)	12.0	5.5	5.0	6.0
Body mass (g)	64	35	50	38
Metabolic rate [ml O_2/(kg × hr)]	900	1,150	1,100	1,150
Body temperature (°C)	34.8	37.0	37.0	37.0

a. Summarize the data from this experiment.

_____

_____

_____

_____

_____

_____

_____

_____

b. Do the data support the claim that leptin is a satiety signal?

_____

_____

c. Explain why the mass of nutrients ingested is considerably more than the increase in body mass.

_____

_____

_____

_____

_____

_____

d. Predict what an injection of leptin would do for an *Ob/ob* (heterozygous) mouse.

_____

_____

_____

_____

_____

_____

e. Select the group of mice above that could represent a phenotype of mice without functional leptin receptors. Explain your answer.

_____

_____

_____

_____

_____

_____

_____

_____

_____

_____

_____

_____

_____

_____

_____

31 Breathing

Chapter Outline

Chapter 31 puts gas exchange in the context of the gases being dissolved in water. Oxygen delivery is required for aerobic respiration, and carbon dioxide removal is required for acid-base balance. The entry of oxygen (O_2) and the exit of carbon dioxide (CO_2) occur via simple diffusion, as these membrane-soluble gases move across cell membranes in the directions predicted by their concentration gradients. Though many factors can determine how fast small, nonpolar molecules like O_2 and CO_2 diffuse, the concentration gradient is the most relevant and most variable determinant of the rate and direction of gas diffusion.

The primary reason that cells are small and that many animals are small and thin is that O_2 is not very soluble in water, and once it is dissolved, it diffuses slowly. Though our atmosphere is slightly more than 20 percent O_2, the maximum O_2 concentration in seawater is always less than 0.002 percent. Due to the time scale that O_2 is used in animals, each cell must be within 100 μm of an O_2 supply. Thus, there is a physiological limit on cell size and strong evolutionary pressure for having an effective circulatory system for O_2 delivery. In contrast to O_2, CO_2 is readily soluble in water, and its concentration gradient is of higher magnitude, so preventing excess CO_2 buildup is easier than acquiring O_2.

Some organisms, such as jellyfish, utilize direct exchange of gases between the cells and the nearby environment, while other larger and more complex organisms, such as fish, need both respiratory and circulatory systems. The respiratory organs of organisms have evolved to maximize gas diffusion, not only between the organism and its environment, but also between the circulatory system and the cells of the organism. Gas diffusion is maximized by large surface areas, short distances, and large concentration gradients.

Gas exchange is maximized by frequent ventilation (breathing), keeping the blood underneath the respiratory tissue moving, and by countercurrent exchange anatomy. Most vertebrate lungs are tidal in nature (i.e., air moves back and forth in the same set of tubes), but birds maximize gas exchange using unidirectional airflow through their gas-exchange surfaces. Some organisms have hemoglobin in their red blood cells, which binds O_2 and takes it out of solution in the plasma, also maximizing the concentration gradient.

As with many systems, homeostatic control of gas exchange is controlled by negative feedback. In mammals, the medulla oblongata in the brainstem senses pH levels. As the level of CO_2 increases in the blood, carbonic acid is formed, so the concentration of hydrogen ions also increases; the resulting decrease in pH is a potent chemical stimulus in a neural reflex that causes vertebrate animals to breathe faster. Should breathing occur too rapidly, too much CO_2 can be lost, and the blood's pH will increase. Chemoreceptors on the aorta and other large blood vessels monitor pH and oxygen levels in the blood. Increased temperature and reduced pH decrease hemoglobin's affinity for O_2. The warm, acidic conditions near active tissues facilitate O_2 delivery (i.e., the "unloading" of O_2) where it is needed.

The emphasis in Chapter 31 is primarily on **Big Idea 2** but includes some of **Big Idea 4**, focusing on the nature of interrelated systems within organisms. The specific parts of the AP Biology curriculum covering **Big Idea 2:** Biological systems utilize free energy and molecular building blocks to grow, to reproduce, and to maintain dynamic homeostasis, include:

• **2.A.3**: Organisms must exchange matter with the environment to grow, reproduce, and maintain organization.

- **2.D.1**: All biological systems from cells and organisms to populations, communities, and ecosystems are affected by complex biotic and abiotic interactions involving exchange of matter and free energy.

- **2.D.2**: Homeostatic mechanisms reflect both common ancestry and divergence due to adaptation in different environments.

The specific parts covering **Big Idea 4**: Biological systems interact, and these systems and their interactions possess complex properties, include:

- **4.B.2**: Cooperative interactions within organisms promote efficiency in the use of energy and matter.

Chapter Review

Concept 31.1 *describes the physical processes governing diffusion, including partial pressures, temperature, and the distance involved. Air has a much higher concentration of O_2 than water by as much as a factor of 10. Thus, extracting O_2 from water is a greater challenge than extracting it from the atmosphere.*

Fick's law, or the law of diffusion for gases, is a tool describing the variables that influence the rate of gas exchange between two locations. Though not part of the AP Biology Curriculum Framework, the equation for rate of exchange (Q) is:

$$Q = DA\frac{P_1 - P_2}{L}$$

1. Explain how each component of this equation affects the diffusion of gases.

   a. *D* (diffusion coefficient): _____

   _____

   b. *A* (cross-sectional area across which the gas is diffusing): _____

   _____

   c. P_1 and P_2 (partial pressures of the gases at the two locations): _____

   _____

   d. *L* (distance between the two locations): _____

   _____

2. Another way of looking at the above equation is to say that $\frac{P_1 - P_2}{L}$ is a partial pressure gradient. Explain why using air rather than water is more effective for respiration.

_____

_____

_____

3. Identify the variable in Fick's law that is most likely to vary in your lungs in a period of one hour, going from rest to exercise. Explain your answer.

_____

_____

_____

4. Describe two characteristics of O_2 that allow it to readily diffuse across cellular and mitochondrial membranes.

_____

_____

_____

_____

5. Assume that you are an oxygen-starved fish with a choice between cold water and warm water. Which water temperature would provide you with greater access to oxygen? Explain.

_____

_____

_____

_____

6. Explain the effect of temperature on the metabolic rate of ectotherms (e.g., fish).

_____

_____

_____

_____

_____

7. Based on your answers to Questions 5 and 6, describe how warm water discharged from a power plant into a lake affects oxygen access for fish.

_____

_____

_____

_____

_____

Concept 31.2 *examines the evolutionary adaptations that maximize respiratory exchange, especially regarding the concentration gradients of the gases. Examples of different systems include external gills, internal gills, lungs, and tracheae. Additionally, countercurrent exchange systems, with the exchange media moving past each other in opposite directions, maximize gas diffusion.*

8. Discuss why fish utilize a countercurrent exchange system in their gills to acquire dissolved oxygen from the environment.

_____

_____

_____

_____

_____

9. Describe how the structure of lungs in a terrestrial animal maximizes the animal's ability to acquire oxygen from the environment.

_____

_____

_____

_____

10. Countercurrent flow aids both gas exchange and temperature regulation. Describe how countercurrent flow in a fish's gills is similar to what is observed in the leg circulation of a penguin: the artery leading away from the body runs adjacent to the vein leading back up from the foot.

_____

_____

_____

_____

_____

11. Birds have been seen flying above Mount Everest in the Himalayas mountain range, well above the altitude where humans can breathe unaided. Describe an anatomical feature of bird lungs that allows such high altitude gas exchange.

_____

_____

_____

_____

_____

_____

_____

Concept 31.3 *discusses the anatomy and function of mammalian lungs. While many of the details of lung anatomy and ventilation are not part of the AP Biology Curriculum Framework, it is important to understand gas exchange, which is often used as an illustrative example for obtaining nutrients and eliminating wastes. This section also covers the regulation of breathing in mammals. Carbon dioxide is very soluble in blood and readily forms carbonic acid, a weak acid, in the blood. Carbonic acid readily dissociates to H^+ ions and bicarbonate ions (HCO_3^-), the latter serving as a buffer against excess acidity in the blood. Breathing is under negative-feedback control by CO_2 concentration in the blood. Along with all other homeostatic systems, you should know the controlled variable, the sensors, the signaling mechanisms, and the effectors in this system.*

12. Describe the forces that pull air into the human lungs.

_____

_____

_____

_____

_____

13. Describe the forces that push air out of the human lungs.

_____

_____

_____

_____

_____

_____

_____

14. Describe the path of an O_2 molecule as it travels from the atmosphere to the mitochondrion inside a human muscle cell. Include an account of each membrane the O_2 molecule passes through, and describe what happens to the atoms within O_2 that are "used" in the mitochondrion.

_____

_____

_____

_____

_____

_____

_____

15. An untreated diabetic who lacks insulin will metabolize fats for energy and produce an excess of acidic end products, lowering the pH of the blood. Predict how this condition would affect the individual's breathing.

_____

_____

_____

_____

_____

_____

16. Hyperventilating, or rapid deep breathing, reduces the amount of CO_2 in the lungs. Explain the dangers of hyperventilating before swimming underwater.

_____

_____

_____

_____

_____

_____

17. Hemoglobin (shown below) serves in O_2 transport. It is a quaternary protein with four subunits. Identify how this protein shows the four levels of protein structure.

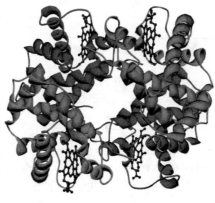

_____
_____
_____
_____
_____
_____
_____
_____
_____
_____
_____
_____

18. Explain why CO_2 is more soluble in blood plasma than is O_2. Include the chemical equation showing the relationships between CO_2, H_2CO_3, H^+ and HCO_3^- in your answer.

_____
_____
_____
_____
_____
_____
_____
_____
_____
_____
_____
_____
_____
_____

Science Practices & Inquiry

In the AP Biology Curriculum Framework, there are seven **Science Practices**. In this chapter, we focus on **Science Practice 2:** The student can use mathematics appropriately. More specifically, we focus on **Science Practice 2.2:** The student can apply mathematical routines to quantities that describe natural phenomena.

Question 19 asks you to use calculated surface area-to-volume ratios to predict which cell(s) might eliminate wastes or procure nutrients faster by diffusion (**Learning Objective 2.6**). Question 20 asks you to apply what you know about impulses to justify the shape of a neuron.

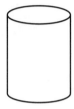

Some useful equations
(h is height or length of a cylinder)
Volume of a cylinder is $\pi r^2 h$
Surface area of a cylinder is $2 \pi r^2 + 2 \pi r h$

19.   Calculate the surface area-to-volume ratio for each of the cells described below.

a. A cylindrical neuron that is 10 micrometers in diameter and one meter long

b. A typical cubic cell measuring 20 micrometers on a side

20. Neurons need to be able to conduct impulses over long distances. Explain how this determines their shape.

_____

_____

_____

_____

_____

_____

_____

_____

32 Circulation

Chapter Outline

If you filled your stomach with glucose and relied on diffusion for its delivery, it would take years, perhaps decades, for the glucose to reach every part of your body. The main benefit of having a circulatory system is that it speeds delivery of diffusible materials to within 100 µm of nearly every cell in the body; over that short distance, diffusion of glucose is at equilibrium in less than five seconds.

Building a circulatory system appears to be a straightforward process. You need plumbing (blood vessels) and a pump (heart). You connect them together, fill the system with blood, turn on the pump, and watch the blood circulate. In reality, a great number of subtle factors, such as the size of the plumbing, the vigor of the pump, and the matching of flow in cases where there are two circuits, present interesting challenges. Given the essential importance of good circulation, evolutionary adaptations have brought this system to a very high level of performance.

Chapter 32 includes **Big Idea 1** and **Big Idea 2**. The specific parts of the AP Biology curriculum covering

Big Idea 1: The process of evolution drives the diversity and unity of life, include:

- **1.B.1**: Organisms share many conserved core processes and features that evolved and are widely distributed among organisms today.

The specific parts covering **Big Idea 2:** Biological systems utilize free energy and molecular building blocks to grow, to reproduce, and to maintain dynamic homeostasis, include:

- **2.A.3**: Organisms must exchange matter with the environment to grow, reproduce, and maintain organization.

- **2.C.1**: Organisms use feedback mechanisms to maintain their internal environments and respond to external environmental changes.

- **2.D.2**: Homeostatic mechanisms reflect both common ancestry and divergence due to adaptation in different environments.

- **2.D.3**: Biological systems are affected by disruptions to their dynamic homeostasis.

Chapter Review

Concept 32.1 *observes that transport—of both "good stuff" (e.g., nutrients) and "bad stuff" (e.g., wastes)—is the immense benefit provided by the development of a circulatory system. The general idea is that a fluid containing solutes needed for cellular function is delivered near the active cells, and the fluid picks up waste products as it passes near those active cells. Other sites in the body, such as the lungs, permit exchange between the fluid and the organism's external environment. Distinction is made between open systems, where the exchange fluid leaves blood vessels during its journey, and closed systems, in which the exchange medium is always contained within blood vessels. The fluid in the closed vessels moves more slowly through the tiniest vessels (capillaries), allowing adequate time for exchange to occur.*

1. Both a grasshopper and a clam have open circulatory systems. Explain what enables the grasshopper to be more active and sustain a higher metabolic rate than the clam.

_____

_____

_____

_____

_____

_____

_____

2. Below is a schematic drawing of a crustacean. Does it have an open or a closed circulatory system? Explain.

_____

_____

_____

_____

_____

_____

_____

_____

_____

3. Discuss which type of circulatory system, open or closed, supports a higher rate of metabolism.

_____

_____

_____

_____

_____

_____

_____

Concept 32.2 *delves deeper into specialized functions in circulation, leading to a description of a "dual" circulation. This process includes a circuit for environmental exchange with the organism and a second circuit that delivers blood throughout the body for gas and nutrient exchange at the active tissues.*

Among vertebrates, the simplest circulatory pump is the two-chambered heart of fish. In this system, all of the blood pumped out of the heart is delivered to the gills to "load" it with oxygen and "unload" its carbon dioxide. The blood vessels in the gills are large enough that there is adequate hydrostatic pressure from the heart's contraction cycles to deliver the blood to the systemic circuit after passage through the gill circulation. Lungfish have a slighter different system, as the development of a small lung to enhance gas exchange has occurred. Associated with the lung is a shunt circulation that moves the circulating blood away from the gills and to the lung. The lungfish's heart and the blood vessels associated with the lung have also undergone evolutionary changes, with a septum separating the atrium so that one side receives blood from the lung and the other side receives the venous return from the body.

Reptiles and adult amphibians have three-chambered hearts, along with two distinct circuits, pulmonary and systemic, that are kept relatively separated by a partial septum in the ventricles. There is some mixing of relatively deoxygenated and fully oxygenated blood, however, and the system does not support a very high metabolic rate.

Birds and mammals, along with crocodilians, have the four-chambered hearts you are probably most familiar with, along with fully distinct pulmonary and systemic circulations.

4. Explain why the volume of blood moving out of your left ventricle per unit of time exactly matches the volume moving out of your right ventricle.

_____

_____

_____

_____

_____

_____

_____

_____

_____

5. Describe a possible explanation for a large blood vessel becoming altered over evolutionary time to function as a chamber of the heart.

_____

_____

_____

_____

_____

_____

_____

_____

_____

_____

_____

Concept 32.3 *focuses on the human heart, describing the right heart and its circuit as the pulmonary circuit, and the left heart and its circuit as the systemic circuit (see diagram). The contraction cycle of the heart is the result of pacemaker cells periodically initiating action potentials, independent of the nervous system. The interval between action potentials can be shortened by signals from the sympathetic division of the autonomic nervous system to increase cardiac output for exercise or emergencies. Similarly, the period of the cardiac cycle can be lengthened by signals from the parasympathetic division, when the person is resting and fed. Action potentials spread from cell to cell in the heart via gap junctions.*

6. Arrange the terms below in the correct anatomical sequence as blood flows from the heart through the body and returns. The starting place (1) is completed for you.

_____	capillaries
_1_	heart
_____	arterioles
_____	venules
_____	arteries
_____	veins

Aorta

Superior vena cava (vein)

Pulmonary artery

To lung

To lung

Pulmonary veins

From lung

From lung

Inferior vena cava (vein)

Descending aorta

7. Describe systole and diastole.

_____

_____

_____

_____

_____

8. Investigators measuring membrane potentials of the pacemaker cells in the heart found that putting drops of acetylcholine onto a beating heart caused its cells to become more hyperpolarized, and the approach to threshold for an action potential was also slower. Describe the effects of these two changes on the overall heart rate, and identify which division of the autonomic nervous system was being modeled in the experiment by the addition of acetylcholine.

_____

_____

_____

_____

9. Epinephrine, also called adrenaline, is a neurotransmitter and hormone. Predict the effects of drops of epinephrine on membrane potentials in the experimental setting described in Question 8, and identify the division of the autonomic nervous system that is modeled by adding epinephrine.

_____

_____

_____

10. Arrange the terms below in the correct sequence of action potentials during one cardiac cycle. The starting place (1) is completed for you.

_____   conducting system (Purkinje fibers)

__1__   sinoatrial (S-A) node

_____   ventricles

_____   atrioventricular (A-V) node

_____   atria

11. A red blood cell moving into the heart from the venous return (vena cava), then to the lungs and back to the heart, and then into the kidneys would pass a number of distinct anatomical landmarks on its journey. Arrange the terms below in the correct anatomical sequence passed by the red blood cell. The starting place (1) is completed for you.

_____   pulmonary vein

_____   pulmonary artery

__1__   vena cava

_____   right atrium

_____   left ventricle

_____   right ventricle

_____   left atrioventricular (bicuspid) valve

_____   right atrioventricular (tricuspid) valve

_____   left atrium

12. The amount of blood in the heart's chambers determines the heart's force of contraction. Explain why and how a stretched heart might contract more forcefully than a heart less stretched. Describe circumstances related to both conditions as your cardiac output varies throughout the day.

_____

_____

_____

_____

_____

13. Like skeletal muscles, contraction of heart muscle is dependent on calcium ions entering the cytosol. Unlike skeletal muscles, where each individual contraction is an all-or-nothing event, heart contraction strength is variable. Explain what this implies for calcium entry into the two contractile tissues.

_____

_____

_____

Concept 32.4 *tours the blood vessels traversed by the blood after it leaves the heart. Blood vessels, with the exception of the capillaries, are surrounded by circular smooth muscle, the contraction of which reduces vessel diameter, thus increasing resistance to blood flow and forcing the blood to flow elsewhere if there is an open, low-resistance vessel to accept it. The regulation of blood vessel diameter, through vasodilation and vasoconstriction, dynamically determines how much blood flows into each part of the body. For example, if you are frightened by a scary noise in the night, sympathetic signals cause vasoconstriction in your kidneys and digestive tract, simultaneously causing vasodilation in large blood vessels in your legs, in case you must flee the danger. Each day, about two liters of plasma are normally lost from the capillaries and are carried as lymph through lymphatic vessels back to the blood.*

14. Starting in the aorta, name, in correct anatomical sequence, the categories of blood vessels that will carry the blood away from and then back to the heart (e.g., arteries → …).

_____

_____

_____

_____

15. Hydrostatic pressure on plasma forces some of it to "leak" out of the capillaries and enter the extracellular space. Explain the force that helps return some of this fluid to the capillaries, and predict what would happen in a patient with abnormally high levels of protein in the blood.

_____

_____

_____

_____

16. Explain how skeletal muscle contraction and one-way valves assist the flow of venous blood.

_____

_____

_____

_____

Concept 32.5 *describes the fluid that is pumped around the circulatory system. This blood is composed of watery plasma and suspended cells, primarily erythrocytes (red blood cells). Erythrocytes are often described as small bags, each containing one million molecules of hemoglobin, the protein that greatly increases the blood's capacity to transport oxygen. Erythrocytes, lacking a nucleus and the genetic code, "live" only four months, and replacements of these cells are always being made. Blood also contains platelets, cell fragments that are stimulated to clump together on exposed collagen by chemical signals released after an injury (a cut). White blood cells, effectors of the immune system, are also present in blood.*

17. Red blood cell shape can be altered by the osmolarity of the plasma. Explain what would happen to erythrocyte volume if the erythrocytes were placed in a beaker of pure water. Predict what changes would take place if erythrocytes were placed in a saltwater solution.

a. Placed in water: _____

_____

_____

b. Placed in hyperosmolar (very salty) solution: _____

_____

_____

18. Describe the possibly fatal sequence of events that could occur if an inexperienced person injected pure water into the veins of a severely dehydrated hiker.

_____

_____

_____

_____

_____

19. Erythropoietin is a hormone that prevents anemia (an impaired ability of the blood to carry oxygen) by stimulating red blood cell production. Explain how a cancer patient who has undergone a fairly toxic round of chemotherapy and radiation treatment would benefit from taking a drug form of erythropoietin.

_____

_____

_____

20. Myoglobin is a muscle protein similar to hemoglobin, but myoglobin has a higher affinity for O_2, so it picks up and holds O_2 as an oxygen reserve in muscle tissue. Human fetal hemoglobin has a higher affinity for O_2 than does maternal hemoglobin, facilitating O_2 transfer in the placenta. With this in mind, label each curve in the graph at the right with the appropriate protein from the following list:

(A) Human hemoglobin

(B) Fetal hemoglobin

(C) Human maternal hemoglobin

(D) Myoglobin

21. Explain the effect of high metabolic activity (e.g., exercise) on the local concentration gradient for O_2 in the blood near an exercising muscle. Compare that to the O_2 gradient in the blood moving through capillaries in the lungs. Include a discussion of the loading and unloading of O_2 on hemoglobin molecules.

_____

_____

_____

_____

_____

_____

Science Practices & Inquiry

In the AP Biology Curriculum Framework, there are seven **Science Practices**. In this chapter, we focus on **Science Practice 1:** The student can use representations and models to communicate scientific phenomena and solve scientific problems. More specifically, we focus on **Science Practice 1.4:** The student can use representations and models to analyze situations or solve problems qualitatively and quantitatively.

For Question 22, you will evaluate the effects of stretching the heart to see how much blood can be pumped with each contraction cycle. You will use models to analyze quantitatively and qualitatively the effects of disruptions to dynamic homeostasis in biological systems (**Learning Objective 2.28**).

22. The length of the heart was varied as the amount of blood pushed out of the ventricle was measured, as shown in the table.

Heart length at beginning of contraction as a percentage of maximum length	Volume of blood per contraction (mL)
35%	3,800
45%	4,200
55%	4,700
65%	5,100
75%	5,700
85%	8,800
100%	10,000

a. Graph the data, placing the independent variable on the *x* axis and the dependent variable on the *y* axis. Connect the points with a smooth curve. Label and scale both axes.

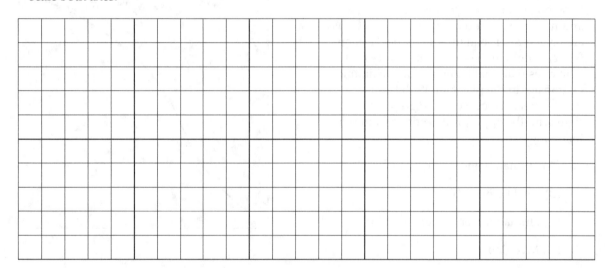

b. Summarize the results shown in your graph.

_____

_____

_____

c. A resting athlete might pump 5L of blood per minute from each ventricle. At maximum effort, that value could jump to 25L of blood per minute. With this in mind, discuss whether or not data from stretching the heart are relevant to real life.

_____

_____

_____

_____

33 Muscle and Movement

Chapter Outline

Acquiring an understanding of skeletal muscle contraction has long been of interest to humankind. This knowledge might provide relief to those who are paralyzed. It could also raise human performance to new heights. Understanding smooth muscle and cardiac muscle contraction are also of considerable interest, as these underlie homeostasis of blood pressure, which impacts all physiological systems. Chapter 33 gives you an opportunity to synthesize your knowledge of excitable cells, the regulation of muscle contraction, and some basic principles of movement.

The chapter includes **Big Idea 3** and **Big Idea 4**. The specific parts of the AP Biology curriculum covering **Big Idea 3:** Living systems store, retrieve, transmit, and respond to information essential to life processes, include:

- **3.E.2**: Animals have nervous systems that detect external and internal signals, transmit, and integrate information, and produce responses.

The specific parts addressing **Big Idea 4:** Biological systems interact, and these systems and their interactions possess complex properties, include:

- **4.A.4**: Organisms exhibit complex properties due to interactions between their constituent parts.
- **4.B.2**: Cooperative interactions within organisms promote efficiency in the use of energy and matter.

Chapter Review

Concept 33.1 *provides anatomical details of skeletal muscle organization. Skeletal muscles, like those you use to maintain your posture, are built of bundles of muscle fibers. Anatomically, these fibers are groups of cells with membranes that merged during fetal development to function together, and this arrangement means they are not replaceable during adulthood. Each muscle fiber has many myofibrils that, at the level of the sarcomeres, contain actin and myosin filaments. Interactions between these filaments are responsible for the shortening of the muscle during contraction. Actin and myosin filaments are long, repeating polymers of actin and myosin proteins, respectively. The myosin molecules have a hinged, cross-bridge section that can bind to actin and then flex, pulling on the actin, causing it to slide. The cross-bridge alternates binding and pulling, using ATP as it does so, in a type of ratcheting pattern. This causes actin to slide and the muscle length to shorten.*

The nervous system contacts the muscle fibers at a synapse called the neuromuscular junction (NMJ). Neuronal activity releases acetylcholine into the NMJ, activating an action potential on the muscle fibers. The action potential causes a brief rise in the concentration of calcium ions inside the muscle cell. Calcium ions bind to proteins, which activates the sliding of actin filaments and shortens the muscle fiber. Relaxation occurs quickly, as the active transport of calcium ions out of the cytosol and back into the smooth endoplasmic reticulum (in muscles this is called the sarcoplasmic reticulum) terminates contraction. Contraction in smooth muscles and cardiac (heart) muscle is also regulated by the arrival and departure of calcium ions in the cytosol.

1. Describe the three proteins that associate with actin in skeletal muscle, and explain how each is altered during a contraction sequence.

_____
_____
_____
_____
_____
_____
_____
_____
_____

2. Describe the two binding sites on the myosin cross-bridge.

_____
_____
_____
_____
_____
_____
_____

3. Explain how rigor mortis occurs. Include in your answer a discussion of how actin and myosin dissociate after normal muscle contraction in a living person.

_____
_____
_____
_____

4. Discuss "excitation-contraction coupling" relative to muscle contraction.

_____
_____
_____

Concept 33.2 *addresses the parts of the body that move as a result of muscle contraction. For vertebrate animals, it is usually the bony skeleton that moves. In other animals, such as earthworms, there is a hydrostatic skeleton—a fluid-filled cavity that changes its shape as fluids are moved by muscle contraction.*

5. Explain what is meant by the observation that our muscles are arranged in antagonistic pairs.

_____
_____
_____

6. Consider the statement, "The skeletal muscles of a person resting in a chair are completely relaxed." Is this statement true or false? Explain your answer.

_____

_____

_____

_____

_____

_____

_____

7. Describe both points of attachment of skeletal muscles to bones.

_____

_____

_____

_____

_____

_____

_____

_____

_____

Concept 33.3 *explores force production by muscles. Muscle contraction is dependent on ATP availability. ATP is hydrolyzed to maintain the gradients of sodium and potassium ions across muscle membranes, power the cross-bridge cycle between actin and myosin, and remove calcium ions from the cytosol when it is time to relax. Therefore, the supply of ATP is an important consideration in how much work a muscle can accomplish. There are different types of muscle that vary in response to their loads and that have differences in energy metabolism. Postural muscles that hold you upright are active most of the time. They hydrolyze a large amount of ATP in accomplishing their work. This "aerobic" muscle, resistant to fatigue, has a large blood supply and a lot of mitochondria for ATP production. In contrast, the bulging muscles of a weightlifter can rapidly generate a great deal of tension, but these muscles are more prone to fatigue as their energy sources are quickly depleted.*

8. Describe the specific meaning of *twitch*, the minimum unit of contraction in skeletal muscles, and discuss the ways that ATP hydrolysis makes a twitch possible.

_____

_____

_____

_____

_____

_____

_____

_____

9. One curve is labeled in the graph below. Add the labels "glycolytic" and "aerobic" to the other curves, and explain what the curves tell us about ATP supplies during a five-minute sustained period of muscle activity.

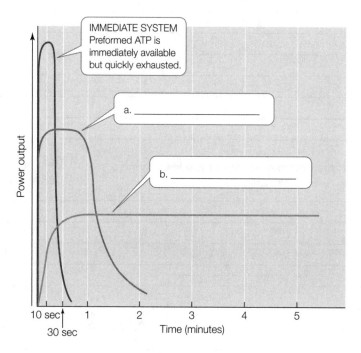

a. _____

_____

_____

_____

_____

_____

_____

b. _____

_____

_____

_____

_____

_____

Concept 33.4 *describes distinctive types of muscle, including vertebrate cardiac muscle.*

10. Describe how action potentials spread from one cardiac muscle cell to the next.

_____

_____

_____

_____

_____

11. Describe the similarities and differences between the proteins that can bind calcium ions in skeletal and smooth muscle.

_____

_____

_____

_____

_____

_____

_____

_____

_____

_____

12. The "catch" muscles in clams and scallops can hold the half-shells closed tightly for long periods of time. Discuss the similarity between the metabolic mechanism for this contraction and rigor mortis.

_____

_____

_____

_____

_____

_____

_____

_____

_____

_____

_____

Science Practices & Inquiry

In the AP Biology Curriculum Framework, there are seven **Science Practices**. In this chapter, we focus on **Science Practice 1:** The student can use representations and models to communicate scientific phenomena and solve scientific problems. More specifically, we focus on **Science Practice 1.3:** The student can refine representations and models of natural or man-made phenomena and systems in the domain.

In Question 13, you will evaluate the effects of muscle stretch on tension development in muscle and then extrapolate this information to another type of muscle. This question will ensure that you are able to refine representations and models to illustrate biocomplexity due to interactions of the constituent parts (**Learning Objective 4.10**).

13. A scientist measured the resting length of a skeletal muscle in its appropriate anatomical position. With an electrode, she then stimulated the muscle to contract, while measuring force generation with electronic detectors. The same measurements were made after the muscle was rearranged to varying lengths, presented here as percentages of resting length.

Length of fibers at beginning of contraction as a percentage of resting length	Force generated as a percentage of maximum force possible
35	10
75	50
100	100
115	100
130	80
150	50
175	10

a. Graph the data, placing "length" on the *x* axis and "force" on the *y* axis, and connect the points with a curve. Label all parts of your graph.

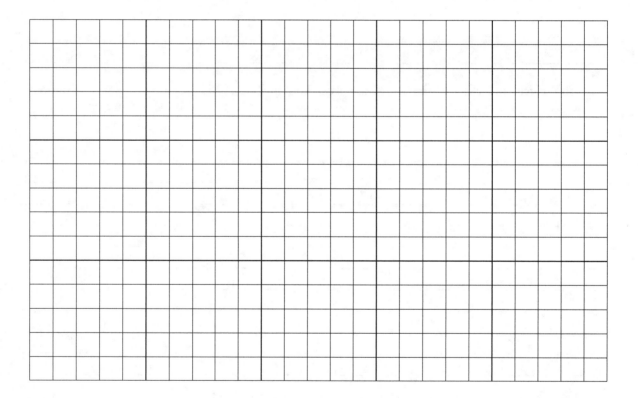

b. Write a caption that explains the meaning of your graph.

_____

_____

_____

_____

c. The drawing at the right shows two possible arrangements of actin and myosin. Assume that one represents muscle that is stretched beyond its resting length and the other is at its resting length. On your graph in *Part b*, draw similar representations showing actin and myosin overlap at three data points (left of middle, middle, and right of middle).

d. Assume that smooth muscle can generate as much force as skeletal muscle but over a much wider range of stretching. Add a curve to the graph to show how you would expect the data for smooth muscle to look if measured similarly. Describe this curve.

_____

_____

_____

_____

_____

_____

_____

_____

34 Neurons, Sense Organs, and Nervous Systems

Chapter Outline

Homeostasis, the dynamic maintenance of optimal conditions, requires sensors and effectors that regulate controlled variables, such as blood pressure. Chemical signaling via hormones is one major signaling route for cellular communication to maintain homeostasis. The other route is the nervous system, discussed here.

While exploring the operations of the brain is a worthy and fun activity, the understanding of individual cells, the neurons, along with the glial cells that support neuronal metabolism, is important to comprehending the overall system. You should find that much of this material is an application of material you have previously learned. You will once again see cellular organelles, membrane structure and function, the sodium-potassium pump, and membrane potentials serving important biological functions. This material is challenging to learn, but spending some time to meet this challenge will open many doors of biological understanding to you.

Chapter 34 includes components of **Big Idea 2, Big Idea 3,** and **Big Idea 4**. The specific parts of the AP Biology curriculum covering **Big Idea 2:** Biological systems utilize free energy and molecular building blocks to grow, to reproduce, and to maintain dynamic homeostasis, include:

- **2.B.1**: Cell membranes are selectively permeable due to their structure.

- **2.C.2**: Organisms respond to changes in their external environments.

The specific parts covering **Big Idea 3:** Living systems store, retrieve, transmit, and respond to information essential to life processes, include:

- **3.D.2**: Cells communicate with each other through direct contact with other cells or from a distance via chemical signaling.

- **3.E.2**: Animals have nervous systems that detect external and internal signals, transmit and integrate information, and produce responses.

The specific parts addressing **Big Idea 4:** Biological systems interact, and these systems and their interactions possess complex properties, include:

- **4.B.2**: Cooperative interactions within organisms promote efficiency in the use of energy and matter.

Chapter Review

Concept 34.1 *details the cellular components of the nervous system, starting with cells called neurons. Neurons are similar to one-way roads in that they carry signals in only one direction. An individual neuron has two functional regions. The highly branched, dendritic region is the information-receiving region. It has transmembrane proteins that serve as receptors to bind chemical signals, called neurotransmitters. In response to a signal, the dendritic region of the cell undergoes a small change in membrane potential, called a graded potential. The second functional region of a neuron is called the axon or axonal region. Neurotransmitter signals are released from its terminus in response to action potentials. Neurons that carry information into the central nervous system (spinal cord and brain) are called afferent neurons, as they affect what happens next in the organism. Neurons carrying commands out of the central nervous system are called efferent neurons, because they effect change by controlling effectors in the body. The neurons located between the afferent and efferent neurons are called interneurons.*

1. Describe the difference between a nerve and a neuron.

_____

_____

_____

_____

_____

2. Describe how a neuron's axon hillock acts as the decision point for whether or not the neuron will undergo an action potential to communicate with its target.

_____

_____

_____

_____

_____

3. Discuss the relative abundance of glial cells and neurons in the brain, and describe two functions of glial cells.

_____

_____

_____

_____

_____

_____

Concept 34.2 *reveals details about neuronal function. Whether neuronal activity is as simple as "Me want cookies!" or as sublime as "I finally understand the Nernst equation," it is a matter of understanding that ion movements across neuronal membranes alter membrane potentials.*

The membrane potential describes the separation of charges inside and outside of neuronal membranes, and these potentials are measured in millivolts (mV). The interior of a neuron, its cytosol, has many protein molecules. Most of these are in the anionic (negatively charged) state, so the inside of the "resting" cell is electronegative relative to the outside of the cell, typically between -50 and -70mV. The resting membrane potential of a "quiet" neuron is anything but resting: it depends on a high rate of ATP hydrolysis, driving the sodium-potassium pump (Na^+-K^+-ATPase). The unequal distribution of charge across the membrane means that it is polarized. Changes that reduce the charge difference across the membrane are called depolarizing changes, and changes that increase the charge difference are said to be hyperpolarizing changes.

The functions of neurons are based on ion movements (especially sodium and potassium ions) across the cell membrane through transmembrane proteins called ion channels. The channels have two major characteristics: selectivity and gating. Selectivity means that a particular ion-channel protein, when it is open, has a single "best" ion that passes through it. For example, skeletal muscles move toward contraction by first opening sodium (ion) channels. Gating means that the opening or closing of the ion channel is like the operation of a gate that opens or closes in response to particular events. Some of the sodium channels on skeletal muscles open only in response to the binding of the excitatory neurotransmitter acetylcholine, following its release from motor neurons. Overall, the sequence leading to skeletal-muscle contraction begins with the opening of "acetylcholine-gated sodium channels." Some of the other ion channels, including those involved in action potentials, are gated by changes in membrane voltage. Voltage-gated sodium channels and voltage-gated potassium channels have been studied most thoroughly.

Knowing that sodium ions are more abundant outside the neuron than inside, and that the inside of the cell has more negative charges than the outside, one can predict that the opening of sodium channels will result in the inward movement of sodium ions, which are positively charged, thus depolarizing the neuron. Correspondingly, the opening of potassium channels will allow potassium ions, more abundant inside the cell than outside, to depart from the cell, thus hyperpolarizing the neuron.

The movement of small numbers of ions across neuronal membranes causes graded potentials, small changes in membrane potential that are most important in the dendritic region of the neuron. Graded potentials spread quickly to nearby areas but decay as they spread. Graded potentials are also summable. In contrast, action potentials are due to large-scale ion movements and to the operation of voltage-gated ion channels. Action potentials are functionally important in the long, thin axonal region of neurons. Action potentials are "all-or-none" events. They do not decay and are not summable.

4. Explain how a "resting" neuron comes to have more sodium ions outside the cell than in the cytosol and to have more potassium ions inside the cell than in the extracellular fluid.

_____

_____

_____

_____

_____

_____

5. Explain what is meant by the term *threshold* in describing neuronal function.

_____

_____

_____

_____

_____

_____

6. The ions considered in studying excitable membranes contribute to the "electrochemical gradient" along the neuronal membrane. Discuss the meanings of "electro-" and "-chemical" gradients.

_____

_____

_____

_____

_____

7. Describe how two or more graded potentials can be added together.

_____

_____

_____

_____

_____

8. Describe how the refractory period makes it impossible for two or more action potentials to be added together.

_____

_____

_____

_____

_____

9. Explain why the concept of threshold does not apply to graded potentials.

_____

_____

_____

_____

_____

_____

10. Explain how the concept of threshold applies to action potentials.

_____

_____

_____

_____

_____

_____

11. Label the graph below with each of the following:

   (A) Peak of increased sodium permeability

   (B) Threshold for an action potential

   (C) Resting membrane potential

   (D) Hyperpolarization (undershoot)

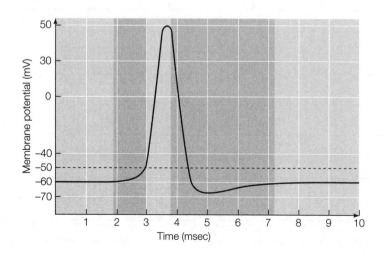

12. Certain cells in the heart have a "sodium leak" channel that allows sodium ions to leak into the cytosol. Describe what this leak does to membrane potential. Because these cells can fire action potentials, include the concept of threshold in your answer.

_____

_____

_____

_____

_____

_____

Concept 34.3 *describes the synapse, the point of communication between two neurons or between an efferent neuron and its target cell(s).*

In a small number of adjacent cells with electrical synapses, the opposing membranes are physically connected via gap junctions that allow an immediate and direct spreading of action potentials from cell to cell. Most cells, though, have a physical gap between the cells in communication and are characterized as chemical synapses.

The signal used in a chemical synapse is often called a neurotransmitter. Neurotransmitters are released from the axon terminal of the neurons sending messages. The released neurotransmitter molecules diffuse across the synaptic space and bind to receptor proteins on the dendritic end of the neurons or cells receiving the message. Upon binding to the neurotransmitter, the dendritic membrane undergoes a change in membrane potential: when the signal is excitatory, the neuron is more likely to "fire" an action potential, but if the signal is inhibitory, it hyperpolarizes and is less likely to fire an action potential. As noted earlier, the key determinant of whether or not the receiving neuron fires an action potential is whether it undergoes enough depolarization to reach the threshold for activating the voltage-gated sodium and potassium channels.

13. For a motor neuron that releases acetylcholine, describe the connection between the arrival of an action potential at the axon terminal and its release of acetylcholine.

_____

_____

_____

_____

_____

_____

14. Speculate on how the "acetylcholine message" is terminated in the neuromuscular junction.

_____

_____

_____

_____

_____

_____

15. Compare the activity of an olfactory neuron, as it samples odorant molecules in the nasal cavity, to chemical communication at a synapse.

_____

_____

_____

_____

_____

_____

_____

_____

16. Assume that learning involves changes in the effectiveness of synaptic communication. Given that assumption, predict how learning may correspond more closely to changes in metabotropic receptors (G protein–linked receptors) than to changes in ionotropic receptors (ligand-gated ion channels). Define the activity of each in your answer.

_____

_____

_____

_____

_____

_____

_____

_____

_____

Concept 34.4 *explores the sensory abilities of animals. In the process of sensory transduction, sense organs convert environmental stimuli to changes in the membrane potentials of sensory neurons, leading to information processing in the nervous system, and possible changes in behavior and physiology.*

Sensory organs, such as the nose, ears, and eyes, allow animals to collect, filter, and magnify the many stimuli encountered from moment to moment. The sensory cells are called chemoreceptors, mechanoreceptors, and photoreceptors. In addition to sensing the outside world, sensory cells monitor the internal environment in key locations, including oxygen concentration in the blood and body temperature.

The arrival of stimuli at sensory cells leads to changes in their membrane potentials, a process called sensory transduction. In this manner, sensory-transducing cells are analogous to dendritic membranes that receive chemical neurotransmitter molecules. Changes in membrane potential are due to the movement of ions across the membranes of the sensory cells/neurons, resulting in graded potentials. To reiterate the focus on sensory reception, these graded potentials are often called receptor potentials. Depending on the sensory modality involved, the receptor potentials can lead to action potentials, which allow for smelling, or graded-potentials that alter neurotransmitter release, which allow for vision and hearing. In both cases, the next neuron in the pathway is altered in its activity, and so on along the pathway into the central nervous system, leading to organismal responses. This contributes to homeostatic regulation.

Mechanoreceptor neurons respond to stretching and deformation of their membranes by altering transmembrane ion traffic, thus generating receptor potentials and initiating transduction. Among their many roles, some mechanoreceptor mechanisms are part of a system that adjusts the strength of muscle contraction so that it can more accurately match load requirements. Mechanoreceptor mechanisms also underlie hearing (audition) and vestibular functions (balance and eye movements).

Vision begins with photosensory transduction. The transducing cells, found in the retina, are the rods and cones, the latter for color vision. In the case of rods, the absorption of photons of light by pigments, such as rhodopsin, is linked to changes in the membrane potential of the photoreceptor cell. In turn, a graded depolarization of the rod changes its secretion of neurotransmitters, altering the activity of the neural pathway leading to visual perception.

The neural signals from different sensory systems are processed in various locations in the brain. (Knowing the specific details of neuroanatomical pathways is beyond the scope of the AP Biology Curriculum Framework.) Organize your studies on the many similarities of sensory receptors in detecting stimuli and then transmitting information via changes in membrane potentials.

17. Ligand-gated channels open or close when a chemical signal binds to the receptor protein associated with the channel. Another class of channels opens or closes in response to mechanical stimulation, such as the physical deformation of the cell in response to external pressure. Propose the transduction mechanism for a sensory process that is due to the operation of mechanically gated ion channels, and identify the type of sensory information provided by that sense.

_____

_____

_____

_____

_____

18. An individual olfactory neuron in a dog's nasal cavity will likely express only one of more than 1,000 odorant-receptor genes, yet it seems dogs are capable of distinguish hundreds of thousands of different odorants. Discuss some possible mechanisms by which this diverse sampling capability might occur.

_____

_____

_____

_____

_____

_____

19. "The world is one gigantic synapse," wrote one olfactory biologist. Describe the meaning of this statement using principles of synaptic communication.

_____

_____

_____

_____

_____

20. Describe the anatomical and functional relationships between the tympanic membrane; the incus, malleus, and stapes; and the cochlear fluid.

_____

_____

_____

_____

_____

21. "Ringing" noises in the ears are not uncommon after a blow to the head. Describe how physical jostling of the hearing apparatus can lead to the perception of sound that does not really exist.

_____

_____

_____

_____

_____

22. As you fill a pail with water, you manage to hold it steady under the faucet even as the mass of the filling pail becomes greater and greater. Describe the sensory feedback system that adjusts the strength of skeletal muscle contraction to match the load of the filling bucket.

_____

_____

_____

_____

_____

23. Describe how the exposure of a rod to a brief flash of light affects its membrane potential and the release of its neurotransmitter.

_____

_____

_____

_____

_____

24. Explain how and why colors are vivid in daylight but dull and grayish at night.

_____

_____

_____

_____

_____

25. Describe what you would expect to see in examining the rods and cones in nocturnal owls compared to birds that are diurnal in behavioral activity.

_____

_____

_____

_____

26. A tumor damaged the bones in a patient's middle ear on the left side of her head, impairing her sense of hearing. After the tumor was removed, the audiologist tested the patient's ability to hear by placing a tuning fork near the left pinna, and then again while touching the vibrating tuning fork to the left side of the patient's forehead. The patient could hear the tuning fork better when it was touching her forehead. When the unaffected right ear was tested, the tuning fork was heard more clearly when it was placed near the right pinna than when it was placed on the right side of the forehead. Refer to the diagram to the right to explain these observations.

Concept 34.5 *describes the vertebrate nervous system. The brain and the spinal cord make up the central nervous system and are organized in a predictable manner. The spinal cord includes neuronal tracts to the brain (afferent pathways) and from the brain (efferent pathways), as well as synaptic contacts and interneurons required for reflexes. An example is the knee-jerk reflex, wherein sensory afferent inputs about muscle and tendon stretch modify the amount of efferent motor outputs on associated muscles.*

The autonomic nervous system controls involuntary physiological functions in the body. It is subdivided into two opposing sections: the sympathetic (exercise and emergency) and the parasympathetic (resting and fed) systems. For example, heart rate is under autonomic influence, with sympathetic signals (epinephrine from the adrenal gland and norepinephrine from sympathetic terminals) accelerating heart rate as appropriate during exercise or emergency, whereas parasympathetic signals (acetylcholine from parasympathetic neurons) slow your heart rate during other times.

27. Describe the anatomical differences between sensory (afferent) and motor (efferent) neurons.

---

28. Describe the functional differences between sensory and motor neurons. Give an example of the stimulus or organ controlled by each.

_____

_____

_____

_____

_____

_____

_____

29. Describe how the following changes in the activity of the autonomic nervous system affect heart rate. Include as many anatomical and neurochemical details as you can.

    a. Increased activity in the sympathetic division:

_____

_____

_____

_____

_____

_____

_____

_____

    b. Increased activity in the parasympathetic division:

_____

_____

_____

_____

_____

_____

_____

_____

30. Discuss the general principles that speaking uses a different part of the brain than does understanding and responding to words.

_____

_____

_____

_____

_____

_____

_____

_____

Science Practices & Inquiry

In the AP Biology Curriculum Framework, there are seven **Science Practices**. In this chapter, we focus on **Science Practice 1:** The student can use representations and models to communicate scientific phenomena and solve scientific problems. More specifically, we focus on **Science Practice 1.4:** The student can use representations and models to analyze situations or solve problems qualitatively and quantitatively.

In Question 31, you will evaluate a model of a synapse and describe how nervous systems transmit information (**Learning Objective 3.45**).

31. Respond to each of the following prompts, using the following terms: graded potential, threshold, and action potential. Assume that the four axon terminals shown in the drawing represent excitatory synapses.

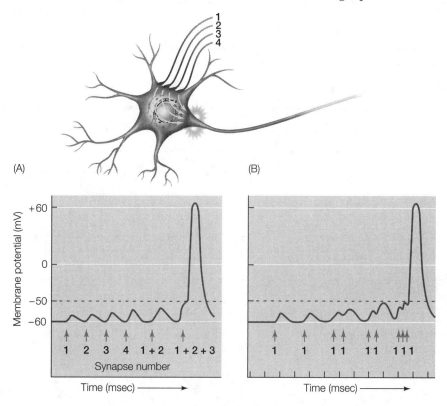

a. Explain how graph A represents spatial summation.

_____

_____

_____

_____

_____

_____

_____

_____

_____

_____

_____

b. Explain how graph B represents temporal summation.

_____

_____

_____

_____

_____

_____

_____

_____

_____

_____

c. Add a fifth inhibitory axon terminal to the diagram, close to the axon hillock, and discuss the effect of its simultaneous activity with attainment of threshold.

_____

_____

_____

_____

_____

_____

_____

_____

_____

_____

_____

_____

35 Control by the Endocrine and Nervous Systems

Chapter Outline

If you have a relative or a friend who has diabetes mellitus, you know someone with an endocrine disease. Insulin is one of many important hormones, the main chemical messengers found in the blood. Produced and released by endocrine glands, hormones travel through the blood and influence the activity of target cells—those cells that have the receptor proteins to bind hormones. The binding of the hormone and its receptor produces a biochemical change in the target cell, thus accomplishing the target cell's role as an effector in a homeostatic system. In this chapter, we will also review the nervous system as a signaling system from Chapter 34.

Big Idea 2 and **Big Idea 3** are central to understanding hormones and neural integration. The specific parts of the AP Biology curriculum covering **Big Idea 2:** Biological systems utilize free energy and molecular building blocks to grow, to reproduce, and to maintain dynamic homeostasis, include:

- **2.C.1**: Organisms use feedback mechanisms to maintain their internal environments and respond to external environmental changes.

The specific parts covering **Big Idea 3:** Living systems store, retrieve, transmit, and respond to information essential to life processes, include:

- **3.A.4**: The inheritance pattern of many traits cannot be explained by simple Mendelian genetics.

- **3.B.2**: A variety of intercellular and intracellular signal transmissions mediate gene expression.

- **3.D.2**: Cells communicate with each other through direct contact with other cells or from a distance via chemical signaling.

- **3.E.1**: Individuals can act on information and communicate it to others.

Chapter Review

Concept 35.1 *explains that neurons and endocrine cells communicate with other cells to carry out their functions of control and coordination. Most intercellular communication takes place by means of chemical signals that are released from a nerve cell (neuron) or an endocrine cell and travel to another cell, called the target cell. The signal molecules bind to receptors on the target cell, triggering it to respond. The responses can affect an animal's function, anatomy, and behavior. Muscle tissue, for example, is subject to both neuronal and endocrine system control. The two systems are specialized to carry out different types of control and coordination. The nervous system and neurons are involved when a fast response is needed, such as pulling a hand away from a hot stove. On the other hand, when a longer, slower response is needed, such as muscle-building and growth, the endocrine system takes on additional importance.*

1. Communication in the endocrine system is sometimes described as slow and broadcast signaling. Describe "slow" and "broadcast" features in the endocrine system.

_____

_____

_____

_____

_____

2. Hormones can reach all of the cells in the body, but only some of the cells change activity in response. Describe the features of a given cell that determine its ability to respond to a particular hormone.

_____

_____

_____

_____

_____

Concept 35.2 *states that hormones are chemicals released by endocrine glands into the blood. Hormones serve as messengers when they reach their receptor proteins on or in target cells. Only cells with the appropriate receptor proteins will be directly altered by the arrival of the hormone—all other (receptor-less) cells are non-target cells. Chemically, most hormones are amines, proteins, or steroids. Descriptions of two insect hormones are presented, reiterating the ancient origin of chemical signaling pathways in animals and plants.*

Receptor proteins are just as important as hormones. Cells that lack receptor proteins for hormone Q cannot show a direct response to hormone Q; it is as if Q were not even there. Receptor proteins are located either on the plasma membranes of target cells (especially true for the receptors of hormones that are proteins, e.g., insulin) or in the cytosol and nucleus of the target cells (especially true for lipid-soluble hormones, e.g., steroids). In both cases, the binding of the hormone to its receptor protein is the event that alters the biochemistry of the target cell, eliciting its "effector" responses for homeostasis.

3. Hormones can act on the cell that produces them (autocrine effect), neighboring cells (paracrine effect), and distant cells after passage in the blood (endocrine, or hormonal, effect). Discuss whether it is possible for a single molecule to work via all three effector routes.

_____

_____

_____

_____

_____

4. Discuss the water solubility and lipid solubility of protein hormones and steroid hormones.

_____

_____

_____

_____

_____

5. In humans, prolactin is a hormone that stimulates milk synthesis in the mammary glands, but in salmon, prolactin is a signal that mediates physiological changes needed for moving from saltwater to freshwater. Discuss how this particular hormone can have very different effects in different organisms.

_____

_____

_____

_____

6. The insect pictured here is the adult reproductive form of the genus *Rhodnius*. The juvenile form of these blood-sucking insects can live up to a week after being decapitated. Molting from the advanced juvenile stage to the adult form takes place seven days after a blood meal. However, when the juvenile is decapitated immediately after a blood meal, the headless juvenile does not show any apparent molting changes, even a full week later, but it is still alive. Explain what this result tells us about the source of a "molting hormone" in these animals.

_____

_____

_____

_____

_____

7. Estrogens are a group of steroid hormones that stimulate growth in many of their target cells. Propose the reasons for testing whether or not a breast cancer tumor in a human mammary gland expresses the gene for the estrogen receptor.

_____

_____

_____

_____

_____

8. Epinephrine is a hormone secreted by adrenal glands when a person is exercising or is profoundly startled. This chemical has opposite effects in different parts of the circulation: it reduces blood flow in the gastro-intestinal tract, but it increases blood flow in large skeletal muscles. Discuss the means by which one signal (epinephrine) can have these two opposite effects (vasoconstriction and vasodilation).

_____

_____

_____

_____

9. Discuss the downregulation of insulin receptors, seen in patients with type II diabetes mellitus.

_____

_____

_____

_____

Concept 35.3 *describes the hypothalamus and the pituitary gland. Along with the hypothalamus in the brain, the pituitary gland plays a central role in orchestrating hormone secretion and allowing hormonal control mechanisms to function in homeostasis. In humans, the pituitary gland has two main parts: the anterior pituitary gland (APG), located near the front of the head; and the posterior pituitary gland (PPG), located closer to the back of the head. Despite their proximity to each other, the APG is made up of specialized epithelial cells arising first in the roof of the embryonic mouth, whereas the PPG is a down-growth from the embryonic brain. The APG and PPG both secrete protein hormones; those from the PPG are released by the nerve endings of neurons from the hypothalamus, and those from the APG are released after the APG cells are stimulated by releasing hormones secreted from the hypothalamus. You will not need to memorize most of the hormonal details in this chapter, but you should work to understand how classes of hormones function.*

10. Explain why the hormones secreted by the anterior pituitary gland are called *tropic* hormones.

_____

_____

_____

_____

_____

11. The stress hormone axis is organized in the pattern shown in the diagram at the right. This axis includes a hypothalamic hormone (CRH) that stimulates secretion by the APG, an APG hormone (ACTH) that stimulates steroid synthesis (cortisol) in the adrenal glands, and adaptive responses, like glucose release from the liver and reduced immune system activity. Explain why the stress hormone axis includes a part that is in the brain. (*Hint*: Think about the many forms of stress in life.)

_____

_____

_____

_____

_____

_____

_____

_____

_____

_____

_____

_____

12. Cortisol has receptors in cells of the immune system and the liver. Cortisol receptors are also found in the hypothalamic and pituitary components of the stress hormone axis. Explain the roles of the hypothalamic and pituitary receptor proteins, referencing the concept of feedback.

_____

_____

_____

_____

_____

Concept 35.4 *provides some examples of mammalian hormones. To analyze a hormone system, review the following:*
- *Source of the hormone*
- *Stimuli that elicit the secretion of the hormone*
- *Cellular location of the hormone's receptor proteins*
- *Link between the target cell response and homeostasis*

Remember that negative feedback requires receptor proteins, too.

13. Thyroid hormones boost metabolism when environmental conditions become more difficult, for example, during cold weather. Explain how boosted metabolism can aid an animal's survival as temperatures decline.

_____

_____

_____

_____

_____

14. The condition called *goiter* often appears as a large swelling of the neck in the region of the thyroid gland. In hypothyroid goiter, the gland is greatly enlarged as it unsuccessfully attempts to make thyroid hormones. Thyroid hormones are normally secreted when the hypothalamus releases thyrotropin-releasing hormone, leading to increased secretion of thyroid-stimulating hormone from the pituitary gland. Address each of the following by circling TRUE or FALSE and then explaining your logic.

   a. Persons with hypothyroid goiter have very high levels of thyroid hormones in their blood.
      TRUE FALSE [*choose one, then explain*]

   _____

   _____

   _____

   _____

   b. Persons with hypothyroid goiter have very high levels of thyroid-stimulating hormone.
      TRUE FALSE [*choose one, then explain*]

   _____

   _____

   _____

   _____

c. Persons with hypothyroid goiter have very high levels of thyrotropin-releasing hormone.
   TRUE FALSE [*choose one, then explain*]

_____

_____

_____

_____

15. Compare the role of androgens in the development of male reproductive systems with that in female reproductive systems.

_____

_____

_____

_____

_____

16. Compare the operation of the hypothalamic–pituitary–gonadal hormone axis before and after puberty, limiting your discussion to male reproduction.

_____

_____

_____

_____

_____

_____

_____

Concept 35.5 *provides an overview of the endocrine systems of insects and other arthropods, such as crayfish and crabs. For example, many insects have antidiuretic and diuretic hormones that control excretion of water by the insect organs that serve kidney functions. Diuretic hormones promote excretion of a high volume of water. Some of the blood-sucking insects secrete diuretic hormones immediately after a blood meal. These hormones promote rapid excretion of much of the water in the blood, thereby concentrating the nutritious part of the meal (the blood proteins) in the gut. The best-understood endocrine systems in insects control growth and development through the action of several hormones: prothoracicotropic hormone (PTTH), ecdysone, and juvenile hormone.*

17. Explain how juvenile hormone affects the maturation of insects.

_____

_____

18. Arthropods (insects and crustaceans) have exoskeletons that must be shed (ecdysis) to allow the animals to grow larger. Explain how an arthropod can shed its shell.

_____

_____

_____

_____

Science Practices & Inquiry

In the AP Biology Curriculum Framework, there are seven **Science Practices**. In this chapter we focus on **Science Practice 5**: The student can perform data analysis and evaluation of evidence. More specifically, we focus on **Practice 5.1:** The student can analyze data to identify patterns or relationships.

Question 19 asks you to analyze data that indicate how organisms exchange information in response to internal changes and external cues, and which can change behavior **(Learning Objective 3.40)**.

19. The time courses of action for different hormones vary widely. Some hormones are released rapidly, establish their effects almost immediately, and are cleared from the bloodstream within minutes. Others are released slowly and remain in the blood for many hours or even days. One way of characterizing the time course of a hormone is to measure its half-life in the blood: the length of time it takes for the blood level of a given hormone to fall to half of the baseline (maximum) following its release (or injection).

The table at the right gives blood concentrations of thyroxine (T_4) following a 600-µg injection of T_4.

a. Plot these data on the grid provided.

Time (hrs)	T_4 (mg /dL)
0	7.5
6	13.7
12	12.3
24	11.1
36	10.7
48	10.3
60	9.9
72	9.5
84	9.3
96	9.1

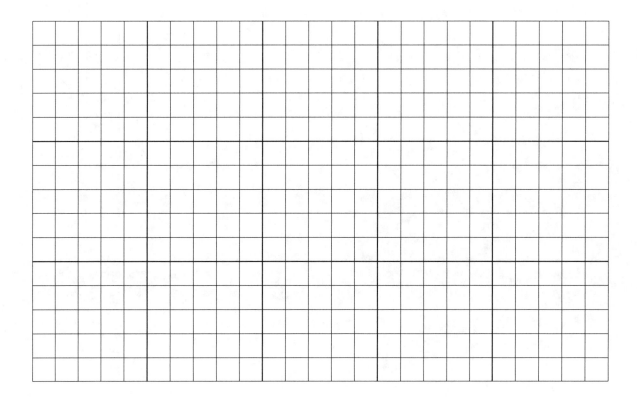

b. Consider what you know about the functioning of T_4. Would you expect this hormone to have a short half-life or a long half-life? Explain your answer.

_____

_____

_____

_____

_____

_____

_____

c. Use your graph to estimate the half-life of T_4 in the bloodstream. Give your answer to the nearest 0.1 hour.

36 Water and Salt Balance

Chapter Outline

36.1 – Kidneys Regulate the Composition of the Body Fluids
36.2 – Nitrogenous Wastes Need to Be Excreted
36.3 – Aquatic Animals Display a Wide Diversity of Relationships to Their Environment
36.4 – Dehydration Is the Principal Challenge for Terrestrial Animals
36.5 – Kidneys Adjust Water Excretion to Help Animals Maintain Homeostasis

Chapter 36 focuses on an essential homeostatic process: the maintenance of the ionic composition and the volume of the extracellular fluid, with an emphasis on the vertebrate renal system. Additional discussion includes the removal of nitrogenous wastes, the inevitable byproduct of our protein-based existence, but the importance of maintaining the extracellular fluid's composition and volume cannot be overstated.

The optimal conditions for life rarely match those of the non-living environment, and cell survival depends on maintaining the correct concentrations of ions and nutrients in the cytosol. Organisms take in nutrients, gases and minerals from the environment in order to condition the blood with the "good stuff" needed by the cells in the body. In turn, the blood conditions the extracellular fluid around the cells, delivering nutrients and oxygen and removing wastes—or the "bad stuff," including carbon dioxide.

Chapter 36 reiterates many parts of the AP Biology Curriculum Framework, especially **Big Idea 2**. The specific parts of the AP Biology curriculum covering **Big Idea 2**: Biological systems utilize free energy and molecular building blocks to grow, to reproduce, and to maintain dynamic homeostasis, include:

- **2.B.1**: Cell membranes are selectively permeable due to their structure.

- **2.D.2**: Homeostatic mechanisms reflect both common ancestry and divergence due to adaptation in different environments.

Chapter Review

Concept 36.1 *establishes the homeostatic emphasis of studying salt and water balance. Osmotic equilibrium, the balancing of dissolved solutes inside the cell with the concentration in the extracellular fluid, provides a starting point for this exploration. Note that osmotic equilibrium or balancing refers only to the number of dissolved solutes, not to the chemical identities of the solutes. For example, the higher concentration of potassium ions inside cells and the higher concentration of sodium ions outside cells are partially offsetting each other when the osmotic balance between the inside and outside of the cell is considered. Osmotic imbalance, depending on whether solutes are more abundant inside or outside the cell, can lead to water loss, or gain, respectively, and impairment or even death of the cell.*

Animals are classified as osmoregulators if they actively regulate the osmolarity of the extracellular fluid and osmoconformers if they do not. Freshwater and terrestrial environments compel organisms to be osmoregulators, and marine invertebrates are the most common examples of osmoconformers. At extreme concentrations of salts, for example, in lakes of greater salinity than is present in seawater, failure to osmoregulate will lead to shrinking of cell volume and eventually death of the cells.

The ratio of the osmolarity of the urine to the osmolarity of the plasma (U/P ratio) is a simple value that describes an organism's capacity to concentrate its waste. Any time this ratio exceeds 1.0, the kidneys, by excreting urine that is saltier than the plasma, are making the plasma more dilute. Conversely, when the urine is less salty than the plasma, the kidneys are making the plasma osmolarity more concentrated.

1. Describe the sequence of osmotic changes that might occur in a marine invertebrate of limited osmoregulatory capacity when it is trapped in a tide pool of ocean water after high tide. Assume that the liquid in the pool, over the course of the next six hours, undergoes the situations described below.

   a. Salinity in the pool remains equal to that of seawater.

   _____

   _____

   _____

   _____

   _____

   b. Rain falls, and the fresh water decreases the salinity of the pool below that of ocean.

   _____

   _____

   _____

   _____

   _____

   c. Water evaporates, increasing the salinity of the pool above that of the ocean water.

   _____

   _____

   _____

   _____

   _____

2. Protein structure can be altered by changes in pH, possibly impairing cellular functions. Bicarbonate ions play an important role as a buffer system to maintain a constant pH in the bloodstream. The kidneys play an important role in reducing the amount of bicarbonate ions lost in the urine. Write the bicarbonate/ carbonic acid dissociation equation, and explain its significance with respect to pH in blood.

   _____

   _____

   _____

   _____

   _____

   _____

3. When ascending to high altitude, mountain climbers can suffer from "respiratory alkalosis" as they hyperventilate abnormally, reducing the level of carbon dioxide in the blood. Explain the relationship between an abnormally fast breathing rate (hyperventilation) and acid-base balance in the tissues.

   _____

   _____

   _____

   _____

   _____

Concept 36.2 *describes nitrogenous waste products associated with amino acid metabolism. The hydrolysis of amino acids releases ammonia, a fairly toxic waste material. For animals that have extensive contact with water, such as bony fishes, diffusion of ammonia from the blood to the water moving over the gills is adequate to remove the ammonia from the body. Other animals, like mammals, convert ammonia to less toxic materials, including urea, while still others, such as birds, convert nitrogenous wastes to uric acid.*

4. Identify the number of nitrogen atoms in one molecule of ammonia, one molecule of urea, and one molecule of uric acid. For the complete catabolism of a protein with 32 amino acids, state how many molecules of ammonia, urea, and uric acid would be produced, assuming that three organisms under study each produce only one of the three nitrogenous wastes listed above.

_____

_____

_____

_____

_____

_____

_____

5. Compare the amount of water required as a solute for the elimination of the three types of nitrogenous waste.

_____

_____

_____

_____

_____

_____

_____

_____

Concept 36.3 *discusses the varied osmotic relationships that animals have with their environments. Animals with body fluids of osmolarity equal to the fluid they live in are said to be isosmotic to their environment, a description limited to marine invertebrates. The osmolarity of bony fish in the ocean is always less than the osmolarity of the ocean water; that is, the fish's fluids are hyposmotic to the ocean. In contrast, all freshwater fish living in an environment of very low osmolarity are hyperosmotic, compared to freshwater.*

6. Propose an explanation for the fact that the body fluids of saltwater fish are more dilute than seawater.

_____

_____

_____

_____

_____

_____

7. Compare the challenges that freshwater and saltwater fish face with respect to the gain and loss of water and ions in their environments.

_____

_____

_____

_____

_____

_____

8. Describe how "water appetite" (the drinking of environmental fluids) changes during the full life cycle of salmon that hatch in freshwater, mature in the ocean, and return to freshwater to mate.

_____

_____

_____

_____

_____

_____

Concept 36.4 *details the risks of dehydration faced by terrestrial animals and describes some of the behavioral, anatomical, and physiological adaptations that enhance their success in arid environments.*

9. Kangaroo rats are rodents found in arid environments where access to water is extremely limited. Describe one of each of the following types of evolutionary adaptations found in these animals.

a. Behavioral:

_____

_____

_____

_____

b. Skin and digestive tract:

_____

_____

_____

_____

c. Renal:

_____

_____

_____

_____

Concept 36.5 *details how the kidneys adjust the amount of water excreted in urine in order to support the homeostasis of ionic composition and volume of the extracellular fluid, and thereby protect the appropriate content and volume of the cytosol in the cells. Hormonal mechanisms serve the regulation of kidney function in mammals.*

Following excess water ingestion and absorption, blood volume becomes abnormally high, so blood pressure increases. In such conditions, the human kidney responds to reduce blood volume and blood pressure by increasing the excretion of copious, dilute urine.

Following blood loss and/or dehydration, a decrease in blood pressure is sensed by baroreceptors in the human kidney and by baroreceptor (pressure-sensitive) neurons in blood vessels. As a result, two hormone systems release signals that increase the reabsorption of fluid from the renal filtrate, thus reducing the volume of urine excreted and conserving the body's water. One such hormone system involves anti-diuretic hormone (ADH), which is secreted from the posterior pituitary gland in response to neural reflexes. These reflexes are activated by decreased blood pressure and by increased osmolarity of body fluids, typical of what occurs during dehydration. The hormone's name describes its action: anti-diuresis, or more plainly, reduction in urine excretion. The resulting ADH-induced increase in the kidneys' water channels (aquaporins) makes it possible for water to be retained at higher levels in the body. A second hormone system responding to dehydration involves hormones from kidneys, liver, and adrenal glands, and is not described here.

Water conservation in amphibians is similar to that in humans. It occurs via an alteration in the water permeability of part of the nephron, a structural unit of the kidney, in response to hormones. In insects, by contrast, the Malpighian tubules form and excrete urine-like fluid from the blood in the open circulatory system.

10. Label the diagram at the right with the following:

(A) Collecting duct

(B) Filtration occurs here

(C) Proximal convoluted tubule

(D) Distal convoluted tubule

(E) Ascending limb of loop of Henle

(F) Descending limb of loop of Henle

(G) Vasa recta

(H) Glucose reabsorption occurs here

(I) ADH receptors are found here

(J) Water permeability is always low here

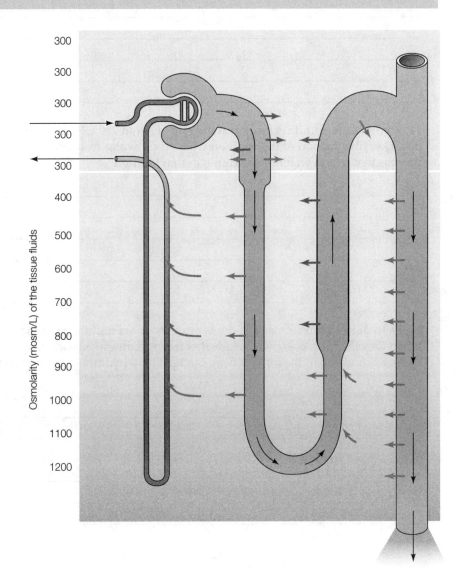

11. Describe the location and operation of Malpighian tubules for the types of organisms that utilize these structures for processing ions and nitrogenous waste.

_____

_____

_____

_____

12. Describe how the rectum of an organism with Malpighian tubules further process ions and nitrogenous wastes, including how these processes affect organismal water balance.

_____

_____

_____

_____

13. Explain how ADH secretion is activated, and describe the consequences of ADH action on its targets.

_____

_____

_____

_____

_____

_____

14. For humans, filtrate is formed at the rate of about 180 L/day, yet urine excretion is only about 2 L/day. Describe the part of the nephron where most water reabsorption (~75%) takes place, and describe the process that drives water reabsorption in that location.

_____

_____

_____

_____

_____

_____

15. Dehydration causes many of the symptoms of overindulging in the consumption of ethanol, even when the ethanol is present at relatively low concentrations, such as in beer. Explain how the consumption of so much water, in the form of beer, can lead to dehydration. Include ADH in your answer.

_____

_____

_____

_____

_____

_____

Science Practices & Inquiry

In the AP Biology Curriculum Framework, there are seven **Science Practices**. In this chapter, we focus on **Science Practice 7:** The student is able to connect and relate knowledge across various scales, concepts, and representations in and across domains.

In Question 16, you are asked to connect what you know about osmotic gradients, water movements, glucose reabsorption from renal filtrate, and neurobiology.

16. As he prepared for his AP test, James found himself making several trips to the kitchen, thirsty and hungry, and frequently using the bathroom. Distracted from his studying, he found the data set at the right in a lab notebook his mom wrote in the 1980s.

Plasma glucose concentration (mg/100 mL plasma)	Reabsorption rate of glucose from renal filtrate (mg/min)
0	0
100	100
200	200
300	300
400	400
500	400
600	400

a. Graph the data, placing "glucose concentration" on the x axis and "reabsorption rate" on the y axis, and connect the points with a curve. Label all parts of your graph.

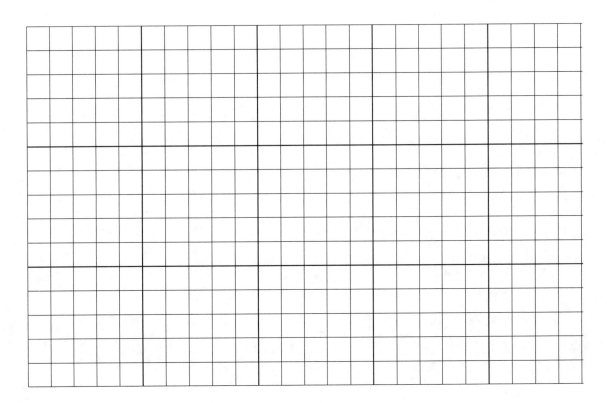

b. Write a caption that explains what is happening in your graph.

_____

_____

c. Examine the data to determine whether or not the phenomenon of saturation can be demonstrated, and state where on the graph you are focusing. Explain what is being saturated and where in the nephron saturation might occur.

_____

_____

_____

_____

_____

_____

_____

d. Present and discuss the evidence that James might be suffering from diabetes mellitus, and relate his symptoms to excessive loss of sodium ions from his body.

_____

_____

_____

_____

_____

_____

_____

37 Animal Reproduction

Chapter Outline

37.1 – Sexual Reproduction Depends on Gamete Formation and Fertilization
37.2 – The Mammalian Reproductive System Is Hormonally Controlled
37.3 – Reproduction Is Integrated with the Life Cycle

Reproduction is a biological imperative for any species of living organism; without reproduction, there are no new individuals, and without new individuals, evolution is not possible. Observe any parents with their offspring and you will see that reproduction is also miraculous, as new individuals come into being, fresh and full of opportunity.

Like plants, animals can reproduce asexually, efficiently making copies of themselves; or sexually, exchanging genetic material with partners to produce offspring with new combinations of adaptations.

Chapter 37 addresses **Big Idea 2** and **Big Idea 3**. The specific parts of the AP Biology curriculum covering **Big Idea 2:** Biological systems utilize free energy and molecular building blocks to grow, to reproduce, and to maintain dynamic homeostasis, include:

- **2.D.3**: Biological systems are affected by disruptions to their dynamic homeostasis.

- **2.D.4**: Plants and animals have a variety of chemical defenses against infections that affect dynamic homeostasis.

The specific parts covering **Big Idea 3:** Living systems store, retrieve, transmit, and respond to information essential to life processes, include:

- **3.A.2**: In eukaryotes, heritable information is passed to the next generation via processes that include the cell cycle and mitosis or meiosis plus fertilization.

- **3.D.2**: Cells communicate with each other through direct contact with other cells or from a distance via chemical signaling.

Chapter Review

Concept 37.1 *describes gamete formation and fertilization. Although sexual reproduction via budding and fission does occur in a few animals, there are simple evolutionary limits when making high-fidelity copies of one genotype/ phenotype. Therefore, most animal reproduction occurs via sexual interactions, though a few species, such as aphids, can alternate between asexual and sexual reproduction.*

The meiotic production of haploid gametes by sexually reproducing animals occurs in a process called gametogenesis. Female gametes, called ova or eggs, are generally much larger than the male gametes, typically called sperm. Gametogenesis of ova is called oogenesis and of sperm, spermatogenesis. In mammals, oogenesis is dependent on the supply of diploid primary oocytes, produced by mitosis during embryonic development, whereas diploid spermatogonia, the male equivalent of the primary oocytes, are mitotically produced throughout adult life. The meiotic progression to haploid sperm occurs within the male gonads, the testes, whereas the progression to haploid secondary oocytes occurs during each ovarian cycle (the menstrual cycle), with the final meiotic step occurring only after fertilization. The interaction of the egg with a single sperm causes the final meiotic step to progress with the resulting union of two haploid nuclei and the formation of a zygote.

The union of sperm and egg is called fertilization. This fusion might occur externally, as in the well-studied sea urchin, or internally, as in all mammals. The molecular "recognition" of a sperm by an egg is chemically mediated for precision and accuracy. Next, the haploid nuclei are brought into close proximity. They fuse to convert the former two haploid nuclei to a single diploid nucleus, a zygote, the single cell that gives rise to new life.

For most animals, the genetic sex of the offspring is determined at the time of fertilization and is dependent on which sex chromosomes are brought together. Exceptions exist, of course, including temperature-dependent sex determination in turtles and crocodilians and sequential hermaphrodism known among several coral fishes.

1. Fisherman used to regard sea stars (starfish) as unwelcome competition for the oysters they sought to bring to market, because sea stars prey on oysters. Accordingly, any sea stars caught while dredging for oysters were cut into pieces and thrown overboard to feed the fishes. Describe how this likely generated the opposite of the desired effect.

_____

_____

_____

2. Some species of aphids alternate between asexual reproduction during spring and summer and sexual reproduction during autumn. Discuss the benefits to aphids of this pattern, in light of the facts that the aphids thrive on fresh green vegetation and only fertilized eggs are able to survive the cold months of winter.

_____

_____

_____

3. Explain whether the budding that enables *Hydra* to reproduce occurs by mitosis or meiosis. Describe this process as it applies to these cnidarians.

_____

_____

_____

_____

_____

_____

_____

4. Mitochondria appear to have once been an independent form of life that formed a symbiosis with a cell ancestral to the eukaryotic cell. Discuss a mother's and a father's likely contributions to the mitochondria of their offspring's cells and describe the cellular process leading up to that result.

_____

_____

_____

_____

5. In humans, aging leads to reduction and then cessation of female reproductive potential, whereas older men remain reproductively able. Provide a detailed description of these differences in reproductive potential.

_____

_____

_____

6. Clownfish, often found as symbionts with anemones, are "sequential" hermaphrodites. Explain.

_____

_____

_____

_____

7. Describe two events in the mechanism that blocks polyspermy in sexually reproducing animals.

_____

_____

_____

_____

_____

_____

_____

_____

8. Some animals deposit their zygotes into the external environment for development, while others retain zygotes internally for development. Provide one example of each pattern, and describe it.

_____

_____

_____

_____

_____

_____

_____

Concept 37.2 *examines the sources and the actions of hormones that coordinate reproductive physiology and behavior. There are many hormones to consider, but the AP Biology Curriculum Framework does not include all of them. Focus your efforts on understanding how the hormones work together as a coordinated whole, through cell communication. Review your notes on signal transduction to gain insight on how the target cells respond to the arrival of hormones.*

In male mammals, spermatogenesis begins at puberty and takes place in the seminiferous tubules in the testes. Hormonal support, from the androgens (including testosterone) and the gonadotropins (including follicle-stimulating hormone), are needed by the Sertoli cells in the tubules to support spermatogenesis. The Sertoli cells respond to the hormones by metabolically supporting the mitotic activity of the spermatogonia and the meiotic events that follow to yield sperm. Following maturation in the epididymis of the testis, sperm are mixed with other glandular products along the reproductive tract, forming semen, which is ejaculated through the penis during orgasm.

In females, oogenesis takes place in the ovaries. Ovarian follicles surround each growing primary oocyte, supporting its growth and maturation, and then the follicle bursts at the time of ovulation, releasing the oocyte near the reproductive tract. In some animals, copulation induces ovulation. Other animals ovulate on a copulation-independent schedule set by oocyte maturation. In either case, ovulated oocytes are swept into the oviducts, where fertilization occurs if sperm are present. Pregnancy requires steroid-hormone support for the uterus. There are numerous methods for avoiding fertilization and pregnancy.

9. For each of the following glandular sources, name at least one hormone that influences reproduction, and describe the conditions that favor secretion of that hormone.

a. Hypothalamus: _____

_____

_____

b. Anterior pituitary gland (APG): _____

_____

_____

c. Ovaries: _____

_____

_____

d. Testes: _____

_____

_____

e. Placenta: _____

_____

_____

10. For each of these glandular sources, describe the target and the method of transduction at the target cells for the hormones you provided in Question 9.

a. Hypothalamus: _____

_____

_____

b. Anterior pituitary gland (APG): _____

_____

_____

c. Ovaries: _____

_____

_____

d. Testes: _____

_____

_____

e. Placenta: _____

_____

_____

11. Describe the tissue source of testosterone in males, and propose two methods for determining which cells in the body are the "target cells" for testosterone effects.

_____

_____

_____

_____
_____
_____
_____

12. Negative feedback is characteristic of most endocrine pathways, including female reproductive physiology. However, there is a brief period in females when that feedback process suddenly reverses. Describe that time, and explain what happens.

_____
_____
_____
_____
_____

13. Draw two curves on Part C of the diagram below to show the cycles of estrogen and progesterone synthesis and release. Explain how these hormones cause the physical changes that occur in the reproductive tract, shown in Part D.

_____   (A) FSH and LH secreted by the anterior pituitary
_____
_____
_____   ⑦
_____
_____   Luteinizing
_____   hormone (LH)
_____   Follicle-stimulating
_____   hormone (FSH)
_____   ⑥
_____   ① ⑩ ⑭
_____
_____   (B) Events in the ovary
_____
_____   Several   Single mature Ovulation   Corpus luteum
_____   follicles start follicle
_____   developing
_____   ④   ⑧
_____   Follicular phase   Luteal phase
_____
_____   (C) Ovarian hormones
_____
_____
_____
_____   (D) Events in the endometrium of the uterus   Highly proliferated and
_____   vascularized endometrium
_____   ⑪   ⑬
_____   Bleeding and sloughing
_____   (menstruation)
_____   ③

Thickness of endometrium

0   7   14   21   28
Day of menstrual cycle

14. Steroid hormone levels, especially those of estrogen and progesterone, support the high metabolic activity in the uteruses of pregnant women. In the first trimester (the first three months of pregnancy) these hormones are synthesized in one anatomical location. During the second and third trimesters, they are synthesized in another location. Describe this sequence.

_____

_____

_____

_____

_____

_____

15. Nursing babies evoke a rapid hormone reflex (oxytocin secretion) in their mothers, greatly enhancing milk release from the mammary glands. Discuss the evolutionarily adaptive value of using rapid hormonal reflexes to quiet a hungry baby.

_____

_____

_____

_____

_____

_____

_____

16. Describe three categories of contraception methods. For each, describe where and how pregnancy is prevented.

_____

_____

_____

_____

_____

_____

_____

_____

17. Describe the primary risk involved in letting parents select the sex of their babies.

_____

_____

_____

_____

_____

_____

Concept 37.3 *discusses how reproduction is an essential part of an animal's life cycle. A full understanding of reproduction often involves asking questions about the life cycle. Does reproduction place limits on the rest of the life cycle? Does the life cycle compel reproduction to take place in certain ways? In humans the reproductive cycle is rigidly linked with mating, which leads directly to fertilization. Many animals, however, have evolved mechanisms of decoupling successive steps in the reproductive process, so that the time that elapses between one step and the next is flexible. Such mechanisms increase options for certain steps to be coordinated with environmental conditions independent of other steps.*

18. For a marine fish enthusiast with a large aquarium, discuss whether it would be better to have semelparous or iteroparous species of fish. Explain your answer.

_____

_____

_____

_____

_____

_____

_____

_____

_____

_____

_____

_____

19. Discuss embryonic diapause as a strategy for living in seasonal environments.

_____

_____

_____

_____

_____

_____

_____

_____

_____

_____

_____

_____

Science Practices & Inquiry

In the AP Biology Curriculum Framework, there are seven **Science Practices**. In this chapter, we focus on **Science Practice 7:** The student is able to connect and relate knowledge across various scales, concepts, and representations in and across domains. More specifically, we focus on **Science Practice 7.2:** The student can connect concepts in and across domain(s) to generalize or extrapolate in and/or across enduring understandings and/or big ideas.

Question 20 asks you to connect how organisms use negative feedback to maintain their internal environments (**Learning Objective 2.16**).

20. The receptors for steroid hormones are similar enough that they sometimes bind to the "wrong" steroids. Prolonged use of prednisone, a cortisol-like drug used to treat inflammation, could possibly reduce fertility. On the partial model shown for a section of the three-part hormone axis regulating the female reproductive tract, show three locations where the effects of prolonged exposure to cortisol would be likely to become apparent, leading to a lack of menstrual cycles (amenorrhea), and describe what hormonal changes an endocrinologist would see in the blood of an affected person. (*Hint*: think about where steroid-hormone receptors are needed for negative feedback to function.)

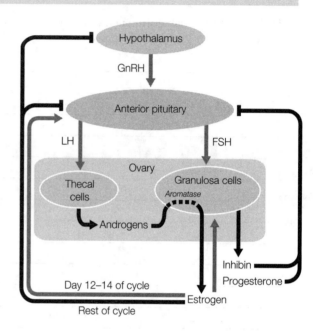

_____
_____
_____
_____
_____
_____
_____
_____
_____
_____
_____
_____
_____
_____
_____
_____
_____
_____
_____
_____

38 Animal Development

Chapter Outline

Differential gene expression acts to organize early development. Even though every cell has the same set of instructions (DNA), the specific genes expressed in each cell depend on the internal and external signals present in and around that cell. Cytoplasmic factors in the zygote, most carried over from the ovum, play important roles in setting up the signaling cascades that orchestrate the major processes of development: determination, differentiation, morphogenesis, and growth. Throughout this chapter, we will see how these processes underlie the development of a multicellular individual from a single cell. The specific names of the developmental phases and embryonic stages are not part of the AP Biology Curriculum Framework, but differential gene expression is a recurring theme.

Chapter 38, which shows how cell communication is fundamental to growth and development, includes three of the four **Big Ideas**. The specific parts of the AP Biology curriculum covering **Big Idea 2:** Biological systems utilize free energy and molecular building blocks to grow, to reproduce, and to maintain dynamic homeostasis, include:

- **2.E.1**: Timing and coordination of specific events are necessary for the normal development of an organism, and these events are regulated by a variety of mechanisms.

The specific parts covering **Big Idea 3:** Living systems store, retrieve, transmit, and respond to information essential to life processes, include:

- **3.B.1**: Gene regulation leads to differential gene expression, leading to cell specialization.

- **3.B.2**: A variety of intercellular and intracellular signal transmissions mediate gene expression.

- **3.D.2**: Cells communicate with each other through direct contact with other cells or from a distance via chemical signaling.

The specific parts addressing **Big Idea 4:** Biological systems interact, and these systems and their interactions possess complex properties, include:

- **4.A.3**: Interactions between external stimuli and regulated gene expression result in specialization of cells, tissues, and organs.

Chapter Review

Concept 38.1 *introduces fertilization as the activation point for the development of a new embryo. The tiny sperm from the male parent and the considerably larger egg from the female parent do not contribute equally to all aspects of the newly formed zygote. For example, the egg is typically the source of mitochondria; all of your mitochondria are of maternal origin. Immediately following fertilization (i.e., the union of maternal and paternal haploid DNA), a complex cascade of events occurs within the cytoplasm. Only a limited set of genes is transcribed during the early cell divisions, with signals controlling gene expression emanating from the cytoplasm.*

1. Draw and then describe an unfertilized frog egg. Include its cortical cytoplasm, its animal pole, and its vegetal pole. Describe the development of anatomical axes that will appear after fertilization happens and development begins.

_____

_____

_____

_____

_____

2. Describe the contributions of the sperm at fertilization, including a brief discussion of the sperm's function in launching early development.

_____

_____

_____

_____

_____

_____

Concept 38.2 *further describes the events following fertilization. This is a period of intense cell division with little to no increase in size of the mass of cells (i.e., the newer cells are smaller and smaller). As the cells divide, a ball of cells forms, which becomes the hollow ball of cells called the blastula.*

3. Distinguish between the two terms in each pair:

a. Zygote and blastula: _____

_____

_____

_____

b. Blastula and blastocyst: _____

_____

_____

_____

c. Incomplete and complete cleavage: _____

_____

_____

_____

Use the diagram of a blastula at the right to answer Questions 4 and 5.

4. Label the ectoderm, endoderm, and mesoderm.

5. Using the appropriate letter from the list below, label the cells in the blastula that will become each organ or system.

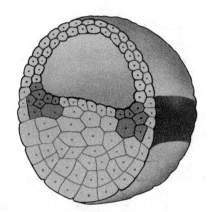

(A) Nervous system

(B) Muscular system

(C) Digestive system

(D) Epidermis

(E) Kidneys and connective tissues

(F) Lungs

6. Pluripotent cells can form any type of cell in an organism's body. Explain why the earliest cells of the blastocyst are pluripotent, and discuss their value in biomedical research.

_____

_____

_____

_____

_____

_____

Concept 38.3 *explains how gastrulation forms the three layers underlying the body plan. The specifics of which cells and which layers form and fold is complex and well-studied, but this is not included in the AP Biology Curriculum Framework.*

The ectoderm is the outer germ layer, formed from the cells remaining on the outside of the embryo. The ectoderm gives rise to the nervous system, including the eyes and ears, and forms the outer or epidermal layer of skin. The innermost germ layer, the endoderm, forms from cells that migrate to the inside of the embryo during gastrulation, later yielding the linings of the digestive and respiratory tracts, the urinary bladder, and other internal organs. The middle layer, the mesoderm, is made of cells that migrate between the endoderm and the ectoderm. The mesoderm gives rise to the blood vessels, muscles, bones, heart, and several other organs. These distinctions result from differential gene expression.

7. Draw a simple diagram of a zygote, blastula, and gastrula of a sea urchin.

Zygote	Blastula	Gastrula

8. While there are many differences between gastrulation of the sea urchin, frog, and chicken, there are also many similarities. Identify three broad similarities and comment on the evolutionary heritage involved.

9. Describe how the formation of mesoderm and endoderm differs between sea urchins and chickens. Discuss which is more similar to human tissue formation.

Concept 38.4 *describes how the major organ systems form through inductive tissue interactions. Formation of the nervous system is used as an example. Once the notochord has formed from mesodermal tissue, it plays a critical role in inducing neurulation, the formation of the neural tube. There are many details in this section, but most are beyond the scope of the AP Biology Curriculum Framework.*

10. Explain how the nervous system arises from ectodermal tissue.

11. Your nerve cells are buried deep underneath muscle tissue, the latter being of endoderm origin. Describe how nerves are formed.

12. Research on signaling proteins in development show that a protein suspected to be involved in a developmental process must be shown to be both necessary and sufficient. Explain.

_____
_____
_____
_____
_____
_____
_____
_____
_____
_____
_____

13. Segmentation can be easily seen in many animals, such as annelids (segmented worms) and arthropods (crabs and insects). Are humans segmented, and if so, how?

_____
_____
_____
_____
_____
_____
_____
_____
_____
_____
_____

Concept 38.5 *examines how the growing embryos of birds and mammals gain nutrition, with comparison of the membranes and exchange surfaces included.*

14. In the diagram of a chick embryo below, label the four membranes (circled) and the embryo, allantois, amniotic cavity, and gut.

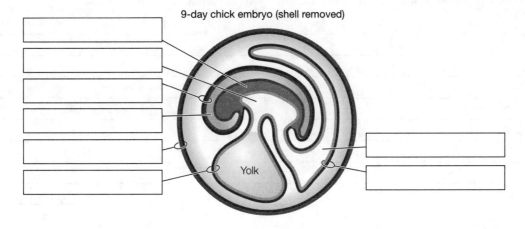

9-day chick embryo (shell removed)

Yolk

15. Describe the similarities between the mammalian placenta and the chicken egg.

_____
_____
_____
_____
_____
_____
_____
_____
_____
_____

Concept 38.6 *addresses the continuation of development throughout life. Some animals look like their parents immediately and undergo direct development to reach full size. Others appear very different and spend part of their lives in one or more forms as they undergo indirect development.*

16. Is human growth and development a form of direct or indirect development? Provide examples in your answer.

_____
_____
_____
_____
_____
_____
_____
_____
_____
_____

17. Many organisms have larval forms. Describe two advantages of having this.

_____
_____
_____
_____
_____
_____
_____
_____
_____
_____
_____

Science Practices & Inquiry

In the AP Biology Curriculum Framework, there are seven **Science Practices**. In this chapter, we focus on **Science Practice 1:** The student can use representations and models to communicate scientific phenomena and solve scientific problems. More specifically, we focus on **Science Practice 1.3:** The student can refine representations and models of natural or man-made phenomena and systems in the domain.

Question 18 asks you to refine representations to illustrate how interactions between external stimuli and gene expression result in specialization of cells, tissues, and organs (**Learning Objective 4.7**).

18. Below is a set of early embryological drawings from several different organisms. A novice embryologist has placed them in an incorrect order. In the blanks below, place them in their correct order, and name the primary feature in each diagram.

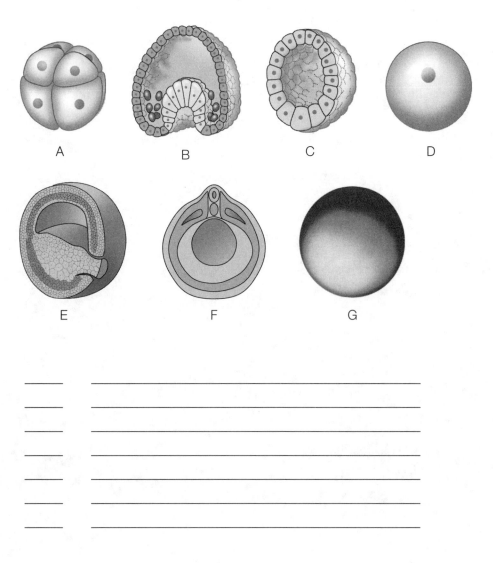

A   B   C   D

E   F   G

_____   _____

_____   _____

_____   _____

_____   _____

_____   _____

_____   _____

_____   _____

39 Immunology: Animal Defense Systems

Chapter Outline

39.1 – Animals Use Innate and Adaptive Mechanisms to Defend Themselves against Pathogens
39.2 – Innate Defenses Are Nonspecific
39.3 – The Adaptive Immune Response Is Specific
39.4 – The Adaptive Humoral Immune Response Involves Specific Antibodies
39.5 – The Adaptive Cellular Immune Response Involves T Cells and Their Receptors

To maintain health and prevent infection, multicellular organisms can mount a coordinated defense against invasion by pathogenic organisms. Pathogenic invaders disrupt homeostasis in their hosts, sometimes even to the point of death. Animal and plant defense systems are abundantly represented in the AP Biology Curriculum Framework, so this chapter is especially relevant to exam preparation. Though this chapter is extremely detailed, memorization of these details (e.g., the structure of specific antibodies) is not expected. Rather, focus on how these ideas are united in immunology.

There are two major levels of defense: innate immunity and adaptive immunity. Diverse, nonspecific, innate defenses protect most animals against invasion. For example, salty skin with its own flora is not often a hospitable environment for additional bacterial growth. In addition, natural killer cells roam the body, attacking invaders as they are encountered and recognized chemically as foreign.

Most multicellular organisms have adaptive immune responses. A major conceptual premise is that an organism's adaptive immunity must distinguish between self and nonself so only the latter will be subject to attack. Activated by the chemical recognition of invaders, B and T lymphocytes are key players in adaptive immunity. Host cells coordinate defense by using chemical signals. Adaptive immunity expressly allows an organism to respond quickly and emphatically to specific pathogens that had been previously encountered and defeated, a sort of chemical memory that thwarts reinfection and forms the basis of modern vaccination practices.

Chapter 39 spans **Big Idea 2**, **Big Idea 3**, and **Big Idea 4**. The specific parts of the AP Biology curriculum covering **Big Idea 2**: Biological systems utilize free energy and molecular building blocks to grow, to reproduce, and to maintain dynamic homeostasis, include:

- **2.D.3**: Biological systems are affected by disruptions to their dynamic homeostasis.

- **2.D.4**: Plants and animals have a variety of chemical defenses against infections that affect dynamic homeostasis.

The specific parts addressing **Big Idea 3**: Living systems store, retrieve, transmit, and respond to information essential to life processes, include:

- **3.D.2**: Cells communicate with each other through direct contact with other cells or from a distance via chemical signaling.

The specific parts covering **Big Idea 4**: Biological systems interact, and these systems and their interactions possess complex properties, include:

- **4.C.1**: Variation in molecular units provides cells with a wider range of functions.

Chapter Review

Concept 39.1 *describes the primary differences between innate (nonspecific) and adaptive (specific) immunity. White blood cells, including phagocytes, leucocytes, and natural killer cells, are involved in both forms of immunity. Cytokines are chemical messengers that coordinate activities of immune-system components.*

1. Identify and label each of the following immune mechanisms as innate (I) or adaptive (A).

____ Stomach acid that destroys ingested bacteria

____ T-cells that destroy viruses

____ Skin defenses that prevent viruses from entering

____ Defensins that destroy invaders with plasma membranes

____ Interferons that prevent viruses from spreading between neighboring cells

____ Antibodies that prevent reinfection by chicken pox

2. White blood cells can be classified as phagocytes or lymphocytes. Explain the similarities and differences between these classifications.

a. Similarities: _____
_____
_____
_____

b. Differences: _____
_____
_____
_____

Concept 39.2 *focuses on the innate (nonspecific) immune system, including the skin, mucus, lysozymes, and defensins. Other innate defenses involving proteins and cellular defenses include phagocytes, natural killer cells, complement proteins, and interferons. Many of these defenses also cause inflammation with more blood flow, swelling due to increased intercellular fluids, and release of chemical signals, which can enhance protective defenses.*

3. Describe how the innate immune system meets a pathogen in each of the following scenarios:

a. A pathogen lands on your skin. _____
_____
_____
_____

b. A pathogen lands in your mouth. _____
_____
_____
_____
_____

c. A pathogen is ingested from a drink of water. _____
_____
_____
_____
_____

4. Describe natural killer cells, and explain how they can be part of both the innate and adaptive immune systems.

_____

_____

_____

_____

_____

_____

5. Describe how the inflammation response aids in fighting infection.

_____

_____

_____

_____

_____

_____

6. Many people take antihistamines to control allergies. Explain how these drugs can reduce allergic responses.

_____

_____

_____

_____

_____

_____

7. Explain how interferons are involved in cell communication. Include sources and targets in your answer.

_____

_____

_____

_____

_____

8. Synthetic cortisol-like drugs (agonists) are often injected into swollen and painful bone-joints (e.g., tennis elbow, pitcher's arm, and arthritic knees). Describe how the immune system responds to the injected agonists, and discuss how this can provide some relief to the patient.

_____

_____

_____

_____

_____

_____

9. Suppose that you were exposed to a newly synthesized "artificial" bacterium and all signs of the bacterium were gone from your body within 24 hours. Assume further that this bacterium is novel enough that it does not share chemical identity signals with other bacteria. Given the time frame in this scenario, decide if your immune system's victory over this bacterium was via innate or adaptive immunity. Be sure to explain some of the ways the bacterium was defeated.

_____

_____

_____

_____

_____

_____

Concept 39.3 *introduces the four premises for adaptive response: specificity, diversity, self-recognition, and memory. Activated T-cells destroy foreign invaders displaying specific antigens. Upon exposure, B cells synthesize specific antibodies that recognize upwards of 10 million different antigens. This diversity is created by DNA changes and mutations after B cells are formed in the bone marrow. Self-recognition is important, so your immune system's attacking cells do not harm the self cells; the latter possess major histocompatibility complex (MHC) proteins on their surfaces as a form of chemical identification.*

10. Define antigens and antibodies.

_____

_____

_____

_____

_____

_____

11. Explain how an individual bacterium can have several antigens.

_____

_____

_____

_____

_____

_____

12. Explain how a single molecule (polypeptide or polysaccharide) can include multiple antigen sites.

_____

_____

_____

_____

_____

_____

_____

13. Severe combined immunodeficiency (SCID) is a genetic disease in which T and B lymphocytes are nonfunctional. Describe a transplant that might establish the production of normal lymphocytes in a patient.

_____

_____

_____

_____

_____

_____

_____

14. Describe two types of disease that are of special concern in SCID.

_____

_____

_____

_____

_____

_____

_____

_____

_____

_____

_____

15. After winter break at a boarding school, many students get sick with the flu or other viruses. Describe the process that often results in adults being more reisitant to sickness than younger people are.

_____

_____

_____

_____

_____

_____

16. Explain how humoral immunity differs from cellular identity, giving a brief example of each type.

_____

_____

_____

_____

_____

_____

Concept 39.4 *describes that the humoral immune response depends on the production of antibodies by the B cells. Antigen-antibody reactions activate effector responses to deactivate the pathogen.*

17. Though you have probably never been exposed to botulism, diphtheria, or their toxins, you are making B cells and antibodies that can recognize these antigens and help protect you from botulism. Explain how the antibodies are produced even though you've had no previous exposure.

_____

_____

_____

_____

_____

18. Discuss how the production of millions of antibodies comes about, and describe the similarities between this process and the idea of introns and splicing.

_____

_____

_____

_____

_____

_____

19. Discuss how the involvement of antibodies leads to the destruction of foreign pathogens or toxins.

_____

_____

_____

_____

_____

_____

Concept 39.5 *describes how the two types of T cells, T-helper cells and cytotoxic T cells, are the basis of cellular immunity.*

20. Describe the main difference between antibodies interacting with pathogens and antibodies interacting with the major histocompatibility complex (MHC) proteins.

_____

_____

_____

_____

_____

_____

21. Explain the roles of T-helper cells and cytotoxic T cells, discussing the key differences between their actions in the immune system.

_____

_____

_____

_____

_____

_____

_____

_____

_____

_____

_____

22. Flu vaccines can induce mild flu symptoms, yet protect against a more difficult case of the flu at a later time. Propose an explanation for each of these effects.

_____

_____

_____

_____

_____

_____

_____

_____

_____

_____

23. Some people describe allergies as an overactive immune response. Explain.

_____

_____

_____

_____

_____

_____

_____

_____

Science Practices & Inquiry

In the AP Biology Curriculum Framework, there are seven **Science Practices**. In this chapter, we will focus on **Science Practice 1:** The student can use representations and models to communicate scientific phenomena and solve scientific problems. More specifically, we will focus on **Science Practice 1.1:** The student can create representations and models of natural or manmade phenomena and systems in the domain.

Question 24 asks you to create representations and models to describe immune responses (**Learning Objective 2.29**).

24. For each of the scenarios below, draw a diagram or flow chart showing how a person's immune system might react to the foreign virus.

   a. While walking down a crowded hallway, someone in front of you coughs without covering her mouth. You feel the spray of the cough on your arm, but you do not get sick.

   b. While swimming in the ocean, you swallow some seawater. Later that night you feel ill and you run a temperature. The next day you're fine.

   c. A child comes down with chicken pox, but his parents do not. Both of his parents had chicken pox as children. (Create two flow charts, one for the son and one for the parents.)

40 Animal Behavior

Chapter Outline

Behaviors are fittingly one of the last topics we examine, as this integrative and organismal chapter incorporates information from most of the other chapters in the book. Behaviors have genetic underpinnings. They have evolved in response to selective pressures and are learned from previous generations. This chapter examines the proximate and ultimate causes of behavior. Proximate explanations often answer "how" questions: How does an organism react to a particular stimulus? How do genetic, physiological, neurological, and developmental mechanisms influence the behavior? Ultimate explanations answer "why" questions, focusing on the evolutionary explanations for behaviors: Why do organisms react the way they do? Why does a particular behavior yield an evolutionary advantage for an individual over others in the population?

Many behaviors are complex and have genetic associations. These ties are studied through molecular genetic approaches. Recall that DNA codes for RNA, which is spliced to make mRNA, which is then translated to guide protein synthesis. Thus, a mutation in a gene can change how an organism reacts to its environment. For example, a mutation in a gene for an olfactory receptor protein can change how an organism reacts to odors in its environment if that gene product alters its capability to detect odors that are relevant to the selection pressures acting on that individual.

The behaviors of animals develop and mature over time as the nervous system and other systems develop. Juvenile behaviors, such as suckling or begging for food, give way to adult behaviors, such as migration and courtship behaviors. Hormones play a large part in the developmental changes in behaviors. Some behaviors develop at specific times in an animal's life. For example, imprinting, a parent–offspring bond, happens only within a few hours of birth in many species. Accordingly, songbirds learn species-specific songs best while very young.

Environmental cues that can influence behavior include circadian rhythms and migration. Circadian rhythms in organisms are based on the rotation of Earth on its axis. Most organisms kept in continuous darkness or in continuous light will exhibit a sleep/wake cycle that repeats approximately every 24 hours. Migratory behaviors are seasonally expressed and temporally guided by visual references, allowing a return to a specific location (homing). Long-distance migration requires the sun, the stars, or the Earth's magnetic field for reference.

Natural selection shapes animal behavior. Every behavior can be examined from the perspective of its cost-benefit ratio, including energetic cost, risk cost, and opportunity cost. How much energy is expended to carry out the behavior? What are the risks of being injured or killed while performing the behavior? What benefits are lost if the behavior cannot be performed? This approach explains why some organisms will sacrifice themselves for the greater good of a colony.

Chapter 40 topics span **Big Idea 2** and **Big Idea 3**. The specific parts of the AP Biology curriculum covering **Big Idea 2:** Biological systems utilize free energy and molecular building blocks to grow, to reproduce, and to maintain dynamic homeostasis, include:

- **2.C.2:** Organisms respond to changes in their external environments.

- **2.E.2:** Timing and coordination of physiological events are regulated by multiple mechanisms.

- **2.E.3:** Timing and coordination of behavior are regulated by various mechanisms and are important in natural selection.

The specific parts covering **Big Idea 3:** Living systems store, retrieve, transmit, and respond to information essential to life processes, include:

• **3.A.3:** The chromosomal basis of inheritance provides an understanding of the pattern of passage (transmission) of genes from parent to offspring.

• **3.D.2:** Cells communicate with each other through direct contact with other cells or from a distance via chemical signaling.

• **3.E.1:** Individuals can act on information and communicate it to others.

Chapter Review

Concept 40.1 *introduces the idea that an animal's nervous system activates and coordinates behaviors. When lizards run, for instance, neurons stimulate contractions in an appropriate pattern in their leg muscles. Similarly, when people have animated conversations, their brains activate their hand movements and facial expressions. According to this viewpoint, although behaviors—such as leg motions and smiles—are fleeting and not in themselves material objects, they have a material basis: they arise from brain tissue, neurons, and the movements of ions that give rise to nerve impulses. When a person speaks, reads, or walks, specific brain regions show evidence of increased metabolism. These types of evidence point to a neural basis for complex behaviors involved in human communication.*

1. Fixed action patterns (FAPs) are expressed by animals without prior learning and are often resistant to modification by learning. Generally, FAPs have a stimulus (sign stimulus) that initiates the behavior. Describe and discuss the sign stimulus for each of the FAPs below.

    a. Mating dances by birds during courtship

_____

_____

_____

_____

_____

_____

    b. Aggression to all red-colored stimuli during breeding season by red-bellied stickleback fish

_____

_____

_____

_____

_____

    c. Moths folding their wings and dropping to the ground when an ultrasonic sound from a bat is encountered

_____

_____

_____

_____

_____

_____

2. Gull chicks instinctively peck at the red dot on a parent's bill, a behavior that induces the parent to regurgitate food into the chick's mouth. In the chart below are the results of an experiment showing the percent of times a model was pecked compared to a control model. Each of the small circles on the bills of the models was red.

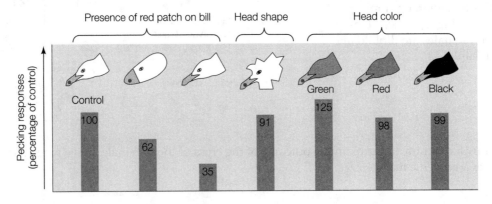

a. Summarize the results of the experiment.

_____

_____

_____

_____

_____

b. Explain how a result of 125 percent is possible.

_____

_____

_____

_____

_____

c. Provide an explanation, based on the data, as to whether the presence of a red dot on the bill or the color/shape of the head is a more effective stimulus for pecking responses.

_____

_____

_____

_____

_____

3. Under certain conditions, FAPs are highly adaptive. Give an example, and describe the benefits.

_____

_____

_____

_____

_____

_____

_____

_____

4. In a honey bee colony, when pupae die, a normal hygienic bee (*uu*, *rr*, or *ur*) will uncap the cell and remove the dead pupae for disposal. Two genes control this behavior, uncapping (*u*) and removing (*r*). (Recall that in honey bees, females are diploid and males are haploid.)

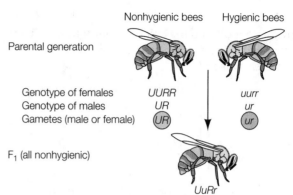

Nonhygienic bees   Hygienic bees

Parental generation

Genotype of females   UURR   uurr
Genotype of males   UR   ur
Gametes (male or female)   UR   ur

F₁ (all nonhygienic)

UuRr

a. Draw a diagram and explain the outcome of the cross of the F₁ female above when she is crossed with a hygienic male.

_____

_____

_____

_____

_____

_____

_____

_____

_____

_____

b. Draw a diagram and explain the outcome of the cross of the F₁ female above when she is crossed with a nonhygienic male.

_____

_____

_____

_____

_____

_____

_____

_____

_____

_____

c. Choose which of the two crosses is more useful in a behavioral study of honey bees, and explain your choice.

_____

_____

_____

_____

_____

5. Circadian rhythms are adaptive. Explain this, including the idea that anticipation of resource availability is of evolutionary benefit.

_____

_____

_____

_____

6. Do all circadian rhythms result in animals being awake during the day? Explain, including at least two selective pressures that promote daytime activity and two selective pressures that promote nighttime activity.

_____

_____

_____

_____

Concept 40.2 *examines learning, which is the ability of an animal to modify its behaviors as a consequence of experiences. Suppose that a mouse living in a forest is less likely to be caught by a predator if it can return to its burrow rapidly. Prior to the mouse's birth, there would be no way to predict the location of that mouse's burrow or landmarks useful for finding it. For this reason, natural selection could not provide inherited information on these particulars. However, natural selection has favored the evolution of learning abilities. A mouse inherits mechanisms by which it can learn locations. Then, during its life, it uses those mechanisms to incorporate specific information on its actual burrow location and useful landmarks into its escape behavior.*

7. Explain the relationship between imprinting and critical period.

_____

_____

_____

_____

8. A researcher frequently wears yellow boots around his research area. Explain why baby ducks will sometimes follow him as though he were their mother, but only when he wears the yellow boots.

_____

_____

_____

_____

9. Discuss the adaptive value of imprinting.

_____

_____

_____

_____

_____

Concept 40.3 *studies how behavior is integrated with the rest of function.*

10. When chased, both frogs and toads respond by hopping away until fatigue prevents them from going any farther—a behavior dependent on the synthesis and subsequent use of ATP during muscle contraction. Frogs hop away at high speeds using anaerobic glycolysis, a biochemical process that produces large amounts of ATP very rapidly but that can't be sustained for long periods of time. Toads use aerobic respiration, a process that produces less ATP per unit of time but that can operate for a much longer period. Suppose you make records of speed and duration for two cases of escape behavior, as in the figure. (These data, though modeled on actual data, are hypothetical.)

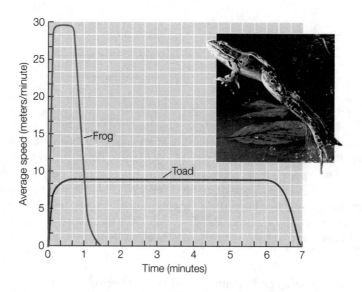

a. Identify the animal that appears to have fatigued more quickly, and propose a mechanism for this rapid fatigue.

_____

_____

_____

_____

b. Propose a mechanism by which increased speed of ATP synthesis causes a more rapid development of fatigue.

_____

_____

_____

_____

c. Identify the animal that traveled farther in this test. Propose a relationship between the speed of ATP synthesis and the capacity to travel long distances. (*Hint*: Determining the number of squares under each graph of speed versus time will allow you to integrate the information and estimate distance traveled.)

_____

_____

_____

_____

Concept 40.4 *examines how movement presents distinctive challenges. The distances covered may be short, such as when animals search for food each day. Some animals, by contrast, travel almost halfway around the globe during seasonal migrations. Moving through space requires that animals meet the challenges of navigation and orientation, ensuring that they can find their destinations and return home. Navigation refers to the act of moving toward a particular destination or along a particular course. Orientation refers to adopting a position, or a path of locomotion, relative to an environmental cue, such as the sun.*

11. Two forms of orientation behavior, taxis and kinesis, have been tested in behavioral studies. Taxis is a directed motion, either forward or away from a stimulus, while kinesis is random motion, which does not result in any particular orientation in relationship to the stimulus. For each of the scenarios below, determine whether the orientation is an example of taxis or kinesis and provide a brief explanation about its adaptive value.

a. Cockroaches will move away from a light source.

b. An insect remains stationary in humid conditions longer than it does in arid conditions.

c. Individual *Euglena*, a flagellate protozoan with chloroplasts, is attracted to light.

12. In a honey bee colony, the queen is the only reproductive female. She mates in flight, stores the sperm, and then uses that sperm throughout her life. Most of the eggs are fertilized and develop into sterile females (worker bees), while unfertilized eggs develop into males. Discuss the adaptive value of the eusocial behaviors of female honey bees.

_____

_____

_____

_____

_____

_____

_____

Concept 40.5 *discusses animals that live in groups. Flocks of birds, schools of fish, and herds of antelopes are just a few examples. Many such groups are considered societies, organized to some degree in a cooperative manner. Note that living in a group tends to make animals more visible, allows diseases to spread, and can quickly deplete food or other resources. Biologists presume that group living has evolved only when it provided advantages that exceed its disadvantages. Physiological advantages of group living are clear in some cases—penguins, for example, reduce their thermoregulatory costs in the cold of winter by huddling together.*

The subject of social behavior includes both the behaviors that integrate individuals into societies and the group behaviors of entire societies. Our focus here is on potential behavioral advantages of group living.

13. Pigeons fly and forage in flocks. The larger the flock, the sooner a predator, such as the goshawk, is detected. Review the graph and use a cost-benefit analysis to decide if there is an optimum size of a flock. Explain your answer.

Goshawk   Wood pigeon

_____

_____

_____

_____

_____

_____

_____

_____

_____

_____

_____

_____

_____

Concept 40.6 *explains that the interactions of genetic, physiological, and environmental factors determine complex behaviors. Circadian rhythms control the daily cycle of behavior and are normally timed to a light/dark cycle. Other environmental cues are used by organisms to navigate, such as orienting to landmarks or celestial objects. Ecologists utilize a cost-benefit approach to study the relationship between behavior, the environment, and fitness. In other words, natural selection shapes behavior based on the sensory and physiological capabilities of animals as well as the environmental stimuli present.*

14. Researchers used artificial selection to produce two strains of hamsters: one with a short circadian period and one with a long circadian period. They wanted to see if swapping tissues between the strains carried the donor's activity pattern with it. They focused their work on two clusters of "pacemaker" neurons, found in the suprachiasmatic nuclei (SCN) of the brain. Destroying the SCNs of adult hamsters caused the animals to become arrhythmic. After several weeks of arrhythmia, scientists transplanted SCN tissue from fetal hamsters into the brains of the adult hamsters whose SCNs had been destroyed. Long-period adult hamsters received tissue from short-period fetuses, and short-period adults received tissue from long-period fetuses. The effects of these treatments on the hamsters' circadian periods are shown in the table below.

	Treatment			
Recipient	None	SCN destroyed	SCN destroyed and short-period transplant	SCN destroyed and long-period transplant
Short-period adult	Short-period	Arrhythmic	Not done	Long-period
Long-period adult	Long-period	Arrhythmic	Not done	Not done

a. Propose a mechanism by which SCN destruction led to arrhythmic behavior.

b. How could the researchers have designed a control for this experiment? (*Hint*: Examine the data closely.) What results would you expect from this?

15. Using the cost–benefit approach, explain the two behaviors below. Be sure to include all three aspects of cost–benefit in your discussion.

a. Sea birds will not defend feeding rights to parts of the ocean, yet they will vigorously defend nesting areas on a beach.

_____

_____

_____

_____

_____

b. Male elephant seals often fight to the death to stake out territories on a beach where females will soon arrive.

_____

_____

_____

_____

_____

Science Practices & Inquiry

In the AP Biology Curriculum Framework, there are seven **Science Practices**. In this chapter, we focus on **Science Practice 7:** The student is able to connect and relate knowledge across various scales, concepts, and representations in and across domains. More specifically, we focus on **Science Practice 7.2:** The student can connect concepts in and across domain(s) to generalize or extrapolate in and/or across enduring understandings and/or big ideas.

Question 16 asks you to connect concepts in and across domain(s) to predict how environmental factors affect responses to information and change behavior (**Learning Objective 2.40**).

16. For each of the scenarios below, identify the type of behavior shown and discuss the environmental cues that lead to these behaviors. Include in your discussion the relationships between genetics, physiology, and the outward behaviors exhibited.

a. Hand-reared, endangered baby cranes are shown an ultralight aircraft when they are born, which is later used to lead the young cranes on their migratory routes.

b. When a female goose notices an egg outside the nest, it begins a repeated movement to drag the egg with its beak and neck. The goose continues to repeat the movements even if the egg is absent, until it reaches the nest, at which point the goose repeats the motion over and over until the egg is returned.

c. In a group of wild turkeys, a subordinate turkey may help his dominant brother put on an impressive display that is only of direct benefit to the dominant turkey.

_____

_____

_____

_____

_____

_____

41 The Distribution of Earth's Ecological Systems

Chapter Outline

41.1 – Ecological Systems Vary over Space and Time
41.2 – Solar Energy Input and Topography Shape Earth's Physical Environments
41.3 – Biogeography Reflects Physical Geography
41.4 – Biogeography Also Reflects Geological History
41.5 – Human Activities Affect Ecological Systems on a Global Scale

An ecological system (biome) is composed of the populations of organisms living and interacting together in a particular environment. Some ecological systems are small, while others can be as large as the boreal forest stretching across much of Canada. A particular ecosystem, such as a small pond, might appear to have well-defined borders, but there are often organisms from neighboring ecosystems, like herons and raccoons, that feed on life in the pond. No ecosystem is completely isolated, particularly from physical parameters like water and sunlight (energy) that constantly move into and out of ecosystems.

An ecosystem develops and exists within its long-term climate trends, primarily patterns of temperature and moisture. On any given day or week, *weather* describes short-term changes in atmospheric conditions. By comparison, long-term averages over many years or decades are known as *climate*. Latitude, elevation, and topography are the primary factors that determine an area's climate and thus the distribution of different types of terrestrial biomes.

Chapter 41 spans **Big Idea 1**, **Big Idea 2**, and **Big Idea 4**. The specific parts of the AP Biology curriculum covering **Big Idea 1**: The process of evolution drives the diversity and unity of life, include:

- **1.B.2**: Phylogenetic trees and cladograms are graphical representations (models) of evolutionary history that can be tested.

- **1.C.2**: Speciation may occur when two populations become reproductively isolated from each other.

The specific parts covering **Big Idea 2**: Biological systems utilize free energy and molecular building blocks to grow, to reproduce, and to maintain dynamic homeostasis, include:

- **2.C.2**: Organisms respond to changes in their external environments.

- **2.D.1**: All biological systems from cells and organisms to populations, communities, and ecosystems are affected by complex biotic and abiotic interactions involving exchange of matter and free energy.

The specific parts addressing **Big Idea 4**: Biological systems interact, and these systems and their interactions possess complex properties, include:

- **4.B.2**: Cooperative interactions within organisms promote efficiency in the use of energy and matter.

- **4.B.4**: Distribution of local and global ecosystems changes over time.

- **4.C.4**: The diversity of species within an ecosystem may influence the stability of the ecosystem.

Chapter Review

Concept 41.1 *introduces the ecological concepts. An ecosystem comprises a biological community interacting with its environment. This concept requires consideration of the interactions within and between biotic (living organisms) and abiotic (physical environment) factors. A community description includes all of the populations in a given area interacting with each other, while a population is one group of individuals of a single species living and interbreeding in a particular location.*

1. Consider this statement by a school principal: "Our school is committed to providing a welcoming environment for our diverse community." Describe two things in this statement that are inaccurate from an ecological/biological perspective.

_____

_____

_____

_____

_____

2. Identify three biotic components found in most ecosystems.

_____

_____

_____

_____

_____

3. Identify three abiotic components found in most ecosystems. Briefly propose a bilogical impact of each component.

_____

_____

_____

_____

_____

_____

4. Interactions between the members of a population of unicellular organisms can be compared to the interactions between the cells of a multicellular organism. Discuss two similarities and two differences between the bacterial community of the human gut and the bacterial community of a forest community.

Similarities:

_____

_____

_____

_____

Differences:

_____

_____

_____

_____

5. Interactions between the members of a population of unicellular organisms often lead to increased efficiency and utilization of energy and matter, much like that seen in a multicellular organism. Explain three benefits that humans gain from "hosting" the microbial community in the human gut.

_____

_____

_____

_____

_____

_____

_____

_____

_____

6. Deep sea vent communities are found at the bottom of the sea floor, typically near diverging plate boundaries where super-heated water issues from the sea floor (see diagram). This seawater typically has a temperature ranging from 60°C to 400°C and is often highly acidic (<pH 3). It contains hydrogen sulfide that many species of bacteria can oxidize to provide energy transfers for chemosynthesis.

One novel organism found in the community of organisms surrounding these deep sea vents is the giant tubeworm. These tubeworms have no mouth or digestive tract, but inside them are billions of bacteria per gram of body tissue.

Describe and discuss the route by which carbon sources needed by the tubeworms and bacteria become available in the deep ocean.

Oceanic zones

_____

_____

_____

_____

_____

_____

_____

Concept 41.2 *discusses the abiotic components of ecosystems. The uneven distribution of solar energy across the Earth's surface sets global wind patterns in motion, which in turn drive the global ocean surface currents. Water and climate diagrams summarize the climate of ecosystems.*

7. Contrast climate change with weather change. Provide an example of each.

_____

_____

_____

_____

_____

_____

_____

8. Describe how Earth's weather patterns are affected by the tilt of the Earth on its axis. Include equatorial and temperate comparisons. Be sure to discuss how much atmosphere the energy from the sun must penetrate to reach Earth's surface at different latitudes.

_____

_____

_____

_____

_____

_____

_____

_____

9. Propose the climatic and biological effects of each of the following alterations:

    a. Earth's tilt changes from 23.5° to 5°.

    _____

    _____

    _____

    _____

    b. Earth's tilt gets reversed.

    _____

    _____

    _____

    _____

    c. Earth's tilt changes from 23.5° to 25°.

    _____

    _____

    _____

    _____

Answer questions 10–13 using the following climate diagrams, which show temperature and precipitation data for three locations.

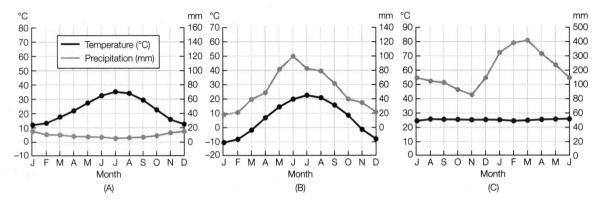

10. Select the diagram (A, B, or C) that best represents climate near the equator, and explain your choice.

_____

_____

_____

_____

_____

11. Select the diagram (A, B, or C) that represents the latitude 30° North, where there is typically a high rate of evaporation from the surface, and dry, warm air sinking to the surface. Identify and describe the biome that would be found here.

_____

_____

_____

_____

_____

12. Select the diagram (A, B, or C) that would have the longest growing season, and explain your choice.

_____

_____

_____

_____

_____

13. Diagram C includes varying precipitation throughout the year. Select the month with the lowest precipitation and discuss why this reduction occurs at that time. Suggest a biome that might be found in a region with this precipitation pattern.

_____

_____

_____

_____

_____

14. Organisms' activities are affected by interactions with abiotic factors. Explain how each of the factors in the table below could affect the behavior and health of the marine organisms shown.

	Coral reef	Fish	Sea otter
Nutrient availability			
Temperature change from 22°C to 18°C (72°F to 64°F)			
Salinity change from 32ppt to 25ppt			
pH change from 8.18 to 8.07			

Concept 41.3 *surveys the major biomes of the world and their physical conditions.*

15. Define the term *biome* and discuss how biomes are determined. Describe the type of biome you live in, linking your description to the definition of that biome.

_____

_____

_____

_____

16. Discuss whether or not the human gut is a biome, and indicate your perception of how small a biome can be.

_____

_____

_____

_____

17. Based on the information in the graph below, describe the annual rhythms of temperature and precipitation for a temperate seasonal forest in the Southern Hemisphere.

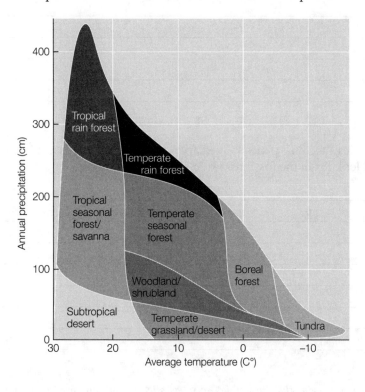

_____

_____

_____

_____

_____

_____

_____

_____

_____

_____

_____

_____

_____

_____

_____

Concept 41.4 *examines the geologic history of Earth, including plate tectonics, in shaping the distribution of organisms we see today. The movement of the plates has shaped our world into seven major biogeographic regions.*

18. Explain how major geological events, such as plate tectonics, impact ecosystem distribution.

_____

_____

_____

_____

_____

_____

_____

_____

_____

19. South American and African tectonic plates moved apart approximately 100 million years ago. Explain what evidence you would look for in the fossil record to support this finding.

_____

_____

_____

_____

_____

_____

_____

_____

_____

Concept 41.5 *addresses the many ways that human activity has affected the complexity and heterogeneity of the world's ecosystems. The previous epochs of life are labeled according to the dominant life form during that time period. Some suggest that we are now in the Anthropocene period, or "Age of Humans."*

20. Describe two human activities that have altered ecosystems, and discuss the effects of the alteration on biodiversity.

_____

_____

_____

_____

_____

_____

_____

_____

Science Practices & Inquiry

In the AP Biology Curriculum Framework, there are seven **Science Practices**. In this chapter, we focus on **Science Practice 6:** The student can work with scientific explanations and theories. More specifically, we focus on **Science Practice 6.3:** The student can articulate the reasons that scientific explanations and theories are refined or replaced.

Question 21 asks you to explain how the distribution of ecosystems changes over time by identifying large-scale events that have resulted in these changes in the past (**Learning Objective 4.20**).

21. Identify two large-scale events (not caused by humans) that have changed the distribution of ecosystems in the past. For each event, describe how the ecosystems changed, and predict how they might change again in the future.

_____

_____

_____

_____

_____

_____

_____

_____

_____

_____

_____

_____

_____

_____

_____

_____

_____

_____

_____

_____

_____

_____

_____

_____

_____

_____

_____

_____

42 Populations

Chapter Outline

Chapter 42 begins with a description of populations of individuals in a species that interact with one another in a given area. Population density and population size are two measures of ecological interest. There are many sampling tools for determining population size, but most involve determining the population density and then multiplying this by the area of the population's habitat.

Populations change over time in response to many factors. At a simplistic level, the change in the size of a population (dN) over time (dt), assuming no immigration or emigration, is the number of births (B) less the number of deaths (D), as shown by this equation:

$$\frac{dN}{dt} = B - D$$

Because it is usually impossible to monitor every individual in a population, ecologists calculate per capita birth and death rates (i.e., the average individual's number of offspring and the average individual's chance of dying, in some interval of time). The difference between these birth and death rates is the per capita growth rate (r). By multiplying r by the population size (N), we obtain an estimate of population-growth rate over time. This is expressed by this equation:

$$\frac{dN}{dT} = rN$$

The life history of a species describes growth, development, reproduction, and death. Life histories are represented as circles beginning with eggs or mating parents and ending with the next generation. Below is a diagram showing the life history of the black-legged tick. Life histories can be very complex, particularly if a species relies on blood meals from other species. Other resources, such as light, space, and temperature, must also be considered.

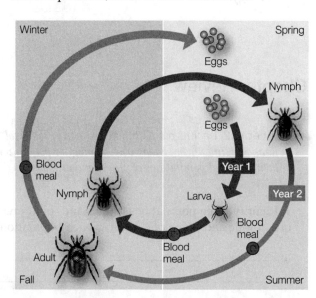

Population growth rates typically fall into two patterns, exponential (multiplicative) and logistic. The equations representing these two models are:

$$\frac{dN}{dt} = r_{max}N \qquad\qquad \frac{dN}{dt} = r_{max}N\left(\frac{K-N}{N}\right)$$

Exponential growth   *Logistic growth*

Most species will grow multiplicatively until they reach their carrying capacity (K). At this point, they will fluctuate up or down in response to resource availability or changing environmental conditions. Rarely do we see a species with a consistent population size at its carrying capacity. Most species show frequent increases or decreases in population.

This chapter includes material relevant to **Big Idea 1**, **Big Idea 2**, and **Big Idea 4**. The specific parts of the AP Biology curriculum covering **Big Idea 1:** The process of evolution drives the diversity and unity of life, include:

- **1.A.1**: Natural selection is a major mechanism of evolution.

- **1.C.1**: Speciation and extinction have occurred throughout the Earth's history.

The specific parts covering **Big Idea 2:** Biological systems utilize free energy and molecular building blocks to grow, to reproduce, and to maintain dynamic homeostasis, include:

- **2.A.1**: All living systems require constant input of free energy.

- **2.A.3**: Organisms must exchange matter with the environment to grow, reproduce, and maintain organization.

- **2.D.1**: All biological systems from cells and organisms to populations, communities, and ecosystems are affected by complex biotic and abiotic interactions involving exchange of matter and free energy.

- **2.D.3**: Biological systems are affected by disruptions to their dynamic homeostasis.

The specific parts addressing **Big Idea 4:** Biological systems interact, and these systems and their interactions possess complex properties, include:

- **4.A.5**: Communities are composed of populations of organisms that interact in complex ways.

- **4.A.6**: Interactions among living systems and with their environment result in the movement of matter and energy.

- **4.B.3**: Interactions between and within populations influence patterns of species distribution and abundance.

Chapter Review

Concept 42.1 *points out that there are many ecological, aesthetic, and ethical dimensions to the study of population dynamics. Humans have long been managing populations, including herds of cattle, fields of crops, schools of fish, and endangered populations of plants and animals.*

1. Identify three populations (plants and/or animals) that are actively managed by humans. Then identify one abiotic and one biotic factor in each population's environment that affect its abundance.

_____

_____

_____

_____

_____

_____

_____

_____

_____

_____

_____

_____

2. Edith's checkerspot butterfly (*Euphydryas editha*) extends from British Columbia and Alberta to Baja California. Many subpopulations of this endangered butterfly went extinct during a severe drought between 1975 and 1977. The only subpopulation that survived was the largest one, on Morgan Hill in the San Francisco Bay Area. The butterfly population is divided into subpopulations, each occupying a patch of suitable habitat. Arrows on the drawing at the right indicate nine colonization events in 1986.

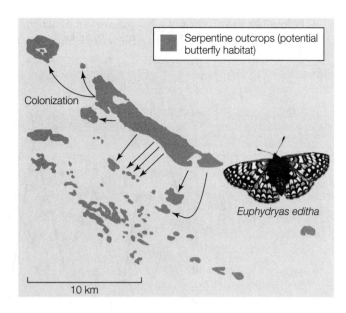

Identify and describe three factors that might prevent this checkerspot butterfly from colonizing an area.

_____

_____

_____

_____

_____

_____

_____

_____

_____

_____

_____

_____

_____

Concepts 42.2 and 42.3 *address the study of demographics, or how populations change over time. Many formulas are given in these sections, but the ones you need to be familiar with are found on the AP Biology Exam equation sheet inside the back cover of this book.*

3. Identify two factors, other than birth and death rates, that affect the size of a population.

_____

_____

_____

_____

_____

_____

4. Below is a graph showing how densities of acorns, rodents (mice and chipmunks), and black-legged tick populations vary over time in a New York State oak forest.

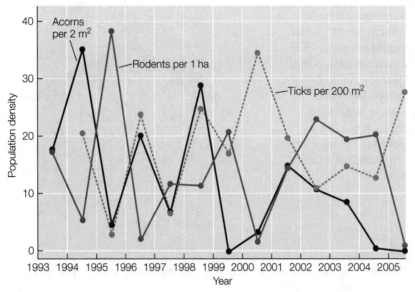

a. Propose and justify the relationship between acorn and rodent densities.

_____

_____

_____

_____

b. Propose and justify the relationship between rodent and tick densities.

_____

_____

_____

_____

c. Ticks are parasites relying on blood meals to reproduce. Propose the effects of changes in one abiotic factor and one biotic factor on tick population numbers.

_____

_____

_____

_____

d. For the year 2000, calculate the number of ticks in the forest if the forest covers 50 square kilometers.

e. Identify two abiotic and two biotic factors that also could influence the population fluctuations seen in the figure.

_____

_____

5. The table below shows the survivorship and fecundity for cactus ground finches born in 1978 on one island in the Galápagos archipelago.

Quantitative Life History for 210 Common Cactus Finches Born in 1978 on Isla Daphne			
Calendar year	Age of bird (years)	Survivorship[a]	Fecundity[b]
1978	0	1.00	0.00
1979	1	0.43	0.05
1980	2	0.37	0.67
1981	3	0.33	1.50
1982	4	0.31	0.66
1983 Increased rain	5	0.30	5.50
1984	6	0.20	0.69
1985 Drought	7	0.11	0.00
1986	8	0.07	0.00
1987 Increased rain	9	0.07	2.20

[a]Survivorship = the proportion of the 210 birds that survived from birth to a given age
[b]Fecundity = the average number of young born per female of a given age

a. Identify the age range when the ground finches in this study were reproducing at their highest rate.

_____

_____

_____

b. Survivorship at age x is the proportion of the original cohort that survived to age x. Calculate how many birds did not make it to one year of age.

c. Propose the relationship between increased rainfall in 1983 and increased fecundity in that year.

_____

_____

_____

d. Fecundity is the average number of young per female. Assume that one-half of the population is female. Calculate the number of young born in 1983.

6. Assume that a population of 25 women and 25 men, all 21 years old, colonizes a previously uninhabited island. Twenty babies are born the following year. In the table at the right, write in possible life table values for these twenty babies.

Year	Age	Survivorship	Fecundity
1	0	1.00	0.00
5			
10			
15			
20			
25			
30			
35			
40			
45			
50			
55			
60			
65			
70			

7. Describe the assumptions you made when giving the survivorship and fecundity values in Question 6.

_____

_____

_____

_____

_____

_____

Concept 42.4 *focuses on the dynamics of population growth rates. Most populations tend to grow at either a logistic or an exponential growth rate. Time is a key consideration here, and even if human imagination is not always able to grasp the passage of time, the mathematics make the conclusions clear.*

8. Explain why populations cannot grow multiplicatively for extended periods of time.

_____

_____

_____

_____

_____

_____

9. The graph below shows growth in the human population over more than 12,000 years.

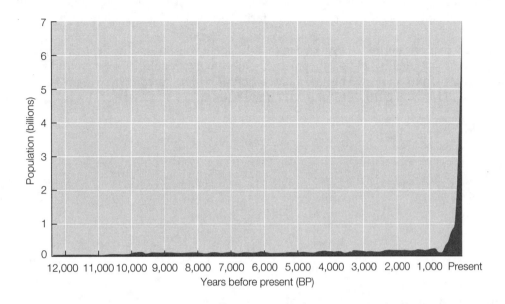

a. Discuss whether the growth in the first 11,500 years should be classified as multiplicative or additive.

_____

_____

_____

_____

_____

b. Discuss whether the growth in the last 500 years on the graph should be classified as multiplicative or additive.

_____

_____

_____

_____

_____

c. Propose an explanation for the fact that the number of human offspring continues to increase over a long period of time.

_____

_____

_____

_____

_____

d. Discuss how the population crash approximately 500 years ago might have affected human genetic diversity.

_____

_____

_____

_____

Questions 10 and 11 refer to an infestation of yellow star-thistle (*Centaurea solstitialis*), a spiny annual plant native to the Mediterranean region. The species, a noxious weed that is unpalatable to livestock, has invaded several regions of the United States, including an imaginary farm operated by Rancher Jane.

10. Jane carefully inspects her ranch every year. In 2012, there was no star-thistle. In 2013, she discovered that one hectare of her ranch's 128-hectare pasture had been invaded. In 2014, she found the weed population had grown to cover two hectares. Based on this pattern, predict how many hectares of her land the star-thistle will infest in 2015, 2016, and 2017 if the pattern is:

   a. growing additively.

   b. growing multiplicatively.

11. Imagine that Jane did not see any star-thistle in 2012, but she discovered in 2013 that the star-thistle population had suddenly infested 32 hectares of her pasture. Calculate how many years she has until the weed completely covers the pasture, if its population is:

   a. growing additively.

   b. growing multiplicatively.

Concept 42.5 *deals with metapopulations, so this section is beyond the scope of the AP Biology Curriculum Framework. Still, it is useful to know that population size of species does change due to more than just births and deaths. Immigration and emigration, as well as habitat fragmentation induced by humans, can be significant factors in population size.*

12. Extinction of populations in small patches can easily occur.

a. Identify a fragmented habitat in your local area.

_____

_____

b. Name the animals found in this habitat, and describe the risks they face.

_____

_____

_____

_____

_____

_____

_____

_____

c. Propose two reasons for the extinction of populations in small patches.

_____

_____

_____

_____

_____

13. Sidewalks can easily divide an area into metapopulations for small organisms, such as snails. Name one organism that might be limited in its distribution because of each of the barriers below, and explain your choice.

a. Parking lot:

_____

_____

b. Small road:

_____

_____

c. Interstate highway:

_____

_____

d. Housing development:

_____

_____

> **Concept 42.6** *discusses that the ability to predict the dynamics of populations contributes to our ability to influence the fates of natural populations. On the AP exam, you will most likely not encounter a specific question about the black rockfish or the Edith's checkerspot butterfly that you read about in this chapter, as they are not listed in the AP Biology Curriculum Framework. However, there will be general population data for you to graph or interpret.*

14. In the study below, moss (dark areas) was scraped off of a rock (light areas) in the pattern shown. In the "insular" or island treatment (I), the patches are surrounded by bare rock that is inhospitable to moss-dwelling small arthropods and thus provide a barrier to recolonization. In the "corridor" treatment (C), the patches are connected to the mainland by a 7-by-2 centimeter strip of live moss. In the "broken-corridor" treatment (B), the configuration is the same as the corridor treatment, except that a 2- centimeter strip of bare rock cuts the moss strip.

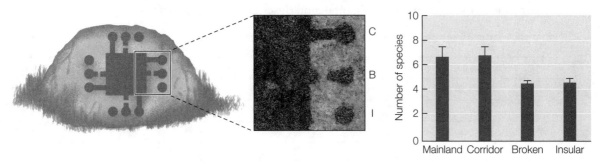

After six months, the number of species of small arthropods was counted in each of the four areas.

a. Summarize the results shown in the graph.

_____

_____

_____

_____

_____

_____

b. Explain the purpose of the broken-corridor (B) treatment.

_____

_____

_____

_____

_____

_____

c. Explain why the experiment should be replicated multiple times before conclusions are drawn.

_____

_____

_____

_____

_____

_____

_____

Science Practices & Inquiry

Question 15 asks you to use data analysis to refine observations and measurements regarding the effect of population interactions on patterns of species distribution and abundance (**Learning Objective 4.19**).

15. Rancher Jane (Questions 10 and 11) is thinking of raising American bison (*Bison bison*) instead of cattle, but she wants to know how well bison will do on her ranch. She buys 50 inseminated female bison and places ten of them, chosen at random, into their own pasture. Using these ten females as a sample, Jane collects demographic data for one year. Use her data in the table at the right to answer the questions below. Show all of your work.

Female #	Alive at end of year?	# of offspring
1	Yes	1
2	Yes	0
3	Yes	1
4	Yes	0
5	No	0
6	Yes	1
7	Yes	1
8	No	0
9	Yes	1
10	Yes	0

   a. What is the total number of births and deaths among this sample population?

_____

_____

_____

_____

_____

_____

   b. What are the estimated birth and death rates for Jane's entire herd of 50 bison, based on this sample?

_____

_____

_____

_____

_____

   c. Based on these estimates, what will the size of Jane's entire herd of bison be at the end of the year?

_____

_____

_____

_____

_____

43 Ecological and Evolutionary Consequences of Interactions within and among Species

Chapter Outline

43.1 – Interactions between Species May Increase, Decrease, or Have No Effect on Fitness
43.2 – Interactions within and among Species Affect Population Dynamics and Species Distributions
43.3 – Species Are Embedded in Complex Interaction Webs
43.4 – Interactions within and among Species Can Result in Evolution

When you watch a butterfly sipping nectar from a flower or a bat swooping and diving after insects at night, you are seeing species interact with one another. The butterfly is drinking the flower's nectar, but it is also moving pollen from flower to flower, helping the plant achieve sexual reproduction. In turn, the butterfly is prey for many species of birds, much as the night insects are prey for the bats. These are but a few of the many and often intertwined relationships among organisms.

As organisms adapt to avoid being eaten, many new novel structures and features evolve. These include protective adaptations like thorns, camouflage, armored shells, and bitter or spicy compounds. As one organism evolves to avoid being eaten, its predator also evolves or adapts to the new defensive mechanisms. For example, as seeds became larger and thicker, bird bills became larger to enable the birds to crack the seeds. These consumer-resource interactions lead to evolutionary "arms races," often with contrary results. Hot chili peppers, for example, synthesize a repellent compound known as capsaicin. While many organisms find this too bitter or spicy to eat, many people enjoy—even prefer—spicy dishes.

Chapter 43 has ideas that span **Big Idea 1**, **Big Idea 2**, and **Big Idea 4**. The specific parts of the AP Biology curriculum covering **Big Idea 1**: The process of evolution drives the diversity and unity of life, include:

- **1.A.2**: Natural selection acts on phenotypic variations in populations.
- **1.C.1**: Speciation and extinction occurred throughout the Earth's history.
- **1.C.3**: Populations of organisms continue to evolve.

The specific parts covering **Big Idea 2**: Biological systems utilize free energy and molecular building blocks to grow, to reproduce, and to maintain dynamic homeostasis, include:

- **2.D.1**: All biological systems from cells and organisms to populations, communities, and ecosystems are affected by complex biotic and abiotic interactions involving exchange of matter and free energy.
- **2.D.3**: Biological systems are affected by disruptions to their dynamic homeostasis.

The specific parts addressing **Big Idea 4**: Biological systems interact, and these systems and their interactions possess complex properties, include:

- **4.A.5**: Communities are composed of populations of organisms that interact in complex ways.
- **4.B.3**: Interactions between and within populations influence patterns of species distribution and abundance.

Chapter Review

Concept 43.1 *notes that species interactions can be positive, neutral, or negative. There are five broad categories of interactions between organisms: competition, consumer-resource, mutualism, commensalism, and amensalism.*

1. For each of the relationships below, indicate in the appropriate column if the first species mentioned (Species 1) is affected negatively (-), positively (+), or not at all (0). Do the same for the second species (Species 2), then write the type of interaction in the third column. The first example is completed for you.

Example	Species 1	Species 2	Type of Interaction
American bison feed on grasses.	+	-	Consumer resource
Wrasses (small fish) clean the teeth of larger fish.			
Mosquito feeds on the blood of a deer.			
Bread mold secretes penicillin that kills local bacteria that generally have little to no effect on the mold.			
A cactus wren builds a nest in a cholla cactus without affecting the cactus.			
A hawk captures a small squirrel for food.			
A rabbit rests in the shade of a small bush.			
Deer create a trail through a forest where they routinely travel.			
Plovers (a bird) remove insects from the backs of large animals.			

2. Many types of trees can be found in a forest. Identify three different biotic factors and discuss how they can affect the growth and health of trees.

_____

_____

_____

_____

_____

_____

_____

_____

_____

3. Explain how predation is different from parasitism.

_____

_____

_____

_____

Concept 43.2 *examines how interspecific interactions affect growth. When two species compete directly with each other for resources, per capita growth rates usually decrease for at least one of the species, one species goes extinct, or resource partitioning occurs.*

4. The intertidal zone along ocean shorelines is teeming with life as species compete for living space. Twice a month, as the moon circles the earth, higher-than normal tides submerge the shoreline, which is normally only splashed by waves.

Two species of barnacles (small crustaceans that filter seawater for food particles in the intertidal zone) exhibit interspecific competition as they compete for space. The rock barnacles, *Semibalanus balanoides*, are found in a narrow range between the lower intertidal zone and the average high-tide line. The stellate barnacles, *Chthamalus stellatus*, are found across a broader range, between the lower intertidal zone and the highest high-tide line.

   a. Draw a diagram of the intertidal zone showing a region where only stellate barnacles are found. Include in your diagram the low-tide line, average high-tide line, and highest high-tide line.

   b. Explain how stellate barnacles can survive above the average high-tide line.

   _____

   _____

   _____

   c. Explain why rock barnacles cannot survive above the average high-tide line.

   _____

   _____

   _____

   d. When the two barnacles are found living in the same location, the rock barnacles grow on top of the stellate barnacles, killing them. Draw a diagram showing what happens when these two species are found together in the intertidal zone.

e. A researcher clears organisms and debris off a patch of rock in the middle of the intertidal zone. Describe what happens as both types of barnacles attempt to colonize that zone.

_____

_____

_____

_____

_____

_____

_____

_____

_____

_____

5. In a forest ecosystem, foxes prey on rabbits and mice, yet foxes are unlikely to consume all of the rabbits. Propose a reason that not all rabbits are eaten.

_____

_____

_____

_____

6. Propose the consequences of two species competing for the same resources in the same location at the same time.

_____

_____

_____

_____

_____

Concept 43.3 *considers how human-introduced species can alter species interactions, using food webs as illustrative examples per the AP Biology Curriculum Framework. Introduced species often establish themselves in environments that lack the regulatory controls found in their native habitats, sometimes resulting in out-of-control growth. Kudzu, purple loosestrife, fire ants, and Eurasian weevil are examples of introduced species that have grown out of control and have altered many ecological relationships in North America.*

Questions 7 and 8 refer to problems with kudzu, an invasive plant species.

Kudzu, *Pueraria lobata,* is a climbing vine native to Japan and China. It is usually classified as a weed, because it climbs over trees and shrubs and grows so rapidly that it blocks sunlight and kills them. Kudzu spreads primarily by rhizomes and by vegetative propagation via runners that form new plants. It can grow at a rate of 0.3m/day in optimal conditions and is now common along roadsides and other areas throughout the southeastern United States.

The plant was introduced to the United States at the Japanese pavilion in the 1876 Centennial Exposition in Philadelphia. In 1935, the Soil Conservation Service began to test kudzu as a solution to the eroded lands in Alabama and Georgia. After a few years, that agency proclaimed that kudzu, with its fast growth and deep roots, could solve the erosion problems of the South. Farmers were paid $8 per acre to plant kudzu and prevent erosion. During the Great Depression, the Civilian Conservation Corps planted over 70 million seedlings of kudzu from Maryland to Texas.

In the 1950s, scientists concerned about kudzu's rapid spread began to classify it as a weed. The damage was already done; by the 1980s, kudzu had covered an estimated 7 million acres of the South, and it continues to spread by 320,000 acres per year.

7. Discuss why kudzu continues to spread so quickly across the United States.

_____

_____

_____

_____

_____

_____

_____

8. Discuss the impact of kudzu on species diversity in afflicted areas.

_____

_____

_____

_____

_____

_____

Questions 9 and 10 refer to the inadvertent introduction of various species, such as the fungus that causes Dutch Elm disease.

Dutch elm disease is caused by a fungus that is spread by bark beetles, quickly killing susceptible elm trees. The fungus is thought to have been introduced to the United States by a shipment of logs from the Netherlands in 1928. Although the name may imply otherwise, Dutch elm disease is most likely native to Asia and was probably introduced to Europe around 1910. Elm trees, once dominant across the forests of the northeastern United States, have been known to survive up to 400 years. Now they rarely live more than 15 years.

9. Identify three ways species are inadvertently introduced to new areas.

_____

_____

_____

_____

10. Describe why the inadvertent introduction of various species has increased over the past century.

_____

_____

_____

_____

Concept 43.4 *explores how interactions between species can affect individual fitness, thus shaping evolutionary changes. The interests of consumer and resource species are at odds with each other, leading to an evolutionary "arms race," in which prey continually evolve better defenses, predators evolve better offenses, and neither gains a lasting advantage over the other.*

11. In the context of evolution, fitness is not how fast you can run a mile or how many push-ups you can perform. Define the term *fitness* in its evolutionary sense, and give an example.

_____

_____

_____

_____

_____

_____

12. Africa's Lake Victoria is home to many different species of *cichlids*. A researcher saw five different species of these fish in one location. Using the concept of resource partitioning, explain how these species can coexist in one place.

_____

_____

_____

_____

_____

_____

_____

13. The Red Queen analogy, based on Lewis Carroll's *Through the Looking-Glass*, originates with the quote "It takes all the running you can do, to keep in the same place." Explain how this analogy could apply to the evolutionary arms race between chili peppers and the animals that eat them.

_____

_____

_____

_____

_____

_____

_____

14. Many believe that plants purposefully produce fruit for other organisms to eat so their seeds will be spread to new locations. Discuss why this is untrue.

_____

_____

_____

_____

Science Practices & Inquiry

In the AP Biology Curriculum Framework, there are seven **Science Practices**. In this chapter, we focus on **Science Practice 4**: The student can plan and implement data collection strategies appropriate to a particular scientific question. More specifically, we focus on **Science Practice 4.1**: The student can justify the selection of the kind of data needed to answer a particular scientific question, and **Science Practice 4.2**: The student can design a plan for collecting data to answer a particular scientific question.

Question 15 asks you to justify the selection of the kind of data needed to answer scientific questions about the interaction of populations within communities (**Learning Objective 4.11**).

15. Some consider the black walnut tree to be an example of an amensal species, as its roots secrete the chemical juglone that harms or kills plants that attempt to grow near it. However, this interaction may also be considered an odd form of consumer–resource if the death of nearby plants removes competition and allows the walnut tree greater access to scarce resources. Design an experiment that would allow you to determine the correct type of ecological interaction between black walnut trees and neighboring plants.

44 Ecological Communities

Chapter Outline

Chapter 44 examines how multiple groups of species interact to form communities. Communities change as the environment changes, with latitude or elevation, and with other factors, such as extinction and colonization, disturbance, and climate change. When disturbances occur in ecosystems, there will likely be changes in the affected communities. Depending on the severity of the disturbance, the original community may or may not return to its native state. Catastrophic disturbances, such as volcanic eruptions, can create entirely new landscapes for colonization by new communities. On a smaller scale, the local extinction of one species may open a window for a small change in community structure.

Energy and materials move within and through communities. Solar energy enters communities as a readily usable, high-energy input, with one output: heat. Thus, energy flows through an ecological community in a one-way direction. Matter, on the other hand, is continuously recycled within the community as organisms consume other organisms, die, and decompose, thereby releasing primary nutrients needed by others in the community. In fact, many of the molecules in your body were not too long ago in an autotroph, maybe in a kernel of corn or a leaf of lettuce. Ultimately, the molecules and atoms that comprise our bodies have been recycled millions of times, as matter is neither created nor destroyed, per the laws of thermodynamics. To put these phenomena succinctly: energy flows and matter cycles.

Estimating biodiversity in an ecological community provides an indication of its health and stability. Biodiversity is measured by both species richness and species evenness. Species richness is simply how many species are in a community. Species evenness is less intuitive; it focuses on how many of each species are present and how individual organisms are spatially distributed in the community. As biodiversity increases, the productivity and stability of a community generally increase, as well.

Humans depend on many ecosystem services provided by different organisms or groups of organisms. For example, pollinators are critical to many forms of agriculture. Without them, many crops will fail to form their fruits or vegetables. Managing and restoring ecosystems while maintaining their health are key facets of research and practice in community ecology.

Chapter 44 spans **Big Idea 1**, **Big Idea 2**, and **Big Idea 4** and looks at how evolution ties in with ecology. The specific parts of the AP Biology curriculum covering **Big Idea 1:** The process of evolution drives the diversity and unity of life, include:

- **1.C.1**: Speciation and extinction have occurred throughout the Earth's history.

The specific parts covering **Big Idea 2:** Biological systems utilize free energy and molecular building blocks to grow, to reproduce, and to maintain dynamic homeostasis, include:

- **2.A.1**: All living systems require constant input of free energy.

- **2.A.2**: Organisms capture and store free energy for use in biological processes.

- **2.D.1**: All biological systems from cells and organisms to populations, communities, and ecosystems are affected by complex biotic and abiotic interactions involving exchange of matter and free energy.

- **2.D.3**: Biological systems are affected by disruptions to their dynamic homeostasis.

The specific parts addressing **Big Idea 4:** Biological systems interact, and these systems and their interactions possess complex properties, include:

- **4.A.5**: Communities are composed of populations of organisms that interact in complex ways.
- **4.A.6**: Interactions among living systems and with their environment result in the movement of matter and energy.

- **4.B.3**: Interactions between and within populations influence patterns of species distribution and abundance.
- **4.B.4**: Distribution of local and global ecosystems changes over time.
- **4.C.4**: The diversity of species within an ecosystem may influence the stability of the ecosystem.

Chapter Review

Concept 44.1 *states that communities are made up of groups of species that coexist and interact with one another within a defined geographic area. The boundaries of some communities are determined by the physical habitat: a pond, for example, defines a community of aquatic species that interact much more with one another than with terrestrial species outside the pond. However, the boundaries between different communities often overlap. For example, raccoons from a forest community will forage for food at a pond's edge, while deer will graze on grass in an open meadow and retreat into the forest for protection. Thus, an ecosystem's boundaries are flexible.*

1. Ecotones are transitional boundaries between ecosystems, such as the border between a grassy area and a forest. This area has a mixture of grasses, shrubs, small trees, and older trees all living in a thin strip. Identify another ecotone and describe the characteristics of the two ecosystems bordering it. Explain how the area includes features of each bordering community.

_____

_____

_____

_____

_____

2. Despite the many decades that have passed since the eruption of the volcano on the Indonesian island of Krakatoa, stable communities of organisms are only now becoming established on the island. Explain why these communities are not identical to the communities present when the volcano erupted in 1883.

_____

_____

_____

_____

3. The new communities on Krakatoa appear to be stabilizing. Discuss whether or not these communities will continue to be stable or change in the future.

_____

_____

_____

_____

_____

Concept 44.2 *examines how communities of organisms change over time. Succession is most dramatic in a community after a major disturbance and is a somewhat predictable progression of species coming and going. In rare circumstances, a new community forms where there are very few preexisting species and little to no soil, such as a lava flow, or a boulder field left by a retreating glacier. Most successional events occur as one population or community replaces another. This is called secondary succession. Climate change, invasive species, and humans are all causes of disturbances that lead to succession.*

4. Recall that free energy is the energy available for use in an ecosystem. Explain how changes in free energy availability can disrupt an ecosystem. Give three examples of possible disruptions, and describe their effects on energy availability. Be sure your examples include a disruption that increases free energy and one that decreases it.

_____

_____

_____

_____

_____

_____

5. For each disruption in Question 4, discuss what effect each departure from preexisting conditions will have on the number and size of trophic levels.

_____

_____

_____

_____

_____

_____

_____

6. Explain how changes in the number of producers, such as reductions caused by disease outbreaks, can affect the number and size of other trophic levels.

_____

_____

_____

_____

_____

_____

Concept 44.3 *describes how energy and matter move through an ecosystem. Remember, energy flows through an ecosystem, and matter is constantly recycled. Autotrophs use solar energy to synthesize chemicals that have potential energy. As consumers eat autotrophs, they utilize this energy for metabolism and store some of the chemicals for future use. A good rule of thumb is the 10 percent rule: the total biomass of each trophic level is about one-tenth that of the level it feeds on.*

7. Identify two examples of free energy in the environment that autotrophs can utilize, and explain how each is used.

_____

_____

_____

_____

_____

_____

8. Dung beetles utilize dung in many ways. Some eat dung, others lay their eggs in it, and some form balls of dung and roll them into their nests. The graph shows how the species composition of dung beetles changes in a pile of dung over time. Describe this process with regard to rollers, dwellers, and tunnelers.

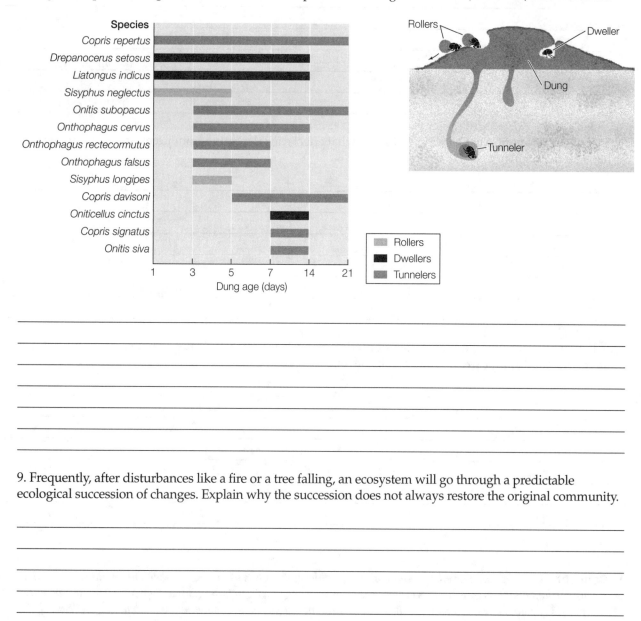

_____

_____

_____

_____

_____

_____

_____

9. Frequently, after disturbances like a fire or a tree falling, an ecosystem will go through a predictable ecological succession of changes. Explain why the succession does not always restore the original community.

_____

_____

_____

_____

_____

_____

Refer to the figure below to answer Questions 10–12. The figure shows a food web for species in the grasslands of Yellowstone National Park.

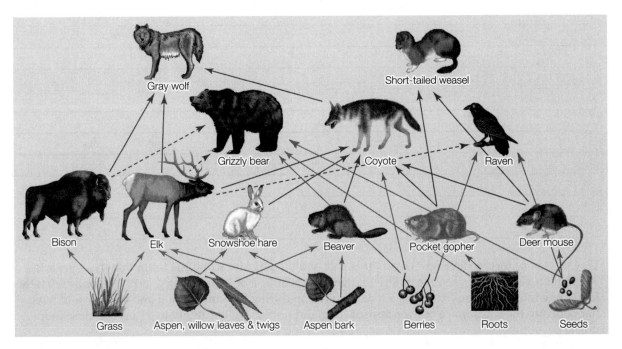

10. Briefly describe what would happen if each of the following groups were removed from the park. Limit your answer to two trophic levels.

a. Coyotes: _____

_____

_____

b. All primary producers: _____

_____

_____

c. All consumers: _____

_____

_____

11. Discuss two possible consequences of adding to Yellowstone Park a new primary consumer that feeds only on grasses.

_____

_____

_____

_____

_____

_____

_____

_____

_____

_____

12. Explain why there are fewer high-level consumers (wolves and weasels) than primary consumers in Yellowstone National Park.

_____

_____

_____

_____

_____

_____

_____

_____

_____

_____

13. One theory for the development of large coal and oil deposits is that the fungi that lived prior to 300 million years ago lacked the ability to digest the cellulose of trees and tree ferns. Describe what the landscape must have looked like in a forest or swamp during this time period and what would have happened to the soil surface of the forests if fungi did not evolve the ability to digest cellulose more quickly.

_____

_____

_____

_____

_____

_____

_____

_____

_____

_____

14. Explain how each of the following abiotic factors can affect the stability of populations.

a. Water: _____

_____

_____

_____

b. Nutrient availability: _____

_____

_____

_____

c. Availability of nesting materials and sites: _____

_____

_____

15. Explain how each of the following biotic factors can affect the stability of populations.

a. Food chains and food webs: _____

_____

_____

_____

b. Species diversity: _____

_____

_____

_____

c. Population density: _____

_____

_____

_____

d. Algal blooms: _____

_____

_____

_____

16. The hypothetical communities of fungi pictured below have 12 individuals each, but they but differ in species richness and relative abundance, both of which affect diversity. Describe where you might find an example of each of these communities in the real world. (Your examples do not need to be limited to just three or four species.)

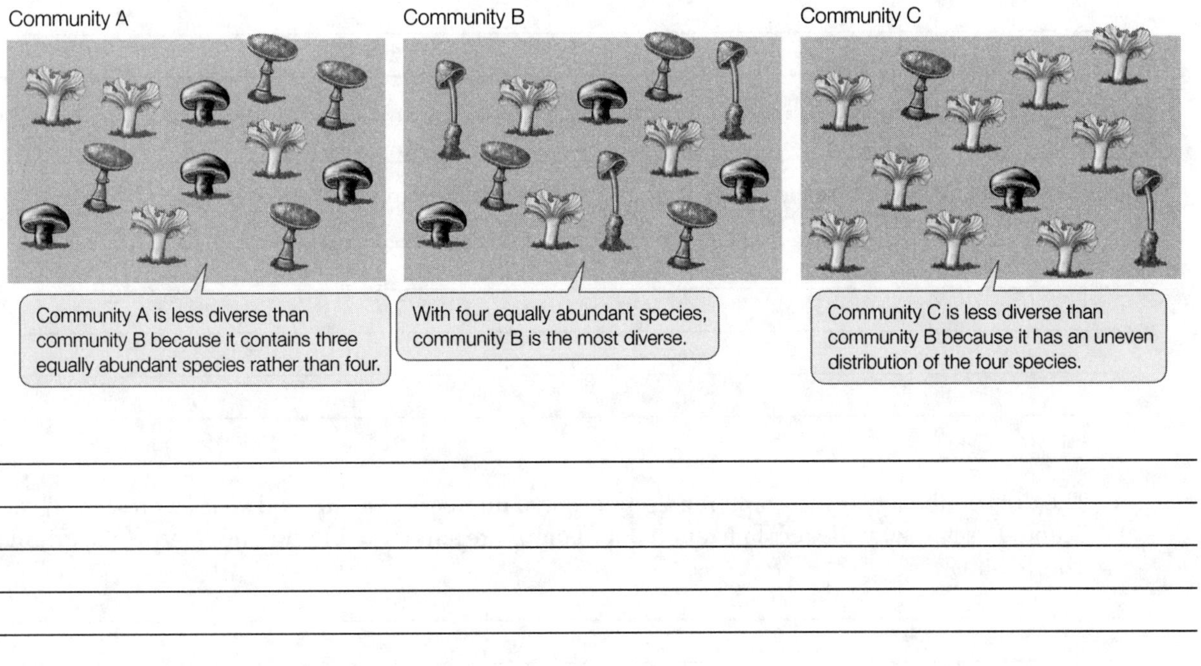

Community A

Community B

Community C

Community A is less diverse than community B because it contains three equally abundant species rather than four.

With four equally abundant species, community B is the most diverse.

Community C is less diverse than community B because it has an uneven distribution of the four species.

_____

_____

_____

_____

_____

_____

_____

_____

Concept 44.4 *discusses some of the factors that influence biodiversity. The study of island biogeography has contributed greatly to our understanding of biodiversity and the structure and function of ecological communities. Islands often have simpler food webs than those found on larger land masses.*

17. By the experimental removal of all arthropods (defaunation) from four mangrove islands of equal size but different distances from the mainland, two researchers were able to observe the process of recolonization. They compared the results by using the predictions of the theory of island biogeography. Below is a graph of their data.

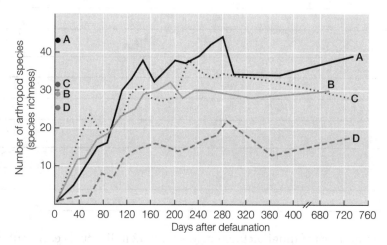

a. Which line would represent an island closest to the mainland? Explain.

_____

_____

_____

_____

_____

b. Why do most of the lines level off after approximately 200 days?

_____

_____

_____

_____

_____

c. The dots on the left of the graph represent original numbers of arthropod species present on each island. Explain why the recolonization populations are similar to but not the same as the original populations.

_____

_____

_____

_____

_____

_____

18. Propose and explain the likely relationship between increased biodiversity and increased stability in ecosystems.

_____

_____

_____

_____

_____

_____

_____

_____

_____

19. Choose two of the disruptions below, and discuss how their human impacts accelerate change at local and global levels. Identify specific organisms, and describe the effects of the disruption on those organisms.

- Logging
- Slash-and-burn agriculture
- Urbanization
- Monocropping
- Infrastructure development (dams, transmission lines, roads)

_____

_____

_____

_____

_____

_____

_____

_____

20. Choose one item from the list below, and discuss how introduced species can exploit new niches free of predators or competitors while devastating native species.

- Dutch elm disease
- Potato blight
- Smallpox [historic example for Native Americans]

_____

_____

_____

_____

_____

_____

_____

_____

_____

Concept **44.5** *explores the value of maintaining and fostering the biodiversity of communities. The demise of many thousands of beehives due to colony collapse disorder has caused alarm. Colony collapse disorder is thought to be a complex interaction among multiple variables, possibly including a fungus and protozoans, but why it happens and where it came from is still a puzzle.*

21. Some ecologists propose buying land in Central America and forming a green belt of vegetation from South America through tropical America. Others propose saving large isolated regions as parks. Discuss which proposal would be more successful for maintaining species biodiversity throughout Central America.

_____

_____

_____

_____

_____

_____

_____

_____

_____

_____

_____

_____

_____

_____

_____

_____

_____

_____

_____

_____

_____

_____

_____

_____

_____

_____

_____

_____

_____

_____

Science Practices & Inquiry

In the AP Biology Curriculum Framework, there are seven **Science Practices**. In this chapter, we focus on **Science Practice 6**: The student can work with scientific explanations and theories. More specifically, we focus on **Science Practice 6.4:** The student can make claims and predictions about natural phenomena based on scientific theories and models.

Question 22 asks you to make scientific claims and predictions about how species diversity within an ecosystem influences ecosystem stability (**Learning Objective 4.27**).

22. Species diversity is impacted by many different phenomena. Choose three of the disruptions below, and explain how each can impact the dynamic homeostasis or balance of an ecosystem.

- Invasive and/or eruptive species
- Human impact
- Hurricanes, floods, earthquakes, volcanoes, fires
- Water limitation
- Increased salinity

45 The Global Ecosystem

Chapter Outline

We are all in this together. Because all of Earth's systems are interrelated, a change in wind patterns over the ocean can cause climate changes around the world. When a large volcano erupts, injecting gases and ash into the upper atmosphere, the effects are felt across the globe for years. A change in climate will alter the productivity of an ecosystem.

Gross primary productivity (GPP) is the amount of energy trapped by the producers in an ecosystem, but not all of this is available to consumers. Much is dissipated as heat energy during the catabolism of fuel molecules. Net primary productivity (NPP) is the amount of energy captured in the tissues of primary producers, so it is a key indicator of the amount of energy available to the next trophic level (consumers). Measurements of an ecosystem's NPP are important descriptors of productivity.

The recycling of elements and nutrients in ecosystems occurs via biogeochemical cycles. Nutrients typically move from one form to another, into and out of major pools and sinks at varying flux rates. Most studied are the water, carbon, and nitrogen cycles.

The biogeochemical cycle of carbon has direct impacts on the world's climate. The increased release of greenhouse gases from human activities is a significant contributor to warmer winters and summers, more powerful storms, and increasingly unpredictable weather. Like a pane of clear glass, the atmosphere allows the passage of most solar radiation, warming Earth's surface. Much of this energy is reradiated as heat energy, but greenhouse gases in the atmosphere prevent it from reaching space. Instead, the energy further warms our atmosphere, causing global climate change.

Climate changes cause many disruptions to ecosystems, such as evolving plant species, shifting migration patterns, and melting polar ice caps. Historically, organisms have substantially changed Earth's atmosphere, most notably resulting from the evolution of photosynthetic organisms and the subsequent release of molecular oxygen gas (O_2). Other physical changes have resulted in warming and cooling trends. But now one species, *Homo sapiens*, is single-handedly causing large-scale deviations. The challenge we face is to minimize human influence on climate change and mitigate the effects of the damage we've already done. This requires a genuine commitment to worldwide cooperation.

Chapter 45 includes **Big Idea 2** and **Big Idea 4**. The specific parts of the AP Biology curriculum covering **Big Idea 2**: Biological systems utilize free energy and molecular building blocks to grow, to reproduce, and to maintain dynamic homeostasis, include:

- **2.A.2**: Organisms capture and store energy for use in biological processes.

- **2.A.3**: Organisms must exchange matter with the environment to grow, reproduce, and maintain organization.

The specific parts covering **Big Idea 4**: Biological systems interact, and these systems and their interactions possess complex properties, include:

- **4.A.6**: Interactions among living systems and with their environment result in the movement of matter and energy.

- **4.B.4**: Distribution of local and global ecosystems changes over time.

- **4.C.4**: The diversity of species within an ecosystem may influence the stability of the ecosystem.

Chapter Review

Concept 45.1 *examines how net primary productivity (NPP) varies with climate change.*

1. Explain why NPP does not measure the rate of exchange between organisms and all of the nutrients they need.

_____

_____

_____

_____

Refer to the diagram at the right to answer Questions 2 and 3.

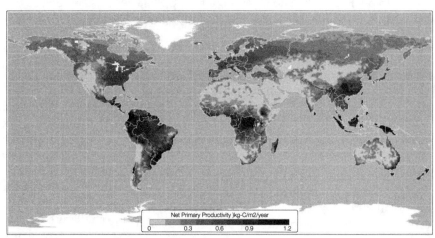

Map courtesy of the Center for Sustainability and the Global Environment, University of Wisconsin—Madison

2. Identify two reasons that NPP is higher in the equatorial regions.

_____

_____

3. Summarize the pattern of NPP across North America, and discuss why these patterns exist.

_____

_____

_____

_____

_____

4. Design an experiment to determine the identity of the limiting nutrient in a grassland ecosystem.

_____

_____

_____

_____

_____

_____

5. Explain why the limiting nutrient in a grassland ecosystem might not be a limiting nutrient in another ecosystem.

_____

_____

_____

_____

_____

Concept 45.2 *identifies and discusses biological, geological, and chemical processes contributing to biogeochemical cycles.*

6. Describe the primary energy source that drives the constant recycling of most matter.

_____

_____

_____

_____

_____

7. Earth is considered an open system with regard to energy. Discuss this concept with attention to free energy and entropy.

_____

_____

_____

_____

_____

_____

_____

_____

_____

8. Earth is considered to be a closed system with regard to matter. Discuss this concept with attention to free energy and entropy.

_____

_____

_____

_____

_____

_____

_____

_____

Concept 45.3 *considers the three most important biogeochemical cycles in ecosystems: the water, carbon, and nitrogen cycles. One result of too much nitrogen runoff from agricultural fields and animal wastes is the cultural eutrophication in bodies of water. This can result in hypoxic or anoxic zones in these ecosystems.*

9. Complete the table below for each of the three major biogeochemical cycles. Sinks are the locations where the nutrient is inaccessible for long periods.

Cycle	Fluxes	Pools	Sinks
Water			
Carbon			
Nitrogen			

10. Draw either the nitrogen cycle or the carbon cycle, showing the major fluxes, pools, and sinks. Include examples of living organisms.

11. Excess nutrients (nitrates) entering a body of water from surface runoff can result in an algal bloom. Explain how the overabundance of algae in a body of water can lead to an anoxic zone (i.e., no dissolved O_2).

_____

_____

_____

_____

_____

_____

_____

12. Though nitrogen gas (N_2) makes up approximately 78 percent of the Earth's atmosphere, it is a limiting nutrient in many ecosystems. Explain why we need to constantly apply nitrogen as fertilizer to agricultural fields, despite its abundance in air.

_____

_____

_____

Concept 45.4 *relates biogeochemical cycles and global climate, with a particular focus on the greenhouse effect and the recent increases of greenhouse gases in the atmosphere.*

Refer to the graph at the right, showing the concentration of carbon dioxide (CO_2) in the atmosphere, to answer Questions 13 and 14.

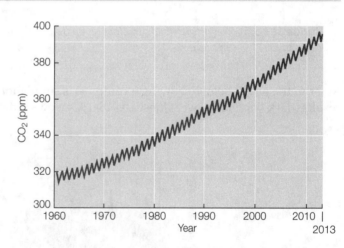

13. Draw a diagram or flow chart that represents the rise and fall of CO_2 in the atmosphere over one year. Assume that the data are from a temperate forest, and include living organisms

14. Calculate the percent increase of CO_2 in the atmosphere between 1980 and 2010.

15. Carbon dioxide is not the most potent greenhouse gas, yet it is the one that is most often discussed. Explain the reason for this.

_____

_____

_____

_____

_____

_____

Concept 45.5 *looks at the effects of global climate change on the Earth's ecosystems and predicts how ecological systems are changing as a result.*

Refer to the graph below, showing a computer's simulation of temperature in the atmosphere and the actual results (dark line), to answer Questions 16–19. Arrows indicate five major volcanic eruptions.

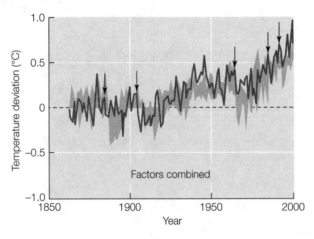

16. Explain the dashed line across the middle of the graph.

_____

_____

_____

_____

_____

17. Discuss what the data show for the ten years following volcanic eruptions, and explain how this change occurred.

_____

_____

_____

_____

_____

_____

_____

_____

_____

_____

_____

_____

18. Discuss what likely happened to ecosystems in the ten years following the volcanic eruptions.

_____

_____

_____

_____

_____

_____

_____

_____

_____

_____

_____

_____

19. There was a major volcanic eruption in Iceland in 2011, and carbon dioxide concentrations have continued to rise. Using the graph below, expand the line to 2020 with these two factors in mind.

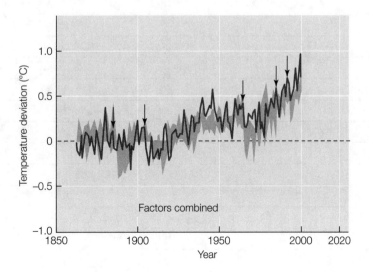

Concept 45.6 *focuses on humans and their impact on the environment, raising the hope that humans can mitigate the damage done.*

20. Interview one or two older members of your local community who have spent the majority of their lives nearby. How has the local climate changed over their lifetimes? Has local vegetation or animal life changed over the years?

_____

_____

_____

_____

_____

_____

_____

_____

_____

_____

_____

_____

_____

_____

21. Imagine that you have been elected president of the United States. What is the first major thing you would do to change how Americans affect climate change? How would you work to influence other global leaders to reduce their greenhouse gas emissions?

_____

_____

_____

_____

_____

_____

_____

_____

_____

_____

_____

_____

_____

_____

Science Practices & Inquiry

In the AP Biology Curriculum Framework there are seven **Science Practices**. In this chapter, we focus on **Science Practice 2:** The student can use mathematics appropriately. More specifically, we focus on **Science Practice 2.2:** The student can apply mathematical routines to quantities that describe natural phenomena.

Question 22 asks you to apply mathematical routines to quantities that describe interactions between living systems and their environment, which result in the movement of matter and energy (**Learning Objective 4.14**).

22. The chart below shows how NPP varies with different ecosystems. Using the entire NPP for terrestrial ecosystems, calculate the percent NPP of temperate forests. Express your answer to the nearest tenth, and record your answer on the grid provided. Show your work.

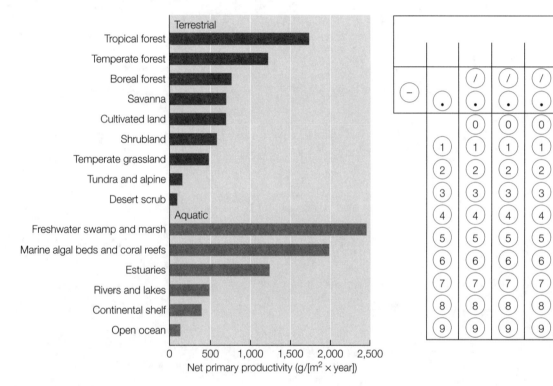

Preparing for the AP® Exam

An Introduction to the New AP® Biology Course

The revised AP® Biology exam, first administered in 2013, is in some ways very different from the former version and in other ways quite similar. Like the exams in previous years, there are multiple-choice and free-response questions. The new exam has a greater focus on the conceptual understanding of biology. Reduced content, additional math-based questions, and an increased emphasis on learning and inquiry make the new AP® Biology course more engaging than ever.

The AP® Biology exam is divided into four **Big Ideas**, all weighted equally on the exam. The topics, shown below, are described in more detail in APCentral's course description at apcentral.collegeboard.com.

1. Evolution
2. Cellular Processes: Energy and Communication
3. Genetics and Information Transfer
4. Interactions

All test questions are defined by the scope of the new **Learning Objectives** in the Curriculum Framework. Content areas including phylogeny, much of plant biology, and many of the human systems have been removed from the required material.

Many of these topics are not required but are given as illustrative examples. For most topics, there are three or four illustrative examples to show how a concept is applied. Your teacher should use at least one example for each topic in your class. Pay close attention to these, and be ready to use them in free-response questions. Plan on reviewing at least one of these examples from each section. As an example, look at **Essential Knowledge 1.A.2**: c. Some phenotypic variations significantly increase or decrease fitness of the organism and the population. To foster student understanding of this concept, instructors can choose an illustrative example such as sickle cell anemia, the peppered moth, or DDT resistance in insects.

A short free-response question could ask you to show how phenotypic variations can increase the fitness of a population using one of these examples.

Format of the AP® Exam

Section I (90 minutes; 50%)

Part A: 63 Multiple-choice questions

Part B: 6 Grid-in questions

Section II (80 minutes; 50%)

2 long free-response questions; 10 points each (25%)

6 short free-response questions; 3–4 points each (25%)

The new AP® Biology exam provides an equation sheet, and you may use a simple, four-function calculator (with square root). You may not use a scientific or graphing calculator. You will record your answers to calculation (grid-in) questions on a grid like the one shown at the right.

The answers to multiple-choice questions are recorded on answer sheets and are graded by computer. You will earn points *only* for correct responses on multiple-choice questions. **There is no guessing penalty for incorrect answers, so answer *all* questions.** In the new AP® Biology test, multiple-choice items have four possible responses, A – D. You will not find answers such as "all of the above" or "none of the above," and there are no negative questions such as "Which of the following is NOT…" As before, questions are in random order.

All of the essays written by AP® Biology students in response to the free-response questions are graded by high school teachers and college professors in June. To standardize scoring, there is a grading rubric for each question, instructing readers how to allocate points for answers. Readers practice scoring and check each other's work for accuracy.

Results fall into one of the following categories on a five-point scale:

5	Extremely well qualified (to receive college credit)
4	Well qualified
3	Qualified
2	Possibly qualified
1	No recommendation

Released free-response questions and their rubrics showing point distributions can be found at APCentral. Be aware that the free-response questions from 2012 and earlier are of the long (10-point) free-response style. Until 2013, there were no short questions. The College Board released a practice exam before the summer of 2013 that has examples of grid-in and short free-response questions.

You can expect to receive your scores in early July. If requested, your scores will be sent directly to colleges and universities, as well. Many colleges and universities accept a score of 4 or 5 for credit and placement. Some colleges will give you credit for a score of 3. You can go online to find out what scores an institution accepts, or contact the admissions office for more information.

Strategies for Preparing for the AP® Exam

- As you study, develop your own shorthand notes and/or acronyms. For example, in studying signaling, you might realize that signaling implies a stimulus to start the signal, a sensor that detects the signal, and receptor-based effector mechanisms that lead to a response. By using the underlined letters in that sentence, the acronym SSRE can help you remember some key ideas about signaling.

- Make reading and writing an integral part of your coursework. *Practice writing essays!* Write an essay on any topic from the course, selected by you or your teacher, using only your memory to guide you. When you're done, open your notes and your textbook to see what you forgot to mention or what you stated incorrectly. Then rewrite your answer. Note how long it takes you to write your answers so you will be better prepared to pace yourself when the real essays have to be written for the exam.

- Start your review two to three weeks before the exam. Make a review schedule and stick to it! Schedule time to take a practice exam, time to review each major unit, and time to review problematic units in more detail.

- Re-try the *Strive* Study Guide exercises, covering up your old answers with blank paper.

- Take a full-length test in advance. Two tests are included at the end of this book.

- Make sure you understand the structure of the exam and how it will be graded.

- Get plenty of sleep the night before the exam so you will be well-rested and alert, ready to focus all of your attention on the test. By this time in your school year, especially if you have worked faithfully on this *Strive* guide, you will know as much biology as you need to know to do well. Cramming late into the night before the exam will not give your brain the time it needs to digest the material and transfer it to long-term memory.

- It is important that you are comfortable while taking the exam. Wear layers in case it is colder or warmer than you expect.

- Bring a snack and some water for break time. Your brain needs energy to work at this level for sustained periods.

Strategies for Taking the Free-Response Section of the AP® Exam

1. First, *read the question very carefully*. Pay particular attention to **bold** and underlined words. They are **important**. Be sure to answer the question that is asked, and *only* that question, and answer all parts of it.

2. Write in sentences and paragraphs. *Writing in outline form will earn you no credit.*

3. A good strategy is to define terms, give an example, and then explain how your example works. Say something about each of the important terms you use. Define the simple terms and the complex terms. Often it is the easy definitions that are left out.

4. Remember not to write something you're not sure about; if you do not write it, you cannot lose points for it.

5. Answer the parts of the question in the order they are given. If an essay is set up with internal parts (e.g., a., b., and c.), answer them that way, and *clearly label each part*.

6. Use a blue or black pen, and write *clearly* and *neatly*. It is foolhardy to confuse the reader with poor penmanship.

7. Use detail that is on the subject and to the point. Include the obvious (for example, "light (photons) is necessary for photosynthesis"). Answer each question thoroughly.

8. If you cannot remember a word exactly, get as close as you can. If you don't have a name for a concept, describe it. Remember, the test is often graded conceptually, so you may well get a point for an idea you have described correctly.

9. Write everything you know about the topic, *but stay on the topic*. No detail is too small to be included, as long as it is to the point. (For example, if a question asks about the structure of DNA, talk about the helix, etc. Do not waste time on RNA, and expression, or Mendelian genetics.) Any time you provide a nugget of truth in a written answer, as long as it is on topic, you have a chance to earn points.

10. Carefully label your diagrams and place them at the appropriate location in the answer section, not detached at the end. Be sure to refer to the diagram in your essay.

11. Widen your margins. This will make the essay easier for people to read.

12. Understand that the exam is written to be difficult. The national average for the essay section will be about 50% correct— 5 points out of a possible 10—on the longer essays. It is very likely that you will not know everything. This is expected, but it is very likely that you do know something about each essay topic, so relax and do the best you can. Write thorough answers.

13. Do not leave blanks. Often on difficult essays the mean will be very low. If you are struggling with a question, it is likely that many others are also struggling. So if you write a little, you may well hit the mean.

DON'T

1. These are not English essays. Don't restate the question. Don't write a rambling introduction or repeat things in your conclusion. These things waste valuable time.

2. Don't waste time on background information or long introductions unless the question calls for historical development or historical significance. Just answer the question.

3. Don't ramble—get to the point!

4. Don't panic or get upset because you are unfamiliar with a question. You probably have read or heard something about the subject; stay calm and think.

5. Don't scratch out excessively. A line through unwanted word(s) should be sufficient.

6. **Don't write in the margins**, especially on the short free-response questions.

7. Don't worry about spelling every word right or using perfect grammar. These things are not graded. It is important for you to know, however, that very poor spelling or grammar may make a bad impression on the grader.

8. Though you won't be graded on handwriting, sloppiness and large loops that cover other letters are difficult to decipher. It is easy for a grader to miss an important word when he/she cannot read your handwriting. If a word cannot be read, it cannot earn a point.

Practice Exam 1

Directions:

Following is a full-length Practice Exam to help you hone your skills for the AP® Biology exam. This exam is comprised of two parts, and answers and sample scoring rubrics follow at the end. It is important that you practice your test-taking skills by simulating real testing conditions. Allocate three hours to take this exam.

1. Take this test in a single three-hour block.

2. Do not use headphones or allow music, phones, texting, or other social media to interrupt you.

3. Allow 90 minutes for Section I; this includes the multiple-choice and grid-in (calculation) questions. Then put this section away. You may *not* go back to it during Section II.

4. Take a 10- to 15-minute break, and have a snack.

5. Take 10 minutes to read over and outline potential answers. Then give yourself 80 minutes to complete Section II. Watch your time carefully, and stop when the time is up.

After you check your results, be sure to go back and review the areas you struggled with. Each question is correlated to a specific Learning Objective in the AP® Biology curriculum framework. Look up the ones you erred on, and study these topics further.

NOTE: For Practice Exam Section I, print out an answer sheet from www.pol2e.com/hs/strive

No portion of this practice test may be copied or posted to the Internet without written permission from the publisher.

GO ON TO THE NEXT PAGE.

BIOLOGY
Section 1
63 Multiple-Choice Questions
6 Grid-In Questions
Time: 90 Minutes

Directions: Each of the questions or incomplete statements below is followed by four suggested answers or completions. Select the one that is best in each case, then fill in the corresponding space on the answer sheet.

1. Hershey and Chase were the first scientists to show that DNA, rather than protein, is the source of heritable information. In their experiment, radioisotope-labelled viruses were used to infect bacteria. Use of which of the following isotopes best justifies, as described, Hershey and Chase's claim that DNA is the source of heritable information?

   (A) Oxygen-18, because the virus uses the oxygen to respire while inside the bacterium.
   (B) Nitrogen-15, because the virus uses nitrogen to assemble amino acids.
   (C) Carbon-14, because the virus uses it to assemble carbohydrates for its cell wall.
   (D) Phosphorous-32, because it was transferred from the virus to the bacterium.

2. Huntington's disease is an autosomal dominant genetic disorder that results in cognitive decline and decreased muscular coordination. The symptoms usually begin at about age 40 and can progress very rapidly. A simple test can determine whether a person carries this trait.

   After learning these things, a young woman whose mother had Huntington's disease is deciding whether or not to have children. Which of the following ethical questions is she likely to ask?

   (A) Is Huntington's disease transmitted as a genetic disorder?
   (B) If she carries the Huntington's mutation, should she be worried about her insurance company declining her coverage in the future?
   (C) Should she undergo genetic testing to determine whether she carries this trait and could pass it on to her children?
   (D) If she carries the trait, is it possible for her to pass it directly to her husband, as with some other diseases?

GO ON TO THE NEXT PAGE.

3. A biologist examined several populations in a forest ecosystem over two weeks. He observed a population of butterflies, the flowers they feed on, and the two species of birds that feed on the butterflies. The data are reflected in the graphs below.

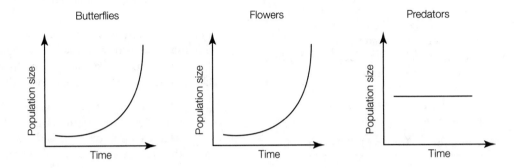

Which of the following best justifies the collection of the data described above?

(A) To determine how a population increases in size, the density of individuals must be measured.

(B) To determine whether the rate of reproduction is logistic or exponential, the constraints on a population must be measured in addition to the population size.

(C) To calculate the overall rate of growth of a population, the limits to population growth by density-dependent factors must be measured.

(D) To determine how a population grows, age-structure diagrams of both predators and prey must be used to study future growth patterns.

GO ON TO THE NEXT PAGE.

4. In an investigation into diffusion, a student submerges an agar cube with phenolphthalein in vinegar (acetic acid). Phenolphthalein changes from pink to clear as the pH turns from basic to acidic. As the vinegar diffuses into the cube, the cube turns from red to clear, so the depth of penetration can be measured. The data presented below represent the depth of diffusion into three different sized cubes after five minutes. The size of each cube is represented as the length of each side.

Size of cube	Depth of diffusion
1 cm	0.4 cm
2 cm	0.4 cm
3 cm	0.4 cm

Based on the data provided above, which of the following best supports the claim that there is an evolutionary constraint on cell size?

(A) The volume of a cell increases as materials diffuse into it, allowing for a faster rate of diffusion.

(B) The formation of organelles increases as cell size increases.

(C) The size of the cube increases as the depth of diffusion increases.

(D) The rate of diffusion is the same regardless of cell size, thus limiting cell size.

5. Most researchers consider DNA to be the original source of heredity, as depicted below:

$$DNA \rightarrow RNA \rightarrow PROTEIN$$

Recent research, however, has shown that this may not be true. Which of the following models supports a revision of the theory that DNA is the original source of heredity?

(A) A variant form of DNA can now be considered the original agent of heredity, because new forms of DNA with different nucleotides have been isolated from fossils.

(B) RNA can now be considered the original agent of heredity, because RNA can self-replicate.

(C) Proteins can now be considered the original agent of heredity, because they are more numerous and can serve more functions.

(D) Individual nucleotides can now be considered the original agent of heredity, because they can be formed in the Miller–Urey apparatus that simulates Earth's original atmosphere.

GO ON TO THE NEXT PAGE.

Questions 6 – 7

Crickets are small insects that are commonly heard chirping on warm summer evenings. The body temperature of these ectothermic insects is dependent on the temperature of the surrounding environment. Ten crickets were placed in a bottle, and a probe was used to measure carbon dioxide (CO_2) as the crickets produced it. The crickets' CO_2 production at 25°C and 40°C is shown in the graph below.

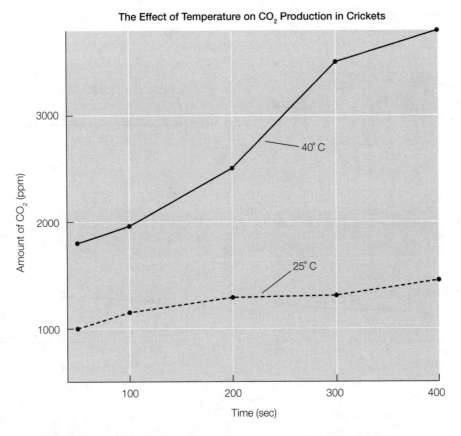

The Effect of Temperature on CO_2 Production in Crickets

6. Which of the following provides reasoning to support the claim that as carbon moves through organisms it is ultimately given off as carbon dioxide?

(A) Crickets are in a dynamic homeostasis with their environment.

(B) Crickets are always growing.

(C) Crickets are reproducing more at higher temperatures.

(D) Crickets are unable to survive below temperatures of 20°C.

7. Which of the following most likely predicts the effect on the respiration rate of crickets if the temperature is decreased to 15°C?

(A) Respiration rate will increase because the crickets will use respiration to warm their bodies.

(B) Respiration rate will increase because the enzymes that catalyze respiration will be closer to their optimum temperature.

(C) Respiration rate will decrease because enzymes that catalyze respiration will have less kinetic energy.

(D) Respiration rate will decrease because the lowered carbon dioxide concentration in the air will cause a decrease in the feedback mechanism regulating respiration.

GO ON TO THE NEXT PAGE.

8. Crickets are ectothermic organisms, meaning that body temperatures are strongly influenced by the external temperature. Mice, however, are endothermic and can dynamically regulate their body temperatures, within limits, as external temperatures vary. Both organisms utilize food energy for respiration and release CO_2 as a by-product of their respiration. Which of the following models best describes the rates of respiration of mice held at 25°C and 40°C?

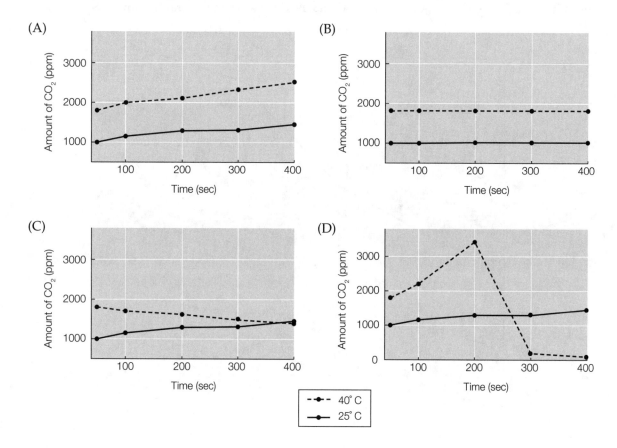

GO ON TO THE NEXT PAGE.

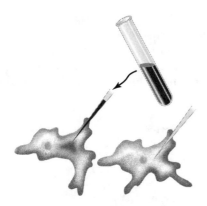

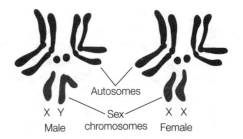

9. Amoebas are single-celled protists that use microfilaments (part of the cytoskeleton) for locomotion. Cytochalasin prevents the *in vitro* formation of microfilaments from its monomers. To investigate whether cytochalasin would have the same effect on microfilament formation in a living system, this drug was injected into living amoebas using a tiny syringe, as shown above. A second group of amoebas was injected with the same volume of fluid that did not contain the drug.

If cytochalasin does prevent the formation of microfilaments in living amoebas, which of the following should be observed in the amoebas injected with the drug?

(A) The amoebas would exist as blob-like organisms with no ability to move.

(B) The amoebas would immediately die due to lack of cytoskeletons.

(C) The amoebas would uptake large amounts of water due to osmosis and rupture.

(D) The amoebas would be able to move normally due to pre-existing microfilaments.

10. The species *Drosophila melanogaster* has four pairs of chromosomes. The gene for eye color is located on the chromosome that also determines sex. The allele for wild-type red eyes is dominant to the allele for white eyes. When a white-eyed female fly is crossed with a red-eyed male, all of the female progeny are red-eyed and all of the male progeny are white-eyed. Which of the following best supports the claim that this trait deviates from Mendel's model of inheritance?

(A) The eye color gene is linked with the sex trait, and males carry only one allele for this trait.

(B) The eye color gene is found as three alleles and only two of these alleles are found in this cross.

(C) The eye color is caused by multiple genes acting together to create one trait.

(D) The eye color is a result of genes located outside of the nucleus in the mitochondria.

GO ON TO THE NEXT PAGE.

11. In an investigation into the effect of light on carbon dioxide production during respiration, a researcher placed ten crickets in a bottle, and an electronic probe was used to measure the amount of carbon dioxide produced by the crickets over a five-minute period. One group of crickets was placed under a bright light source, while a second group was placed under a dim light. A heat sink was used in front of the bright light source so that both groups of crickets would experience the same external temperature.

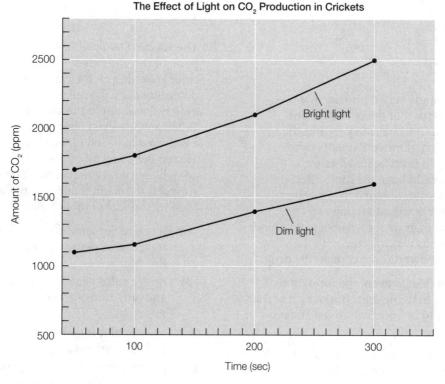

The Effect of Light on CO_2 Production in Crickets

Based on the data shown, which of the following describes the crickets' rate of respiration?

(A) It was greater under the bright light source.

(B) It decreased because of the bright light source.

(C) Dim light reduced the rate of oxygen utilization by approximately one-third.

(D) The rates in the two lighting conditions were very similar.

GO ON TO THE NEXT PAGE.

Questions 12 – 14

Tube #	Temperature (°C)	Time needed for disk to float (sec)
1	25°	18
2	30°	12
3	35°	15
4	40°	18
5	45°	25
6	50°	116
7	55°	>120

In an investigation into the effect of temperature on enzymatic activity, a researcher ground chunks of potato in a blender to extract the enzyme catalase. Disks of filter paper were soaked in the potato catalase extract. The filter paper disks were then pushed to the bottom of tubes of hydrogen peroxide (H_2O_2) solutions at different temperatures. As catalase reacted with H_2O_2, bubbles of oxygen gas (O_2) formed on the paper disks, causing the disks to float. The time it took for the disk to rise to the top of each tube was measured. (Room temperature was approximately 25°C.)

12. Based on the data, which of the following best describes the optimal temperature for the activity of catalase?

    (A) 25° C
    (B) 30° C
    (C) 45° C
    (D) 50° C

13. In environments warmer than room temperature, which of the following environmental modifications will likely increase the rate of reaction of catalase with H_2O_2?

    (A) Decreasing the concentration of carbon dioxide gas
    (B) Increasing the enzyme concentration
    (C) Increasing the concentration of oxygen gas
    (D) Increasing the pH

14. Which of the following best describes the results observed in tube #7?

    (A) The activation energy of the reaction was doubled.
    (B) The activation energy of the reaction was lowered.
    (C) The optimal temperature of the enzyme was reached.
    (D) The shape of the catalase molecule was changed.

GO ON TO THE NEXT PAGE.

Questions 15 – 16

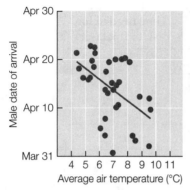

Pied flycatchers spend the winter months in northern Africa. It the spring, they migrate back to the Netherlands in northern Europe, where climate change has increased the air temperature over a 34-year period. The graph above shows the arrival dates for male pied flycatchers arriving in the Netherlands, along with the average air temperature at the time. Each dot corresponds to one year, and the calculated line is the overall regression of arrival date and temperature. (Air temperatures were measured each year and averaged to get the temperatures shown.)

15. Which of the following best describes the change in behavior of the pied flycatcher in response to the external cue of rising environmental temperatures?

   (A) There is a correlation between arrival date and air temperature, as male pied flycatchers arrive in the Netherlands earlier each successive year.

   (B) The data in the graph are too scattered to suggest any conclusions.

   (C) Increased air temperatures directly cause male pied flycatchers to arrive earlier.

   (D) There is a direct correlation between the arrival dates of male and female pied flycatchers.

16. If the researchers wanted to refine this experiment by examining the behavior of the pied flycatchers with respect to other abiotic features, which of the following would be appropriate to study?

   (A) Population density, biofilms, and nutrient availability

   (B) Salinity, pH, water, and nutrient availability

   (C) Availability of nesting materials and competition with other birds for nesting sites

   (D) Symbiosis and other predator–prey relationships

GO ON TO THE NEXT PAGE.

Questions 17 – 18

Students performed an investigation using dialysis tubing with various solutions to study the properties of varying substances as they move across membranes. Each solution listed below was placed into a dialysis tubing bag, which was then immersed in distilled water. The percent change in mass of the dialysis tubing bag was calculated after 30 minutes.

Treatment	Solution in tubing	% Change in mass
1	Albumin (0.001M)	+0.05
2	Glucose (1M)	+2.88
3	Sodium chloride (1M)	+0.82
4	Sucrose (1M)	+4.83
5	Water	+0.15

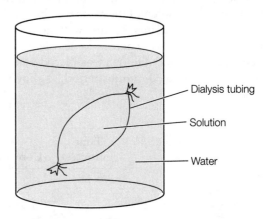

17. Which of the following most likely explains the difference between the results for sodium chloride (NaCl) and those for glucose ($C_6H_{12}O_6$)?

(A) Sodium chloride ions are smaller and thus diffuse out as water diffuses in.

(B) The sodium chloride has a greater electronegativity than the glucose, and thus water diffuses in at a faster rate.

(C) Sodium chloride ions are larger than glucose ions, so water diffuses easily through the membrane.

(D) The sodium chloride has less solubility in water than the glucose, thus more water diffuses into the dialysis bag.

18. Which of the following best describes the role of Treatment 5 in the investigation?

(A) It serves as a comparison to see if other factors may have influenced the results.

(B) It increases the number of repeated trials.

(C) It gives the students practice in filling and weighing dialysis bags.

(D) It increases the range of the independent variables.

GO ON TO THE NEXT PAGE.

Questions 19 – 21

During transpiration, water evaporates from airspaces in a plant's leaves and escapes through small pores called stomata. The stomata stay open to allow the entry of carbon dioxide, a necessary reactant in photosynthesis, but this results in significant water loss.

A student investigated how environmental conditions affect the loss of water by using four plants of the same species. Each had the same number and size of leaves. One plant served as a control and was kept at room temperature in a location with no air movement. A second was placed in front of a fan to simulate a gentle breeze blowing across the leaves. A third was placed in front of a strong light providing additional heat and light, and a fourth was placed in a very humid environment. The student measured and recorded water loss over a 30-minute period, as shown in the chart below.

Time (minutes)	Water loss (mL)			
	Control	Wind	Strong light	High humidity
0	0.0	0.0	0.0	0.0
10	0.0026	0.0063	0.0093	0.0012
20	0.0055	0.0106	0.0132	0.0020
30	0.0079	0.0154	0.0170	0.0029

19. Based on the data, which plant showed the greatest rate of transpiration over the 30-minute period?

    (A) Control
    (B) Wind
    (C) Strong light
    (D) High humidity

20. Which of the following best supports the decision to use the same types of plants with the same amount of surface area?

    (A) This makes it possible to replicate the experiment over and over again.
    (B) All plants will have the same number of stomata and the same potential for water loss.
    (C) Use of a common plant makes it possible to compare data on water loss.
    (D) It is important to limit the number of variables in an experiment to measure the effect of change.

21. Plants have made several types of adaptations to control water loss through their stomata. Which idea represents a refinement of the experiment testing the ability of plants to control water loss through stomata?

    (A) Creating an artificial plant with small holes in the leaves to compare with living systems
    (B) Forcing the plants to close their stomata and then measuring their water loss
    (C) Developing an alternative biochemical pathway in plants to reduce the impact of lowered carbon dioxide levels on photosynthesis
    (D) Using a magnifying lens to view the opening and closing of stomata under varying environmental conditions

GO ON TO THE NEXT PAGE.

22. Which of the following supports the claim that organisms utilize free energy to maintain organization, grow, and reproduce, but within any one ecosystem, there are different strategies to utilize energy?

    (A) Coral polyps rely on symbiotic algae to capture sunlight and convert it to chemical energy.

    (B) Onion cells have compounds that regulate mitosis, ensuring that the chromosomes have replicated prior to mitosis occurring.

    (C) Compared to larger organisms, smaller organisms typically have higher rates of metabolism.

    (D) Stanley Miller's apparatus simulating the Earth's early atmosphere showed that complex organic molecules could form abiotically from smaller inorganic precursors.

23. Which of the following correctly pairs researchers with their contributions to the discovery of the structure of DNA?

    (A) Wilkins and Franklin: provided clear images of DNA utilizing X-ray crystallography

    (B) Watson and Crick: first suggested DNA is the agent of heredity

    (C) Avery and MacLeod: used radioactive proteins and DNA with viruses that show DNA is the agent of heredity

    (D) Hershey and Chase: elucidated the double helical nature of DNA

24. Organisms exhibit complex properties due to their constituent parts. When one part of a cell becomes defective, other parts or functions of the cell may also malfunction. Parkinson's disease is one such example. The actual cause of Parkinson's disease is unknown, but most research indicates that it is caused by the death of neurons in the brain that normally release the neurotransmitter dopamine. New research indicates that most afflicted neurons in some Parkinson's patients also have defective nucleoli, where RNA polymerases make the constituent parts of ribosomes. To evaluate whether or not the defective nucleoli were contributing to Parkinson's, which of the following might the scientist study as a possible direct cause of the cell having defective nuceoli?

    (A) Mitochondria could no longer produce ATP.

    (B) Enzymes could no longer be produced.

    (C) DNA could no longer be replicated.

    (D) Osmosis would not be able to move water across membranes.

GO ON TO THE NEXT PAGE.

25. Using a computer sensor to measure water loss, a scientist examined the contribution of each structural component of a plant to the plant's total water loss over a two-week period. The data are shown below.

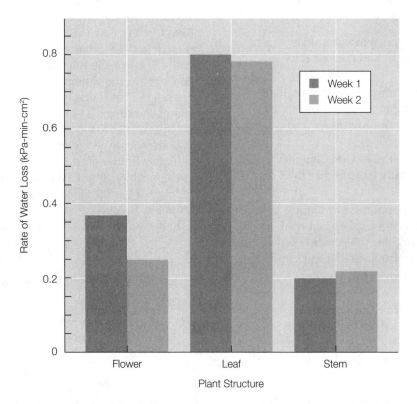

Based on the data, which of the following is a reasonable conclusion about the rates of water loss in different parts of the plant?

(A) Week 1 was warm and windy, and Week 2 was cool and windy, causing differences in transpiration.

(B) The flower began to lose petals in Week 2, which resulted in a lower rate of transpiration.

(C) Because stems and flowers lack stomata, there is no water loss by transpiration in these structures.

(D) Leaf surface area accounts for a higher rate of transpiration than do flowers and stems.

GO ON TO THE NEXT PAGE.

Questions 26 – 27

Polymerases add new nucleotides based on complimentary pairing. The basics of the mechanism of action for these polymerases are shown in the figures below.

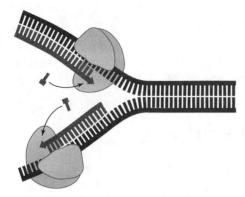

DNA polymerase copies both strands of DNA

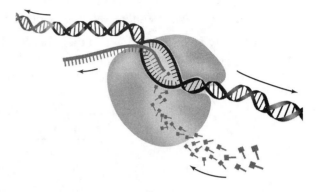

RNA polymerase copies one strand of DNA

26. Based on these models, which of the following best describes a major difference between the copying mechanisms of DNA polymerase and RNA polymerase?

(A) DNA polymerase copies in both $3' \rightarrow 5'$ and $5' \rightarrow 3'$ directions, while RNA polymerase copies only $3' \rightarrow 5'$.

(B) DNA polymerase makes a replica of the original strand of DNA.

(C) Because RNA polymerase is only performing transcription, it requires less energy than DNA polymerase.

(D) DNA polymerase is aided by proteins during replication, while RNA polymerase needs no additional molecules for transcription.

27. A researcher claims that DNA polymerase is an enzyme responsible for copying DNA. Which of the following pieces of evidence about mutations best supports the researcher's claim?

(A) A mutation in an intron of the DNA for this protein would cause the shape of the enzyme to change.

(B) A mutation in an exon of this gene might cause a change in the shape of the enzyme, leading to a change in the efficiency of the enzyme.

(C) A mutation causing an intron to become an exon will have little to no effect on the efficiency of the enzyme.

(D) A mutation in the code for the enzyme's final protein structure will lead to enhanced ability of the enzyme.

GO ON TO THE NEXT PAGE.

28. The polymerase chain reaction (PCR) is a biochemical technology that is used to make thousands or millions of copies of DNA from just one or a very few copies of DNA. The method imposes cycles of repeated heating and cooling on the reaction, allowing the separation of the DNA strand and enzymatic replication of the DNA. Primers (short DNA fragments) containing sequences complementary to the target region along with a DNA polymerase are key to enabling selective and repeated copying. As PCR progresses, the DNA generated is itself used as a template for replication, setting in motion a chain reaction in which the DNA template is exponentially copied.

PCR is usually accomplished with a thermocycler. DNA polymerase enzyme (Taq polymerase) is able to function despite the high temperatures of a PCR machine. During PCR, DNA is heated to separate the DNA strands and then cooled to allow the enzymes to replicate the DNA. Below is a typical sequence for a thermocycler reaction series.

Step	Temperature	Time (name of step)
Initial denaturation	95°C	30 seconds
30 cycles	95°C 45–68°C 68°C	15–30 seconds (denaturation) 15–60 seconds (annealing of primers) 1 minute/Kb (replication)
Final step	68°C	5 minutes

Based on the data, which of the following claims can be made about Taq polymerase?

(A) It is an enzyme found universally in most organisms.

(B) It is found in humans, whose body temperatures are about 37°C.

(C) It is absent in any organism whose internal temperature exceeds 68°C.

(D) It was found in thermophilic bacteria that thrive in hot springs near 100°C.

GO ON TO THE NEXT PAGE.

29. In an investigation of osmosis, a researcher soaked an egg in vinegar for 24 hours to remove the hard shell but leave intact a semi-permeable membrane. The egg was then placed in distilled water for three days. The results are shown in the diagram below.

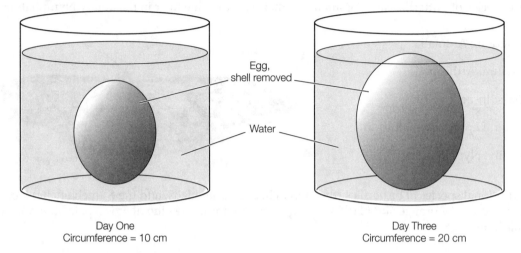

Day One
Circumference = 10 cm

Day Three
Circumference = 20 cm

Which of the following best explains the increase in egg circumference?

(A) The solutes inside the egg are at a higher concentration and actively pull in water through the selectively permeable membrane, via proteins.

(B) The water outside the egg is at a higher concentration and is causing the active transport of solutes outside of the egg as water moves in.

(C) The membrane expands due to a lower solute concentration outside the egg.

(D) Water moves into the egg through membrane proteins (aquaporins) because the solutes of the egg are at a higher concentration.

GO ON TO THE NEXT PAGE.

Questions 30 – 33

The blue tiger butterfly (*Tirumala limniace*), a pale-blue insect with black markings, is pictured below. Three different species of butterflies are classified together with the blue tiger in the family Nymphalidae:

- Kingdom: Animalia

- Phylum: Arthropoda

- Class: Insecta

- Order: Lepidpoptera (butterflies)

- Family: Nymphalidae

Courtesy J.M. Garg

Three additional species of butterflies (the monarch, the painted lady, and the Kamehameha) look very similar, based on the orange and black marking on their wings. The blue tiger is a pale blue color with black markings.

The table below provides more information about these four butterfly species.

Name	Coloration	Location	Subfamily
Blue tiger (B)	blue/black	India, SE Asia	Danaini
Kamehameha (K)	orange/black	Hawaii	Nymphalini
Monarch (M)	orange/black	North America, Australia	Danaini
Painted lady (P)	orange/black	North America, Australia, Asia, Europe	Nymphalini

GO ON TO THE NEXT PAGE.

30. Which of the following cladograms most accurately depicts the most parsimonious relationship of these butterflies, based on their classification?

(A)

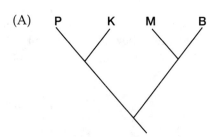

(B)

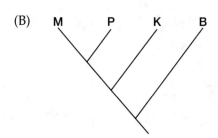

(C)

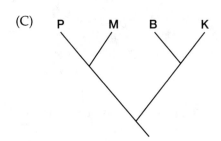

(D)

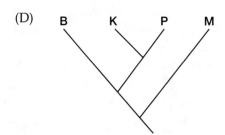

31. Based on the data, which two species are likely to have the most similar DNA?

(A) Blue tiger (B) and Kamehameha (K)

(B) Monarch (M) and Kamehameha (K)

(C) Painted lady (P) and Kamehameha (K)

(D) Monarch (M) and painted lady (P)

32. Which of the following pieces of evidence would be most valuable to an evolutionary biologist who wanted to validate the accuracy of the phylogenetic trees of butterflies?

(A) Knowledge of which of the four species of butterflies can interbreed

(B) A comparison of DNA sequences from the four butterflies

(C) A comparison of the proteins found in each of the four butterflies

(D) A more detailed range map of where each butterfly is found

33. A group of students in the United States raised painted lady butterflies in their classroom to study energy dynamics. At the conclusion of the study, they had 60 adult butterflies that they wanted to release outdoors. Their teacher told them that this was not a good idea. Which of the following best supports the teacher's reasoning?

(A) The painted lady would be an introduced, or non-native, species.

(B) The large number of these butterflies could disrupt the local population.

(C) The butterflies might cross-breed with local butterflies to form a new species.

(D) The butterflies might interbreed with local blue tigers and create new subspecies.

GO ON TO THE NEXT PAGE.

34. CO_2 emissions into the atmosphere from the burning of fossil fuels are causing ocean acidification. As carbon dioxide dissolves into seawater, carbonic acid is formed by the following reaction:

$$CO_2 + H_2O \rightleftharpoons H_2CO_3 \rightleftharpoons HCO_3^- + H^+$$

Ocean-dwelling organisms are negatively affected. Forming calcium carbonate shells becomes much more difficult in the presence of more acidity, which can dissolve calcium carbonate. A new study examining the global ecosystem from the North Pacific provides evidence that the oceans are becoming more acidic on a large scale, as shown in the graph below.

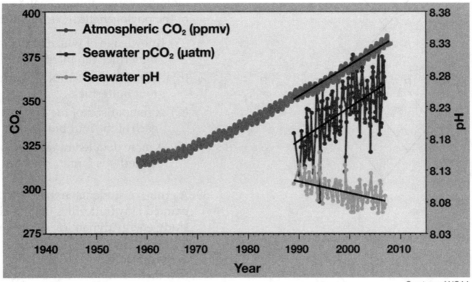

Courtesy of NOAA

Which of the following most likely predicts the consequence of the rising CO_2 levels on the marine trophic level(s)?

(A) The increase in atmospheric CO_2 is directly related to an increase in atmospheric temperature, and this increase in temperature will increase the overall primary productivity of the ocean ecosystem.

(B) Primary producers (phytoplankton) which make shells from calcium carbonate, will be affected first, since their shells are rapidly dissolved by acidic conditions.

(C) Primary consumers (zooplankton) will be affected only if the increase in CO_2 levels continues for at least another 60 years.

(D) Marine organisms will evolve new mechanisms to keep their shells from eroding in response to the rising atmospheric CO_2 levels.

GO ON TO THE NEXT PAGE.

35. The notch signaling pathway is part of a highly conserved cell signaling system present in most multicellular organisms. It is present in all mammals. The notch receptor is a membrane-spanning protein that has external and internal functional regions. Signal proteins (ligands) bind to the external portion, causing the internal domain to release and enter the cell nucleus. This leads to an increase in the expression of specific genes.

The external notch receptor is normally triggered via direct cell-to-cell contact, in which the transmembrane proteins of adjacent cells directly contact the notch receptor. Notch binding allows groups of cells to organize gene expression in patterns that allow the formation of large structures and tissues in the body.

Which of the following scientific questions best supports the claim that notch proteins and other signaling proteins are highly conserved?

(A) If cell signaling processes evolved separately many times, are notch proteins found in mitochondria?

(B) If all organisms share a line of descent, are notch proteins also found in protists?

(C) The imperfect nature of DNA replication and repair increases variation, so how do notch proteins vary from one organism to another?

(D) How do notch proteins allow plant cells to communicate through plasmodesmata of plants?

GO ON TO THE NEXT PAGE.

Questions 36 – 37

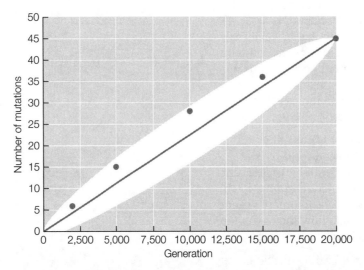

The figure above shows a lineage of *Escherichia coli* bacteria that were propagated in the laboratory for 20,000 generations. Genomes were sequenced from individuals sampled at various points during the experiment to be compared with the genome of the ancestral clone. The line represents a constant rate of mutation accumulation.

36. Based on these data, which of the following is the most valid conclusion?

    (A) The accumulation of mutations is a result of genetic drift caused by natural selection.

    (B) Mutations accumulate in populations in a continuous, nearly constant fashion.

    (C) The mutations will result in new phenotypic variations for which the environment can select.

    (D) The straight line represents a population that is in Hardy–Weinberg equilibrium.

37. If the researchers were to allow this population of *E. coli* to grow for another 10,000 generations, which of the following best approximates how many total mutations would accumulate over the entire 30,000 generations?

    (A) 15
    (B) 28
    (C) 45
    (D) 65

GO ON TO THE NEXT PAGE.

Questions 38 – 41

Hybrids of two different species generally have lower fitness, and individuals that breed only within their own species will leave more surviving offspring than will individuals that interbreed with another species.

A researcher observed that individuals of the perennial flower *Phlox drummondii* have pink flowers across most of its range in Texas. However, where *P. drummondii* is found in sympatry with its close relative, the pink-flowered *P. cuspidata*, *P. drummondii* usually has red flowers. No other *Phlox* species has red flowers.

The researcher studied the effect of prezygotic isolating mechanisms on the production of red flowers, proposing that a prezygotic isolating mechanism may reduce the chances of hybridization between the two species.

The figures below show the average percent of seeds produced by nine populations of *P. drummondii*. The error bars in the graph represent the 95% confidence intervals ($\pm$ 2 SEM) of the sample means.

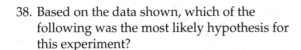

P. drummondii flower color	Number of progeny (seeds)		
	P. drummondii	Hybrid	Total
Red	181 (87%)	27 (13%)	208
Pink	86 (62%)	53 (38%)	139

Mean number of seeds produced by red
and pink *P. drummondii* and hybrid phlox

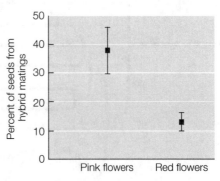

Percent of seeds produced by
P. drummondii from hybrid matings

38. Based on the data shown, which of the following was the most likely hypothesis for this experiment?

   (A) If there are more red flowered *P. drummondii* in the field than pink flowered *P. cuspidata*, then the pink flowers will hybridize more readily.

   (B) Pink flowered *P. cuspidata* will readily hybridize with red flowered *P. drummondii*.

   (C) Red-flowered *P. drummondii* are incapable of hybridizing.

   (D) Red-flowered *P. drummondii* are less likely to hybridize with *P. cuspidata* than are pink-flowered *P. drummondii*.

39. Using the graphed data above, determine the approximate value for the standard error of the mean (SEM) for the pink-flowered *P. drummondii*.

   (A) 4
   (B) 8
   (C) 16
   (D) 38

40. Which is the best conclusion to draw from the data?

   (A) Red-flowered *P. drummondii* are incapable of hybridizing with other *Phlox* species.

   (B) Red-flowered *P. drummondii* produce more seeds than pink-flowered *P. drummondii* plants.

   (C) Hybrid pink-flowered *P. drummondii* produce more flowers than red-flowered plants.

   (D) Red-flowered *P. drummondii* hybridized 38 percent of the time with *P. cuspidate*.

41. Which of the following correctly describes what the error bars represent?

   (A) 95 percent confidence that the range includes the actual sample mean

   (B) The values of data that fall outside of two standard deviations

   (C) 95 percent confidence that the range includes the true mean of the population

   (D) The number of replicates in the experiment

GO ON TO THE NEXT PAGE.

Questions 42 – 43

The figure below is a phylogenetic tree of mammals, based on molecular data. It is accompanied by the original and current distribution of each taxon. A timeline of major continental drift events over the past 150 million years is shown below the tree.

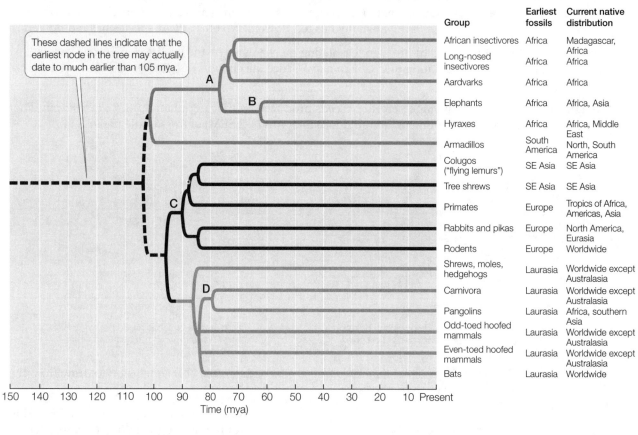

Group	Earliest fossils	Current native distribution
African insectivores	Africa	Madagascar, Africa
Long-nosed insectivores	Africa	Africa
Aardvarks	Africa	Africa
Elephants	Africa	Africa, Asia
Hyraxes	Africa	Africa, Middle East
Armadillos	South America	North, South America
Colugos ("flying lemurs")	SE Asia	SE Asia
Tree shrews	SE Asia	SE Asia
Primates	Europe	Tropics of Africa, Americas, Asia
Rabbits and pikas	Europe	North America, Eurasia
Rodents	Europe	Worldwide
Shrews, moles, hedgehogs	Laurasia	Worldwide except Australasia
Carnivora	Laurasia	Worldwide except Australasia
Pangolins	Laurasia	Africa, southern Asia
Odd-toed hoofed mammals	Laurasia	Worldwide except Australasia
Even-toed hoofed mammals	Laurasia	Worldwide except Australasia
Bats	Laurasia	Worldwide

These dashed lines indicate that the earliest node in the tree may actually date to much earlier than 105 mya.

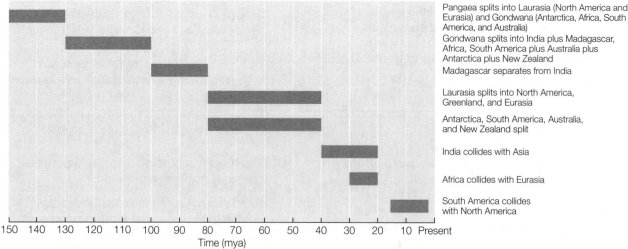

Pangaea splits into Laurasia (North America and Eurasia) and Gondwana (Antarctica, Africa, South America, and Australia)

Gondwana splits into India plus Madagascar, Africa, South America plus Australia plus Antarctica plus New Zealand

Madagascar separates from India

Laurasia splits into North America, Greenland, and Eurasia

Antarctica, South America, Australia, and New Zealand split

India collides with Asia

Africa collides with Eurasia

South America collides with North America

GO ON TO THE NEXT PAGE.

42. Which lettered node on the tree most clearly connects molecular data to an event of continental separation?

   (A) A
   (B) B
   (C) C
   (D) D

43. Based on an analysis of the data, which of the following groups of mammals appear to have dispersed to new areas following removal of a barrier to dispersal?

   (A) Aardvarks
   (B) Rabbits and pikas
   (C) Bats
   (D) Tree shrews

44. Which of the following best represents a four-chromosome cell that is undergoing mitosis?

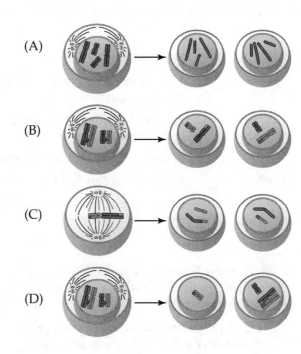

(A)

(B)

(C)

(D)

GO ON TO THE NEXT PAGE.

Questions 45 – 46

The enzyme HMG CoA reductase (HR) catalyzes a first step in the synthesis of cholesterol. The table below shows how various treatments affect HR levels in liver cells.

TREATMENT	AMOUNT OF HR PROTEIN
1. Actinomycin D, a drug that inhibits RNA polymerase II	Reduced
2. Suberoylanilide hydroxamic acid, a histone deacetylase inhibitor	Increased
3. Bortezomib, a proteasome inhibitor	Increased
4. High level of cholesterol	Reduced
5. Azacytidine, inhibitor of DNA methylation	Increased

45. Which of the following is the most likely explanation for the reduction of cholesterol during Treatment 1?

    (A) RNA polymerase lays down a short primer sequence before DNA replication can occur.

    (B) RNA polymerase is the enzyme that modifies ribosomes post-transcriptionally.

    (C) RNA polymerase is necessary to create mRNA, which is translated into the enzyme HR.

    (D) RNA polymerase is responsible for copying RNA multiple times before leaving the nucleus.

46. Which of the following is the most likely explanation for the reduction of cholesterol during Treatment 4?

    (A) Cholesterol at high levels inhibits the enzyme HR via negative feedback.

    (B) At high levels, cholesterol binds to itself, decreasing its concentration in the bloodstream.

    (C) Cholesterol sends positive feedback to the enzymes responsible for synthesizing cholesterol.

    (D) At high concentrations, cholesterol stimulates repressor enzymes.

GO ON TO THE NEXT PAGE.

47. In an investigation of natural selection, male widowbirds were captured and their tails were either artificially lengthened by gluing on feathers or artificially shortened by cutting feathers. In a control group, tail feathers were cut and replaced at their normal length to control for the effects of capture and tail-cutting. The males were released and observed as they established territories and mated with females. The number of successful nests in each male's territory was then recorded and graphed, as shown.

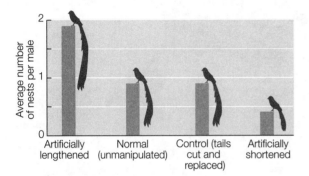

Which of the following is the most likely conclusion connecting genetic variation in the male widowbirds to the phenotype for this population?

(A) Genetic drift in widowbirds caused the birds with artificially shortened tails to produce more nests.

(B) Stabilizing selection in widowbirds is creating a population of longer tails.

(C) Sexual selection in widowbirds has favored the evolution of long tails in the males.

(D) Tail length has little to no effect on the number of nests produced.

48. The chemical reaction for cellular respiration is represented by the equation below.

$$C_6H_{12}O_6 + 6O_2 + 6H_2O \rightarrow 6CO_2 + 12H_2O$$

The rate of respiration of germinating seeds is performed by measuring oxygen and carbon dioxide gases. Which of the following best predicts the rate of carbon dioxide production in germinating seeds?

(A) It is equal to the rate of oxygen consumption.

(B) It is six times the rate of oxygen production.

(C) It is half the rate of oxygen consumption.

(D) It varies with the rate of oxygen consumption.

GO ON TO THE NEXT PAGE.

49. House mice did not live in North America before European colonization. They arrived as stowaways on European ships, presumably in random groups. A researcher trapped wild house mice at five locations from Florida to Maine, indicated by arrows on the map at the right. She paired males and females from each location to obtain lab-born, lab-reared offspring. All mice were born and raised in exactly the same lab environment.

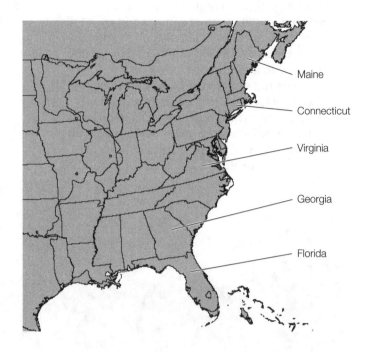

The scientist set up a formal experiment to test nest-building at two temperatures by house mice from the five locations. Nest-building was measured by finding the weight of cotton mice used to build four nests. The researcher found that mice from progressively northern (colder) areas tended to build much bigger, warmer nests at cooler temperatures.

This result points to evolution by natural selection of a genetically controlled, behavioral propensity for wild mice to build warmer nests in colder locations where they would be particularly advantageous.

GO ON TO THE NEXT PAGE.

Which model most accurately represents the evolution of nesting behavior in the mice?

(A)

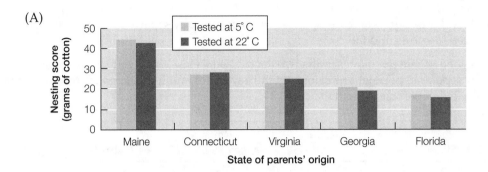

(B)

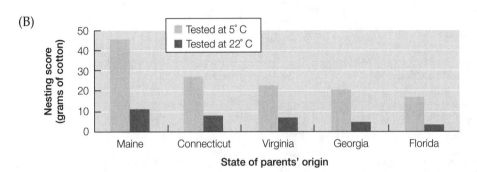

(C)

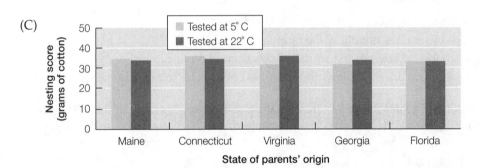

(D)

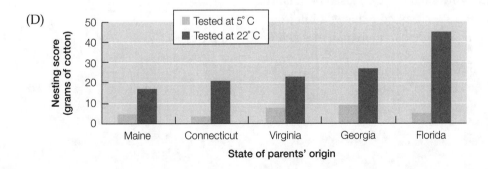

GO ON TO THE NEXT PAGE.

Questions 50 – 51

The leopard frogs *Rana berlandieri* and *Rana sphenocephala* usually have non-overlapping breeding seasons in areas where they are found together. Where the species are geographically separated from each other, however, both species breed in spring and fall.

After a new pond was created where the ranges of the two species were close together but still separated, frogs from the previously separated populations colonized the new pond and hybridized. Sampling at this newly constructed pond yielded the following data.

Life Stage	*Rana berlandieri*	*Rana sphenocephala*	F1 Hybrids
Recently hatched tadpoles (spring year 1)	155	125	238
Late-stage tadpoles (summer year 1)	45	55	64
Newly metamorphosed froglets (fall, year 1)	32	42	15
Adult frogs (year 2)	10	15	1

50. Which of the following best justifies the selection of the data showing that the two species of leopard frogs are reproductively isolated?

    (A) A pre-zygotic mechanism causes the F1 froglets to go blind.
    (B) A pre-zygotic mechanism does not allow the tadpoles to develop.
    (C) A post-zygotic mechanism prevents the adult hybrids from surviving.
    (D) A post-zygotic mechanism does not allow the sperm of one species to fertilize the egg of another.

51. Based on the number of adult *Rana berlandieri* frogs in the pond in year 2, which of the following supports the claim that genetic drift was responsible for altering the genetic make-up of this population?

    (A) Predation caused there to be fewer frogs after year 2.
    (B) Neutral mutations resulted in a decreased population.
    (C) Non-selective processes resulted in fewer adult frogs.
    (D) Disruptive selection resulted in more tadpoles and fewer adult frogs.

GO ON TO THE NEXT PAGE.

Questions 52 – 53

Eukaryotic cells have a nucleus and other membrane-bound compartments. A group of scientists wanted to trace the path that the enzyme lipase follows between its site of synthesis and its final destination within a liver cell. First, the scientists exposed cultured liver cells to radioactive amino acids for three minutes. The amino acids entered the cells and became incorporated into all proteins synthesized during that time period. Then the unbound radioactive amino acids were removed, so any proteins synthesized subsequently were not radioactive. At five-minute intervals after the brief exposure to radioactive amino acids, some of the cells were broken open and analyzed to measure how much radioactive lipase was in each organelle at each time. The table shows the results.

Time (minutes)	Percentage of radioactive lipase			
	Endoplasmic reticulum (ER)	Golgi apparatus	Lysosomes	Ribosomes
5	5	0	0	95
10	25	10	0	65
15	75	20	5	0
20	25	55	20	0
25	0	65	35	0
30	0	25	75	0
35	0	0	100	0

52. Based on the data, which of the following is the most likely pathway that lipase took in the cell?

(A) Ribosome → ER → Golgi → Lysosome
(B) ER → Golgi → Lysosome → Ribosome
(C) Ribosome → Golgi → ER → Lysosome
(D) Lysosome → Ribosome → ER → Golgi

53. Which of the following best describes the importance of internal membranes of the cell to the formation of lipase?

(A) Internal membranes provide passageways through the cell, allowing for cell-to-cell communication.
(B) Internal membranes compartmentalize the internal spaces in the cell, facilitating intracellular metabolic processes.
(C) Internal membranes increase the surface area for the absorption of nutrients.
(D) Internal membranes protect the nucleus and allow for regulation of DNA expression.

GO ON TO THE NEXT PAGE.

54. Animals require a constant source of energy to maintain homeostasis. The mechanisms used to take in and digest food are varied, but the digestive tracts of many animals show phylogenetic patterns and relationships. Some animals, such as jellyfish and coral, have primitive mouths with two-way tracts that also serve as anuses. Other animals have separate mouths and anuses with one-way tracts. The digestive tracts of four animals are shown below.

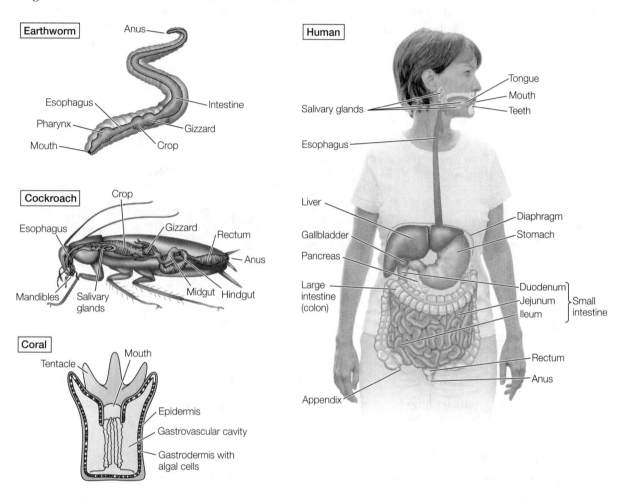

Which cladogram best supports the claim that three of these animals share a more recent common ancestor, based on their digestive tracts?

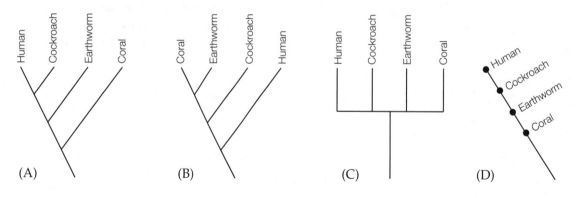

GO ON TO THE NEXT PAGE.

55. Which of the following would best support a scientific explanation that DNA is the primary source of inheritance?

    (A) Evidence that all living organisms contain DNA

    (B) Evidence that DNA is replicated semi-conservatively by enzymes

    (C) Watson and Crick's model of DNA showing DNA being antiparallel with a double helix

    (D) Hershey and Chase's experiment showing viral DNA with radioactive P entering bacterial cells

56. A change in genotype may or may not be associated with a change in phenotype. Below are four possible changes. Which might be subject to natural selection when expressed as a phenotype?

    (A) A neutral mutation in the telomere of a chromosome

    (B) A mutation that causes a plant to live a month longer after producing its last seeds

    (C) A mutation in an intron deleting five nucleotides

    (D) A mutation that causes seed germination to occur earlier in the spring

57. Gregor Mendel arrived at his two laws of inheritance by developing a series of hypotheses, then testing them using peas. Each of his crosses involved a simple trait with two different alleles for each gene. Identify the statement below that correctly explains a genetic trait that cannot be accounted for by Mendelian genetics.

    (A) A variety of flowers occurs in one of two colors: pink and red.

    (B) A gene for coat color in Labrador retrievers has two forms: black and brown.

    (C) A fruit has three forms: round, oval, and long, based on a difference in just two alleles.

    (D) A cross in corn involves two genes and four types of kernels: wrinkled yellow, wrinkled purple, smooth yellow, and smooth purple.

GO ON TO THE NEXT PAGE.

58. Many animals that face uncertain food availability have evolved a tendency to collect and store more food than they can eat right away. Desert seed-eating rodents, such as the Merriam's kangaroo rat (*Dipodomys merriami*), will harvest as many seeds as they can find and bury the seeds in shallow deposits scattered around their territories. In some years, the plants in the desert environment produce few seeds, and the kangaroo rats eat all the seeds they have stored. In other years, the kangaroo rats store more seeds than they are able to eat, and the uneaten seeds germinate; they have been "planted." In those years, the plant species whose seeds kangaroo rats favor increase in abundance. When periods of drought occur over multiple years, many grasses and local plants will show signs of decline with less abundance.

Which of the following investigations could scientists use to gather data to analyze the effect of the Merriam's kangaroo rat on the patterns of distribution of local plants in the environment?

(A) Enclose a large plot of land with a rodent-proof fence and remove all rodents except the Merriam's kangaroo rats from the fenced area. Measure the population of kangaroo rats over the next year.

(B) Enclose several large areas of land with rodent-proof fences in three locations that are widely spaced apart. Remove all other rodents from the fenced plots. Monitor the temperature, rainfall, and area covered by local plants in each location.

(C) Enclose several large plots of land with rodent-proof fences and remove the Merriam's kangaroo rats from half the plots. Monitor the fenced areas over several years, and compare the area covered by local plants in plots with and without kangaroo rats.

(D) Enclose a large area with rodent-proof fences and remove all Merriam's kangaroo rats form the area while leaving all other rodents and animals. Over the next several years, monitor the area covered by local plants.

59. DDT, a potent insecticide, was first used during World War II to help prevent the spread of mosquitoes and malaria among troops and civilians. In 1955, the World Health Organization began spraying DDT in earnest to eradicate malaria around the world. Mosquitoes resistant to DDT first appeared in India in 1959 and are now found throughout the world.

In an experiment, a researcher examined the effects of DDT on mosquitoes. Those that survived exposure to DDT for more than one hour were labeled resistant.

Month	0	8	12
Mosquitoes resistant to DDT	4%	45%	77%

Which of the following best describes the cause of the mosquitoes' rapid rise in resistance?

(A) Some mosquitoes were resistant to the DDT and left more offspring than others through natural selection.

(B) Natural selection created the variation needed by the mosquitoes to become resistant to the DDT.

(C) Genetic drift caused a shift in the frequency of the resistance genes, leaving more resistant mosquitoes to reproduce.

(D) Resistant mosquitoes were accidently introduced into the experiment after six months.

GO ON TO THE NEXT PAGE.

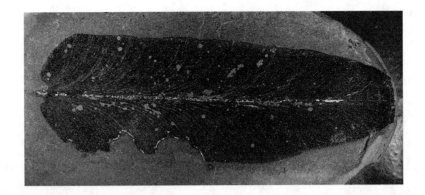

60. The figure above shows a fossilized fern leaf. The margins of the leaf appear to have been chewed by insects. Which of the following investigations would provide data that could be used by a paleontologist to further refine his evidence about this fossil and best use this fossil to support biological evolution?

   (A) Date the rocks from above and below the fossil using radiometric data and the chemical make-up of the minerals to determine the age of the fossil fern.

   (B) Match the bite marks in the leaf to insects found today, then look for fossils of today's insects in the fossil record.

   (C) Examine fern leaves that were found in younger rocks, and compare the size of the leaves with this one.

   (D) Extract DNA from the minerals of the fossilized fern and compare the DNA of the fossil with that of modern-day ferns.

GO ON TO THE NEXT PAGE.

Questions 61 – 63

Giant squid axons are large enough to be useful in the study of neuronal physiology. Electrodes can be inserted into the axons to measure the charge inside and outside of the axon, as shown below. An axon is induced to transmit a signal. The figure shows the normal sequence of charge as the signal is generated and passes down the axon.

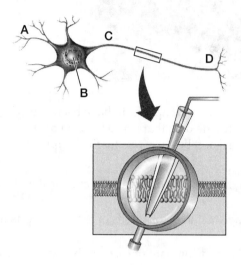

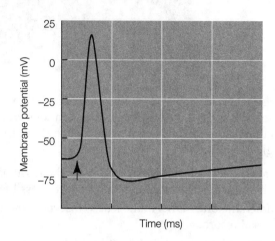

61. The arrow in the graph above shows the membrane potential just before a neuron fires. When the neuron is alive but inactive, what membrane potential should be detected at location D in the diagram?

    (A) 15
    (B) 0
    (C) –62
    (D) –76

62. The neuron above is stimulated to fire an action potential at its normal location inside the squid's body. Based on letters in the diagram, which of the following best indicates the firing sequence?

    (A) B → C → D
    (B) B → A
    (C) A → B → C → D
    (D) D → C → B → A

63. Many axons have a myelin sheath that develops over time and acts as an electrical insulator. This increases the speed of the electrical charge, enabling people to have greater eye-hand coordination and to do tasks more quickly. Which part of the nerve cell in the figure becomes myelinated?

    (A) A
    (B) B
    (C) C → D
    (D) B → C

GO ON TO THE NEXT PAGE.

Directions: The next six questions, numbered 121–126, require numeric answers. Determine the correct answer for each question and enter it in the grid on your answer sheet. Use the following guidelines for entering your answers.

- Start your answer in any column, space permitting. Unused columns should be left blank.

- Write your answer in the boxes at the top of the grid and fill in the corresponding circles. Mark only one circle in any column. You will receive credit only if the circles are filled in completely.

- Provide your answer in the format specified by the question. The requested answer may be an integer, a decimal, or a fraction, and it may have a negative value.

- To enter a fraction, use one of the division slashes to separate the numerator from the denominator, as shown in the example below. Fractions only need to be reduced enough to fit in the grid.

- Do not enter a mixed number, as this will be scored as a fraction. For example, 2 1/2 (two and one-half) will be scored as 21/2 (twenty-one halves).

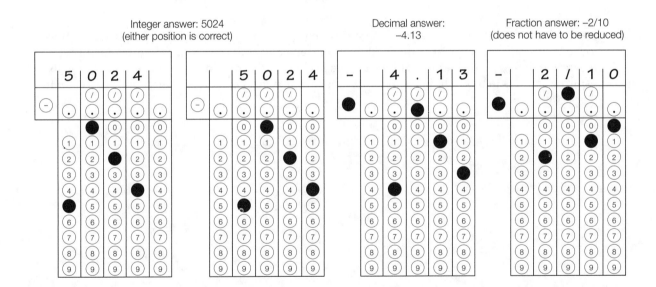

Integer answer: 5024
(either position is correct)

Decimal answer:
−4.13

Fraction answer: −2/10
(does not have to be reduced)

GO ON TO THE NEXT PAGE.

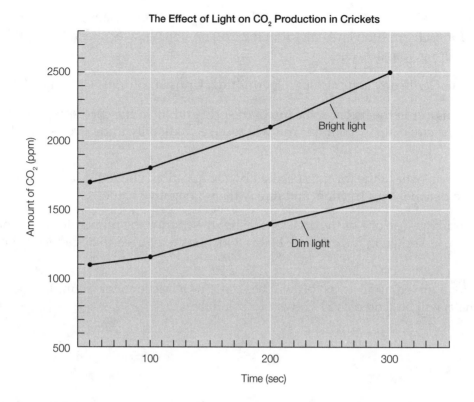

The Effect of Light on CO_2 Production in Crickets

121. Energy flows through an ecosystem as organisms convert food into energy. The graph above shows how crickets utilize energy from the food they consume and convert it to carbon dioxide during respiration. Based on the data, calculate the rate of change in carbon dioxide concentration due to the respiring crickets in bright light between 100 and 200 seconds. Give the answer to the nearest tenth of a second.

GO ON TO THE NEXT PAGE.

122. A student set up a simple experiment to determine how much energy is transferred from one trophic level to the next by using caterpillars (butterfly larvae). Eleven caterpillars were placed in a jar with leaves for food. The caterpillars consumed 14.58 grams of plant material, which has an energy value of 14.355 kcal. The caterpillars themselves increased in mass by 2.64 grams, which has an energy value of 2.178 kcal.

Calculate the percent of energy that was transferred from the producers to the consumers and is currently found in the biomass of the caterpillars. Give your answer to the nearest tenth.

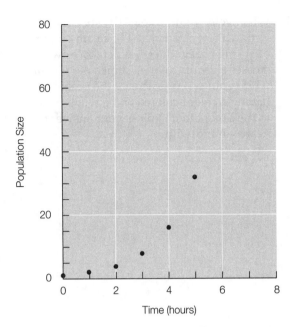

123. A researcher inoculated a growth medium with a single bacterium that grew exponentially, generating the data in the graph above. Using these data, approximate the number of bacteria that will be found on the plate at the six-hour mark. Express your answer to the nearest whole number.

GO ON TO THE NEXT PAGE.

124. When yellow guinea pigs (I^y) are crossed with white guinea pigs (I^w), cream-colored offspring are produced. A pet store owner crosses a cream-colored guinea pig with a white guinea pig. Calculate the probability of having a cream-colored and a white offspring in the same litter. Express your answer to the nearest hundredth.

125. A recessive dilute gene in cats results in kittens that are gray instead of black, which is the dominant color. To test this, a researcher mated two heterozygous black cats (Bb) several times and predicted that there would be 22 black kittens and 6 gray kittens. Calculate the chi square value for the expected results of this cross. Express your answer to the nearest hundredth.

GO ON TO THE NEXT PAGE.

126. In corn, white kernel color is a recessive allele and yellow is a dominant allele. A random sample from a population that is in genetic equilibrium shows that 1,255 are yellow and 249 are white. Calculate the percentage of heterozygotes in this population. Express your percent to the nearest tenth.

END OF SECTION I

IF TIME REMAINS, YOU MAY CHECK YOUR WORK.

DURING THE ACTUAL EXAM, YOU WILL NOT BE ABLE TO GO ON TO SECTION II UNTIL TOLD TO DO SO. FOR THIS PRACTICE EXAM, PUT AWAY SECTION I, TAKE A SHORT BREAK, THEN GO ON TO SECTION II.

BIOLOGY
Section II
8 Questions
Planning Time—10 minutes
Writing Time—80 minutes

Directions: Questions 1 and 2 are long free-response questions that require about 22 minutes each to answer and are worth 10 points each. Questions 3–8 are short free-response questions that require about 6 minutes each to answer. Questions 3–5 are worth 4 points each and questions 6–8 are worth 3 points each.

Read each question carefully and completely. Write your response in the space provided for each question. Only material written in the space provided will be scored. Answers must be written out in paragraph form. Outlines, bulleted lists, or diagrams alone are not acceptable.

1. Some humans are able to identify or recreate the pitch of a sound without a reference tone. Individuals with this ability are said to have absolute, or perfect, pitch. These individuals can often identify a specific pitch played on an instrument, sing a named pitch, or reproduce bars of music in the correct key several days after hearing it. They do these things with 70%–99% accuracy, as compared to 10%–40% for individuals who do not possess absolute pitch. Increased language capabilities, specific handedness, a lack of drug or alcohol use, or study of a second language are often characteristics of individuals with absolute pitch. Absolute pitch has often been linked to a critical period, early in childhood, and has therefore been thought to be impossible to acquire after childhood.

   A group of researchers was investigating the ability of a drug, valproate (VPA), to improve an adult's ability to identify pitch. Twenty-four healthy, right-handed, adult males (ages 20–24) who were not known to have perfect pitch made up the test group. Twelve individuals took VPA and twelve took a placebo, a substance containing no VPA. The test subjects completed two dosing regimens (Investigation 1 and Investigation 2), each lasting two weeks. Each test subject received the placebo or VPA in the first investigation and the alternate regimen in the second investigation. The subjects then listened to 18 instrument-generated sounds of various pitches. The results obtained by the researchers for both tests are shown in the table below. (Individuals could respond correctly three times by chance alone.)

INVESTIGATION 1				INVESTIGATION 2			
TEST GROUP A: VPA		TEST GROUP B: PLACEBO		TEST GROUP A: PLACEBO		TEST GROUP B: VPA	
Mean number of correct responses	Standard error of the mean (SEM)	Mean number of correct responses	Standard error of the mean (SEM)	Mean number of correct responses	Standard error of the mean (SEM)	Mean number of correct responses	Standard error of the mean (SEM)
5.09	0.7	3.50	0.5	3.33	0.2	2.75	0.8

GO ON TO THE NEXT PAGE.

ADDITIONAL PAGE FOR ANSWERING QUESTION 1

GO ON TO THE NEXT PAGE.

ADDITIONAL PAGE FOR ANSWERING QUESTION 1

_____

_____

_____

_____

_____

_____

_____

_____

_____

_____

_____

_____

_____

_____

_____

_____

_____

_____

_____

_____

_____

_____

GO ON TO THE NEXT PAGE.

ADDITIONAL PAGE FOR ANSWERING QUESTION 1

GO ON TO THE NEXT PAGE.

2. White-tailed deer prefer to feed on the young trees along the edges of forests. The trees produce many seeds that birds, mice, squirrels, and chipmunks eat. Lizards prey on small insects that eat the leaves of plants and bushes.

A research team studied the population dynamics of white-footed mice and eastern chipmunks in an eastern deciduous forest. The study investigated the environmental factor that triggers the dramatic once-in-a-decade outbreaks of invasive gypsy moths that defoliate oak forests in the eastern United States. The researchers made the claim that the outbreaks start when the moths escape predation-related population control by mice and chipmunks, which eat moth pupae.

In 1991, soon after the study began, one of the field assistants contracted Lyme disease, an infection caused by bacteria of the genus *Borrelia*. Epidemiologists discovered that Lyme disease is transmitted by bites from *Borrelia*-infected black-legged ticks. Tick hosts include white-tailed deer, birds, lizards, and small mammals, as well as humans.

The research group turned their attention to black-legged ticks as the disease vectors (organisms that transmit pathogens). The researchers had already been counting ticks on live-trapped mice and chipmunks. Now they began to investigate the relationship between increased host population size and tick abundance and infection rate.

They discovered that small mammals are the primary reservoir for *Borrelia*, because they can harbor the bacteria without getting sick. Ticks are not infected when they hatch from eggs as larvae; they become infected as larvae or nymphs when they bite infected hosts.

(a) **Construct** a food web including at least ONE producer, ONE primary producer, and ONE secondary consumer for the deciduous forest ecosystem described above. **Describe** the direction of energy flow between all organisms within the food web.

(b) When predation-related population control strategies fail, states often attempt to manage gypsy moth movement by stopping their migration through with trapping and insecticide use. **Predict** the long-term effect on the relative productivity of the producers. **Predict** the consequence to the squirrel population if this strategy is effective for several years.

(c) **Describe** the type of symbiotic relationship between ticks and the *Borrelia* bacteria. **Predict** the effect on rodent population size when oaks produce a big acorn crop. **Predict** the consequence of the change in the rodent population size on the tick population size.

THIS PAGE MAY BE USED FOR TAKING NOTES AND PLANNING YOUR ANSWERS.
NOTES WRITTEN ON THIS PAGE WILL NOT BE SCORED.
WRITE ALL YOUR RESPONSES ON THE LINED PAGES.

GO ON TO THE NEXT PAGE.

PAGE FOR ANSWERING QUESTION 2

GO ON TO THE NEXT PAGE.

ADDITIONAL PAGE FOR ANSWERING QUESTION 2

_____

_____

_____

_____

_____

_____

_____

_____

_____

_____

_____

_____

_____

_____

_____

_____

_____

_____

_____

_____

_____

_____

GO ON TO THE NEXT PAGE.

ADDITIONAL PAGE FOR ANSWERING QUESTION 2

_____

_____

_____

_____

_____

_____

_____

_____

_____

_____

_____

_____

_____

_____

_____

_____

_____

_____

_____

_____

_____

_____

_____

_____

GO ON TO THE NEXT PAGE.

ADDITIONAL PAGE FOR ANSWERING QUESTION 2

_____

_____

_____

_____

_____

_____

_____

_____

_____

_____

_____

_____

_____

_____

_____

_____

_____

_____

_____

_____

_____

GO ON TO THE NEXT PAGE.

3. Many early sharks and various lobe-finned fishes, including the tetrapod transitional species leading to amphibians, evolved during the Devonian period (419–359 million years ago). While most scientists support this evolutionary pattern, much of the fossil record has not yet been discovered documenting this transition.

   (a) **Predict** what scientists will find to be the time period during which transitional species most likely lived. **Justify** your prediction.

   (b) The fossil record provides one piece of evidence for common descent of organisms. **Describe** TWO pieces of evidence for common descent, other than fossil evidence.

PAGE FOR ANSWERING QUESTION 3

_____

_____

_____

_____

_____

_____

_____

_____

_____

_____

_____

_____

_____

_____

_____

_____

_____

_____

_____

GO ON TO THE NEXT PAGE.

4. In animals, internal and external signals regulate a variety of physiological responses that synchronize with environmental cycles and cues. Fireflies, a type of flying insect, use bioluminescent flashes as part of their mating ritual. Scientists have observed that males tend to flash while flying, and females sit in the bushes and selectively respond by flashing back. Male fireflies produce flashes of light of different duration, intensity, and frequency. Researchers have made the claim that males respond with varying aggression to other males with varying flashing patterns.

Pose a hypothesis about what male firefly behaviors may lead to successful mating. **Identify** the appropriate independent and dependent variables for the investigation. **Describe** the length of time the researchers should conduct the investigation.

PAGE FOR ANSWERING QUESTION 4

_____

_____

_____

_____

_____

_____

_____

_____

_____

_____

_____

_____

_____

_____

_____

_____

_____

_____

GO ON TO THE NEXT PAGE.

5. The graph at the right shows the rate of an enzyme-catalyzed biochemical reaction at 37°C. In this reaction, hydrogen peroxide (H_2O_2), a substrate, is degraded by catalase, an enzyme. Varying environmental conditions can vary the enzyme kinetics.

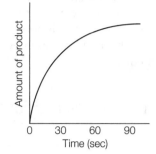

(a) Using the axes below, **draw** the predicted effects on the amount of product that results when the reaction occurs in each of the following conditions. (The original line is included for comparison.)

- The environmental temperature is reduced to 20°C.
- After 30 seconds, a competitive inhibitor is added to the solution.

(b) **Justify** your prediction for each of these environmental changes.

PAGE FOR ANSWERING QUESTION 5

GO ON TO THE NEXT PAGE.

6. Several independent lines of evidence shed light on the origins of life on Earth. While researchers continue to investigate these data, there remain several competing hypotheses. **Describe** ONE testable scientific hypothesis about the natural origin of life, from inorganic molecules to eukaryotic cells. **Describe** TWO pieces of evidence supporting this as a scientific hypothesis about the origins of life on Earth.

PAGE FOR ANSWERING QUESTION 6

_____

_____

_____

_____

_____

_____

_____

_____

_____

_____

_____

_____

_____

_____

_____

_____

_____

_____

_____

_____

GO ON TO THE NEXT PAGE.

7. Soil microbial communities have the metabolic and genetic capability to adapt to changing environmental conditions in a very short period of time. Generation of variation in microbial communities is faster than that in animal communities. **Describe** TWO mechanisms by which microbes, but not animals, can increase genetic variation. **Describe** ONE mechanism common to both microbes and animals that can increase genetic variation.

PAGE FOR ANSWERING QUESTION 7

_____

_____

_____

_____

_____

_____

_____

_____

_____

_____

_____

_____

_____

_____

_____

_____

_____

_____

_____

_____

GO ON TO THE NEXT PAGE.

8. Auxin is a plant hormone that is synthesized in the shoot tip of a seedling as a response to light. As part of this response, the seedling stem bends toward a light source (phototropism), and auxin diffuses down the shoot in a unidirectional fashion. In an investigation into phototropism, oat seedling shoots approximately 20 mm long were exposed to light from one side. Researchers observed the seedlings after six hours and recorded the response to light. Variable lengths of the seedlings were covered with foil to block the light. The results are shown below.

REGION COVERED	Response to light
1. Entire shoot uncovered	+
2. Entire shoot covered (20mm)	−
3. Top 5mm of shoot covered	−
4. Top 10mm of shoot covered	−
5. A 5mm band, 5–10 mm from the top covered	+
6. A 5 mm band, 10–15mm from the top covered	+

Response to light in oat seedlings after six hours of light exposure.
A positive response to light required bending beyond 30° from vertical.

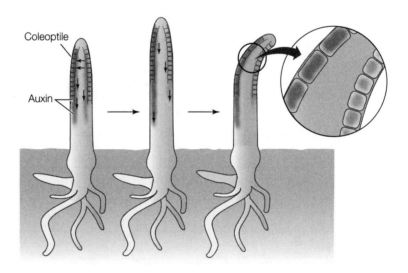

Auxin is produced in the shoot tip as a response to light.
The light stimulates cell expansion on the side of the shoot farthest from the light source.

On the figure provided on the following page, label "incoming light" to **specify** the direction of the light that is causing the seedling to bend.

Identify the control group in the investigation. **Describe** the role of this control group.

GO ON TO THE NEXT PAGE.

PAGE FOR ANSWERING QUESTION 8

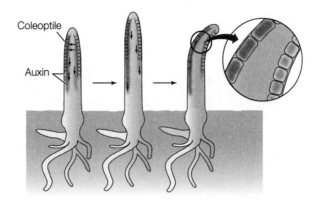

_____

_____

_____

_____

_____

_____

_____

_____

_____

_____

_____

_____

_____

STOP

END OF EXAM

**IF TIME REMAINS,
YOU MAY CHECK YOUR WORK ON THIS SECTION.**

_____

Section I Answer Key

MULTIPLE-CHOICE ITEMS

#	Answer	LO		#	Answer	LO
1	D	3.2		33	B	4.13
2	C	3.13		34	B	4.21
3	B	4.11		35	B	3.1
4	D	2.7		36	B	1.4
5	B	1.29		37	D	1.3
6	A	2.3		38	D	1.11
7	C	2.3		39	A	1.1
8	C	2.1		40	B	1.2
9	A	4.6		41	C	1.2
10	A	3.15		42	D	4.20
11	A	2.9		43	B	4.20
12	B	4.17		44	A	3.7
13	B	4.17		45	C	3.21
14	D	4.17		46	A	3.21
15	A	3.40		47	C	3.26
16	B	2.22		48	A	2.5
17	A	2.12		49	B	1.13
18	A	2.23		50	C	1.23
19	C	2.24		51	C	1.8
20	B	2.23		52	A	2.13
21	D	2.22		53	B	2.13
22	A	2.2		54	A	2.26
23	A	3.2		55	D	3.1
24	B	4.8		56	D	3.24
25	D	2.15		57	C	3.16
26	B	3.3		58	C	4.19
27	B	3.6		59	A	1.1
28	D	3.5, 4.17		60	A	1.10, 1.12
29	D	2.11		61	C	3.43
30	A	1.19		62	A	3.45
31	C	1.18		63	C	3.45
32	B	1.17				

GRID-IN ITEMS

#	Answer	Acceptable Range	LO
121	3.0	3.0 – 3.5	4.14
122	15.2	15.1 or 15.2	4.14
123	64	52 – 70	4.12
124	.25	.25	4.12
125	.19	.18 or .19	3.14
126	48.3	48.0 – 48.4	1.1

SAMPLE GRID-IN CALCULATIONS

121. $3.0 - 3.5$

$$\frac{y^2 - y^1}{x^2 - x^1} = \frac{2100 - 1800}{200 - 100} = 3.0$$

122.   15.2 (credit given for 15.1 or 15.2)

$$\frac{2.178}{14.355} \times 100\% = 15.2\% \text{ (credit given for 15.1 or 15.2)}$$

123.   64 (acceptable range is 55–70)

This is not a straight line with an increasing slope; an answer below 55 is too close to a straight line continuing this curve.

124.   .25

The probability of a cream is 0.5 and the probability of a white is 0.5.
Multiply the probabilities to find the probability of both together: $0.5 \times 0.5 = 0.25$

125.   .19 (or .18)

Observed	Expected	$(o-e)^2$	$(o-e)^2/e$	
22	21	1	1/21	.0476
6	7	1	1/7	.1429
				.1905

126.   48.3%

$$\frac{249}{(1255 + 249)} = .1656$$

$q^2 = .1656$

$q = .4069$

If $p + q = 1$, then $p = .5931$

$2pq = .4827$ or 48.3% (credit given for 48.0, 48.1, 48.2, 48.3, or 48.4)

Section II Sample Scoring Rubrics

1. This is a 10-point question.

    (a) 1 pt –   Appropriately plotted bars

          1 pt –   Appropriately plotted SEM bars

          1 pt –   Appropriately plotted chance performance

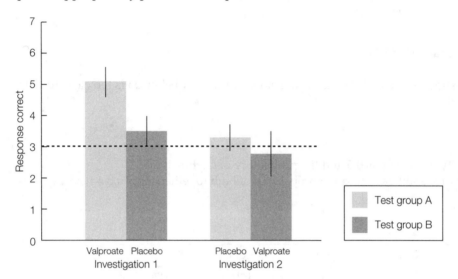

    (b) 1 pt –   To ensure that the individual results were due to VPA and not chance/placebo effect

          1 pt –   Similar language abilities (e.g., not bilingual)

                   Similar handedness

                   Lack of drug/alcohol use

    (c) 1 pt –   Investigation 1

          1 pt –   Non-overlapping error bars in Investigation 1

          1 pt –   For participants who received VPA first, there was a significant effect of treatment.

                   There was no difference between VPA and placebo for the individuals who received the placebo first.

    (d) 1 pt –   VPA treatment improved an adult male's ability to identify pitches.

          1 pt –   With VPA, critical period can occur during adulthood, not only in childhood.

2. This is a 10-point question.

(a) 1 pt – Producer: trees/seeds

2 pts – Primary consumer: deer, birds, mice, squirrels, chipmunks, insects

1 pt – Secondary consumer: lizards

1 pt – Arrows/description correctly showing energy flow from producers to consumers

(b) 1pt – Decreased primary productivity/fewer acorns produced by trees/decreased primary productivity/less food

1 pt – Increased competition of squirrels/decreased squirrel population size

(c) 1 pt – Commensalism/ticks are not affected by the bacteria, but the tick bite transmits the bacteria to the deer

1 pt – Increased rodent population size

1 pt – Increased tick infestation

3. This is a 4-point question.

(a) 1 pt – Between 419 and 359 million years ago

1 pt – Between ages of last known fish and earliest known amphibians

(b) 2 pts – Must include correct type of evidence and matching description from any two of the four rows below.

Type of Evidence	Description
Molecular	Comparison of amino acid sequences / Comparison of DNA sequences
Embryological	Comparison of embryological structures
Biogeography	Comparison of distribution patterns
Anatomical	Comparison of homologous structures

4. This is a 4-point question.

1 pt – Hypothesis: To achieve successful mating, males flash in one or more of the following ways: rapidly/slowly; high frequency/low frequency; bright/dim; variable pattern/consistent pattern.

1 pt – Independent variable [IV]: Flashing characteristic

1 pt – Dependent variable [DV]: Reproductive success or number of fireflies

1 pt – Length of time: Multiple generations (in order to measure reproductive success)

5. This is a 4-point question.

(a)

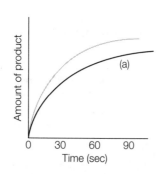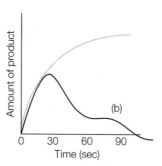

1 pt –   The curve showing the effects of reducing the temperature to 20°C shows a reduction in the rate of product formation due to reduced molecular interactions (less kinetic energy) at cooler temperatures. (Parallel to original curve; Vmax can still be reached but will take longer.) One line with a positive slope, below the original line, is acceptable.

1 pt –   The curve showing the effects of adding a competitive inhibitor at t = 30 seconds demonstrates reduced activity in the reaction, due to competition for the binding site. Slope until 30 seconds (varies based upon substrate concentration); Vmax can still be reached if there is sufficient substrate; K_m increases (*Note*: The shape of this may vary, but it will show a marked decrease at 30 seconds, possibly to zero, depending on how much competitor there is versus substrate.)

(b) 1 pt –   When reduced to 20°C, cooler temperatures reduce the number of collisions. (Heat of the molecules will decrease; Fewer energetic collisions per unit time; Increase K_m of enzyme.) (*Note*: Justification must match curve.)

1 pt –   When competitive inhibitor is added, there is competition between the substrate and the inhibitor for the active site. (*Note*: Justification must match curve.)

6. This is a 3-point question.

1 pt –   There are several acceptable hypotheses, including:

- Initial: Formation of organic precursors; Hydrothermal vents; Clay/hard surfaces; joining of monomers to make polymers
- Process: Formation of proto-cells; Formation of heredity; Earth is very old, this took hundreds of millions of years
- Prokaryotes: Initial prokaryotes formed
- Eukaryotes: Eukaryotes formed

2 pt–   Evidence (must be related to stated hypothesis):

- Initial: Primitive Earth provided inorganic precursors from which organic molecules could have been synthesized; Presence of available free energy and the absence of a significant quantity of oxygen; Miller-Urey apparatus
- Process: RNA world evidence; Radiometric dating techniques
- Prokaryotes: Cyanobacteria fossils, stromatolites; Universality of DNA
- Eukaryotes: Endosymbiosis, chloroplast and mitochondrial DNA; Lateral gene transfer

7. This is a 3-point question.

  2 pt –   Microbes only (any two of the three below):

   • Transformation: uptake of exogenous DNA from the environment
   • Transduction: introduction of foreign DNA into the bacterial chromosome by a bacteriophage
   • Conjugation: DNA transferred from one bacterial cell to another

  1 pt –   Common to microbes and animals:

   • Errors in DNA replication

8. This is a 3-point question.

  (a) 1 pt –

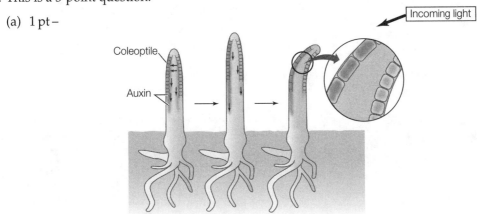

  (b) 1 pt –   Group 1 is the control group.

    1 pt –   The control group ensures that the bending is due to the presence of light/the results are attributable to the experimental variable.

Correlation of Free-Response Questions to the Curriculum Framework

Question #	LO's Covered	Number of Points
1	3.33, 3.47, 3.31, 2.5	10
2	4.15, 2.3, 4.16, 2.24	10
3	1.11, 1.21, 1.9	4
4	2.35	4
5	4.17	4
6	1.26, 1.31	3
7	4.7	3
8	3.29, 3.30	3

Practice Exam 2

Directions:

Following is a full-length Practice Exam to help you hone your skills for the AP® Biology exam. This exam is comprised of two parts, and answers and sample scoring rubrics follow at the end. It is important that you practice your test-taking skills by simulating real testing conditions. Allocate three hours to take this exam.

1. Take this test in a single three-hour block.

2. Do not use headphones or allow music, phones, texting, or other social media to interrupt you.

3. Allow 90 minutes for Section I; this includes the multiple-choice and grid-in (calculation) questions. Then put this section away. You may *not* go back to it during Section II.

4. Take a 10- to 15-minute break, and have a snack.

5. Take 10 minutes to read over and outline potential answers. Then give yourself 80 minutes to complete Section II. Watch your time carefully, and stop when the time is up.

After you check your results, be sure to go back and review the areas you struggled with. Each question is correlated to a specific Learning Objective in the AP® Biology curriculum framework. Look up the ones you erred on, and study these topics further.

NOTE: For Practice Exam Section I, print out an answer sheet from www.pol2e.com/hs/strive

No portion of this practice test may be copied or posted to the Internet without written permission from the publisher.

GO ON TO THE NEXT PAGE.

BIOLOGY

Section I

63 Multiple-Choice Questions

6 Grid-In Questions

Time: 90 Minutes

Directions: Each of the questions or incomplete statements below is followed by four suggested answers or completions. Select the one that is best in each case, then fill in the corresponding space on the answer sheet.

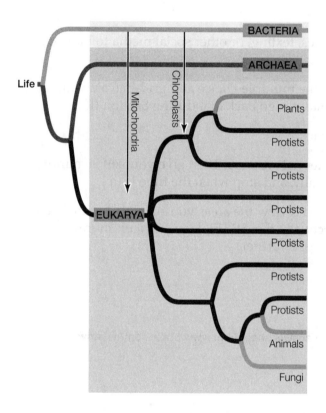

1. The tree of life is a common depiction for the evolution of life from a common ancestor. Which of the following further supports the idea that life has evolved from a common ancestor?

   (A) Aerobic respiration relies on oxygen gas.

   (B) Aerobic respiration is common to many life forms.

   (C) All cells use stomata to regulate their internal environments.

   (D) All living organisms use DNA to store genetic information.

2. Chlorophyll (pictured above) is an important pigment involved in photosynthesis. Its structure is highly amphipathic with a hydrophilic ring structure and a very hydrophobic tail structure. Chlorophyll is found

   (A) inside the stroma of chloroplasts.

   (B) in the thylakoid membranes of chloroplasts.

   (C) in the cytoplasm of plant cells.

   (D) inside the hydrophobic region of cell membranes.

GO ON TO THE NEXT PAGE.

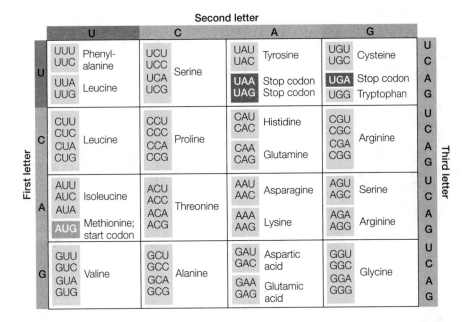

3. Choose the sequence that would be a "silent mutation" of an RNA strand composed of the following nucleotides:

AUG AAA CAA AGC

(A) AUG AAG CAA AGC
(B) AUG CAA AGC
(C) UAG AAA CAA AGC
(D) AUG AAA CAA GAC

GO ON TO THE NEXT PAGE.

4. Meiosis results in the formation of gametes in vertebrates. One of the important side effects of meiosis is the incredible diversity produced as a result of this process. Which of the diagrams below depicts the formation of diversity during meiosis?

(A)

(B)

(C)

(D)

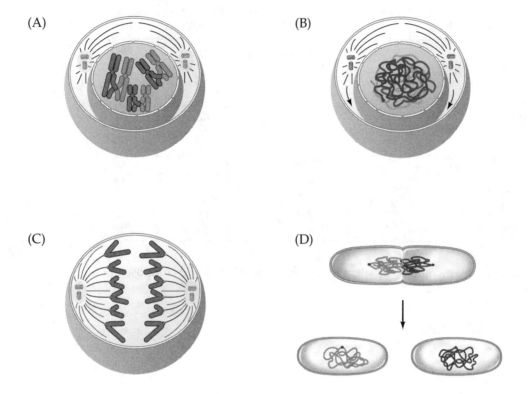

GO ON TO THE NEXT PAGE.

5. Select the model that accurately illustrates how genetic information is translated into a polypeptide.

(A)

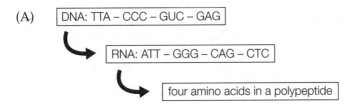

DNA: TTA – CCC – GUC – GAG

RNA: ATT – GGG – CAG – CTC

four amino acids in a polypeptide

(B)

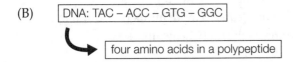

DNA: TAC – ACC – GTG – GGC

four amino acids in a polypeptide

(C)

RNA: AUG – UGG – CUC – CCG

DNA: TAC – ACC – GTC – GGC

four amino acids in a polypeptide

(D)

mRNA: AUG – ACC – CUC – CCG

four amino acids in a polypeptide

GO ON TO THE NEXT PAGE.

Questions 6–9

The protein leptin, a product of the obese gene (*ob*), is implicated as a hormonal signal in energy homeostasis. It is secreted by adipose (fat) cells: as they get larger, more leptin enters the blood. Leptin binds to receptor proteins on hypothalamic neurons, triggering behavioral changes that decrease food intake. In some individuals, genetic mutations that interfere with leptin signaling are associated with the development of obesity.

6. Choose the mechanism that is most like the relationship of leptin and food intake.

   (A) Increased levels of estrogens cause a gonadotropin surge in the middle of the ovarian cycle.

   (B) Clumped platelets at the site of an injury lead to a reduction in blood leakage.

   (C) In an action potential, the initial influx of sodium ions leads to more influx of sodium ions.

   (D) A person shivering from being cold stops shivering as the body heats up.

Codon (5′ – 3′)	131	132	133	134
Wild-Type mRNA	CGA	UUA	UGA	AUA
Mutated mRNA	CGA	UUA	UAA	UA_

Second letter

	U	C	A	G	
U	UUU UUC Phenyl-alanine / UUA UUG Leucine	UCU UCC UCA UCG Serine	UAU UAC Tyrosine / UAA Stop codon UAG Stop codon	UGU UGC Cysteine / UGA Stop codon UGG Tryptophan	U C A G
C	CUU CUC CUA CUG Leucine	CCU CCC CCA CCG Proline	CAU CAC Histidine / CAA CAG Glutamine	CGU CGC CGA CGG Arginine	U C A G
A	AUU AUC Isoleucine AUA / AUG Methionine; start codon	ACU ACC ACA ACG Threonine	AAU AAC Asparagine / AAA AAG Lysine	AGU AGC Serine / AGA AGG Arginine	U C A G
G	GUU GUC GUA GUG Valine	GCU GCC GCA GCG Alanine	GAU GAC Aspartic acid / GAA GAG Glutamic acid	GGU GGC GGA GGG Glycine	U C A G

First letter (left axis), Third letter (right axis)

7. Several different mutations affect leptin signaling in humans. Select the category of mutations that would likely cause the portrayed defect in the mRNA of the leptin-receptor gene.

   (A) Frameshift

   (B) Nonsense

   (C) Missense

   (D) Point

GO ON TO THE NEXT PAGE.

8. Though the hormone leptin has a metabolic function in amphibians, it also appears to be a factor in mate selectivity by toads. One hypothesis is that toads with a plentiful food supply, resulting in elevated secretion of leptin, will have adequate energy to successfully reproduce.

High Water		Low Water	
No Leptin	**Leptin Injection**	**No Leptin**	**Leptin Injection**
Prefer own species	Prefer other species	Prefer other species	Prefer other species

Select the research question that could be plausibly generated by the data in the table.

(A) How does leptin activity affect mate selection in a particular species of toad?

(B) What is the effect of water height on leptin production?

(C) Why does decreased leptin production have no impact on mate selection?

(D) What effect does leptin activity have on habitat selection in toads?

9. Select the organelle dysfunction that is most likely responsible for an individual in whom leptin insensitivity is due to defective insertion of leptin receptors in cell membranes.

(A) Abnormal proton pumps in the mitochondria

(B) Accumulation of misfolded proteins in the endoplasmic reticulum

(C) Failure of the lysosomes to produce an enzyme

(D) Nutrient deficiencies causing disruption of the chloroplasts

GO ON TO THE NEXT PAGE.

10. Signal transduction is the process by which a signal is converted to a cellular response. Signaling cascades relay signals from receptors to cell targets, often amplifying the incoming signals, resulting in appropriate responses by the cell. Which model below expresses the key elements of a signal transduction pathway with secondary messengers that are essential to the function of the cascade?

(A) G-proteins act as intermediaries between a receptor and an effector and can bind to three different molecules and activate the protein effector.

(B) The binding of an epinephrine molecule leads to the production of many molecules of cAMP, thus activating many enzyme targets leading to the release of glucose molecules from glycogen.

(C) Steroid hormones are lipid-soluble and readily pass through the membranes of target cells, beginning the cascading events when they reach receptors inside the target cells.

(D) Protein kinase receptors on the surface of a liver cell can bind to the hormone insulin and activate a cascade of enzymatic reactions, eventually catalyzing glucagon to release glucose.

11. Meiosis is a type of cell division that consists of two nuclear divisions. Which of the following best represents how the process of meiosis has evolved to serve its function(s)?

(A) Meiosis results in two daughter cells with the same number of chromosomes as their parent cells.

(B) Meiosis produces four sperm cells with the haploid number of chromosomes inside each cell.

(C) Meiosis produces a gastrula from the zygote that is genetically similar to the parent cell.

(D) Meiosis halves the nuclear chromosome content and generates diversity.

12. Natural selection can act on characters with quantitative variation in several ways. The graph shows the distribution of birth weight and mortality. Which statement best describes the type of selection shown?

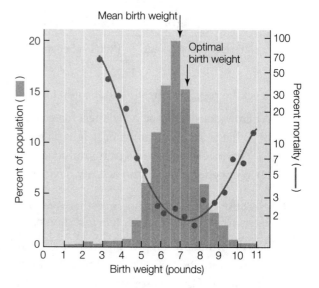

(A) Human birth weight is influenced by disruptive selection because some babies born at either extreme for this trait may still survive.

(B) Human birth weight is influenced by directional selection because the optimal birth weight for babies is between 7 and 8 pounds, shifted slightly from the middle of this graph.

(C) Human birth weight is influenced by stabilizing selection because babies that weigh more or less than average are more likely to die soon after birth.

(D) Human birth weight is not influenced at all by natural selection because humans are able to control almost every aspect of their environment.

GO ON TO THE NEXT PAGE.

Questions 13–15

The figures below show annual data collected in Yellowstone National Park for elk (herbivore) and aspen (tree) populations from the early 1900s to the present. Prior to the 1920s, a strong wolf presence in the park kept the elk population in check (wolves feed on a variety of large mammals, including elk). By 1926, the wolves had been eliminated from Yellowstone, and in 1995, they were reintroduced.

(A)
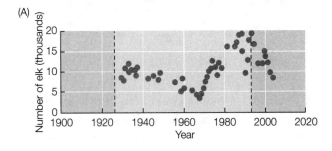

(B)
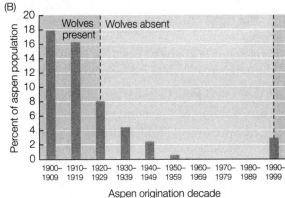

13. According to the data, which statement best explains what happened to the aspen population from the 1920s through the 1990s?

    (A) The presence of wolves prior to 1920 made the soil incapable of supporting the aspen population.

    (B) In the absence of wolves, browsing (eating) by elk prevented the establishment of young aspen trees.

    (C) The population of aspen is dependent on a high density of elk.

    (D) The decrease in population of big herbivores was most likely responsible for the decline of the aspen forests within this time frame.

14. According to the data, which statement best describes the dynamics of these three populations in Yellowstone since 1920?

    (A) Predators play a key role in determining the presence and abundance of many species.

    (B) Removing predators from a community is generally the most ecologically sound way to ensure the survivorship of the herbivore species.

    (C) Reintroducting wolves in 1995 was unlikely to have had an effect on the regeneration of aspen forests.

    (D) The removal of elk from the community would have been an equally sound environmental practice, which would have led to the regeneration of the aspen forests.

15. Which scenario could enable scientists to determine if wolves are a keystone species in Yellowstone National Park?

    (A) Count the number of aspen trees over the next 50 years, now that wolves have been reintroduced to the park.

    (B) Fence off half of the park to keep wolves out, and determine the ratio of wolves to aspen trees in each area to see if the wolves have an effect on the population of aspen trees.

    (C) Fence off a large area of the park from wolves that is very similar to the area inhabited by the wolves, and monitor the number of different species in each area.

    (D) Monitor the growth of the wolf population each year to determine whether they are maintaining a stable population (K selected) or increasing at a logarithmic pace (r-selected).

GO ON TO THE NEXT PAGE.

Community A   Community B   Community C

16. The diagram above shows three hypothetical communities of fungi with varying species richness and abundance. Which of the following statements about these communities is accurate?

(A) Community A is more diverse than community B because it has more individuals of each species.

(B) Community B is more diverse than community C because it has four equally abundant species.

(C) Community C exhibits the same diversity as community B because they each have four species present within the community.

(D) Since each community is composed of the same number of individual organisms, species diversity cannot be determined.

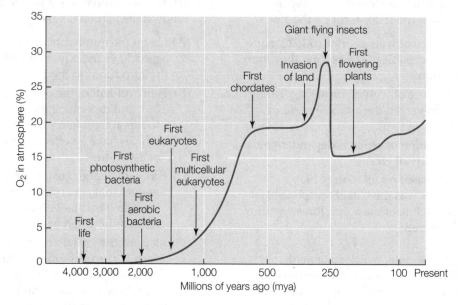

17. The graph above illustrates that changes in the concentration of atmospheric oxygen over millions of years have strongly influenced, and have been influenced by, living organisms. Choose the prediction that is scientifically compatible with the data.

(A) The presence of chordates in a community tends to increase the available oxygen concentration in the atmosphere.

(B) The presence of flowering plants in a community tends to decrease the available oxygen concentration in the atmosphere.

(C) The removal of insects from a community increases the density of the flowering plant population.

(D) The upper limit on body mass in poikilothermic animals is influenced by the availability of atmospheric oxygen.

GO ON TO THE NEXT PAGE.

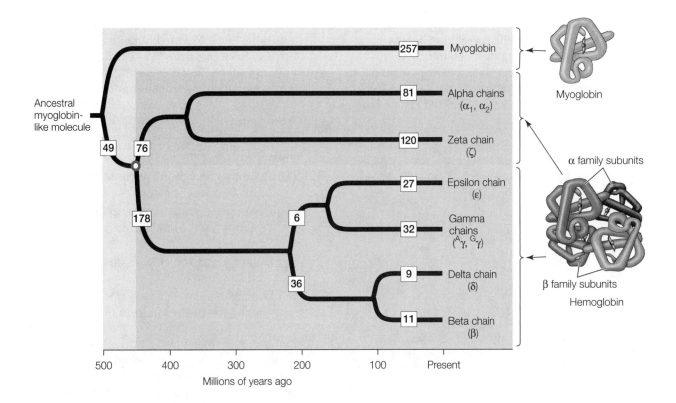

18. This gene tree shows the divergence of the globin molecule from an ancestral myoglobin-like molecule to the present time. The boxed numbers indicate the estimated number of DNA sequence changes along that branch of the tree. Choose the best interpretation of the data presented.

(A) Hemoglobin and myoglobin are estimated to have diverged 450 million years ago.

(B) The alpha chains and the zeta chain are estimated to have diverged 450 million years ago.

(C) The α-globin and β-globin gene clusters are estimated to have diverged 450 million years ago.

(D) The epsilon and beta chains are estimated to have diverged 450 million years ago.

GO ON TO THE NEXT PAGE.

19. Genome size varies tremendously among organisms, with some correlation between genome size and organism complexity. The graph below displays data for the percent of the genome encoding functional genes. Which statement accurately describes the visual data display?

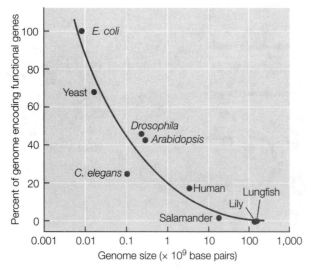

(A) Most of the DNA of bacteria and yeasts encodes RNAs or proteins, but a large percentage of the DNA of multicellular species is non-coding.

(B) Most of the DNA of multicellular species encodes RNAs or proteins, but a large percentage of the DNA of unicellular species is non-coding.

(C) Most human DNA, unlike unicellular organisms, encodes important proteins.

(D) The overall size of the genome of bacteria and yeasts is considerably larger than the genome size of multicellular species.

20. Movement of an organism is a direct attribute of two systems interacting with each other. An organism analyzes the localized environment and determines when and where to move by unleashing an action potential triggering a release of calcium ions in a cell specialized for movement, leading to a contraction. Which two systems in an organism contribute to this coordinated effort?

(A) Respiratory and circulatory
(B) Nervous and muscular
(C) Immune and muscular
(D) Respiratory and muscular

21. Gardeners know that mulching a garden with a thick layer of shredded organic material helps to foster the growth of established plants and prevent weeds from germinating. After applying mulch, a gardener notices that the established plants grow faster and very few weeds grow up through the mulch. Which is a logical hypothesis as to why few weeds grow up through the mulch?

(A) Toxic compounds are released through the decomposition process.

(B) Decomposing mulch uses up many of the soil nutrients, preventing weeds from growing.

(C) Decomposing mulch uses up oxygen and reduces light levels.

(D) Decomposing mulch uses up CO_2 needed by the weeds for photosynthesis.

22. Plants require many trace nutrients and minerals, such as copper, nickel, and magnesium. Many enzymes and processes stabilize and make ATP biologically active with the use of magnesium. Which of the following requires magnesium?

(A) Xylem cells, for transport of water in vascular bundles

(B) Aquaporins, for diffusion of water in cell membranes

(C) Plasmodesmata, allowing the movement of cytoplasm from cell to cell

(D) Chlorophyll, for photosynthesis in chloroplasts

23. A researcher measured the amount of DNA in a group of cells immediately following mitosis and found an average of 8 picograms of DNA per nucleus. How much DNA would the cells have during the S phase of mitosis?

(A) 4 picograms
(B) 7 picograms
(C) 15 picograms
(D) 24 picograms

GO ON TO THE NEXT PAGE.

Questions 24–26

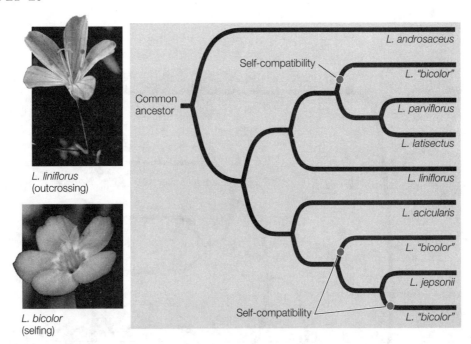

L. liniflorus
(outcrossing)

L. bicolor
(selfing)

The figure above shows a portion of phylogeny of the *Leptosiphon* (a flowering plant in the phlox family) genus. The dots represent three separate occasions when the self-compatibility characteristic (the ability of flowers to regularly fertilize their ovules using their own pollen) evolved in this plant genus.

24. According to the figure, which of the following represents a monophyletic group?

    (A) *L. androsaceus, L. "bicolor," L. parviflorus*
    (B) *L. liniflorus, L. acicularis, L. "bicolor," L. jepsonii*
    (C) *L. androsaceus, L. jepsonii, L. "bicolor"*
    (D) *L. "bicolor," L. parviflorus, L. latisectus*

25. What is the best explanation for the *L."bicolor"* species name showing up in three different locations within the phylogeny of this plant genus?

    (A) Convergent evolution of self-compatibility originally fooled taxonomists into classifying three separate species as *L. "bicolor."*
    (B) In order to eliminate confusion, taxonomists gave all three of the self-compatible species in this plant genus the same scientific name.
    (C) The phylogeny suggests that the exact same species evolved three different times over the course of history.
    (D) The phylogeny suggests that the three species are actually varieties of the same plant species on different branches of the phylogenetic tree.

26. Which of the following would be a plausible technique for scientists to determine if the three separate groups of flowers known as *L. bicolor* are indeed one species or three separate species?

    (A) Compare the flower structure of *L. bicolor* specimens with that of other members of the *Leptosiphon* genus.
    (B) Compare DNA or protein sequences of *L. bicolor* specimens with other species of the *Leptosiphon* genus.
    (C) Compare the height of different *L. bicolor* specimens with other members of the *Leptosiphon* genus.
    (D) Compare the gross productivity of different *L. bicolor* specimens with other members of the *Leptosiphon* genus.

GO ON TO THE NEXT PAGE.

Question 27

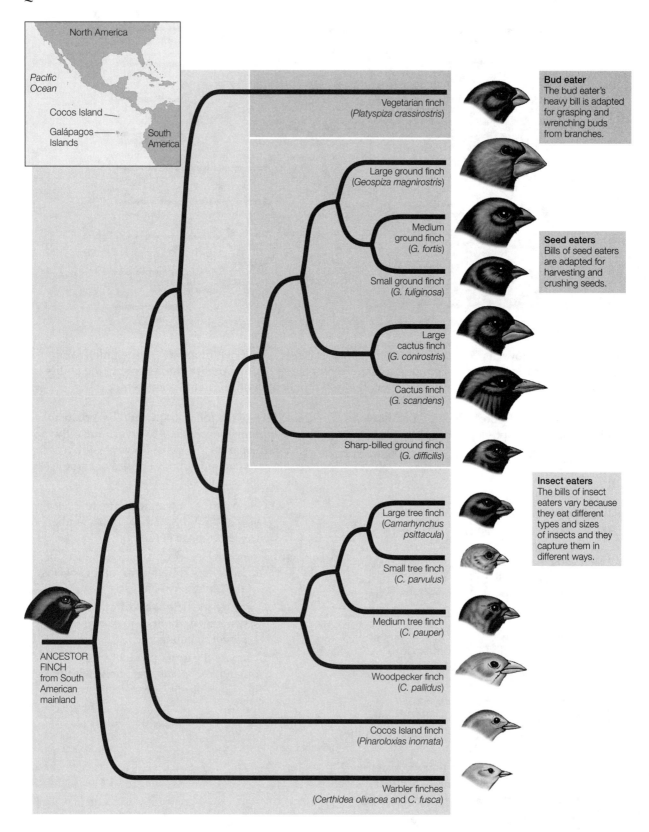

Bud eater
The bud eater's heavy bill is adapted for grasping and wrenching buds from branches.

Seed eaters
Bills of seed eaters are adapted for harvesting and crushing seeds.

Insect eaters
The bills of insect eaters vary because they eat different types and sizes of insects and they capture them in different ways.

North America

Pacific Ocean

Cocos Island

Galápagos Islands

South America

Vegetarian finch (*Platyspiza crassirostris*)

Large ground finch (*Geospiza magnirostris*)

Medium ground finch (*G. fortis*)

Small ground finch (*G. fuliginosa*)

Large cactus finch (*G. conirostris*)

Cactus finch (*G. scandens*)

Sharp-billed ground finch (*G. difficilis*)

Large tree finch (*Camarhynchus psittacula*)

Small tree finch (*C. parvulus*)

Medium tree finch (*C. pauper*)

Woodpecker finch (*C. pallidus*)

Cocos Island finch (*Pinaroloxias inornata*)

Warbler finches (*Certhidea olivacea* and *C. fusca*)

ANCESTOR FINCH from South American mainland

GO ON TO THE NEXT PAGE.

27. The different species of Darwin's finches shown in the phylogeny at the left have all evolved on islands of the Galápagos archipelago within the past 3 million years. All are from a single South American finch species that colonized the islands. The islands are far apart, and they have a variety of environmental conditions. Which of the following statements best represents the type of speciation that gave rise to these fourteen finch species?

(A) Sympatric speciation
(B) Allopatric speciation
(C) Post zygotic isolating mechanisms
(D) Behavioral isolation

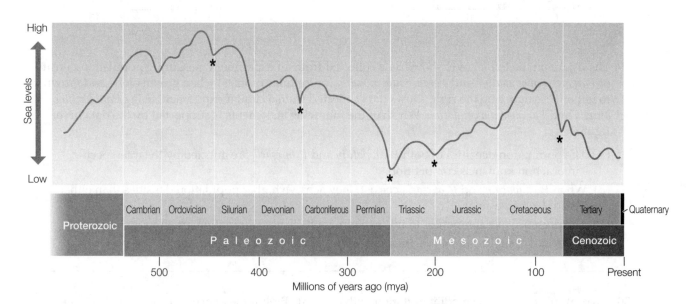

28. Asterisks in the figure above indicate five mass extinctions in the history of life on Earth. During each mass extinction, a large proportion of the species living at the time disappeared. The graphed line represents sea level rise and fall. Using information available in the figure, which of the following is a true statement about the extinction events?

(A) The extinction at the end of the Permian period was the most devastating.
(B) There were three distinct extinction events that occurred during the Mesozoic era.
(C) Each of the mass extinctions coincides with a lowering of sea levels.
(D) Each of the eras (Proterozoic, Paleozoic, Mesozoic, and Cenozoic) ended with a mass extinction event.

GO ON TO THE NEXT PAGE.

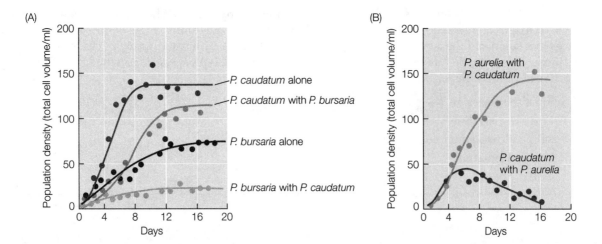

29. The figure on the left (above) shows data collected from an experiment measuring population density of *Paramecium caudatum* and *Paramecium bursaria* (unicellular protists) when grown alone and grown together. The figure on the right shows data collected from a similar experiment using *Paramecium aurelia* and *Paramecium caudatum*. Which of the following statements is supported by the data in the figure?

(A) The population densities of both *P. caudatum* and *P. bursaria* are affected by the interspecific interaction known as competition.

(B) When *P. caudatum* and *P. bursaria* coexist, they achieve higher population densities than either would achieve alone.

(C) The presence of a competitor in this experiment increases population growth rate.

(D) *P. aurelia* population densities are unaffected by the presence of *P. caudatum*.

---

30. An example of a recessive point mutation with a significant effect on phenotype is the one that causes sickle-cell disease. Which statement predicts the change in phenotype that occurs if two sickle-cell trait carriers have a child who is homozygous recessive for sickle-cell disease?

(A) A chromosomal mutation resulting in a homozygous recessive individual for that gene will have a heterozygous advantage over the other genotypes.

(B) Point mutations in coding regions of DNA are silent and will not result in a genetic disorder.

(C) An individual who has two copies of the gene for sickle-cell disease will have defective, sickle-shaped red blood cells.

(D) The sickle-cell allele differs from the normal allele by one base pair, resulting in a polypeptide that differs by many amino acids from the normal protein in the red blood cells.

31. Bioluminescence in a species of bacteria requires a specific density of bacterial cells. Select the best explanation of the cell-to-cell communication that accounts for this phenomenon.

(A) One species of bacteria can release chemical substances that are sensed by another species of bacteria, causing both species of bacterial cells to emit light.

(B) At low population densities, the bacteria cannot secrete the critical concentration of the chemical signal needed to evoke the bioluminescence response.

(C) Bioluminescent bacteria are able to create light when one bacterial cell comes in contact with another bacterial cell of the same species.

(D) The concept of quorum sensing is used as an explanation for the activities involved in forming biofilms.

GO ON TO THE NEXT PAGE.

32. Which of the following is the best explanation of a deviation from Mendel's models of the inheritance of traits?

    (A) Only one copy of a rare allele is needed for expression in males, while two copies of the rare allele must be present for expression in females.

    (B) A male with an X-linked gene can pass it on only to his sons.

    (C) A daughter carrier for an X-linked mutation can pass the mutation on only to her sons.

    (D) Sex-linked disorders are "linked" to the sex of the organism.

33. Nervous tissue transmits information by electrochemical processes, generating action potentials and chemical communication at synapses. Which statement describes what occurs when a nerve process transmits information to a muscle cell?

    (A) The hormone epinephrine (adrenalin) increases blood flow to a muscle cell, which in turn causes the muscle cell to secrete acetylcholine and the muscle fibers to contract.

    (B) A sensory neuron's axon will stimulate the sodium-potassium pump in a muscle cell membrane to begin pumping sodium ions out of the muscle cell, and the muscle cell will contract.

    (C) When an action potential arrives at the neuromuscular junction, acetylcholine will diffuse from the neuron process and move across the synaptic cleft to a muscle-cell membrane receptor.

    (D) Acetylcholine contains calcium ions that bind to troponin in the muscle fiber allowing myosin cross bridges to form, which results in muscle contraction.

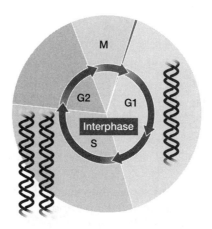

34. During the cell cycle shown in the diagram above, DNA is transmitted from one generation to the next. Which portion of the cell cycle makes it possible for identical copies of DNA to be passed on to each daughter cell?

    (A) G0 or resting phase

    (B) G1 or first growth phase

    (C) S or synthesis phase

    (D) G2 or second growth phase

35. One of the unifying features of life is that DNA is almost universally used as the primary means of carrying genetic information. Some viruses, such as HIV (which can cause AIDS), utilize RNA to carry their genetic information. Which of the following illustrates why the HIV virus is not a deviation from the idea that DNA is the universal carrier of genetic information?

    (A) The HIV virus carries an enzyme called reverse transcriptase that converts the RNA of HIV to a DNA code.

    (B) The membrane surrounding the HIV virus is derived from the host cell machinery.

    (C) Viruses are not considered to be living organisms, and they utilize different molecules to carry their genetic codes.

    (D) Viruses are surrounded by a protein capsule that is coded for by the host cell DNA.

GO ON TO THE NEXT PAGE.

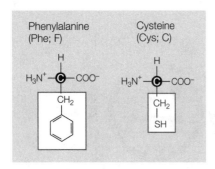

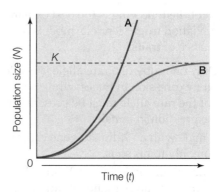

36. The illustration above shows the structure for two amino acids: phenylalanine and cysteine. Which of the following explains what could happen if a substitution mutation of phenylalanine for cysteine occurs?

    (A) Both have a small R group, so there will be little to no change in the function of the protein.

    (B) Both phenylalanine and cysteine have very polar side groups, so there will be little to no change in the protein shape.

    (C) The sulfur in cysteine forms disulfide bridges that will no longer occur, causing major changes in the shape and stability of the protein.

    (D) The R group of phenylalanine will interact with an aqueous environment, causing a change in the secondary structure of the protein.

37. The functions of macromolecules are an outgrowth of the structure of their sub-units. Which of the following macromolecules is correctly paired with its structural determining properties?

    (A) RNA: the shape of the molecule determines the sequence of its protein.

    (B) Protein: the shape of the molecule determines its function.

    (C) DNA: the sequence of monomers determines how much energy the molecule can carry.

    (D) Carbohydrate: the sequence of monosaccharides determines the shape of the molecule.

38. The graph above shows two typical growth-rate patterns. The curve marked "B" depicts a logistic growth curve that is typical for many large mammals. Which of the following best supports the claim that this curve levels out?

    (A) A population's density rarely exceeds the carrying capacity.

    (B) The logistic growth model is generally a result of density-dependent controls.

    (C) The population reached a maximum and crashed, due to limited available resources.

    (D) Large mammals are limited in their population size because of their high metabolic rates.

GO ON TO THE NEXT PAGE.

Questions 39–40

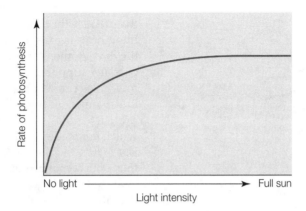

39. As shown in the graph above, the rate of photosynthesis increases as light intensity increases, until a maximum is reached. After this point, additional light does not increase the plant's rate of photosynthesis. Which of the following is a correct explanation for this phenomenon?

   (A) The intense sunlight causes the enzymes for photosynthesis to denature and stop functioning.

   (B) The increased shade caused by the plant's growth slows its rate of photosynthesis.

   (C) Increased light increases the formation of hydrogen ions, and the acidity slows the plant's growth.

   (D) The plant's light-harvesting apparatus becomes saturated and cannot make use of additional light.

40. A student wants to test the idea represented in the graph above. Which of the following would be the best method?

   (A) Expose a group of plants to different-colored lights and measure their change in height after a week.

   (B) Expose a group of plants to sunlight throughout the day and measure their change in height after a week.

   (C) Expose three different groups of plants to low-, medium-, and high-intensity light and measure their change in height after a week.

   (D) Expose a plant to sunlight throughout the day and measure the rate of CO_2 production after a week.

GO ON TO THE NEXT PAGE.

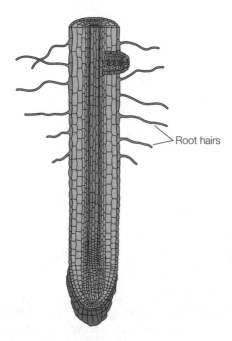

Root hairs

41. Roots hairs, extensions of the membrane of epidermal root cells,

    (A) enhance water conservation by closing the stomata on windy days, much like hair cells in the cochlea move in response to ripples in the cochlear fluid.

    (B) increase a plant's surface area for water absorption in much the same way as the intestinal villi increase the surface area for nutrient absorption in animals.

    (C) protect the root tissue from insect attack, much like nasal hairs protect the nasal cavity from insect attack.

    (D) reduce water loss from the roots, much like tight junctions between epithelial cells in the skin reduce water loss.

42. Choose the most likely set of quantities related to a specific human gene.

    (A) 2,378 nucleotides in DNA; 191 nucleotides in mRNA; 191 amino acids in protein

    (B) 2,378 nucleotides in DNA; 573 nucleotides in mRNA; 191 amino acids in protein

    (C) 2,378 nucleotides in DNA; 2,378 nucleotides in mRNA; 793 amino acids in protein

    (D) 2,378 nucleotides in DNA; 793 nucleotides in mRNA; 264 amino acids in protein

43. The origin of life on our planet is a persistent question in biology, one based on the premise that life arose from non-life. One hypothesis is that an "RNA world" preceded the development of proteins. This idea is partially support by observations that RNA molecules can work together in an enzyme-like manner. Since the origin of cells, however, protein synthesis takes place in ribosomes, which are made up of proteins and ribosomal RNA (rRNA). The RNA code for some of these ribosomal proteins has been recently analyzed, and this code appears to be as old, evolutionarily, as the rRNA molecules in the ribosome. This suggests that

    (A) amino acids did not play a role in synthesizing the ribosomal proteins.

    (B) DNA must have originated prior to the development of the ribosome, and a "DNA–RNA world" preceded the development of protein synthesis.

    (C) the rRNA and the ribosomal proteins coded by RNA have worked together since the origin of the ribosome.

    (D) protein synthesis in the pre-cellular world was directly controlled by DNA without the involvement of RNA.

44. A cell that can give rise to the entire organism, including the extra-embryonic membranes, is considered to be a totipotent cell. Choose the statement that correctly represents this idea.

    (A) A "theme" of science-fiction movies is that having any cell from an adult organism allows scientists to produce clones of that organism.

    (B) Cells below the epidermis continually create new skin cells.

    (C) Gametes are continually created by germ cells in the gonads.

    (D) Cells in the nasal cavity generate olfactory neurons.

GO ON TO THE NEXT PAGE.

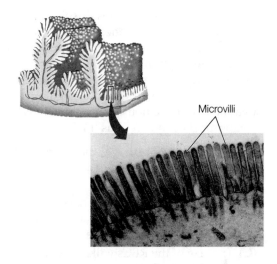

Microvilli

45. The figure above depicts the convoluted folding of the small intestine lining. On each fold are fingerlike projections, called *villi*, that are depicted in the upper diagram. The lower diagram shows an enlargement of the cells on the surface of the villi with their fingerlike projections, called *microvilli*. Which best describes the small intestine's primary cooperative role?

(A) The increased surface area-to-volume ratio of the small intestine lining plays a cooperative role with the other organs of the digestive system to aid the organism in the efficient absorption of matter.

(B) The increased number of cells in the lining of the small intestine allows the small intestine to play a greater cooperative role in circulating signals throughout the organism.

(C) The large number of extensions allows the small intestine to play a cooperative role with the organism to aid in the filtration of waste products as they move through the intestine.

(D) The large cavities between the villi allow the small intestine to play a cooperative role with the organism to form pockets that aid in the storage of food.

46. Maurice Wilkins and Rosalind Franklin's contribution to the discovery of the structure of DNA is often overlooked in favor of Watson and Crick, who are usually given credit for discovering the structure of DNA. Which claim below best represents the contribution of Wilkins and Franklin?

(A) They first suggested that DNA is the agent of heredity.

(B) They provided clear images of DNA utilizing X-ray crystallography.

(C) They used radioactive proteins and DNA with viruses to show that DNA is the agent of heredity.

(D) They discovered the double helical nature of DNA.

47. A culture of cells is poured into a high-speed blender with a mixture of oil and water. After the blender runs for several minutes, the fluid is allowed to settle. Next, the oily portion is separated from the watery portion. Which of the following most accurately predicts the results of this process?

(A) The watery component will include RNA, proteins, and enzymes; the oily component will include ions, membranes, and steroids.

(B) The watery component will include enzymes, membranes, proteins, and RNA; the oily component will include ions and steroids.

(C) The watery component will include ions, proteins, and steroids; the oily component will include enzymes, membranes, and RNA.

(D) The watery component will include enzymes, ions, proteins, and RNA; the oily component will include membranes and steroids.

GO ON TO THE NEXT PAGE.

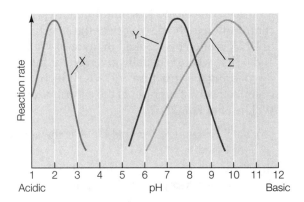

48. The graph above shows reaction rates for three enzyme-catalyzed reactions: X, Y, and Z. Assume that these enzymes are active in the digestive tract and that their activity releases nutrients that can be absorbed. Enzymes in the stomach are activated by hydrochloric acid, while a buffer from the pancreas neutralizes this acidity in the intestines. Which statement about this process is most accurate?

   (A) Enzyme X is denatured at pH 2, enzyme Y is denatured at pH 7.5, and enzyme Z is denatured at pH 9.6.
   (B) Enzyme X activates enzymes Y and Z.
   (C) Enzyme X is inhibited by feedback inhibition, and enzymes Y and Z are enhanced by feed-forward activation.
   (D) Enzyme X is normally active in the stomach, whereas enzymes Y and Z are active in the small intestine.

49. The hydrolysis of ATP, often called the currency of chemical energy in cells, is represented by this reaction:

   $$ATP + H_2O \rightarrow ADP + P_i + \text{free energy}$$

   Choose the most accurate description of this reaction.

   (A) The free energy released by this reaction can be used for cellular work.
   (B) The hydrogen and oxygen atoms from the H_2O substrate are converted to phosphorus.
   (C) The hydrolysis of ATP is an endergonic reaction.
   (D) This reaction describes how light activates chlorophyll.

50. The concentration of solutes dissolved in blood plasma is a particular concern when giving intravenous fluids to a patient. Suppose that a dog suffering from dehydration is brought into an emergency animal hospital. Which best describes the dog's RBCs at the beginning of treatment and one hour after treatment with an appropriate intravenous fluid?

   (A) The RBCs will be larger than normal at the beginning of treatment and will become smaller after treatment.
   (B) The RBCs will be normal-sized at the beginning of treatment, and many will likely burst after treatment.
   (C) The size of the RBCs will not be affected by dehydration or treatment.
   (D) The RBCs will be smaller than normal at the beginning of treatment and will become larger after treatment.

51. Mitosis occurs during the cell cycle but does not constitute the complete cell cycle. Choose the event that is part of the cell cycle but not part of mitosis.

   (A) The cell's DNA is replicated.
   (B) The paired sister chromatids separate and move toward opposite poles.
   (C) The chromosomes line up across the middle of the cell.
   (D) The nuclear envelope forms around each set of chromosomes.

GO ON TO THE NEXT PAGE.

52. The relatedness of all living things on earth stems from the fact that all forms of life have

    (A) the capacity to capture light energy.
    (B) cell motility based on flagellar contraction.
    (C) instructions coded in nucleotide sequences.
    (D) nuclei with surrounding membranes.

53. Mutations on the X-chromosome of a male offspring can be inherited from

    (A) the father only.
    (B) the mother only.
    (C) either the mother or the father.
    (D) the father, but only if the mutation does not affect reproductive function.

54. Researchers believe that they have extracted a new hormone from pancreatic cells. When attempting to characterize the hormone they find that it is fat-soluble. Predict the most likely mechanism of action for the hormone's target cells.

    (A) The hormone causes the target cells to respond rapidly, but the response is short-lived.
    (B) The hormone rapidly triggers action potentials in the hypothalamus.
    (C) The hormone binds to receptor proteins on the surface of the target cells.
    (D) The hormone moves into a cell and causes changes in gene expression in the nucleus.

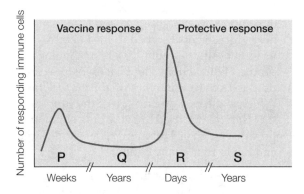

55. The cells of the immune system speed the body's recovery following infection and reinfection. Choose the interval, as shown on the graph above, in which memory cells guide the production of antibodies.

    (A) P
    (B) Q
    (C) R
    (D) S

56. Photosynthesis includes two sets of reactions. One set is directly light dependent, while the other set, called the Calvin cycle, is only indirectly dependent on light. Which of the following lists has products of the Calvin cycle?

    (A) Excited chlorophyll, ribulose bisphosphate carboxylase (rubisco), and electrons
    (B) Carbon dioxide, hydrogen ions, and water
    (C) Oxygen, ATP, and NADPH
    (D) Glucose, ADP, and $NADP^+$

GO ON TO THE NEXT PAGE.

57. Insulin is a hormone released by the pancreas in response to eating sugary foods. Its actions help glucose get absorbed in the body by its target cells. Humulin™, a biotechnology product with actions identical to insulin can be used to treat certain types of *diabetes mellitus*. Which is the best description of the procedure that is currently used to make biotechnology products, such as Humulin™, on a scale large enough to treat many patients?

   (A) A normal copy of the gene of interest is inserted into the genome of a farm animal, and the mRNA of interest is isolated from the animal's blood, urine, or milk.

   (B) Patients undergo gene-transfers to replace a defective copy of a gene with one that is not mutated.

   (C) Bacteria undergo transformation and ligation to incorporate genes whose products are of interest.

   (D) The insulin hormone is isolated from the urine of horses that are genetically bred to overproduce this hormone.

58. Although molecular nitrogen gas (N_2) makes up about 78 percent of the atmosphere, nitrogen is a limiting nutrient in many ecosystems. Plants cannot absorb nitrogen gas (N_2) and assimilate it into amino acids. Nitrogen atoms, in various molecular forms, move through the nitrogen cycle. Which of the following organisms are capable of using N_2 directly?

   (A) Bacteria
   (B) Protists
   (C) Insects
   (D) Fish

Questions 59–63

Behavioral and genetic studies of fruit flies (*Drosophila*) have implicated similar genes and genetic networks in the behaviors of other organisms, including humans. In one such experiment, fruit flies were bred and raised for ten generations with one of two diets: chocolate-flavored food ("*choc* flies") and cinnamon-flavored food ("*cinn* flies"). They were then tested for their mating preferences.

59. Which prediction indicates that the diet the flies were raised on could lead to the formation of a new species?

   (A) Male and female cinn flies were unable to detect the odor of cinnamon.

   (B) Female cinn flies showed little interest in mating with males, regardless of the males' diet.

   (C) Male choc flies showed little interest in mating with females, regardless of the females' diet.

   (D) Male and female choc flies and cinn flies mated only with flies of their own diet group.

Untethered "test" subjects	Tethered "choice" partners	Number of matings
Cinn Males (n = 20)	Cinn Females	16
	Choc Females	4
Cinn Females (n = 20)	Cinn Males	14
	Choc Males	6
Choc Males (n = 20)	Cinn Females	5
	Choc Females	15
Choc Females (n = 20)	Cinn Males	3
	Choc Males	17

GO ON TO THE NEXT PAGE.

60. The table above shows hypothetical data for an experiment with the fruit flies described in Question 59. The data reflect observations of mating behavior when a "test" fly is offered one tethered "choice" mate from each diet type. Which of the following is most likely a correct interpretation of the data?

(A) Test flies chose mates from the group with the opposite diet.

(B) Flies' mating preferences are likely based on a single, recessive gene.

(C) Over the generations, reproductive isolation developed between the two populations.

(D) Chemical odors attracted flies to mates with similar dietary backgrounds.

61. Suppose that 20 test subjects from each diet type were tested in a new setting. In this round, only one "choice" partner was available to each "test" subject. Which prediction about this experimental round is supported by the original data?

(A) Test flies will mate more readily with partners in their own diet group, though cross-mating will occasionally occur.

(B) Test flies will mate readily and exclusively with partners in their own diet group.

(C) Mating will occur in all combinations, due to the absence of alternatives for expressing preferences.

(D) The pacing, sequence, and details of all mating interactions will be identical.

62. Consider that the isolation between the two populations in these studies continued for hundreds of generations, rather than just ten generations. Which of the following predictions would support the conclusion that the two populations will become independent species?

(A) The results would change very little for either population; most flies would mate readily with either population within a few generations.

(B) The offspring of flies from either diet group would be unlikely to show any mating preference for the other diet group.

(C) After having diverged genetically for so many generations, the two populations of flies would now readily mate with partners in diet groups different from their own.

(D) A limited number of matings would continue to be possible between two individuals of different diet groups, but no viable offspring would emerge from such matings.

63. In further studies, differences in food preference and copulatory behavior were observed between the two fruit fly populations. If the groups were combined in an environment with chocolate food resources physically separated from cinnamon food resources, the two populations of flies might continue to diverge. Over time, the flies would likely first differ in the

(A) ability to see colors.

(B) anatomy of the reproductive system.

(C) ability to fly.

(D) anatomy of the respiratory system.

GO ON TO THE NEXT PAGE.

Directions: The next six questions, numbered 121–126, require numeric answers. Determine the correct answer for each question and enter it in the grid on your answer sheet. Use the following guidelines for entering your answers.

- Start your answer in any column, space permitting. Unused columns should be left blank.

- Write your answer in the boxes at the top of the grid and fill in the corresponding circles. Mark only one circle in any column. You will receive credit only if the circles are filled in completely.

- Provide your answer in the format specified by the question. The requested answer may be an integer, a decimal, or a fraction, and it may have a negative value.

- To enter a fraction, use one of the division slashes to separate the numerator from the denominator, as shown in the example below. Fractions only need to be reduced enough to fit in the grid.

- Do not enter a mixed number, as this will be scored as a fraction. For example, 2 1/2 (two and one-half) will be scored as 21/2 (twenty-one halves).

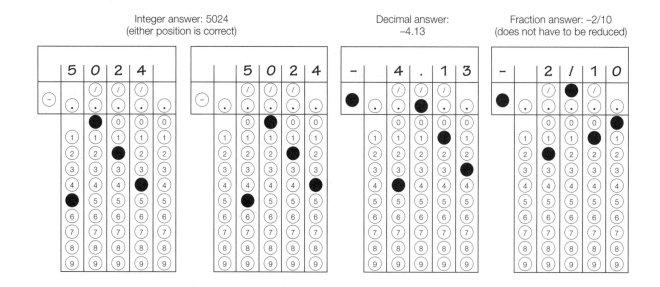

Integer answer: 5024
(either position is correct)

Decimal answer:
−4.13

Fraction answer: −2/10
(does not have to be reduced)

GO ON TO THE NEXT PAGE.

121. The storage roots of radishes (the part of the plant that we eat) can be long, round, or oval. Geneticists crossed long and oval radishes, which produced 348 long radishes and 356 oval radishes. A cross between round and oval radishes produced 195 round and 189 oval radishes. A cross between two oval radishes produced 51 long, 112 oval, and 41 round radishes, and crosses between long and round radishes produced only oval radishes.

A researcher hypothesizes that the oval radish is heterozygous for the shape gene. Calculate the chi-squared value using the data set from these test crosses that best supports this hypothesis. Give your answer to the nearest hundredth.

122. In sheep, black wool is a recessive trait. In a flock of 250 sheep, 12 sheep were found to have black wool. Calculate the percent of the population that is heterozygous for this trait. (Assume that the population is in Hardy–Weinberg equilibrium.) Give your answer to the nearest tenth.

GO ON TO THE NEXT PAGE.

123. Fiddler crabs are common residents of saltmarshes, feeding on dead, partially decomposed saltmarsh grass (detritus). A group of students randomly sampled one-square-meter quadrats in six locations and counted the number of fiddler crabs in each plot. The data are presented in the table below.

Quadrat	Fiddler crabs
1	16
2	5
3	12
4	7
5	2
6	8

Calculate the average number of fiddler crabs one would expect to find in a 100-square-meter plot. Give your answer to the nearest whole number.

GO ON TO THE NEXT PAGE.

124. A human cell can be fused to a mouse cell in the laboratory, forming a single large cell, called a *heterokaryon*. As a test of the fluid mosaic model, this phenomenon was used to find out whether membrane proteins can diffuse throughout the plasma membrane.

A human cell and a mouse cell were fused together to form a heterokaryon. Initially the mouse and human membrane proteins were on opposite sides of the heterokaryon. As time progressed, the proteins rapidly diffused throughout the membrane. An experiment repeated at different temperatures yielded the following results:

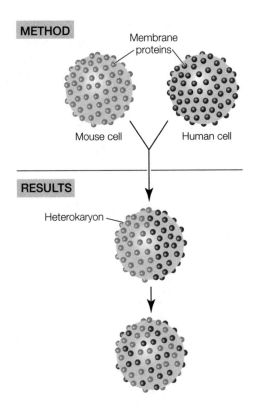

Temperature (°C)	Cells with mixed proteins (%)
0	0
15	8
20	42
25	77

Calculate the rate of change from 15°C to 20°C. Give your answer to the nearest tenth per degree Celsius.

GO ON TO THE NEXT PAGE.

125. As an action potential moves along a neuron, a sudden influx of Na$^+$ ions causes a brief reversal of membrane potential. Shortly after the reversal, the membrane potential is briefly more negative than it was prior to the onset of the action potential, a phase called the *undershoot*. Examine the graph below to determine the minimum membrane potential during the undershoot. Record your answer in the grid.

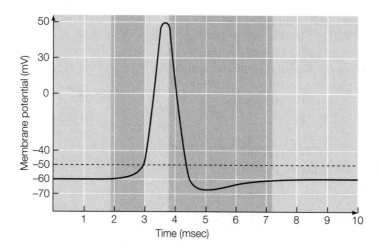

GO ON TO THE NEXT PAGE.

126. The axon of a giant squid can be up to 1mm in diameter and up to 2 meters in length. Calculate the surface area-to-volume ratio for this cell. Express your answer to the nearest whole number as a fraction over 1 (as in X/1).

Some useful equations

Surface area of a circle = πr^2

Volume of a cylinder = $\pi r^2 h$

Surface area of a cylinder = $2 \pi r^2 + 2 \pi r h$

Surface area of a cube = $6 \times$ length $\times$ width

Volume of a cube = length $\times$ width $\times$ height

1,000 mm = 1 meter

END OF SECTION I

IF TIME REMAINS, YOU MAY CHECK YOUR WORK.

DURING THE ACTUAL EXAM, YOU WILL NOT BE ABLE TO GO ON TO SECTION II UNTIL TOLD TO DO SO. FOR THIS PRACTICE EXAM, PUT AWAY SECTION I, TAKE A SHORT BREAK, THEN GO ON TO SECTION II.

478

BIOLOGY
Section II
8 Questions
Planning Time—10 minutes
Writing Time—80 minutes

Directions: Questions 1 and 2 are long free-response questions that require about 22 minutes each to answer and are worth 10 points each. Questions 3–8 are short free-response questions that require about 6 minutes each to answer. Questions 3–5 are worth 4 points each, and questions 6–8 are worth 3 points each.

Read each question carefully and completely. Write your response in the space provided for each question. Only material written in the space provided will be scored. Answers must be written out in paragraph form. Outlines, bulleted lists, or diagrams alone are not acceptable.

1. The graph below shows the absorption-wavelength curves for two different organisms: *Ulva* (a green algae) and purple sulfur bacteria.

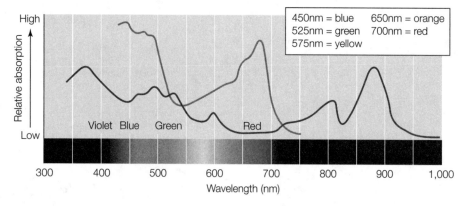

(a) **Label** the two curves for *Ulva* and purple sulfur bacteria on the graph.

(b) **Explain** how purple sulfur bacteria can carry out photosynthesis.

(c) Assume that a newly discovered species of algae has evolved in the same region as the two shown, but it is not in competition with either of them for light. On the original graph, draw this new algae's expected absorption-wavelength curve, paying close attention to the wavelengths of maximum absorption. **Justify** the shape of your curve with an explanation.

(d) **Discuss** how each of the three light-harvesting photosynthetic pigments in your answer above is specifically affected by the energy spectrum of light.

GO ON TO THE NEXT PAGE.

THIS PAGE MAY BE USED FOR TAKING NOTES AND PLANNING YOUR ANSWERS.
NOTES WRITTEN ON THIS PAGE WILL NOT BE SCORED.
WRITE ALL YOUR RESPONSES ON THE LINED PAGES.

GO ON TO THE NEXT PAGE.

PAGE FOR ANSWERING QUESTION 1

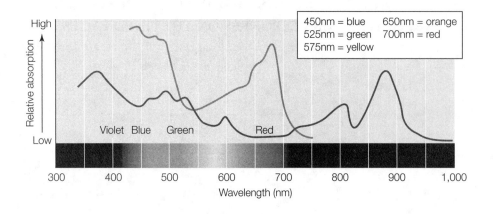

_____

_____

_____

_____

_____

_____

_____

_____

_____

_____

_____

_____

_____

_____

_____

_____

_____

_____

GO ON TO THE NEXT PAGE.

ADDITIONAL PAGE FOR ANSWERING QUESTION 1

GO ON TO THE NEXT PAGE.

ADDITIONAL PAGE FOR ANSWERING QUESTION 1

_____

_____

_____

_____

_____

_____

_____

_____

_____

_____

_____

_____

_____

_____

_____

_____

_____

_____

_____

_____

_____

_____

GO ON TO THE NEXT PAGE.

ADDITIONAL PAGE FOR ANSWERING QUESTION 1

_____

_____

_____

_____

_____

_____

_____

_____

_____

_____

_____

_____

_____

_____

_____

_____

_____

_____

_____

_____

_____

GO ON TO THE NEXT PAGE.

2. Sexual reproduction is the primary mode of reproduction among eukaryotes, including humans.

   (a) **Discuss** THREE genetic and/or evolutionary benefits of sexual reproduction.

   (b) **Discuss** TWO genetic and/or evolutionary costs of sexual reproduction.

   (c) Among the approximately 23,000 human genes, about 35 are found in only one sex. **Identify** the chromosome on which these are found, and **propose** a function for these genes.

   (d) During sexual reproduction, mutations occasionally disrupt the normal development of an individual. Klinefelter syndrome is a condition in which an individual has a Y chromosome and two X chromosomes. **Construct** a diagram that shows how this arrangement of sex chromosomes occurs. Be sure to **explain** your diagram with written text.

THIS PAGE MAY BE USED FOR TAKING NOTES AND PLANNING YOUR ANSWERS.
NOTES WRITTEN ON THIS PAGE WILL NOT BE SCORED.
WRITE ALL YOUR RESPONSES ON THE LINED PAGES.

GO ON TO THE NEXT PAGE.

PAGE FOR ANSWERING QUESTION 2

_____

_____

_____

_____

_____

_____

_____

_____

_____

_____

_____

_____

_____

_____

_____

_____

_____

_____

_____

_____

_____

_____

_____

GO ON TO THE NEXT PAGE.

ADDITIONAL PAGE FOR ANSWERING QUESTION 2

_____

_____

_____

_____

_____

_____

_____

_____

_____

_____

_____

_____

_____

_____

_____

_____

_____

_____

_____

_____

_____

_____

GO ON TO THE NEXT PAGE.

ADDITIONAL PAGE FOR ANSWERING QUESTION 2

_____

_____

_____

_____

_____

_____

_____

_____

_____

_____

_____

_____

_____

_____

_____

_____

_____

_____

_____

_____

_____

_____

_____

_____

GO ON TO THE NEXT PAGE.

ADDITIONAL PAGE FOR ANSWERING QUESTION 2

_____

_____

_____

_____

_____

_____

_____

_____

_____

_____

_____

_____

_____

_____

_____

_____

_____

_____

_____

_____

_____

GO ON TO THE NEXT PAGE.

3. Flowering in plants is often dependent on a critical period of darkness or light. Cocklebur plants typically flower in the fall when there is a critical dark period (inductive period) and the night is longer than the day.

In plants, the seasonal flowering signal moves from leaf to bud. Phytochrome, the receptor for photoperiod, is in the leaf, but flowering occurs in the shoot apical meristem. To investigate whether there is a diffusible substance that travels from leaf to bud, James Knott masked a single leaf, as shown in the diagram at the right. The masked leaf was then "exposed" to the inductive dark period. With just one leaf masked, the plant flowered, while plants with no leaves masked did not flower.

In related experiments, six plants were grown in each of the conditions shown below. Except for the first group, assume that all of the plants were exposed to the inductive dark period for 30 days.

METHOD
Grow cocklebur plants under long days and short nights. Mask a leaf on some plants and see if flowering occurs.

Masked leaf

Control — Plant with masked leaf

RESULTS
If even one leaf is masked for part of the day—thus shifting that leaf to short days and long nights—the plant will flower.

Burrs (fruit)

Masked leaf

Condition	Number of plants that flowered
No inductive dark period, intact plant	0
Inductive dark period, intact plant	6
Inductive dark period, all leaves removed	0
Inductive dark period, all but one leaf removed	6

(a) **Describe** the physiological mechanism that prevented the leafless plants from flowering.

(b) **Propose** a modification of the experiment to explore whether plants with more leaves intact and exposed to the inductive dark period flower sooner.

(c) **Predict** whether the necessary duration of exposure would be different for the intact plants than for the plants with only one leaf, and **justify** your prediction.

GO ON TO THE NEXT PAGE.

PAGE FOR ANSWERING QUESTION 3

_____

_____

_____

_____

_____

_____

_____

_____

_____

_____

_____

_____

_____

_____

_____

_____

_____

_____

_____

_____

_____

GO ON TO THE NEXT PAGE.

4. The diagram below shows the relationship between the diversity of a grassland area and the plant biomass produced over a three-year period.

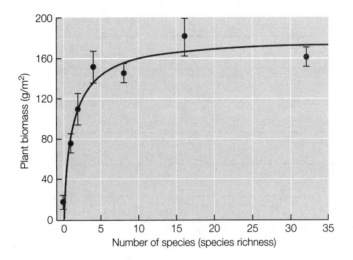

(a) Briefly **explain** what biodiversity measures.

(b) **Summarize** the information shown in the graph.

(c) **Explain** the reason for this correlation between biomass and biodiversity.

PAGE FOR ANSWERING QUESTION 4

_____

_____

_____

_____

_____

_____

_____

_____

_____

_____

_____

GO ON TO THE NEXT PAGE.

ADDITIONAL PAGE FOR ANSWERING QUESTION 4

_____

_____

_____

_____

_____

_____

_____

_____

_____

_____

_____

_____

_____

_____

_____

_____

_____

_____

_____

_____

GO ON TO THE NEXT PAGE.

5. The introduction of new species often has devastating consequences on native populations. **Select** ONE of the following, and **describe** the organism and how it was introduced. **Identify** TWO consequences of its introduction by humans to a region it did not formerly occupy.

- Dutch elm disease
- Potato blight
- Smallpox

PAGE FOR ANSWERING QUESTION 5

_____

_____

_____

_____

_____

_____

_____

_____

_____

_____

_____

_____

_____

_____

_____

_____

_____

_____

GO ON TO THE NEXT PAGE.

6. In higher eukaryotes, the chemical ouabain can impair the activity of the sodium–potassium pump (Na^+-K^+-ATPase). Impaired sodium pumping can, in turn, impair cellular processes that depend on a gradient of sodium ions across the cell membrane. In lower doses, ouabain can have therapeutic effects following cardiac arrest. Would they be the same? **Predict** the effects of ouabain on nerve cells from a giant squid and from a mouse. **Justify** your prediction.

PAGE FOR ANSWERING QUESTION 6

_____

_____

_____

_____

_____

_____

_____

_____

_____

_____

_____

_____

_____

_____

_____

_____

_____

_____

_____

GO ON TO THE NEXT PAGE.

7. Plants and animals are influenced in many ways by environmental conditions, including seasonal and long-term temperature changes.

(a) **Choose** ONE plant and ONE animal, and **describe** how seasonal changes in temperature affect the phenotype of each.

(b) **Describe** how the plant and animal identified above are likely to respond to climate change.

PAGE FOR ANSWERING QUESTION 7

_____

_____

_____

_____

_____

_____

_____

_____

_____

_____

_____

_____

_____

_____

_____

_____

_____

_____

GO ON TO THE NEXT PAGE.

8. A population's ability to respond to changes in the environment is affected by its genetic diversity.

   (a) **Describe** how genetic diversity is beneficial to the long-term survival of a population.

   (b) **Choose** ONE of the species below, and **discuss** why that population is at risk of extinction.
   - California condors
   - Black-footed ferrets
   - Prairie chickens
   - Tasmanian devils

PAGE FOR ANSWERING QUESTION 8

_____

_____

_____

_____

_____

_____

_____

_____

_____

_____

_____

_____

_____

_____

_____

_____

_____

GO ON TO THE NEXT PAGE.

STOP

END OF EXAM

IF TIME REMAINS,
YOU MAY CHECK YOUR WORK ON THIS SECTION.

———————————————————

Section I Answer Key

MULTIPLE-CHOICE ITEMS

#	Answer	LO		#	Answer	LO
1	D	1.17		33	C	3.45
2	B	4.4		34	C	3.9
3	A	3.6		35	A	3.3
4	A	3.10		36	C	4.1
5	D	3.4		37	B	4.2
6	D	2.16		38	B	4.13
7	A	3.25		39	D	2.5
8	A	2.21		40	C	2.4
9	B	4.5		41	B	2.7
10	B	3.36		42	B	3.3
11	D	3.12		43	C	1.30
12	C	1.4		44	A	3.5
13	B	2.24		45	A	4.18
14	A	2.28		46	B	3.2
15	C	2.23		47	D	2.10
16	B	4.19		48	D	4.17
17	D	1.9		49	A	2.1
18	C	1.2		50	D	2.12
19	A	1.10		51	A	3.8
20	B	4.8		52	C	1.32
21	C	2.5		53	B	3.17
22	D	2.8		54	D	2.11
23	C	3.11		55	C	2.29
24	D	1.18		56	D	2.1
25	A	1.14		57	C	3.5
26	B	1.17		58	A	4.16
27	B	1.20		59	D	1.25
28	C	1.20		60	C	1.24
29	A	4.13		61	A	1.26
30	C	3.24		62	D	1.22
31	B	3.34		63	B	1.22
32	A	3.15				

GRID-IN ITEMS

#	Answer	Acceptable Range	LO
121	2.94	2.90 – 3.00	3.14
122	34.2	33 – 35	1.1
123	833	830 – 835	4.19
124	6.8	6.8	2.11
125	-68	-66 – -69	2.12
126	4/1	3.8 / 1 – 4.2 / 1	2.6

SAMPLE GRID-IN CALCULATIONS

121.   2.9 – 3.0 (actual is 2.94)

122. $q2 = 12/250 = .048$
       $q = .219; p = .781$
       $2pq = 2 (.219)(.781) = .342$ or 34.2% (34.3% is also acceptable)

123. $50/6 = 8.33$ crabs
       $m^2 \times 100 \ m^2 = 833$ crabs

124. $\dfrac{Y2 - Y1}{X2 - X1} = \dfrac{DV = \% \ mixed}{IV = temp} = \dfrac{42 - 8}{20 - 15} = 34/5 = 6.8$

125.   –68 (acceptable range is –66 to –69)

126.   SA : Volume

For a cell of length 2 meters (h) and diameter of 1 mm (r = .5mm)
(*Hint*: Convert 2 meters to 2,000 millimeters)

SA $= 2 (3.14)(r)^2 + 2 (3.14)(r)(h)$
      $= 2 (3.14)(.5 \ mm)^2 + 2 (3.14)(.5 \ mm)(2,000 \ mm)$
      $= 1.57 + 6280$
      $= 6,281.57$

Volume $= (3.14)(.5 \ mm)^2 (2000 \ mm)$
         $= 1,570$

SA : V ratio would be $= 6,281.57 / 1,570 = 4:1$ (Gridded as 4/1)

Section II Sample Scoring Rubrics

1. This is a 10-point question.

   (a) 1 pt –

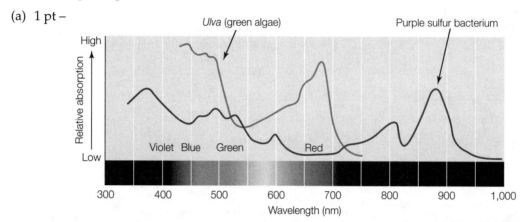

   (b) 1 pt   The purple sulfur bacteria do not produce oxygen from water (H2O), as green plants do.

   1 pt –   The purple sulfur bacteria produce sulfur from hydrogen sulfide (H2S).

   1 pt –   The bacteria are able to do this as electron donors.

   (c) 1 pt –   Answer includes any curve added to the graph that shows a pattern in which relative absorption peaks at wavelengths different from the peaks of green algae and purple sulfur bacteria.

   1 pt –   Lack of "competition for light" by hypothetical species explains that its peaks of relative absorption are different from the peaks on the curve for the Ulva and purple sulfur bacteria.

   1 pt –   It does not absorb at all wavelengths.

   (d) 1 pt –   Green algae's pigment, chlorophyll, absorbs at about 450 and 650 nm for photosynthesis.

   1 pt –   Bacteriochlorophyll, in purple sulfur bacteria, is activated at a long wavelength (~880 nm).

   1 pt –   Putative pigment of fictional bacteria is activated at the point indicated on student's graph.

2. This is a 10-point question.

   (a) Maximum of 3 points from the following:

      1 pt – Offspring can vary from parents.

      1 pt – Crossing over and recombination can produce diverse assemblages of genes.

      1 pt – Crossing over and recombination can "repair" harmful mutations.

      1 pt – It speeds up the rate of evolutionary change.

   (b) Maximum of 2 points from the following:

      1 pt – Crossing over and recombination can separate adaptive genes from each other.

      1 pt – Female parents invest heavily in offspring whose genes have been "diluted" by fathers.

      1 pt – It can be hard to find a mate and to accomplish gamete exchange.

      1 pt – Having two parents required for each offspring slows population growth rate.

   (c) 1 pt – Male humans have a Y chromosome, females do not.

      1 pt – The Y chromosome has about 35 genes on it, all related to testicular function, and determination of maleness—specifically the SRY gene is one gene that is unique to the Y chromosome.

   (d) Klinefleter can be caused in two ways. Either a normal ova (X) is fertilized by an abnormal sperm (XY) or an abnormal ova (XX) is fertilized by a normal sperm (Y). The student earns:

      1 pt – for a diagram correctly showing nondisjunction during meiosis creating either an abnormal sperm with X and Y chromosomes or an abnormal ova (XX).

      1 pt – for the diagram at conclusion showing creation of a zygote with an abnormal and a normal gamete.

      1 pt – for an explanation that correctly describes the points above shown in the diagram.

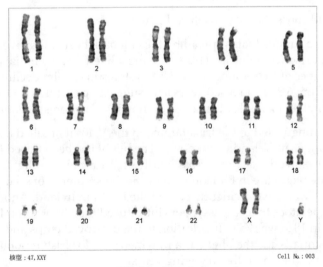

核型 : 47, XXY   Cell No. : 003

Klinefelter Karyotype

3. This is a 4-point question.

   (a) 1 pt –   Leaves produce a chemical signal that promotes flowering, so without leaves, no cytochrome was produced.

   (b) 1 pt –   Have multiple plants with varying numbers of leaves exposed to the dark period.

   (c) 1 pt –   Intact plants with multiple leaves should produce more cytochrome, causing flowering to occur sooner.

       1 pt –   Without leaves there's no photosynthesis to provide the energy needed to produce the cytochrome.

4. This is a 4-point question.

   (a) Biodiversity is the variety of species present in a given community. Biodiversity encompasses two ideas:

       1 pt –   the number of individuals in each species present

       1 pt –   the number of different species present (species richness)

   (b) 1 pt –   As the number of plant species increases in a test plot, plant biomass also increases, up to a point, at which maximum supportable productivity is possible. The upper limit is on how much sunlight can reach the plants in the community under consideration.

   (c) 1 pt –   The primary explanation for increased biodiversity supporting greater biomass is that there are more niches for plants and animals to live in. A greater variety of species allows for different plants with different functional roles. Different plants have different traits with varied adaptations. Some perform better in cooler weather and some better in the shade, while others have varying associations with nitrogen fixing bacteria.

5. This is a 4-point question. Only one may be answered; the first one attempted is scored.

       1 pt –   A description of the organism, including why it is harmful

       1 pt –   An explanation of how it was introduced

       1 pt –   One consequence of its introduction

       1 pt –   A second consequence of its introduction

Dutch elm disease is a fungus that is spread by the elm bark beetle. It arrived in North American on trees accidently imported from Europe (1928), but most likely had its initial origins in Asia. The disease greatly altered the types of trees found in the USA. Interestingly, elm declines have also been noted in the fossil record from 6,000 and 3,000 years ago, suggesting that this is not the first time this has happened. This is another example of succession showing how forests change over time.

The potato blight, a fungus, led to the Irish famine in the 1840s that killed a million or more people. The origin of this fungus in Ireland is unknown. The blight has been traced to the Toluca Valley in Mexico and probably spread via wind across North America causing blights in 1843 and 1844. The earliest records of the blight are in Philadelphia in 1843. A shipment of seed potatoes bound for Belgium in 1845 may well have accidently caused the blight in Ireland. Another possibility is that clipper ships using potatoes to feed passengers introduced the blight. Crop loss in Ireland in 1845 was up to 50% and in 1846 was 75%. In addition to the destroyed crops and resulting loss of life due to famine, many historians cite the blight as a rallying cause for Irish republicanism and the resulting Irish independence movement in the following years.

Smallpox is due to a virus that causes a serious, and sometimes fatal, infection of the skin. It has been part of human civilization for centuries, but ~150,000 people in North America died as a result of the smallpox epidemic of the late 1700s. There is also evidence that earlier travelers to North America inadvertently introduced the virus to native populations, wiping out millions of native North American Indians well before Christopher Columbus arrived. Some accounts also have European settlers deliberately giving infected blankets to native North American populations as germ warfare.

6. This is a 3-point question.

   1 pt – The effects would be the same for mice and squid.

   1 pt – Ouabain inhibits Na+/K+-ATPase, reducing the sodium gradient across the membrane.

   1 pt – Any process utilizing the sodium gradient can be impaired (e.g., calcium storage, any type of sodium-dependent secondary active transport, the generation of action potentials).

7. This is a 3-point question.

   (a) 1 pt – Any seasonal plant can be chosen. Possible answers include fruiting, leaf drop (deciduous species), responses to drought, etc.

   1 pt – Any animal in a seasonal environment can be chosen. Possible answers include seasonal reproduction, seasonal changes in metabolic rate, hibernation, etc.

   (b) 1 pt – Climate change could disrupt the seasonal patterns, extending some physiological processes too late in the season and causing the individual to suffer a reduction in fitness. For plants, earlier budding and flowering are current trends. For both animals and plants, habitation ranges may shift as average temperatures change.

8. This is a 3-point question.

   (a) 2 pts – Genetic diversity lets plants and animals "hedge their bets" on what phenotype, to the extent determined by genotype, might be successful when environmental conditions shift.

   (b) 1 pt – California condors: Very few reproductive individuals persist; they might not have enough genetic diversity to survive a disease outbreak. OR

   Black-footed ferrets: A lack of undisturbed natural areas with prey (prairie dogs) has taken this predator to the edge of extinction. OR

   Prairie chickens: Habitat loss (tall-grass prairies) has greatly curtailed its numbers; it lacks adequate undisturbed areas for mating and rearing chicks. OR

   Tasmanian devils: Transmissible parasitic cancer has caused declines of up to 65% in areas across Australia. This is density-dependent, transmitted by one devil biting another. Pathology is still unknown. This is genetic drift reducing the diversity of the population.

Correlation of Free-Response Questions to the Curriculum Framework

Question #	LO's Covered	Number of Points
1	2.5	10
2	3.27, 3.28, 3.12	10
3	2.35, 2.36, 2.37	4
4	4.27	4
5	4.21	4
6	1.16	3
7	4.23 and 4.24	3
8	4.25	3

Notes

Notes

Notes

Notes

Notes

Notes

Notes

Notes

Notes